Beyond Employment

Beyond Employment

Household, Gender and Subsistence

Edited by Nanneke Redclift
and Enzo Mingione

Basil Blackwell

© The International Sociological Association Research Committee on Urban and Regional Development 1985

First published 1985

Basil Blackwell Ltd
108 Cowley Road, Oxford OX4 1JF, UK

Basil Blackwell Inc.
432 Park Avenue South, Suite 1505,
New York, NY 10016, USA

British Library Cataloguing in Publication Data

Beyond employment.
   1.   Industrial sociology
   I.   Redclift, Nanneke   II.   Mingione, Enzo
   306'.36   HD6955

   ISBN 0–631–13448–4
   ISBN 0–631–13903–6 Pbk

Library of Congress Cataloging in Publication Data

Beyond employment.
   Bibliography: p.
   Includes index.
   1.   Informal sector (Economics)—Addresses, essays,
lectures.   2.   Households—Economic aspects—Addresses,
essays, lectures.   I.   Redclift, Nanneke.   II.   Mingione, Enzo.
HD2341.B43 1985   339.4'1   84-12491

ISBN 0-631-13448-4
ISBN 0-631-13903-6 (pbk.)

Typeset by Alan Sutton Publishing Ltd, Gloucester
Printed in Great Britain by T.J. Press Ltd, Padstow

Contents

Introduction:
Economic Restructuring and
Family Practices

The essays in this collection share a common concern with a broader analysis of the crisis of conventional patterns of employment, as these have been conceived since the nineteenth century. Their purpose is to examine the interrelationship between post-industrial economic and technological change and the struggle for livelihood at the level of household and community. In doing this they are critical of previous functionalist and dualist approaches to the economic system, and consider the interaction of practices and ideologies of class, kinship and gender with this changing labour process from a variety of vantage points. They also draw, implicitly or explicitly, on recent feminist analysis to suggest the need for a new conceptualization of work and a challenge to orthodox interpretations of economic activity. Each chapter discusses a specific regional case. By bringing them together we suggest that they can be read as diverse aspects of an international process.

During the 1960s, it was assumed that the uneven nature of capitalist development and its imperfect penetration of the non-Western world had given rise to radical differences between advanced and developing economies (Wrigley 1967). The latter were seen as transitional forms, in which the traditional or backward elements continued to survive in uneasy coexistence with modern or advanced modes of production. In the 1970s, however, it became clear that the deteriorating land-tenure situation, and the structural dependence of the South on the North, were likely to lead to paths of transition that were very different from those experienced during the period of European industrialization. The economy of the bazaar would not necessarily be transformed, and because of the historical preconditions established by the early industrialization of the North, there was no single evolutionary pattern that all areas would eventually follow.

The rapid urbanization of Third World cities, and the continuing inability of the nascent industrial sector to absorb the 'surplus' population into the capitalist labour force, drew increasing attention to the alternative survival strategies offered by the so-called 'informal economy'. It was evident that a majority of households were largely supported by various forms of hawking, street trade, petty commodity production, reciprocal, kin-based exchange and service activity. Although they were now no longer characterized as 'traditional' or backward, this population was seen as marginalized by the processes of dependent development.

The marginality debate was heavily influenced by the concern with the spatial crisis of the Third World city and the housing question. The geographic separation between the formal built environment of the city and the self-constructed shelter of squatter areas, together with the often sharp discrepancies between areas of legal and illegal land tenure in terms of access to services and infrastructure, reinforced a rigid, bi-sectoral model of the urban economy. The informal sector and 'casual' ways of working, outside the statistically defined labour force, thus became synonymous with poverty and insecurity, and were given physical location in the shanty towns and squatter settlements.

When these assumptions were subjected to empirical scrutiny, however, it proved difficult to formulate exclusive criteria for the definition and identification of each sector, and clear-cut boundaries between the two were elusive. A closer examination of the activities that had been taken as characteristic of informality also revealed that, far from being marginal or residual, they were connected by myriad strands to the capitalist economy proper, recycling its products, provisioning its workers, supplying elements of its production processes and reproducing its labour force. Certainly it was often possible to identify differences of wage rates, contractual status, ease of access, protective legislation and security, capitalization and size of operation between the two sectors. These characteristics, however, were not exclusive, and the evidence for separate economies was far from convincing. The sectors proved to have shifting parameters that varied according to context. Further empirical research revealed, moreover, that physical areas were not always coterminous with types of work, and households themselves were difficult to characterize along sectoral lines, making use of multiple strategies to ensure their survival (Garcia et al. 1982). These strategies, in turn, were differentiated by gender and by stage in the domestic cycle.

Critics of dualism (Bromley & Gerry 1979; Moser 1978; Tokman 1979) thus suggested that as a representation of the real world the concept implied a misleading homogeneity, while as an analytic category it led to static typological exercises that failed to illuminate underlying processes and interconnections. A renewed interest in the articulation of modes of production within Marxist theory stimulated a re-evaluation of the role of non-capitalist forms, arguing that they were subsumed by, though subordinated to, capitalism and essential for its continued evolution. Neo-dualist interpretations (Portes 1978; Portes & Walton 1981) saw the informal sector as a specific feature of dependent capitalism and a necessary feature of the accumulation process.

Ironically, at about the same time as this critique was being developed, the effects of the recession in the advanced industrial countries and the growing potential of technological decentralization, produced increasing dissatisfaction with formal waged employment as a comprehensive basis for class analysis. If growth was no longer to be seen as inevitable nor perhaps as even desirable, in some political programmes, the alternatives for survival in a no-growth society took on a new importance. Other forms of exchange, of goods, labour or cash, which evaded fiscal control and were often labelled 'black' or 'underground' received increasing attention. Feminist analysts had argued that it was in the interests of the State covertly to support the privatization of domestic labour as a hidden subsidy to the costs of reproducing the labour force. Neo-Marxist debates on the theory of value and Marxist feminist dissatisfaction with the limitations of productionist approaches suggested that a reconceptualization of the labour process was necessary.

Thus the European discovery, or rediscovery, of a world of work 'outside' capitalist relations of production can be seen as both a consequence of the changes produced by the process of restructuring and an effect of redefining what is to be counted; partly an empirical response to contemporary change and partly a paradigmatic shift. The extent and significance of unwaged work and the value generated by it are seen by the contributors to this volume both as masked by the limitations of previous androcentric theoretical frameworks and as emergent features of the new post-industrial order. Correspondingly, these new structures of work and employment are seen by some as the vanguard of an alternative life-style, and by others as exploited by and subordinated to capital. Both these perspectives are represented here; by bringing them together we hope to provide a clearer picture of the range of historical contexts in which theoretical positions are generated.

Analyses of peripheral economies have tended to see the relationship between capitalist and 'non'-capitalist, or informal or domestic modes of production, however defined, as basically predatory. They are, with a few exceptions (Lipton 1980), generally pessimistic about the political and economic outcomes for the populations involved. As Gerry and Connolly argue, the policy emphases and political rhetoric of support for self-help (ILO 1972), which were a direct result of the earlier studies of the effectiveness of the survival strategies of the poor, and which are now being picked up to legitimize the Rightist policies of the retreat of the State in Europe, offered a pseudo development 'solution' which ignores the causes of inequitable distribution.

In contrast, the emergence of this question in the recent work on the restructuring of advanced industrial societies has sometimes stressed the liberating potential of the escape from capitalist relations of production, the release from the alienation of work (Friedmann and Ehrhart 1982; Szelenyi 1981) and the individualistic search for creative alternatives. The feminist analysis of work has not generally shared this perspective however and several of the contributors to this collection question its universality in the light of their specific data.

Despite this diversity, the authors represented share a sceptical view of monocausal, functionalist or economicist explanations of current trends. These critical positions are applied to a variety of geographical and social contexts, yet, rather than being incompatible, we argue that they must be conjugated together to overcome the static and ahistorical nature of much previous work. The contributions on patterns of social reproduction (Mingione, Redclift), processes of industrial informalization (Pinnarò and Pugliese), modes of service provision (Gershuny), household strategies (Roldán, Cornuel and Duriez, Pahl and Wallace), the contradiction between everyday practices and structural processes (Godard, Cornuel and Duriez), the social construction of the sexual division of labour (Roldán, Redclift) and the manipulation of political discourse (Gerry, Connolly) approach this common problem at different levels of analysis. They suggest the overlapping dimensions of the practices of social reproduction in the context of economic recession or underdevelopment. Activities organized through the relations of reproduction, of kinship and community, have always existed in hidden and invisible form, though varying in time and space. Here, we are interested not only in the detection of these practices 'beyond employment' but also in exploring the extent to which they adjust, counterbalance or disintegrate under the effects of the decline or continuing structural absence of capitalist relations. It is important, too, that they should be seen as political options and co-opted by political discourse and not simply as solutions to household survival or individual subsistence problems.

Setting these technological and economic developments in their local and historical context underlines the importance of looking at different cultural styles of reproduction and their interaction with industrial processes and available labour-market options. The boom in microprocessing, for example, has been facilitated in part by the use of women as unskilled secondary workers and by the ideology that certain types of work are particularly appropriate for them. When this is coupled with high male unemployment, the demand for foreign exchange and the need of governments to create some form of employment safety valve to mitigate household poverty, a profitable environment for transnational expansion can be created by the removal of tariff barriers and protective legislation (Pearson & Elson 1981).

On the other hand, where the effects of recession are marked, its impact may be partially concealed by a class-based tradition of self-help, a domestic orientation and, for the new middle classes, by a certain pre-existing stake in the consumer market. Here, at least, it would appear to be the middle and stable working classes which are able to derive some benefit from informalization and the shift in service provision out of the State and into the private sector. For the unemployed, however, the ability to make use of alternative solutions to their survival needs appears to be increasingly problematic. Gershuny notes a trend towards a combination of formal employment and medium-to-large income, and a general increase in the time spent in self-service provision. Pahl and Wallace, in the context of their specific case study, both confirm and revise this hypothesis, showing how these emerging patterns are themselves highly differentiated and applicable principally to the stable income population and the shrinking labour aristocracy.

Thus, although access to certain resources and particular domestic structures can maximize the total income, there are clearly limits to the optimistic thesis that technological change will bring about a generalized increase in access to the system. In some labour-market settings, certain groups may be vulnerable at both the employment and the self-provisioning levels. It is not only in the Third World that the loss of a cow may pitch a household from the ability to scrape together a livelihood into a permanent state of indebtedness. The fragility or resilience of survival is partly a legacy of the accumulation permitted by the past. The cushioning effect of early industrialization and the corresponding State ideologies that have historically been its outcome in Western Europe can help to defer the process of decline. Nevertheless, it is clear from the material presented here that, even in the comparative security and affluence of Europe, a mortgage default, the break up of traditional community networks or the run-down of the public sector can lead to the disintegration of the whole pattern and the loss of an adequate livelihood by some households.

Here we should stress the ambiguity of the concepts of 'survival' and 'reproduction' in absolute terms. Empirical studies of the household reveal a very wide range of different forms of an often contradictory nature. Patterns of incorporation in the wider economy are multiple, and the ideology of household unity may conceal a diverse set of internal interests (Harris 1981; Roldán this volume; Stolcke 1981). The concept of household practices attempts to offer an empirical account of these changing cultural styles, while the analysis of patterns of social reproduction suggests a way of linking the contradictory domain of the household to the total economy. More work is needed to develop a theoretical approach that can link this deconstructed grouping with a given economic and political structure.

An implicit biologism has been apparent in some recent approaches to this topic, which infer that the system exists to reproduce itself and that the nature and form of this reproduction is somehow constant. What we are interested in here, however, are the contradictions that may arise as patterns of consumption come into conflict with changing economic realities: opening options for some, foreclosing them for others, securing survival in affluence for a minority and making day-to-day subsistence problematic for many. Survival cannot be defined or measured at a given level, and the ideological construction of what is adequate, may have a powerful impact on felt levels of poverty, although they are frequently misleading in reality. To take but one example, given the media-assisted spread of Western-based patterns of commoditization, there is growing evidence that traditional, non-Western diets come to be experienced as less adequate than the consumption of refined foods despite the actual nutritional superiority of the former. The correlation between prestige and food-consumption habits is well documented. It is not simply that the components of an adequate level of reproduction are culturally determined, rather that they are not static but shifting and changing in response to these pressures. Any account of the impact of macro-economic change must take account of these issues, both within and between households. As Roldán points out, even slight improvements in the material level of existence of the household as a whole may be won at the expense of internal contradictions and emotional stress for some of its female members. Levels and styles of reproduction, such as the allocation of a limited income for the education or clothing of children, rather than the immediate consumption or entertainment of the adults, are, as the Mexico case makes clear, a focus of conflict within the domestic unit. There are hidden costs in these choices which often convert them into struggles for sets of values that are basically in opposition.

The analysis of possible combinations of time, income, skills and resources as the main sources of organization for survival, shows that certain combinations of work can be highly prejudicial and problematic for some members of the household, even while guaranteeing their subsistence. These patterns may be particularly common in self-employed households and in areas in which 'self-employed industrialization' predominates, such as that described by Mingione for Southern Italy, where very long hours of work are coupled with very long hours of domestic labour to produce considerable stress. In this sense, time is squeezed to its limits in accommodating to the need for increased resources (Redclift). Several recent cross-cultural studies have documented the different pressures on the time use of men and women, in which the latter have predominantly shorter resting hours, greater intensity and fragmentation of work and more frequent recourse to multiple simultaneous occupation. Roldán gives some evidence of the complex time-patterning involved in combinations of domestic and income-generating work.

These accounts indicate that time has a different meaning for each sex, and economic change may affect the time use of men and women in different ways. They also show that there are patterns of reproduction that are partly modified or subsumed by economic development and partly maintained. Economistic accounts that imply that the household responds only to economic pressure and rationality must be qualified by the evidence of the persistence of activities and forms of sexual division of labour as culturally valuable. Household food production, for example, is sometimes maintained even when no longer economic to do so; or the ideology that the work of women in agriculture implies loss of status may continue to be significant, even when feminization processes run directly counter to it. There is no necessary line of cause and effect in these arrangements and we are only now beginning to understand some of the dimensions involved. The British studies presented in this volume suggest that some renegotiation of the domestic division of labour may be occurring, if only in a piecemeal way. Other British research finds less evidence of this (Morris 1983) and much of the literature on developing countries argues that the over-exploitation of women is increasing with economic and technological change (Loutfi 1980; Palmer 1979; Rogers 1980). The local context, household structure and domestic cycle are obviously crucial factors here. Families in the expansion phase consume a considerable amount of time in child care, while couples without children have a wider range of options for generating resources, both through income-generating and self-provisioning activities. Single, female-headed households with children are not always able to capitalize on available resources, not only because of time constraints but also because of culturally instituted notions of gender-appropriate activities. However, low-income, female-headed households may utilize welfare benefits and kin-based reciprocity, where available, to greater advantage without resident males, because they are already deprived of access to forms of work with a higher rate of return to labour. They may of course choose this for quite other reasons and there is obviously no simple trade-off between economic benefits and ideological options.

In earlier studies of urban poverty, exchanges through kin were seen as a crucial coping mechanism. Once again there are major differences in the kinds of transfers that are made in different class contexts, whether they are of money, goods, or services. The household as a residential unit may not necessarily be the most significant area. Extended family networks need not be spatially bounded, and remittances from distant migrant members may be a crucial component of the reproduction of certain low-income groups. Goods and services can by definition only be exchanged by those in comparative proximity, while among the middle and upper classes, long-term and inter-generational transfers of financial resources, creating non-reciprocal investments through time, are likely to be more important. All these have different implications for the reproduction of the household. Furthermore, these patterns have class bases and themselves contribute to processes of stratification, though the dynamics of this may be very different from traditional conceptions.

Many of the chapters make some reference to the importance of the inter-relationship between the State, political movements and consciousness; only Cornuel and Duriez, Gerry and Godard elaborate on this relationship. The complexities of the connection between the State and economic development have been widely analysed, but little has been said on the inter-relation between the State, patterns of social reproduction and economic activities. It is clear that State operations are both affected by, and affect, reproduction patterns and the possibilities of capital accumulation in different settings.

In the case of Southern Italy, for example, (Mingione, Pinnarò/ Pugliese), the State appears to be under increasing pressure to provide both formal employment solutions for the growing surplus population and also to expand the provision of public assistance. This leads to a largely inefficient provision of welfare services which continue to be provided in petty commodity and informal ways and through kin and female care, and which are very unevenly distributed among different strata of the poor. Similarly, Connolly stresses how the Mexican situation is characterized by the translation of employment pressures into a mythical attention by the State to informal/household solutions which tend to be highly unsatisfactory and contradictory.

Gershuny's hypothesis on the shift from State provision of services to self-provision, read in conjunction with Gerry's political observations and Pahl and Wallace's specific analysis of the Sheppey situation, supports the view that the recent strategies of the industrialized State, such as privatization and strong ideological support for communal self-help activities, are an essential part of the politics of deindustrialization. The response to this in terms of socio-political movements also gives evidence of the varying impact of informalization on different classes and local environments. Resistance to the expansion of the informal sector in favour of the re-expansion of the industrial labour force outlined for Naples (Pinnarò and Pugliese) and the confrontation over informalization in Mexico (Connolly) are both in contrast with the 'small is beautiful' thesis and the rise of Green movements in Western Europe (Gerry).

Thus, there are both links and contradictions between the State and the market, and a growing conflict between the demands of various fractions of capital and national interests has emerged in the last ten years. In Italy, for example, there is a clear conflict of priorities between the State and the corporations. While the State tries to apply pressures for the creation of national jobs, the corporations argue that their economic survival depends on the migration of their capital to sources of cheap labour. With the increasing mobility of capital, technological restructuring and labour saving have become world-wide goals, but they have a different impact, depending on region, sex, class, age and ethnic group. In the British context, it has been argued that unemployment has had little political impact, partly because it is cushioned by the State, and the standards of living and levels of consumer investment of previous decades. Its effects are simply felt less severely in the early 1980s than they were in the 1930s. On the evidence of the cases documented here, we would argue that this may certainly reflect the situation of white, adult males who were previously skilled, industrial primary workers. Such groups may be able to draw on certain reserves that were not available to their counterparts during the Depression. On the other hand, for minorities – the young, recent immigrants, women and the 'casual' poor of developing countries – the situation may be very different. The experience of unemployment and the ability to continue to produce some form of subsistence clearly varies in accordance with these categories.

The hypothesis suggested by Gershuny, and documented along class lines by Pahl and Wallace, suggests that even a minority of the unemployed who are less badly affected by the recession may suffer greatly from the fact that they lose access to the 'do-it-yourself' society, in which self-provisioning is based on a regular income which can be invested in home ownership, durable consumer goods and the tools for the job.

Underlying processes of polarization, along differet axes from those of traditional class cleavage, appear to be developing, and in their turn conditioning the likely response to change. Frequently they are masked by conventional ideologies about gender, skills and family life. In this book we examine a necessarily selective range of outcomes, but in doing so we suggest that some points of generality do exist, and attempt to provide the basis for an alternative to the assumptions of uniformity that have been current. By setting the issue in an international context it becomes clear that these processes are relevant not simply as an aberration from the 'normal' workings of the capitalist system or as a result of its imperfect penetration of subsistence economies but as an intrinsic aspect of its development, having different emphases at different historical moments and in different locations. We would also take issue with simplistic models of 'centres' and 'peripheries', looking to a more complex view of regional differentiation in which there are many lines of force and nuclei of accumulation. It is a paradoxical feature of late capitalism that trends towards decentralization only disperse labour, but in fact contribute to increased functional integration by reaching outwards to workers, resources and markets. Far from being a symptom of fragmentation, this is the result of increasing concentration and hegemony.

While the analyses of the decline of the industrial working class by Gorz, Bahro and others have clear implications for our understanding of alternatives to formal employment, we suggest in this book that these 'new' forms of work do not necessarily lead to a Utopia of purposeful leisure-time pursuits but themselves result in social dislocation. The misleadingly aggregated model imposed by a sectoral analysis cannot capture the complexities of these patterns of penetration and needs to be replaced by a closer attention to the relations of appropriation, both of labour or time and of resources, through which the reproduction of material life is assured.

Part I

Critical Approaches to the
Social Relations of Production

1

Social Reproduction of the Surplus Labour Force: The Case of Southern Italy

Enzo Mingione

Introduction

The recent attention given by social scientists to the diffusion of informal activities in industrialized countries can only be fully understood by considering its relationship to three other scientific concerns which have emerged during the last decade. These concerns are: (1) current changes in the employment structure, in particular an increase in the unemployment rate as a persistent and long-lasting trend; (2) the feminist critique of the conceptualization of work, especially the increasing attention given to the role of unpaid domestic activities in the development of industrial societies; and (3) the controversial role of the State in shaping economic and social relations, particularly the nature, impact and prospects of different welfare provisions in connection with the fiscal crisis of the State (O'Connor 1973).

Jallade concludes his introduction to a recent debate on *Employment and Unemployment in Europe* with the following remark: 'the employment difficulties of Western Europe . . . are not transitory but, rather, the outcome of the economic, social and cultural values that have prevailed in recent years' (1981:39). Current changes in employment trends are connected with the general rate of economic growth,[1] which fell from the high level of the 1950s and 1960s (ten per cent per year or more) to the low level of the 1970s (five per cent per year or less). It is difficult to state with precision whether we face a definitive change to a long phase of zero or slow growth or whether this is only a transitory phenomenon. Although existing arguments in favour of the first eventuality are not totally convincing, this hypothesis appears much stronger than the second one. Stagnation has been the 'norm' now for a fairly long period and there appears to be little likelihood of re-establishing a generalized high economic growth rate. Moreover, social organization has changed considerably in the last ten years in order to adapt itself to a long-term period of stagnation.

Two trends explain the general phenomenon of employment crisis: (1) the creation of new jobs cannot keep up with the discontinuation of old jobs, nor can it meet the new labour supply resulting from the baby boom of the 1950s and 1960s as well as from social groups (mainly women) which were inactive in the previous decades; and (2) the employment structure is becoming more and more characterized by fragmentation, Balkanization[2] and the emergence of modern double and informal employment.

The present incapacity of the system to create new jobs has two faces: (1) the absolute decrease of employment in manufacturing industries (deindustrialization as a combined result of new labour-saving technologies and of various forms of industrial relocation and restructuring); and (2) the relatively slow and more selective increase of formal employment in the service industries, both public and private. In principle these employment tendencies are independent of stagnation. Technological labour saving, restructuring and industrial relocation increase when industrial investments increase. Hence, at this stage of development, economic recovery implements further employment crisis and consequently stagnation tendencies are renewed because of over-production or over-increase of State expenditure.

The probable consequence of these trends for the employment structure of the industrialized countries, in the likely case that they will continue and remain uncombatted or inefficiently combatted, is a consistent increase of the unemployable or under-employed surplus population. In underdeveloped countries, the formation of a large surplus population increasingly located in urban areas will continue, as industrial relocation and local developments involve only a minority of regions and a relatively small portion of the population.

As we will argue later, these assumptions imply that the survival strategies of these two sections of surplus population are becoming crucial in shaping the present and future problems of societies. It is within this context that informalization processes eventually take place and are observed and analysed.

The welfare intervention of the State[3] has two aspects which it is important to distinguish. The first includes direct provision of collective services, i.e. efficient public transport, low-cost housing, health, education, etc., which are oriented to the socialization of some of the costs of 'better' reproduction patterns of the labour force. The general aims of these interventions are: (1) a contribution to the formation of a qualitatively better (more productive) labour force; (2) maximization of the supply of labour following the changing and contradictory requirements of different sections of capital accumulation (e.g. child-care provisions to increase the supply of women workers, efficient health provisions to decrease the time out from work of the sick); and (3) diversion of the money spent on such services towards other consumption items (i.e. mass consumption of durable goods).

The second aspect of welfare intervention contributes money or basic consumption items (e.g. food stamps) for the survival of the surplus population (the unemployed, disabled, poor and aged). Thus, the part of the surplus population which is not of immediate interest as far as labour demand is concerned is maintained in a 'frozen' state. At the same time the aggregate demand does not fall too sharply and political concensus is maintained.

During the 20 years of post-war economic expansion, governments of the industrialized countries have been able to spend increasing amounts of money on direct provision of collective services and, at the same time, consolidate adequate expenditure on the surplus population. While the living standards of the workers were improving the relation between productivity and the cost of labour was kept favourable for capital accumulation and the risks of over-production were minimized (at least within industrialized areas). The negative effects and contradictions of these development patterns were shifted towards the underdeveloped countries and regions, where surplus population expanded, survival became increasingly difficult and consensus and political order were very problematic.[4]

The present difficulties are mainly related to the contemporary pressures of two tendencies: the decrease of available financial resources due to stagnation, increased international competition and changes in the international division of labour; and the rapid increase of the surplus population which is supposed to be the recipient of the second form of intervention. It is interesting to note that what has been called a tendency towards the dismantling of the Welfare State is often a drastic cut in the first form of expenditure described above, compensated for by increases in the second form of expenditure, where an increasing number of recipients may be facing a decreasing State contribution per capita in real terms (Harloe & Paris 1982).

If these are long-term tendencies, the future prospects are rather worrying. While State expenditure is trapped by the necessity to freeze, with at least partial support, an increasingly large surplus population, the cuts in the provision of socialized services will worsen the living standards of the population and will force the adoption of every possible informal/cheap survival solution (instead of the revival of a no longer convenient market[5]). This probable picture is very different from the optimistic view that some authors have expressed regarding the information process as a new alternative to the oppression of capitalist development (Heinze & Olk 1982; Szelenyi 1981).

negative prospects

Social Reproduction of the Labour Force and Different Forms of Work

The discussion so far explains why there has been a growing scientific attention towards the diffusion of forms of work which have been called 'informal', 'irregular', 'underground', 'black' or by other names.[6] It explains also the importance of the recent feminist emphasis on the role of unpaid domestic work in the development of industrial societies and the great variation in time and space concerning its extent and specific labour processes.[7] Some attention is being devoted also to the importance of non-monetary, voluntary transactions, such as solidarity contributions among friends, relatives and neighbours, as a consistent long-lasting input for the survival of large strata of the population – the social economy (Lowenthal 1975, 1981).

Two important questions have emerged as a consequence of this wave of studies. It is now essential to define and take into consideration forms of work other than the 'formal', recorded employment which has been the almost exclusive object of every traditional study in social science. Consequently, it has become necessary to develop an approach which allows interpretation of the different meanings of these various human activities in the context of different patterns, times and local historical conditions of

industrial development. These two questions are strictly connected
in the sense that any consideration and definition of such activities
which have only a descriptive impact would prove inadequate and
insufficient in the face of the urgent need to interpret their roles and
trends within different patterns and at different stages of industrial
development. My choice has been (see also Mingione 1983) to adopt
and revise the Marxist theory of social reproduction of the labour force.

The basic elements of the Marxist theory of social reproduction of
the labour force are embedded in the concept of the labour force as a
special commodity (special in the sense that it creates new value and
is not directly produced by capital) and in the theory of the
industrial reserve army/surplus population. Although the epistemo-
logical and practical importance of this section of Marxist thinking
is undeniable and has become very evident recently, it has remained
largely undiscussed until the last ten years.

The assumptions adopted in this specific approach to the problem
of social reproduction of the labour force are the following:

(1)   The patterns of social reproduction of the labour force
(intended in a broad sense to be inclusive of present, future and
potential wage-work) affect the capital accumulation process in two
different ways: they determine the costs, quantities and qualities of
the labour supply, both at present and in a generation span; and
they contribute to fixing the limits to the consumption capacity
(commodification process) of goods which are essential to the
survival of the population.

(2)   Although these patterns are strongly affected by different
capital operations, they are not under the direct control/command
of capital (Thrift 1983). They depend on pre-existing, socio-
historical conditions and, to a certain extent, on a degree of choice
among different options by the individual unit of reproduction –
the household (e.g. some households continue to process or grow
food for self-consumption even when it is no longer convenient from
a strictly economic point of view).

(3)   The influence of capital on the social-reproduction patterns of
the labour force is not only limited by the interference of other
conditions and options but it is also bound to be extremely
controversial. The main capital input is the structure of labour
demand, as articulated in numbers and qualities (levels of work
productivity) of jobs. The interconnection between the complex
specific structure of the demand and the complex specific patterns of

social reproduction will result in a wage/income structure and in a specific capacity of monetary expenditure on subsistence goods and services produced and sold on the market (patterns of monetary consumption/commodification). The disequilibrium between these two contemporary results gives rise to two parallel contradictions. Accumulation accompanied by high rates of commodification (a disproportionate increase of unproductive jobs and expenditures) tends to increase the cost of reproduction of the labour force at rates highly problematic for capital. Accumulation accompanied by a disproportionate expansion of excess/surplus population (this is the fundamental meaning of the Marxist theory of the industrial reserve army) results in insufficient commodification and strong over-production tendencies. The complexity of the world system (a shift of the second contradiction towards the underdeveloped countries) and the intervention of the State in industrialized countries have concealed these contradictions and postponed their disruptive effects during periods of sufficient growth rates. However, they have become more evident now with the emergence of the problems we have mentioned in the previous section.

Using this approach, the most important questions still to be answered concern the significance and contradictions that the reproduction of the relative surplus population is beginning to acquire. The umbilical cord of industrialization or of employment growth had permitted the categorization of the relative surplus population as a reserve industrial labour force and the underde-veloped area as a site of future industrial expansion. With its rupture, the reproduction of vast, increasingly urban masses, seems to be pointless and to presage survival in a poverty to which, at least as far as industrial employment is concerned, there is no solution. In this sense the cycle of reproduction of the labour force is already shattered: it no longer constitutes the link between the cycle of accumulation of capital, on the one hand, and the various subsist-ence economies and societies, on the other. This is the starting-point for the elaboration of our hypothesis that the increasing complexity and articulation of present-day societies gives rise to a process of social fragmentation, in which the reproduction of diversified social sectors are incompatible, mutually antagonistic and give rise to new and irrevocable contradictions.

The importance for industrial development of differentiated levels of labour cost/productivity/income is immediately clear; however, it remains to be ascertained how these levels are produced in the various reproductive spheres and social, economic and cultural contexts. Thus, possibilities of a complementary relationship between specific forms of social reproduction and labour costs and quality useful for the expansion of the industrial process acquire a fundamental importance. In this sense, the question of rural and pre-capitalistic societies, domestic work, and the role of the State in social reproduction, particularly in the reproduction of the labour force, constitute fundamental elements for the determination of the costs and the incomes of labour, and of the rhythms and quality of development of the economy and society.

We shall now proceed to propose, in a preliminary and hypothetical manner, a rearticulation of the concept of 'human activities useful for individual and collective reproduction'.

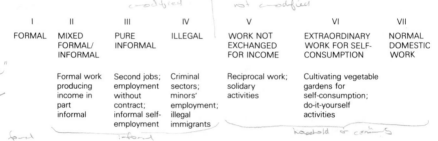

I	II	III	IV	V	VI	VII
FORMAL	MIXED FORMAL/ INFORMAL	PURE INFORMAL	ILLEGAL	WORK NOT EXCHANGED FOR INCOME	EXTRAORDINARY WORK FOR SELF-CONSUMPTION	NORMAL DOMESTIC WORK
	Formal work producing income in part informal	Second jobs; employment without contract; informal self-employment	Criminal sectors; minors' employment; illegal immigrants	Reciprocal work; solidary activities	Cultivating vegetable gardens for self-consumption; do-it-yourself activities	

Figure 1.1   Spectrum of human activities contributing to reproduction (complex hypothesis)

My classification as illustrated in figure 1.1, starts from the Gershuny and Pahl (1979) tripartition (formal: informal: domestic or household). I have broken down this tripartition further to distinguish more clearly between activities that have a largely different meaning, either for the monetary economy and accumulation process or for family organization and reproduction cycle.

The differential between the first four categories and the last three is immediately evident. Different balances between the two groups mean different costs of reproduction and levels of commodification. The differences among the four categories of paid work are more complicated to spell out. Formal work is fully observable in both the employment and income structure. In a highly regulated and controlled society it reflects the fundamental cost of labour within the reproduction process (possibly complemented by various kinds of State contribution) and the monetary consumption capacity. It also fully contributes to the State fiscal system. Mixed work is detected as a source of income but does not express in full the income/cost of labour and the consumption capacity and partially cheats the fiscal system. Pure informal work is not detected and recorded and largely cheats the fiscal system. We will assume that it has a lower ratio of income per worked hour (possibly reflected in a lower cost of the product if the quality is the same) in respect to formal work, which means consistent important consequences in reproduction patterns and in consumption capacities. Illegal work is distinguished because it is very heterogenous, difficult to detect, and different from other informal activities in terms of who practices it, the levels and stratification of income and its disruptive capacity against the State. Reciprocal and supportive activities are deductions from the time of one household in favour of the survival of another household, so that they do not enter the reproduction patterns of the provider but the ones of the receiver. Finally, the distinction between normal (intended as an historically changing concept) and extra-ordinary work for self-consumption is not clear enough because it changes over time and space. However, it is important to distinguish the operation of everyday domestic life from the repair, maintenance and improvement or farming activities, which require specific skills or long periods of training and/or operation, so that the extra-ordinary activities are either optional for households with a sufficient income or forced by the insufficiency of income.

Different combinations of the activities included in the spectrum affect the levels of subsistence and social reproduction and thus, on the one hand, the costs and productivity of labour and, on the other, the structure and expansive potential of the consumption capacity of a determinate society. Diversified combinations of the spectrum affect social organization and conflict and, above all, the concrete prospects of the development of different types of milieux.

Tentative Historical Discourse on the Reproduction Process

I recognize that qualitative changes in the social reproduction process are extremely important and at the same time very difficult to acknowledge in a generalized way. In this sense the results of my analysis are bound to be approximate and hypothetical. Among other questions which contribute to a certain degree of uncertainty, there is the impact of changing and stratified levels of labour productivity. In this respect it is practically impossible to express the whole range of stratification at different times and to avoid an

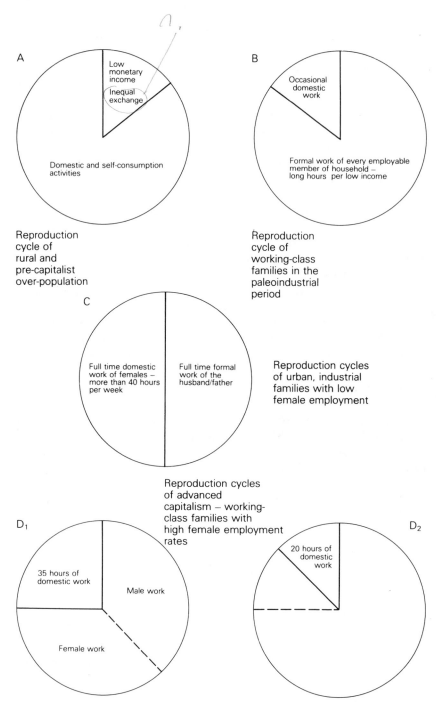

Figure 1.2   Reproduction cycles in different historical places and social ambits

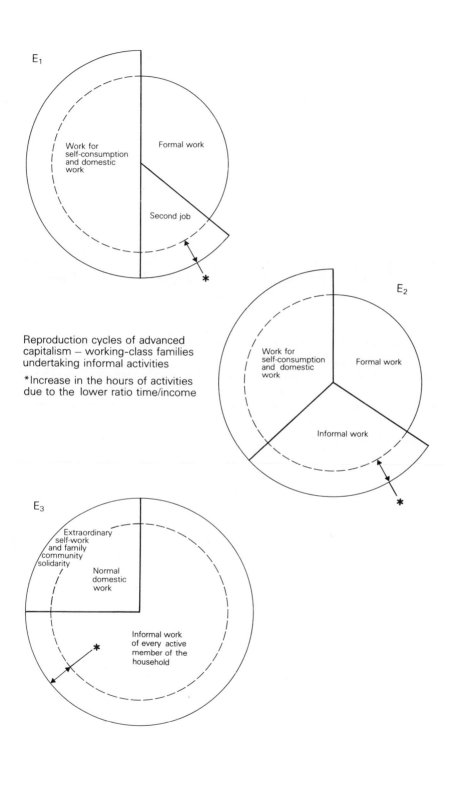

E₁

Work for self-consumption and domestic work

Formal work

Second job

*

Reproduction cycles of advanced capitalism – working-class families undertaking informal activities

*Increase in the hours of activities due to the lower ratio time/income

E₂

Work for self-consumption and domestic work

Formal work

Informal work

*

E₃

Extraordinary self-work and family community solidarity

Normal domestic work

Informal work of every active member of the household

*

explanation which is causally circular. In short, increased productivity of work is reflected in increased income per worked hour and consequently in increased monetary reproduction costs of the more productive labour force and consistent qualitative changes in the labour reproduction process. Alternatively, it could be argued that improvement in the qualitative standards of social reproduction of the labour force allows the formation of a potentially more productive labour force. I would argue that the problem of original causation is not so relevant as long as we recognize that there is strong intercausality between the two processes. A small push from one side may thus be reflected in a consistent acceleration of changes on both sides, if the historical conditions are ripe and there are no barriers to interaction between the two processes (e.g. consistent State intervention which redistributes the benefits of increased productivity to different areas of social reproduction). Historical evidence shows that State intervention has various possible consequences which should be investigated specifically.

I shall argue later that there have been at least two important historical transitions concerning the patterns of reproduction and the levels of labour productivity, and another one may be now under way.[8] The first is connected with the legal abolition of child employment and the decrease in female employment which established the modern form of unpaid domestic work within the workers' households. The second transition is connected with a new increase in women's employment rates, in particular for married women, which is again largely reflected in changes in social reproduction patterns. The present one reflects employment difficulties, i.e. the structural increase of the surplus population in industrialized countries, the diffusion of informal activities, etc.

Our visual expression of reproduction cycles (figure 1.2) does not show the qualitative changes which need to be taken into consideration separately. It is also difficult through this visualization to express different ratios of productivity/income with sufficient precision. From this point of view my considerations must be considered provisional and approximate.

The unit of reproduction (the household) disposes above all of working capacities which, with a limited freedom of choice, conditioned by the historical phases of development and by the socio-cultural background of the unit, it can apply either to working activities that provide a monetary income with which to purchase goods and services for subsistence, or to working activities that directly provide goods and services useful for subsistence (activities for self-consumption or domestic work). Furthermore, the unit may also be able to count on resources from outside, such as assistance from the State or from public bodies (in terms of income or of services and goods) or on contributions in the form of income or free goods and services provided by private individuals or bodies (gifts from relations, inheritances, working help, neighbourhood solidarity, solidarity between friends and colleagues, charity, etc.).

The combination of work for self-consumption and work for income acquires a fundamental importance because it constitutes the reason for the connection between the reproductive cycle of the unit and the general process of accumulation/development. In the context of this connection it is possible to recognize a historical duality in the cycles of reproduction: on the one hand, the reproduction of the labour force directly active in the process of capital accumulation, where, albeit with different historical and geographical combinations, working activity for income is considerable; and, on the other hand, the reproduction of the surplus labour force where, whether the population is urban or rural, work for self-consumption is prevalent and the monetary cost-income of subsistence is minimum.

In the context of reproduction of the active labour force the points of balance between the levels of work for self-consumption and the levels of work for income can vary greatly in different societies. One of the most important factors in conditioning the combination is the qualitative and quantitative structure of labour demand. There is a considerable historical difference between the reproductive balances determined in the presence of early-industrial labour demand, based on very long working hours, particularly low hourly remuneration and the indifferent use of women and minors, and the balances that have gradually developed in the course of the present century, in the presence of an increasingly selective and stratified labour demand, shorter working hours and increasing salaries and productivity of work. In the early-industrial context (see figure 1.2, B), once the pre-industrial productive communities had been abandoned, work for self-consumption was necessarily reduced to the minimum, while the subsistence levels of working families remained extremely low.[9] The costs of labour reproduction were kept low by the presence of a large amount of relative over-population, but even the quality of labour and productivity remained at a relatively low level. Owing to very low living standards and very long working hours, the average life span was short, there was a high rate of infant mortality and the physical endurance of the workers was fairly limited.[10]

From this early situation one passes to a different one based on a more accentuated selectivity of labour demand (e.g. laws against employment of minors) and on a progressive shortening of working hours, with parallel increases in income which reflect more than proportional increases in productivity. The standard of living of the workers' families increases, together with the need to dedicate a part of the working potential of the family to work for self-consumption. Domestic work in the modern sense of the term (Ingrosso 1979) established itself even in the context of working-class families. It is important to note that the solution generally adopted for the reproduction of the labour force in a manner more suitable to the requirements of industrial development was the allocation of a considerable amount of unpaid female labour to domestic work. This 'solution' tended to keep the cost of the reproduction of labour low, but it imposed a discriminatory selectivity on labour demand/supply and withdrew from the field of direct activity of capitalistic accumulation a whole series of activities that remained non-socialized and external to the logic of the market of goods and services.

The reproductive cycles tended to change, assuming one of two different forms, the fortunes of which varied according to historical phase and social context. The first (figure 1.2, C) was based on very high quotas of domestic work, on the assignment of the greater part of the female labour force to unpaid domestic activities, and thus on a supply/demand of female labour which, at least in the non-agricultural sectors, was very limited. The second (figure 1.2, D) was founded on the need to continue to supply the market with large quotas of female labour, and thus on the limitation of domestic activities which was compensated for by the purchase of substitutive goods or services or by public assistance contributions. Furthermore, a certain quota of these domestic activities, difficult to reduce, were carried out, by members of the unit (mainly women) in addition to their full-time work.

In the first case the cost of reproduction of the labour force is lower than in the second, not only in terms of total salaries but also in total social cost. However, the actual degree of propensity to accumulate is clearly less because the reproductive unit's capacity of monetary consumption is smaller and many reproductive goods and services remain private and outside the accumulation circuit and socialization processes. This explanation is useful in understanding the complex link between the structure of the reproduction cycles and the more general process of economic development.

Even though one cannot talk of a generalized historical change from the first to the second model of reproduction after the Second World War, it can nevertheless be affirmed that the second model found a more radical expression in the industrialized countries lacking large internal reserves of labour, apart from women tied to domestic activities. In these cases it became convenient to promote the release of a part of the female labour force and the importation of an immigrant labour force from less developed countries.

The switch from the prevalence of one model to the other, on the other hand, was slower and more controversial in countries possessing internal labour reserves, e.g. Southern European countries such as Italy. In any case the considerable and differentiated change-over from cycle C to cycle D in many industrialized areas after the Second World War helped to accelerate the rhythms of economic growth, to increase the difference between the development rhythms of different areas, and to render much more complex the stratification of costs and modalities of reproduction of the labour force. These areas ranged from the least developed where the quota of monetary consumption remained low, to semi-peripheral areas where female employment in non-agricultural activities remained low owing to the large proportion of women tied to domestic activities, to the more advanced areas in which private work for self-consumption was reduced to the minimum and the service-industry sector, both public and private, underwent a great expansion.

There can also be considerable differences between the more advanced cycles of reproduction of the labour force. In the extreme case (figure 1.2, D_2), high income and the efficiency of public and community services permit a considerable reduction of the time spent on domestic activities (15–20 hours per week at most), with an almost optimum application of both male and female working capacity for income earning. However, there also exist numerous cases of reproduction cycles which are very problematical. In these cases (figure 1.2, D_1), the domestic work level is high (between 20 and 35–40 hours per week) and, in view of its unequal sexual distribution, women find considerable difficulty in combining their domestic work with efficient full-time outside employment; the result is more absenteeism, less professionalism and a working career handicapped by unfavourable discrimination. I would also suggest that in principle the historically socially established assumption that female labour reproduction patterns include a higher quota of domestic unpaid work is the fundamental reason for the persisting job and wage discrimination against women.[11]

Before considering the present situation, we shall raise an important problem concerning the role played in the reproduction cycles by different sizes and qualities of households. It is a complicated point because both size and quality change over time and space, so that generalizations are rather dangerous.

We can assume in general but with consistent and important exceptions (Paci 1980), that industrial development progressively dissolves large households, based on extended families, in favour of much smaller ones, based on nuclear families.[12] This process has important consequences for the organization of reproduction cycles, and in particular of domestic activities. Large households are engaged in a high number of hours of domestic work (which, however, may involve a lower per capita quota in relation to smaller units) and are usually able to provide much more (extraordinary) domestic production than nuclear families. This transition from large to smaller units has different times and rhythms in different regions: we can even assume that in some areas (rural regions in Italy, France, Spain, Greece, etc.) it has not yet completely taken place.

Demographic trends also have a great influence. In general, the population of the industrialized regions is ageing, while birth and marriage rates are decreasing. This means that there is a steady increase of very small households composed of one or two people, either young or old but predominantly the latter. This process influences the reproduction cycles because in general these households enjoy monetary incomes below the average and are compelled to engage in consumption or production activities classified as III to VI in figure 1.1. Welfare State services are required to assist the reproduction of these households and prevent their meeting serious difficulties and weakening both the consensus base and the consumption capacity. This means a continuous increase in the demand for State welfare intervention. On the other hand, the total absence of State intervention and housing shortages in large cities may prevent the diffusion of small households. Forced cohabitation by adults of different ages often leads to problems and conflict.

In addition to these trends, a consistent increase of single-parent households, particularly the number of households headed by women – singles, divorcees or widows, has been noticed in various countries. This tendency, combined with the persistence of job/ wage discrimination against women and the historical assumption of unequal sexual division of domestic work, may also mean increasing pressures for State intervention.

It should be clear that while my hypothetical reproduction cycles are mainly based on time-budgets of middle-aged couples with school-age children, I am well aware of the predominant importance of different kinds of households, in terms of the number of cohabitants, family relations and age groups. From what has just been said, it is possible to argue that the present trends tend to modify the household structure in a complex way but that, in any case, they contribute to the diffusion of informal and irregular activities.

Informalization and Social Reproduction

I shall now proceed to consider the last decade, the complex effects of the economic crisis on reproduction cycles and, above all, the feedback from the reproductive to the economic sphere, with particular emphasis on the impact of the informalization processes on reproduction.

The most important effects of the recent economic crisis on the various reproductive cycles of the labour force derive from the high rate of inflation and from the complex rearticulation of the employment structure (i.e. increasing unemployment, above all of young people; increasing non-employment of young and old people; Balkanization of the labour markets; spread of various types of informal activities). Furthermore, the fiscal crisis of the State plays an important part in modifying the circumstances of social reproduction.

I have argued elsewhere (Mingione 1983) that the combination of inflation and reduced formal employment tends to move the balance between work for self-consumption and work for income in favour of the former, thus leading to a reduction of aggregate demand and accumulation capacity. Taking for granted this process of circular transmission of the crisis, from the productive to the reproductive system (where there is no diminution in the cost of labour sufficient to revive the economy as a whole on account of the segmentation of the labour markets) and back to the productive system, I shall now consider the main changes of social organization in the context of the processes of reproduction of the labour force.

The various reproduction units find themselves, to a greater or smaller extent, faced by the problem of the diminution of the monetary quota used for the purchase of goods and services for subsistence. This is often accompanied by a lowering of the quality and the quantity of the public reproductive services owing to the fiscal crisis of the Welfare State. The tendency of work for self-consumption to increase, rather than generally diminish the costs of reproduction of the labour force, increases the gap between the cost of 'guaranteed' labour, which increases with the inflation rate but is counter-balanced by the decrease in the number of workers, and the cost of the remaining labour force, employed or potential. Even if one takes for granted the reduction in the standard of living of a large number of households, which in any case is reflected in the reproduction cycles by the increase of work for self-consumption compared with monetary incomes, the various units, in the various socio-economic ambits, must seek to re-balance reproduction by means of various combinations of two possible solutions: an absolute increase of work for self-consumption, including that exchanged with neighbours, friends and relations and various forms of informal activities (or occasional formal activities providing a low income).

The spread of informal activities has a number of common characteristics with regard to the cycles of reproduction. In that they are phenomena of labour supply or availability of independent labour, informal activities are one of the consequences of the employment crisis, in the context of which unemployment and non-employment increase without a parallel decrease in the cost of reproduction of guaranteed labour. The availability for informal work thus increases and, at the same time, the cost of reproduction of this sort of labour decreases, for the very reason that the increase in the quota of domestic work resulting from the crisis concerns above all informal work. In this sense, both in general and on average, informal working activities reveal a ratio between gross income and working times lower than that found in formal working conditions. There are exceptions, e.g. some second jobs require professional qualifications.

The lower time/income ratio (i.e. the lower cost of labour) fits in, in the various forms of decentralization and subcontracting, with the need of the economic units to limit or reduce the average cost of labour, even though they are unable to do this in the concentrated units in which they continue mainly to operate.

The second characteristic common to nearly all informal activities is the complex role that they assume with regard to the functioning of the State and public organizations. The evasion of certain obligations of a fiscal, social or contributory nature, and even those of a legal nature, where the employment of minors, the carrying out of dangerous work without taking due safety measures and the employment of illegal immigrants are concerned, is a common characteristic of informal activities and continues to make them practical for the entrepreneur and advantageous for the consumer. Apart from the reduction in revenue (and thus of spending capacity) of public bodies, the spread of informal activities considerably reduces the possibilities of public control and State intervention with regard to reproduction cycles, which become increasingly varied and complex. If the informal workers avoid payment of taxes and other legal contributions, the State finds itself obliged to ignore the requirements deriving from the social reorganization founded on the spread of informal activities. On the other hand, some governments may enjoy the fact that the diffusion of informal activities partially substitutes government intervention (e.g. self-building for public housing, baby-sitting for cash instead of public institutions for child care). Informalization involves, therefore, the development of accentuated and diversified tendencies towards social fragmentation which derive from the schizophrenic nature of the relationship between the increasingly complex structure of social reproduction, the process of public intervention and the cycle of formal capitalistic accumulation.

Informalization introduces two types of contradictions that could have radical consequences with regard to the prospect of social conflict. An increasing degree of incongruence is due to the fact that many households are reproducing formal and informal labour at the same time. This fact may in turn produce competing antagonistic pressures which the households are unable to meet. This contradiction is more common in the highly industrialized cities, where there is an increase of second jobs (Gallino 1982) and informal activities on the part of members of the family of stable formal workers in order to obtain complementary incomes. These serve to counter-balance the erosion of income due to inflation, formal unemployment and the deterioration of services and public assistance. Working commitments within the family unit not only tend to increase, thus taking up nearly all available leisure time, but also to be distributed in a discriminative and inequitable manner. This occurs in the case where the formal worker has an informal second job and the other member of the couple is confined to domestic work (including extraordinary domestic work and non-domestic subsistence work such as the cultivation of a vegetable garden) (figure 1.2,E_1). In fact, domestic work time is extended in a manner proportional to the difficulty of organizing reproduction in a complex situation. Increases in working hours and the unequal distribution of work loads (figure 1.2,E_2) also occur when one member of the couple has a formal job and the other an informal one. The sex, age and ethnic division between informal/formal activities varies from area to area, depending on the relative strength and protection that specific groups enjoy in the labour market and formal employment structure. Strong members will be better suited for formal employment and second jobs while weak ones will have to rely on informal, sporadic and low paid jobs.

The second contradiction concerns the difficulty of combining the increase in work for self-consumption necessary for reproduction with the lower working hours/income ratio usual in the case of informal working activity (figure 1.2,E_3). This contradiction is more common where there are systematic concentrations of informal working activities. The most interesting examples are the areas of peripheral industrialization: small concerns making use of forms of informal employment, e.g. indirectly remunerated work by collaborating members of the household in family business; avoidance of paying the legal minimum salaries and Social Security contributions, out-work; and subcontracting. In these cases it is probable that the whole cycle of reproduction depends, as far as monetary income is concerned, on informal or mixed employment. In fact, in zones in which systems of small industrial concerns have developed, the presence of particular social conditions which assume a great importance in the context of reproduction, has been noted (Bagnasco 1977; Paci 1980). The combination of informal employment or, at any rate, of employment with a low ratio between working hours and income, and the need to dedicate relatively long hours to domestic activities implies the existence of particular organizational forms of the reproduction unit and the presence of solidarity at the level of the community, relations or friends. Only an enlarged and compact family structure or a rigorously organized syndicate with interests in both production and reproduction could maximize the utilization of labour on two fronts, both of which are very demanding. This contradiction also tends to confine the spread of economies with a high degree of informalization to the areas in which these preconditions already exist. One can exclude the possibility of the spread of this type of development in regions or social ambits which are already very degraded or marginal, i.e. where there exists neither the economic nor the social possibility of combining a complex reproduction of an informal labour force available to work long hours with the reproduction of the same by means of burdensome hours of work for self-consumption.

Although it is impossible to explain in a simple manner the influence of informal work on the cycle of reproduction, we can point to three combinations of particular interest: (1) the informal work is carried out as a second job by the single earner of income while the 'housewife' suffers a notable increase in time spent on domestic work in order to permit the single earner to carry out the double activity (figure $1.2, E_1$); (2) there is a combination of a formal and informal job, carried out by different persons, and an increase in work for self-consumption needed to meet the more difficult reproduction requirements (figure $1.2, E_2$); (3) a prevalence of informal activities and the necessity of long hours of work for self-consumption, require, in addition to great sacrifices and a well-structured organization on the part of the reproduction unit, forms of solidarity at family, friendship or community level (figure $1.2, E_3$). In all three cases activity times are very heavy, discriminate greatly between the sexes and the various age groups and give rise to social contradictions that are one of the final results, in the reproductive context, of the employment crisis.

The Informal Sector in Southern Italy

In terms of population, Southern Italy is the single, largest backward area in an industrialized country. However, in the course of the last three decades, while this state of underdevelopment has remained, some very important social changes have taken place. The region is now very diversified and it is accordingly more appropriate to speak not of a 'Southern question' but of a number of different questions. Some agricultural areas remain characterized by backward, fragmentary and subsidized productive structures, while others have benefited from extensive processes of agricultural modernization. The strategy of 'growth poles', mainly applied by State-owned petrochemical and steel industries, has not led to widespread industrialization as expected but to the creation of islands of advanced industrial relationships, similar to those established in the industrial cities of the North. Different again is the complex mixture of modern and technologically advanced industries (from Alfasud to Aeritalia), of a large sector of informal and home-based activities, in part traditional artisan and in part the result of advanced decentralization of exporting sectors (e.g. women's shoes), and a very composite service-industry sector that has developed in the Naples area.

The characteristic that remains common to a large part of the South is the presence of a high level of over-population, a key factor of marginality. However, the modes of social reproduction of the various strata in the different parts of the South have become increasingly differentiated. This is a reflection of the crisis of the accepted means of confronting the over-population problem which functioned more or less efficaciously in the first 20 years after the Second World War. This model was based on the combination of a high level of out-migration, widespread financial assistance on the part of the State to families with insufficient income, housing renewal and public works, and some capital-intensive, industrial decentralizations. However, the survival strategies of the surplus population were based above all on the possibilities of out-migration. Precarious employment, the informal sector and a 'jack-of-all-trades' existence constitute a phase of transition prior to emigration, stable, formal employment and conversion to industrial work. The surplus population and its typical survival strategies could be considered an area of social transition from which it was possible to cherish more or less well-founded hopes of emerging in the course of a few years.

The curtailing of out-migration possibilities in the 1970s and the employment crisis of heavy and manufacturing industry in general, radically modified this situation and rendered it more differentiated and complex. The modes of survival of the surplus population crystallized, became permanent strategies of social reproduction and, as such, even more differentiated in consequence of the need to adapt to the various local opportunities, traditions and characteristics. The character assumed by the informal sector in this situation differs from that which has developed in the industrialized areas and also from the one which has existed for a number of decades in the cities of the underdeveloped countries. Compared with the industrialized areas, the informal sector in South Italy has longer roots and traditions, involves different social strata, and is characterized by a less complementary relationship with the working class, in the narrow sense, and by greater poverty. On the other hand, there is a fundamental difference from the situation in the underdeveloped countries. It seems reasonable to accept the view of Portes and Walton (1981), concordant with most of the literature concerning the informal sector in the cities of underdeveloped countries, that the existence of various informal activities explains both the survival of a large surplus population and the salary differences between formal industrial workers in these countries and those in the industrialized countries. The complementary possibilities offered by the coexistence of formal incomes and greater access to informal consumption or to forms of self-consumption reduce the costs of reproduction of a labour force which is not notably less productive than that of the industrialized countries (Portes & Walton 1981: 67–106). In the South the situation is different. The salary levels of the working class employed by large and medium-sized industry are the same as in the rest of Italy. Trade unionism among these Southern workers is just as strong as it is among the workers of Northern and Central Italy. The cost of labour and the pugnacity of the workers' movement in the South are no less than in the rest of Italy, at any rate in those industrial sectors which have not succeeded in reorganizing themselves by means of an intense, systematic and widespread recourse to informal relationships (work carried out in the home, irregular work contracts, intense self-exploitation of independent work). The existence of a high level of over-population is reflected above all in the modes of reproduction (survival strategies) of the workers in the informal sector, with no major elements of a nature complementary to the lifestyle of the working class employed in the formal sectors. The findings of surveys of the workers at the poles of development carried out in the 1970s confirm these observations.

Our survey (Mingione 1977) of the workers of the petrochemical industry in the Syracuse area revealed that the workers in general worked very little in the informal sector. The workers were nearly all males, did not have a second job, nearly all the wives were full-time housewives and consumption styles were largely based on formal relationships. Even those of direct agricultural origin and having peasant relatives had severed almost all their links with the countryside: they did not make any working contribution in the periods when the demand for agricultural labour is highest, nor did they receive any significant amount of foodstuffs free of charge or at special prices. A more recent confirmation of this situation is provided by a comparison between the survival strategies in the social environments we selected for the investigation of informal activities and the findings of the survey of a control sample of 36 families of workers employed by medium-sized companies in an area of the Calabria region. The workers' families revealed a very low level of informal supplies and the particular domestic services about which we were enquiring. In over 70 per cent of the workers' families, by far the greater part of the work of mending and maintenance of clothing was not carried out in the home. Likewise, over 70 per cent of the families resorted to a specialized craftsman for repair works involving plumbing, carpentry and masonry.

Although there is perhaps not sufficient evidence to justify this conclusion, it may be reasonable to say that the stable working class in the South has relatively little need to work in the informal sector, for the very reason that it combines the income and the employment guarantees typical of an industrial area and the subsistential saving possibilities typical of an area with a high level of over-population. In the industrialized areas, the spread of certain forms of informal activity tends to involve and modify the survival strategies of the working class in the wide sense, strategies rendered increasingly problematical by the employment crisis and the high inflation rate. Moreover, while the informal sector in underdeveloped countries constitutes a complementary element in the reproduction of labour, having a structural effect on the cost of living and thus on the cost of labour, in its role Southern Italy relates mainly to the mode of reproduction of the by now chronic strata of surplus population.

The combination of informal activities/consumption, subsidized incomes and funds supplied by emigrants explains the survival of a large stratum of marginalized, urban population already reduced to a state of semi-definite exclusion from the accumulation of industrial capital. This stratum has a marked internal stratification ranging from the new middle classes (independent workers with privileged access to informal activities who, by evading payment of taxes and Social Security contributions and by working very intensively, obtain incomes which are high in comparison with their relatively low monetary consumption) to a sub-stratum condemned to reproduce aberrant forms of poverty from generation to generation. The fundamental matrices of this social environment are the specific forms of industrial accumulation and the distorted forms of operation of the Welfare State in these zones. As far as the first of these matrices is concerned, the interpretation of Graziani (1978) seems to me to be reasonable. This author maintains that in the South there has been development without increase of employment in manufacturing industry. Industrial development tends to handicap local industry and craftsmen; local consumers come to prefer the increasing number of products brought in from outside.

The activities of the State and of public bodies have been no less important in the determination of the character of the informal sector in the South. As regards the two fundamental fields of operation of the Welfare State – monetary subsidies to needy families and the direct or indirect production of services – the former play a considerable and distorted part in the South, whereas the latter are systematically inadequate. In the absence of a programme of subsidies for the poor, the State has distributed a disproportionate number of disablement pensions. These, when given to poor people who are not disabled, have the advantage of creating and perpetuating political support. Throughout the South, the number of disablement pensions is much greater than that of old-age pensions and in some provinces they are paid to about 50 per cent of the adult population. If, in addition, one considers the part played by old-age pensions and unemployment allowances (very small amounts but in certain sectors, such as the building sector, important as payments), one gets an idea of the contribution the State makes towards the maintenance of a very large part of the surplus population. The income deriving from State subsidies is, in any case, never enough to ensure the survival of a family. The result has been the development of a complementary relationship between State-assistance policy and the spread and crystallization of the informal sector in the South. An important aspect of this complementary relationship is the absence, inadequacy or inefficiency of public-assistance services in every field from public housing, education, transport and health to assistance services for children under school age and for the old. Whereas families of medium and high income can make up for these shortcomings by resorting to private services or to public services outside the local area (it is well known that rich Southerners go to Rome, Milan or Florence for medical treatment), the less well-off have to resort to the informal sector, to 'making-do' or to 'doing-it-yourself'. Thus, in the South, instead of public-housing activity, there has been a spread of self-built housing, instead of kindergartens a variety of inter-parental arrangements, always informal and non-professional, for the care of pre-school children, and so on. The informal sector, in the cities we considered, is particularly active in the fields of building, the retail trade and domestic and personal services. It is not very evident in the manufacturing field, though this is probably not true of certain areas on the Adriatic side or of the Naples area (Collidà 1979; Pinnarò & Pugliese this volume).

In our investigation we have sought above all to identify the possible forms of informal activity and to understand the part that they play in the survival strategy of the various strata of the surplus population.[13] We chose five urban areas of different characteristics in Sicily and Calabria in which, in view of their poor and marginal character and their detachment from employment in the local formal industries, we hypothesized the presence of a large proportion of informal activities. We distributed to a non-representative sample of the resident population a complex questionnaire[14] which included a part relating to the family and an articulated 'budget-time' form for each adult with an income. Since the sample was non-representative, the findings are of qualitative and quantitative descriptive interest but cannot be used to measure the presence of informal activities or to define precise chains of causality.

The main characteristics of the areas selected are as follows: Messina 1 was a municipal residential hotel, subsequently demolished and inhabited by relatively young and very marginalized families, mostly of occasional and unqualified workers in the building trade; Messina 2 (Santa Lucia sopra Contesse) is a low-cost public area on the outskirts of Messina to which a number of low-income families living in very precarious and marginal housing conditions have been transferred; Reggio Calabria is likewise an area of prevalently cheap public housing on the outskirts of the largest Calabrian city; at Milazzo and Barcellona, after Messina the two largest towns in the province, the survey was carried out in the old town centres, in which there is a great mixture of social fabrics with a prevalence of marginality that is reflected in the serious state of decay of the dwellings. Both Milazzo and Barcellona were considered because they differ greatly one from the other. Milazzo is an old trading and fishing port with a troubled industrial history. A large refinery was installed nearby in the 1960s but in the last five years this has been in a state of serious crisis and has started to dismiss large numbers of employees. A little further off there is the factory, established in the 1950s, of Italy's largest mechanical-optical concern, but this too is passing through a very critical phase. A very large number of interviews were carried out in Milazzo in order to throw light on the complexity of a pronounced industrial crisis in a traditionally backward area. Barcellona, on the other hand, is a large agricultural market town in which various attempts have been made in the last ten years, with dubious success, to establish small and medium-sized industries, with mainly local or regional capital.

The Informal Sector and Social Reproduction in Southern Italy

The general analysis of the quantitative findings of our survey, also interpreted in a qualitative light on the basis of the questionnaires and other information available concerning the areas in question, confirms the hypothesis that the informal sector plays an important part in these areas of social marginality but differs according to the specific characteristics of the local community (tables 1.1 and 1.2).

However, it should be made clear immediately that we did not find more than a slight and sporadic presence of systematic informal activities associated with the decentralization and reorganization of manufacturing industries, a typical feature of peripheral industrialization in Central and North-Eastern Italy (Bagnasco 1977, 1981a; Paci 1980) and presumably also in the Naples area (Pinnarò & Pugliese this volume) and along the Southern Adriatic strip. In the course of our survey we found only two cases of this type: a network for the home-production of wigs, organized on the basis of a relationship between semi-independent craftsmen and a large commercial company and embroideresses working at home for a large textile industry based in the North.

In our areas the most common manifestation of the informal sector is in the building trade. A large number of occasional workers manage to survive on a small amount of 'unofficial' work in the fields of private building modifications and maintenance and, increasing in importance, of illegal or irregular self-construction of buildings. A smaller number of specialized craftsmen, nearly always working unofficially, manage to gain fairly large incomes.

In the most evident difference between the five areas considered was the one between the very homogeneous and marginalized case of Messina 1 and the other four, in which the social fabric is more mixed and complex.

The inhabitants of Messina 1 were nearly all couples with children, the ages of the parents ranging between 20 and 40 years, and the males employed occasionally and informally in the building trade as labourers. The wives/mothers were nearly all full-time housewives obliged to remain in the home because of the need for subsistential savings, in view of the sporadic and low earnings of their husbands, and to look after a large number of children of pre-school age, there being no public-assistance services

Table 1.1 Income earners over 14 in five areas of the Mezzogiorno

Variable	Messina 1	Messina 2	Reggio Calabria	Barcellona	Milazzo	Total
Individual cases (N)	17	44	58	49	131	299
Individuals per household	1.2	2.75	2.1	1.8	2.1	2.0
Cases of informal work (%)	82.3	22.7	29.3	30.6	29.0	31.4
Formal white/blue-collar workers (%)	11.8	36.3	50.0	53.1	34.35	39.5
Individuals who do no informal work (%)	17.6	77.2	75.9	57.1	71.0	67.5
Individuals who do no domestic work (%)	64.7	81.8	13.8	51.0	38.9	43.8
Pensions and allowances (%)	64.7	20.4	36.2	26.5	37.4	34.4
Females with income (%)	17.6	47.7	37.9	38.8	38.2	38.5
Under 25 years old with income (%)	29.4	47.7	32.7	20.4	30.5	31.8
Over 65 years old with income (%)	0.0	6.8	15.5	6.1	12.2	10.4
Illiterate or without any school certification (%)	23.5	25.0	15.5	22.4	37.4	28.1

Table 1.2   Results of the survey on householders in five areas of the Mezzogiorno

Variable	Messina 1	Messina 2	Reggio Calabria	Barcellona	Milazzo	Total
Households (N)	14	16	28	27	63	148
Without help from non-cohabitant relatives (%)	85.7	68.7	32.1	33.3	52.4	50.0
Internal making of clothes (%)	28.6	37.5	7.1	51.8	30.1	30.4
Internal mending and repairs of clothes (%)	92.8	62.5	50.0	70.4	87.3	87.4
Informal or household activities (%) for:						
Plumbing	78.6	31.2	50.0	33.3	49.2	47.3
Masonry	92.8	56.2	67.8	37.0	49.2	55.4
Painting	100.0	37.5	96.4	37.0	63.5	65.5
Carpentry	85.7	25.0	42.8	29.6	44.4	43.2
Electrical repairs	85.7	37.5	82.1	59.2	47.6	58.8
Solidarity Relations with neighbours (%)	64.3	25.0	32.1	37.0	63.5	35.1
Females do 100% of domestic activities within the house (%)	92.8	100.0	42.8	88.9	88.9	81.7
Couples with children (%)	71.4	87.5	64.3	85.2	66.7	72.3
Extended Families (%)	21.4	12.5	28.6	7.4	19.0	18.2
Less than 0.50 rooms per capita (%)	92.8	18.7	32.1	25.9	36.5	37.2

of this type in the area. The few working women (three cases) worked unofficially as maids by the hour and relied on domestic help from their daughters aged over ten.

In this specific case of a high degree of informalization, linked to casual and unofficial work in building and to very low and irregular earnings, some interesting coincidences may be observed: the very low level of female employment; a high proportion of complementary public-assistance incomes (pensions and allowances); a greater degree of isolation with regard to the help and solidarity of relatives living elsewhere and, a high degree of self-consumption and informal consumption with regard to all services of house and clothing maintenance, but not to the making of clothes. Even though we are not in a position tò generalize, it is possible to draw certain hypothetical conclusions concerning the more markedly marginal social fabric of the Southern urban areas, a fabric which tends to coincide with urban poverty. The very low working incomes deriving from occasional and/or informal activities find an indispensable complement in State allowances and pensions (in this case never old-age pensions because the sample did not include old people). This means that the spread of informal activities providing a very low level of income is not an alternative to State assistance but rather, necessitates the persistence and the extension of State assistance as an indispensable complement aiding the survival of the poorer families. On the other hand, the level of these contributions can be kept low because they constitute complementary incomes rather than the sole income of the poor families. It is important to remember, however, that whereas initially this complementarity was a provisional survival strategy, pending emigration or the finding of formal employment at an adequate salary, this form of survival now tends to endure.

The result is that the social stratum involved becomes larger because the new poor (young nuclei and recent immigrants from the countryside) are added to, instead of replacing, the old poor. This poses serious questions as to the capacity of the State, already undergoing a serious fiscal crisis, to undertake new commitments, and the capacity of an informal sector with a narrow base to provide complementary incomes to increasing numbers of the population.

The second observation that can be made relates to the connection between the low level of female activity, whether formal or informal, and the structure of subsistential savings. It seems reasonable to affirm that, in a situation of low income and a very difficult labour market, women are deterred from looking for external work and obliged to carry out extremely laborious domestic functions. This is confirmed by the findings of the survey as a whole, in which desire for 'the creation of new jobs for women' always ranked very low among the measures of economic policy for this stratum of the population. Unlike the situation in the underdeveloped countries (Portes & Walton 1981), the survival strategy does not contemplate additional incomes earned by women in informal activities and in the direct production of subsistential goods by rearing animals, cultivating small, urban, vegetable allotments, laundering and mending in the home, some hours of domestic service or unofficial work in petty commerce. In the South women seem to be engaged full time in the attempt to achieve reductions in monetary consumption by means of careful spending, searching for the cheapest prices and shopkeepers who will give credit, domestic DIY when the cost of the relative services is too expensive, and other solutions which require considerable time, such as collaboration with other women in looking after children, and which do not leave enough time for the carrying out of a paid activity.

I shall now comment on the other areas, which is more difficult because the social fabric in these areas is less homogeneous.

The Messina 2 and Reggio Calabria areas are fairly similar because both are areas of cheap public housing with a large proportion of workers and office workers employed full time in formal jobs. This has the effect of reducing to below the average the proportion of informal activities, which are engaged in only occasionally and for short periods of time. This further confirms our hypothesis that regular workers in the South very rarely have two jobs and that the combination within families of formal and informal workers is infrequent. The latter is more common in Reggio Calabria than in Messina 2 and does not necessarily relate to the wife of the head of the family so much as to other adult, male members of the group (this is also a reflection of the above-average presence of extended non-nuclear households). Furthermore, Reggio Calabria differed from all the other areas by virtue of its different, and for the South unusual, distribution of domestic work. The percentage of adults having an income and not contributing to the performance of domestic work is very low (13.8 per cent as against an average of 43.8 per cent) and the proportion of households in which the domestic work is not all carried out by the wife/mother or by other women is accordingly high (67.2 per cent as against an average of 18.3 per cent). This difference is difficult to explain because it is not accompanied by a higher level of external female activity (which in fact is below the average and higher only than that of Messina 1), nor by the presence of a high proportion of young people (which is only slightly above the average and much lower than in Messina 1). Neither can the difference be explained by the large proportion of formal employees, because at Barcellona this is associated with a typically unbalanced distribution of domestic work, carried out almost exclusively by the women. Probably the explanation lies in a number of factors: the higher proportion of non-nuclear households; the smaller proportion of couples with small children; and, above all, the higher proportion of all-male (unmarried, separated, divorced) households. In this sense Messina 2 is at the opposite end of the scale; there is a rigid distinction between domestic work and work to earn an income. Of interest here is the fact that a fairly high proportion (13 out of 21) of women working outside the home do no domestic work. This, too, is practically impossible to explain becuse it is extremely unusual and this situation was found only at Messina 2 (of the 115 females with an income in the sample, 43 did over 20 hours of domestic work weekly and nearly 75 per cent of the 21 who did no domestic work were found at Messina 2). The only explanation that can be given is that the situation is linked to the presence in the area of a high proportion of young people with an income, including unmarried daughters with a job who do not help their mothers with the domestic work.

It is of interest to consider the role played by the various types of informal activities and consumption in the social reproduction of these complex situations. Messina 2 has a relatively low proportion of informal activities and in general a lower level of informal consumption. There were only ten people engaged in informal work – five males and five females. The males worked in the building sector and one of them was an irregular craftsman who can be considered to fall into a middle class of informal activities (he worked more than 40 hours weekly and earned a fairly high income). The women worked as domestic helps by the hour or as irregular shop-assistants. The consumption of informal services and self-consumption are considerably below the average, with the exceptions of building work and, in particular, of home manufacture of clothing. The first exception can be explained by the fact that a large proportion of the local inhabitants have a close professional connection with the building trade. The high proportion of clothing manufacture in the home is less easy to understand, unless it is explained by the fact that the clearer subdivision of domestic work leaves the housewives sufficient time for this activity, being less taken up with other reproductive activities than the housewives of Messina 1. As in Messina 1, but to a smaller degree, the households of Messina 2 are mostly detached from relationships of solidarity and help from relatives, but in this case the absence of family solidarity is not compensated for by a greater degree of community solidarity.

At Reggio Calabria, as we have said, we found a greater mingling of regular and irregular work within the household, though not in the form of double jobs which are uncommon. The informal activities are equally distributed between men and women and are of the same nature as at Messina 2. In this case the isolation from relationships of family solidarity is less marked than in the other areas. This could be due to an earlier pattern of urbanization than in Messina or to a more compact urban structure facilitating contacts (as also in Barcellona and, to a smaller degree, in Milazzo).

The utilization of self-consumption and of certain informal subsistential services is in general more 'modern', with some contradictions. Intrafamily making of clothes is almost nonexistent and very little of the work of clothes' maintenance is done internally. On the other hand, members of the household and informal consumption play an important part in the work of maintenance of the dwelling, above all where electrical repairs and repainting of rooms are concerned. Here again it is probable that this is largely due to the existence of an informal building trade which for years has specialized in unofficial work and in construction for the people involved.

The case of Barcellona is interesting because, together with a large proportion of formal workers and office-workers, there is a proportion of over 30 per cent of informal workers. Here one finds not only double jobs but also many households which include both formal and informal workers. The informal workers are mostly women (twelve as against seven men) who work as home-helps or have irregular employment in commerce; two work at home for the decentralized wig-making enterprise mentioned above and two are farm-workers. The men are all occasional building labourers. Self-consumption and informal consumption are in general below the average, except with regard to clothes-making in the home, which here reaches the high of 51.8 per cent. The only possible explanation of this is the fact that Barcellona still has a prevalently agricultural character and the practices typical of a rural family have been retained. It can also be added that in Barcellona, despite its close physical and historical relationship with the countryside, there is a very high proportion of couples with children and the lowest proportion of extended households of non-nuclear character. This could be due to the relatively less serious housing shortage and to the possibility of continuing to receive help from, and to maintain contacts with, relatives living in the country.

We dedicated particular attention to the case of the Borgo Antico of Milazzo in order to throw light on a situation in which the traditional existence of an informal sector is combined with a serious and persistent industrial and employment crisis. The large number of cases considered does not permit at this stage a qualitative interpretation of the results but only some preliminary comments. Despite the centrality of the Borgo Antico of Milazzo in relation to industrial development, which has, however, for years been in a condition of crisis, the proportion of the inhabitants formally employed is relatively low, a little over one-third, and higher only than in Messina 1. On the other hand, the proportion of informal workers is not very high. As in Barcellona, the informal jobs are mainly for women; the men work in the building trade and as costermongers. There are, however, no double jobs and the division between formal and informal activities is more clear-cut.

The social fabric which we found at Milazzo seems to be the most complex. Apart from some medium-income households, very few compared with the other areas with the exception of Messina 1, we found a wide variety of households with low or very low incomes. The relatively high proportion of persons receiving subsidies (37.4 per cent) reflects the less distinct borderline of poverty. Furthermore, there are also a large number of adults who are illiterate or lacking educational qualifications. Informal supplies and self-consumption are distributed in a fairly regular manner. They are at a high level, as is to be expected in the case of the obsolescent city centre of a Southern town in the throes of an industrial crisis, but never at an extraordinarily high level. Of note, is the high level of solidarity between neighbouring families, a reflection of the age and stability of the city centre.

Preliminary analysis confirms the view that the informal sector is not capable of providing the social environments hardest hit by the employment crisis with easy alternative means of survival. This negative hypothesis seems even more plausible with regard to the South, where the informal sector seems to have a limited economic basis. It has solid, traditional roots which limit the possibilities of 'modernization'. The only possibility of expansion/renovation lies in the field of self-construction building. This had a great boom in the 1970s as the only large-scale solution to the growing need of housing in the South, in view of the absence of public building activity and the traditional lack of interest of the private building trade in the poorer sectors of the market (Ginatempo & Fera 1982). From a strictly economic point of view there is reason to doubt the ability of the informal sub-sector of self construction and unofficial building to continue to expand so as to provide a means of survival for a growing over-population. On the contrary, however, the great volume of buildings constructed in the past ten years and the increasingly limited geographical mobility of the population, together with the decreasing birth rate in the South, suggest that the sector is unlikely to expand.

The other aspect of the informal sector in the South, once again from a strictly economic point of view, is even more closely linked to a recessive cycle. This relates to irregular trading work and personal services, above all to the middle classes (e.g. domestic help by the hour, services in the home, repairs and maintenance works, dress-making, etc.). Inflation and economic recession affect the demand for informal services on the part of the intermediate income groups in a contradictory manner. A deterioration in the standard of living determines a considerable reduction in the highly elastic demand for superfluous service. This occurs above all when the price of the services cannot be further reduced by competition between the workers, without the income obtained being insufficient to justify the work. The clearest example of this is supplied by the situation of supply and demand with regard to household help.

Apart from the unfavourable ideological connotation of this type of work, if the income to be obtained from it is below a certain amount it is more advantageous for women in the South to stay at home because by so doing they can earn more in the form of subsistential savings. Thus, even in the South, there is the paradox of not inconsiderable immigration of maids from the underdeveloped countries, despite the existence of a large local over-population.

With regard to goods and services for which the demand is stable, the question is whether the informal sector is able to organize a supply which is acceptable as an alternative to the formal supply, permitting maintenance of the standard of living and at the same time a certain saving of money. This is certainly a difficult problem. It seems to me, however, that in the South the informal sector has already done all, or almost all, it is capable of doing to provide an alternative supply to meet the demand for goods and services on a local scale. The possibility of further expansion could depend on peripheral, industrial decentralization of the type carried out by small and medium-sized manufacturing industries in Central and North-Eastern Italy, in the southern Adriatic strip and in the Naples area. However, the high degree of marginalization of the social fabric and the relatively high costs of subsistence constitute serious obstacles. It is indicative that so far industrial decentralization has avoided these areas of the South in favour of Third World localities, such as Taiwan, Singapore, North Africa and some Latin American countries, where there is an equal degree of marginalization but subsistence costs are notably lower.

Finally, it would be useful to consider some general hypotheses concerning the social consequences of the character of the informal sector in the South and its progressive transformation from being a transitory phase of a surplus population subsequently to be absorbed by a process of industrialization to being a definitive survival strategy for an increasing over-population. First, it should be borne in mind, that, if the existence of a large informal sector involves a lower degree of commodification in relation to the more advanced areas, the high level of State subsidies to individuals permits a relative overcommodification in favour of certain durable goods which have characterized the industrial development of Italy. In all five areas over 90 per cent of the families possessed a radio, a refrigerator and a black-and-white or colour television set; over 60 per cent and in Messina 2 and Barcellona almost all of them, had a car or a motor cycle and a washing-machine (also owned by all the families in Messina 1). Ownership of bicycles, cameras, gramophones, tape-recorders, electric mixers and sewing machines is common (over 60 per cent except in Messina 1).

The findings of our survey make it possible to hypothesize a number of contradictory social processes, in part peculiar to the informal sector in the South and in part also common to the industrial areas and, more frequently, to the underdeveloped countries.

The first hypothesis relates to the social role of women. There are two problem areas both connected with the poor prospects of employment in the formal sector. There is a considerable tendency towards domestic work, which increases according to the poverty of the household, and a parallel tendency towards work in the informal sector. The first assumes the form of a particularly perverse cycle which has its origins in the social pressures which are discharged on poor Southern families. The lack of public-assistance infrastructures and the need to make considerable subsistential savings, combined with bad relationships in the labour market, with the consequences of poor employment prospects and low salary levels, oblige the mothers/wives to undertake a very heavy load of domestic work. Many girls socialized in this environment leave school early in order to replace their mothers and to allow them to work as domestic helps by the hour or to carry out dressmaking or laundering works in the home. The cycle reproduces a social environment based on a low level of external female employment and occasional male work at a low income level. On the other hand, where informal female work is undertaken, it is notable that a high labour supply, with consequent competition and low incomes, is accompanied by a demand which has a very narrow structural base. It has little to do with the productive decentralization of manufacturing industries and depends almost exclusively on domestic service, household services for private citizens, the retail trade and seasonal agricultural work; this is also because women play no part in the largest organized branch of the informal sector in the South − the building trade.

The second hypothesis concerns children and young people. Here two opposite, but equally perverse, cycles operate. The first involves the working of minors. Children leave school or neglect their schooling in order to contribute to the survival of the family, either by means of unpaid family work or by means of badly paid work (shop-boy, agricultural work, etc.). In this way they remain illiterate or semi-literate and do not even learn a trade. This leads to the reproduction of a generation of poor casual workers, unqualified and semi-literate. There is a large number of semi-literates in our sample of adults with an income; this is not due to a large proportion of old people so much as to the low level of education of the intermediate age groups and of the young (this can immediately be seen in the data relating to Messina 1, Messina 2 and Milazzo).

The other aspect of the youth question lies in the fact that those young people who, at the cost of great effort on the part of their families, complete their schooling do not succeed in finding jobs conforming to their expectations and educational qualifications. Only the State and para-State organizations offer acceptable employment prospects (relatively low salaries but a high degree of stability, which makes them very attractive to the youth of the South). However, young people who have grown up in these marginalized social environments find it difficult to compete for State employment against members of the middle and upper classes who have access to the system of 'recommendations' and political favouritism which governs the allocation of these jobs. This creates a notable tendency towards underemployment and informal employment which tends, at least in a large number of cases, to be transformed into a permanent condition.

We thus have an informal sector which tends to reproduce and to extend itself but which has limitations that prevent it from insuring the survival of even the existing surplus population. This necessitates a high level of monetary assistance from the State to needy families, which plays an indispensable role in the social reproduction of marginality. The complementary relationship between the informal sector and State assistance assures social reproduction in terms of low commodification but with a monetary consumption potential which is relatively high and oriented towards certain durable goods. These are usually produced outside the local area and are typical of the model of industrial development of Italy and Western Europe, being indispensable working instruments for the marginal family (or as in the case of television sets and radios necessary for social integration).

The existence of a large informal sector does not lead automatically to a reduction in the cost of formal work because of the obstacle constituted by the unitary nature of the national employment structure. It does, however, affect the standard of living both of the stable formal workers in the South and of the middle classes. The former, benefiting from a number of reproductive savings, are less inclined to have a double job (due also to the strong competition coming from the labour supply of the surplus population) or to favour the employment of other members of the household. The latter benefit from certain informal services at low cost, e.g. domestic services, clothes made to measure and maintenance services for the dwelling, which are difficult or impossible to obtain in Central Italy and the North.

Even in the present situation, the effect of the informal sector in the South, in the sense of an unfair economic redistribution in favour of the middle and upper classes, is evident. However, the most serious political question relates to the prospect, which the informal sector does not seem to offer, of ensuring a permanent subsistential basis for a growing surplus population. In this respect, the future of Southern Italy seems to be trapped in a cul-de-sac. The State cannot afford to increase its public assistance, the manufacturing and service industries do not offer new employment possibilities and cannot give rise to further migratory movements, and the informal sector appears to be incapable of expansion in the context of the industrial decentralizations currently in course but which lie in the direction, even in the case of Italian manufacturing industries, of countries of the Third World which offer considerably more advantageous conditions.

Notes

1 We do not discuss here the desirability of quantitive growth or the necessity to change the patterns of economic development (see Gershuny 1978). We assume that fast growth was no longer possible in the 1970s and at the beginning of the 1980s as it had been in the previous decades. We should also mention that, in any case, the relation between development and creation of new jobs had deteriorated, as a consequence of the world-scale redistribution of manufacturing industries, employment and technological labour-saving.

2 The term 'Balkanization' of labour markets has been used to express the fact that different layers of supply and/or demand of labour tend to become divided and do not intercommunicate. As a consequence, an excess supply of certain kinds of labour would not affect the wages of other kinds of workers. In this work we will mainly refer to the most recent developments of the American theorization of segmented labour markets (Edwards et al. 1976, 1979; Edwards 1982) and to the Italian contributions of Paci (1973, 1982) and others (Bagnasco 1977; Bruno 1979; Brusco & Sebel 1982).

3 State intervention is certainly wider and more complex. In this context I have limited my attention to those sectors of State intervention which have a direct impact on the reproduction patterns of the labour force (and surplus population). In doing so I am conscious of overlooking the repressive apparatus, the interventions to improve the reproduction of fixed capital or the internal structure of the state bureaucracy itself and the redistributive impact of the taxation system in favour of some layers of the middle class.

4 This point will be considered with the analysis of the development/ underdevelopment process. Due to the drain on local resources by foreign capital, underdeveloped states were unable to freeze and keep under control a fast-increasing surplus population created by the very penetration of capital in the local markets. (This is also because increases in the aggregate demands are reflected in increased imports and not local production capacities.) The underconsumption/overproduction tendencies of capitalist development are thus shifted in the underdeveloped countries where they are reflected in the persistence of poverty, very cheap labour-reproduction patterns and

unstable social and political situations. Finally, the present persistent stagnation can be interpreted as the repercussion on the world system of the vast underconsumption tendencies created by industrial restructuring in capital's quest for less and less expensive labour, combined with a diminished capacity to raise surplus profits in the underdeveloped countries and their expenditure in the expansion of unproductive sectors in the developed countries (an underaccumulation process).

5 Often the market is unable, for various reasons, to provide the services and goods which are no longer provided by the State. This is because market provision is either too expensive for the consumption capacities of large layers of population (e.g. housing and education for the not so well off) or because the demand is strictly local and not convenient for capital operations (e.g. child care). Thus, in many cases, the retreat of State provision does not produce the advocated return of the market but a consistent diffusion of informal and do-it-yourself activities.

6 It is particularly difficult to spell out the origins and exact meanings of the terms used by different authors. 'Informal Sector' was first used with regard to Third World cities (see Bromley and Gerry [1979] for critical references to this literature). 'Irregular economy' (Ferman & Berndt 1981; Ferman et al. 1978; Ferman & Ferman 1973) and 'informal economy' (Bagnasco 1981b; Cornuel 1980; Gershuny & Pahl 1979; Heinze & Olk 1982) may be considered synonymous. 'Underground' or 'subterranean economy' has been used with a more pronounced emphasis on illegal practices (*Business Week* 1978, 1982; Gutman 1977, 1978a, b, 1979a, b, 1980), with the exception of Rosanvallon (1980) and CENSIS–ISFOL–CNEL (1976) where the use of this term is very similar to the one given by other authors to irregular and informal. The recent use of the term 'shadow work' by Illich (1981) is confusing because it included very different activities, done either for cash or for self-consumption. I agree with Pahl and Wallace (this volume) that the term informal economy is misleading, like the term 'household economy' (Burns 1975, 1977), because it assumes that there are various distinct economies.

7 The relation between the commodification and technological innovation processes on one side and the changes in quantity and quality of domestic work on the other is still very controversial. In principle I would agree with Gershuny (this volume, 1983) that there has been a long-term reduction in the time spent on housework in working-class households. This reduction is also connected with the return to employment of married women. The time spent on housework varies consistently between full-time housewives and employed women (see also Vanek 1974).

8   It may be worthwhile to investigate the possible coincidence of my periodization of different patterns of social reproduction of the labour force with the long waves of labour processes hypothesized in the recent work of Edwards et al. (1982). In this sense the proletarianization phase could be reflected in the indiscriminate employment of children and women; the homogenization with the abolition of child work and with the decrease of female employment and the creation of modern domestic work within working-class households; and the segmentation with a consistent return to paid employment of married women. If this is true, the present crisis of the segmentation patterns would coincide with the diffusion of informal activities, which thus assume a fundamental role in the reorganization of the capitalist labour process.

9   As correctly pointed out by Ingrosso (1979), domestic work, in the modern sense of the term, was nearly absent in the early-industrial working-class families, while it already existed in the middle classes.

10 See the reports on the English paleo-industrial working class in Engels (1969) and in the first volume of Marx (1976).

11 As a consequence of adopting this approach, I would argue that gender discrimination in the job structure is directly related to the socially and historically enforced assumption that female labour includes a higher rate of unpaid domestic work, and consequently I would reject different Marxist explanations (Humphries 1977). I would argue that this is the specific mode of incorporation of the patriarchical patterns of male domination (pre-existing in the history of most societies) into capitalist relations of production.

12 It is probably true, as Litwak (1960) argues, that solidarity relations among different households of relatives form a 'modified extended family'. In order to create this condition it is nevertheless necessary that different nuclei continue to live relatively close. When high geographical mobility separates the residences of nuclear families the modified extended family tends to be less present. As will be shown, my survey shows very dishomogeneous results in different areas of South Italy.

13 The purpose of our investigation was to identify a sufficient number of survival solutions based on a combination of informal work, public assistance and large amounts of domestic work. For this purpose we did not make use of a methodology of a strictly qualitative nature (a few detailed descriptions of family life) because it would not have provided our survey with an adequate horizontal extension. On the other hand, the determination of a representative sample for a quantitative survey presented great difficulties. We therefore settled for an ambiguous solution, midway between the two methodologies, by distributing a structured questionnaire to a fairly large sample of families and individuals living in particular

urban areas in the South. Naturally, the sample is not representative of over-population in general (impossible to define with certainty). Our findings are indicative and descriptive of the existence of different and complex survival solutions. As such, they permit the formulation of hypotheses, to be verified by successive quantitative and qualitative research, but they cannot be generalized to provide a definitive interpretation of the situation and role of informal activities in the towns of Southern Italy.

14   The questionnaire consists of two parts. The first part concerns the household: number of members, structure of the family nucleus, number of rooms in the dwelling, whether it is rented, owned or sold with the right of redemption, the type and quality of the dwelling and the approximative specification of the subdivision in terms of percentage of the domestic work between the members of the family. Further questions are: Does the family own or cultivate a piece of land? Does the family include minors of under 14 years who perform paid work? How are the relationships with the neighbours? How are repairs and maintenance of the dwelling carried out? How does the family obtain clothes, maintain them and mend them? What durable goods does the family possess? Does the family have solidarity relationships with relatives who are not members of the household? Does the family have working relationships with friends or relatives engaged in agricultural activities and does it receive agricultural products from them? Finally, the respondents were asked for an opinion concerning the priority they attributed to various measures which improved their standard of living.

The second part relates to information concerning all adult (over 14-years-old) individuals with an income deriving from work, a pension, subsidy or other. In particular we asked the following questions: Does the individual work? Is he in search of work because he is unemployed or it will be his first job? Is he a pensioner? Does he receive a pension or a subsidy and, if so, of what type? What are the average number of weekly hours dedicated to different types of work (formal, informal, occasional, unpaid non-domestic, domestic work or commissions), searching for work, leisure activities and study and cultural activities. Information is requested concerning the type of employment from the employed, the type of work sought from those looking for work, the last type of work from pensioners and from everyone, whether they have or have had a second occupation or job, part-time, occasional or seasonal, and what its characteristics are.

2

The Politics of the Informal Sector: A Critique
Priscilla Connolly

The category 'informal sector' has been powerful enough to impose a conceptual affinity on such diverse subjects as domestic industry, women's labour, minority firms, the family and the labour force and dual modes of relating to work. This conceptual affinity, the reason why all these topics have been discussed under one heading, stems less from their respective theoretical contents than from their original identification with one particular field of analysis or 'sector'. The wide variety of names which have been given to this sector (e.g. 'second', 'irregular', 'black', 'hidden', 'autonomous', 'marginal') reflects the differing criteria used for distinguishing it from its opposite (e.g. 'modern', 'formal', 'heteronomous', 'capitalist', 'monopolic'). These differences do not, however, negate the underlying premise that one part of social reality may be conceived as a system whose distinctive characteristics differentiate it from the 'normal' economic structure.

This chapter does not set out to propose another name for this 'other' sector, nor is it primarily aimed at offering new arguments in support of one or other existing theoretical approaches. Instead, the discussion is centred on the practical implications of the sociological tendency to cluster a wide variety of phenomena under one category, in this case the informal sector as applied in relation to employment and labour conditions.

My doubts about the informal sector's usefulness or convenience began to arise for two reasons. In the first place, from the point of view of its political and ideological implications in Mexico, it became increasingly evident that this category continues to exert an inordinate influence in the everyday interpretations of the problems of poverty and employment while, at the same time, plays an important part in the justification provided for government policies on these issues. The analysis of this aspect was essentially based on press reports, government policy statements, opinions expressed in congresses, seminars and other public events and, lastly, on the plans and programmes issued by the government, the official party and political organizations of opposition. The period studied is from 1980 to 1983.

The second critical area concerns the taxonometric criteria derived from the various conceptual constructs of informal sector, which proved to be frankly inoperable for the purposes of empirical research. This was manifest in a project whose initial objective was, precisely, to determine the needs of Mexico City's informal population regarding training programmes and material aids. The impossibility of identifying a study objective in these terms, both theoretically and empirically, not only implied a radical revision of the theoretical bases of the project[1] but also led to the discovery that the explanations given in many previous empirical studies were often biased by the informal sector and its related concepts. This was reflected in highly eclectic data reading and also, in some cases, in erroneous interpretations of the results.

Considering the two aspects together – the use of informal sector in public discourse and its continuing reproduction in research practice – this concept, like other generalizing categories, such as marginality and 'the crisis', may be considered as fundamental semantic media whereby theoretical production is materialized. At the same time, they translate social practice into abstract concepts: the ultimate task of the social scientist. Here, the term informal sector and its synonyms are found to be extraordinarily powerful; it could be argued that this force is in direct relation to the importance of the social issue they refer to. For, in the context of the Third World, informal sector is not really about minority groups, anomalies or exceptional cases but rather touches on the fundamental problems of development, employment and poverty.

To illustrate and evaluate the ideological and discursive function of the concept of the informal sector, I start with a brief comparison between its origins and implications in advanced capitalist countries and in Latin America. Some more specific applications of the informal sector terminology in Mexico are then reviewed, especially the way that this concept influences common understanding of poverty and unemployment and its role in public policy declarations. Next I

examine some of the empirical bases to the informal sector, again
with reference to Mexico City. Finally I review the major theoretical
outlooks which have emerged out of the marginal–informal debate
and which are beginning to overcome the need for an informal
sector in Mexico. Apart from the opening comparison, the text
references throughout are mainly limited to published sources and
other material which have been circulating in Mexico. This consideration is relevant to the analysis, as the diffusion of certain
works (and not others) will largely determine, and perhaps be determined by, the practical uses they encounter.

The Origins of 'Informal Sector' and its Applications in Government Policy

The acceptance of informal sector as a general category does not
imply its coherence as a theoretical system. On the contrary, it
would seem to consist more of an indefinite agglomeration of partial
causal relations referring to a wide variety of social phenomena. The
initial selection of these phenomena and the way they are labelled
and explained will depend on the importance granted to particular
social problems or on institutional priorities. The criteria which are
used to define the informal sector or similar categories, and thus
their conceptual content, will therefore respond to the specific
context in which research is taking place.

The informal sector in the developed world: employment disguised as unemployment

The advanced capitalist countries have seen a recent proliferation of
studies of the informal sector, 'underground economies', etc., an
interest which apparently responds to a preoccupation over the loss
of fiscal revenues and social security contributions, due to the
existence of economic activities which do not observe the legal and
institutional norms. Thus, a whole series of production relations are
classified as black, irregular and so forth, simply because they are
excluded from national accounts and tax registers. As the major
problem is thought to be one of calculating the monetary value of
such activities and their corresponding contribution to national
income, some authors see no need to distinguish between clandestine wage-labour (sweat-shops) and independent, free-lance or
family work.[2] In other texts, in which some attempt is made at
classifying the various types of production relations, these are
considered merely to represent the different forms in which the

informal, 'clandestine' or 'parallel' economy is manifest and thus reaffirm the existence of this sector, as such, in terms of the legal status of the activities in question.[3]

Given the economic and political situation which gave birth to this type of study — empty public treasuries facing increasing demands for social expenditure, unemployment, economic recession and the emergence of austerity policies — one can hardly be surprised by the conclusions they offer. The main implications of the informal sector are: (1) the national growth rates, calculated exclusively on the basis of the formal sector, are underestimated (things are not as bad as they seem); (2) the unemployment figures are exaggerated, as many of those receiving unemployment benefits are in fact gainfully employed; (3) the inflation index is also overestimated, as prices in the informal sector tend to be 20 to 40 per cent lower than in the formal sector; and (4) taxes are too high, as this is what drives many activities into the underground economy (Feige 1981; Gutmann 1979; Vázquez Arango 1981). It is easy to guess what kind of policy measures are derived from these arguments, or are justified a posteriori on the same grounds.

The influence of this type of economic diagnosis is not only to be found in monetary and public-expenditure policies. It also seems to weigh heavily in sociological conceptualizations of the informal sector in advanced capitalism. Essentially, this is always thought to operate in detriment to the formal economy, the 'establishment' and economic planning, while generally benefiting the individuals involved in informal sector activities.

Whether this is considered to be beneficial or not depends on the position of each author. For neo-Keynesian economists, the informal sector is 'the sickness which seems to affect not only the economies of the entire developed world, but also, the economic profession itself' (Feige 1981:137). Evidently, the magnitude of the 'unrecorded economy' threatens the *raison-d'être* of econometric modelling based on official statistics. Those who are less enthusiastic about State intervention and economic planning, on the other hand, regard the informal sector with hopeful admiration. For Milton Freidman 'the clandestine economy is a real life-belt: it effectively limits collective coercion . . . allowing individuals to get round the restrictions imposed by government on personal enterprise' (quoted in de Grazia 1979:480). However, the extreme Right is not alone in considering the informal sector as a road to salvation. After making the distinction between 'black labour, the modern form of slavery imposed on the clandestine workers' and the 'black work that you choose to do on your own accord', Bosquet (1980:41) writes: 'In black work (the workers) find a true profession, an autonomy, the possibility of being useful and appreciated for their skills and knowledge'; in another text the same idea becomes a central political argument for the 'post-industrial revolution' (Gorz 1982). Some social scientists share this vision of the informal sector's revolutionary potential. For Gershuny (1979:48) 'the recognized existence of a marginal sector could lead to upheavals in the social order', while Pahl (1980:17) suggests that 'as the informal economy flourishes . . . it seems that some workers are slipping out of their chains and walking out of the system's front door.' An alternative interpretation is that the informal sector is a 'safety valve which allows the population to cope with unemployment' (de Grazia 1979).

Behind the wide diversity of political significance an underlying common denominator pervades the interpretation of the informal sector in the developed world. This is the dualist idea, expressed most clearly by the economists, which projects the image of a 'subsystem' in opposition to (and generally to the disadvantage of) the formal economic system.

The Latin American informal sector: unemployment disguised as employment

The way the informal sector is perceived in advanced capitalist countries seems to be the exact opposite to its homonym in the developing world. The various occupational situations classified as informal are seen as the unfortunate result of the system: in this case, the victim is the set of individuals who are engaged in such occupations, while their plight is blamed ultimately on the formal economy. This difference is fundamental because, even though certain shared characteristics could be identified, the developed and underdeveloped informal sectors necessarily fulfil widely differing theoretical and ideological roles; as concepts they respond to different social and political preoccupations.

In countries where national statistics are generally regarded with scepticism, the fact that vast areas of economic activity are not officially recorded is no particular cause for alarm. Neither is the extralegality of these activities (though this is used as a complementary defining criteria for informality). Societies with colonial pasts, in particular, are accustomed to the Law not being rigorously and ubiquitously enforced. In other words, there exists an historical asynchronism between the legal system and the actual social relations to which, supposedly, this refers. Tax evasion is seen as a problem but this is related principally to defaults or frauds committed by companies and individuals, rather than to the loss of revenues from any underground economy. So this kind of concern is not the prime motivator in the search for the informal sector either. Instead, it may be safely assumed that the category 'informal' and similar terminologies have emerged as a response to the manifest urban poverty in countries which are undergoing rapid industrial growth with concurrent urbanization.

In this respect, it is relatively easy to recognize the direct descendence from economic dualism and marginality. Most of the prime Latin American exponents of the informal sector (STPS/ PNUD/OIT 1977; Tokman 1979) take as a starting point a critique of the marginality theories expounded in the late 1960s (Lessa 1970; Nun 1969; Quijano 1971) and they explicitly admit to many areas of common ground which are present in both concepts. Other authors, who never adopt the term informal but whose works have been influential in relation to this, prefer to keep the adjective marginal, enriched with revised theoretical content: the 'occupational marginality' of Muñoz and others (1977) or Kowarick's 'marginal forms of insertion in the productive structures' (1977). All these may be considered as intermediate stages which evolve into the more recent approaches which concentrate on the articulation between the modern, capitalist sector and the non-modern sector, whether this be the 'inferior circuit' (Santos 1975), the 'autonomous sector' (Singer 1980) or whatever.[4]

In spite of the wide divergence of outlooks and theoretical emphases that have emerged from this progression, two common assumptions persist throughout. The first concerns the social problem which inspires this type of enquiry – *the need to explain the impoverishment of increasing numbers of people, simultaneous with economic growth.* No one really questions the idea that the informal sector is basically comprised of the 'have nots'. The second common assumption is similar to that underlying the advanced capitalist informal sector: the dichotomic distinction between the formal or modern pole and the backward or non-modern.

A demonstration of these persistent underlying premises, with their logical inferences, may be found in the practical criteria used by almost all the writers mentioned in identifying their object of study. In this, there seems to be a general consensus to the effect that informal sector employment is characterized by the following attributes, all of which may be deduced from the two basic assumptions mentioned.

1   As a definitive point of departure, informal implies low direct income and the absence of indirect income (health, housing and social security benefits).
2   Consequently, as low incomes mean less-than-minimum wages and thus the non-observance of labour laws, informality is also identified with illegality. This is not, however, necessarily associated with criminal activities.
3   Related to the question of illegality, another qualifying characteristic of informality is *'eventualidad'* (casual labour), a term which (in Spanish) is, in itself, highly ambiguous, as it refers to at least three kinds of situations:[5] (a) full-time, permanently employed wage-earners who are *'eventuales'* because they are not under a permanent contract and therefore are relatively unprotected by the labour laws, may be fired without compensation, etc; (b) people who work occasionally, for whatever reason; and (c) people who work part-time, as these are generally included with the above in statistical sources.
4   Closely related to low incomes and extralegality, the absence of workers' organization is also considered to be symptomatic of informality, a condition usually reduced to not being unionized.
5   The non-compliance with labour and other legislation, which refer essentially to the wage relation and the organization of private enterprise, is also associated with production relations (e.g. non-salaried work) where these are not applicable. This connection is reinforced by the identification of low incomes with backwardness or lack of modernity. Thus, informal sector is equated with empirical observations of small production units with simple division of labour and technology, scarce capital investment and/or non-capitalist production relations, such as petty-commodity production, *'artesanal'* establishments,[6] family businesses and independent or self-employed workers.
6   Consequently, 'informal' work has a low productivity index and is highly competitive in the market.

Apart from these criteria which identify an informal sector in terms of an inferred set of production and employment relations, other definitions are also applied. These are inherited directly from marginality and refer exclusively to characteristics of the labour supply which have been found to correlate with low incomes:

7   Low educational levels or lack of institutional training, which
    are generally thought to mean absence of job skills and
    specialized experience.
8   A predominance of rural immigrants in the urban informal
    sector as these tend to have less education and job skills.

Beyond these empirical definitions, the basic line of enquiry is
naturally directed at how the modern pole generates, makes use of,
subordinates and over-exploits the employment in the non-modern
sector. A key element in this is the association between these
informal occupations and unemployment. However, unlike the
propositions emanating from the First World, where the informal
sector is employment disguised as unemployment, *the informal sector
in the Third World is unemployment disguised as employment.* This idea is
crystallized in another set of terms, such as underemployment and
suboccupation. Although these concepts had already been invented
in relation to employment theories for advanced capitalism, in their
application to 'poor countries', they acquired fundamentally different meanings (Myrdal 1975).[7] Among other distinctions, both
unemployment and subemployment in this context refer primarily
to the population, rather than to the redundance of productive
capacity, or to the underutilization of trained workers.
    Once the chain of causal relationships between poverty, subem-
ployment and unemployment has been established, the study of the
informal sector logically focuses on the causes of unemployment,
identified as a real, but invisible, phenomenon. There seem to be no
doubts here that the marginal occupations, the autonomous sector,
etc., are the result of the modern sector's incapacity to absorb the
labour force (e.g. Hugon 1980:3; Kowarick 1977:85; PREALC
1981:8; Tokman 1979: 74). It is true that some recent researchers
have begun to question 'as something obvious that the Latin
American economic growth bears with it a structural tendency
towards increased unemployment' (Muñoz & de Oliveira 1979: 45).
However, in Mexico at least, the authors who have been most
widely read are unanimous in blaming urban poverty or marginality on the fact that vast sectors of the population have not been
absorbed into the capitalist (or modern) productive structure
(Castells 1973: 12, 1981b: 150; Singer 1980: 21; Touraine 1977:
1113).
    The incapacity of the modern economy to assimilate the available
labour force is attributed to a series of causes, which may be briefly
outlined as follows.

First, the urbanization resulting from high demographic growth rates and rural immigration is considered to be excessive in relation to industrial development. The image of hordes of peasants vainly seeking city employment and the unbalanced spatial distribution of the population is brought into play. In addition, the idea of a superfluous labour supply gives rise to the interpretation of informal sector as 'survival strategies' (Lomnitz 1975; Moser 1981).

Second, on the side of labour demand, industrial growth is generally thought to be insufficient in relation to the expansion of commercial and service employment: the much feared terciarization of the economy. This is based partly on the observation that the proportion of urban population employed in industrial production is less than that registered during the initial phases of the first Industrial Revolution. In addition, the inadequate industrial growth is related to a double confusion surrounding the characterization of the informal sector as unproductive.[8] If the modern sector is, by definition, the most productive, this is not only interpreted in terms of the productivity of labour but also the idea of actual material production is implied. Thus, the modern sector tends to be equated with industrial production, while the informal sector or subemployment is held to be responsible for the excessive terciarization. To add to this muddle, the Marxist distinction between productive and unproductive work is invoked, giving rise to common interpretations which establish these types of equivalences: modern sector means capitalist exploitation of wage-labour in industrial production; informal sector means non-capitalist social relations in the production of services and in commercial activities.

In the third place, the general cause for the insufficient demand for labour is attributed to the capital-intensive development model in the modern industrial sector. This is then immediately related to the implantation of imported technologies in the hands of foreign capital. Thus, in the last instance, it is economic dependence and the monopolistic international firms (or the erroneous national policies which have encouraged their establishment) which are depicted as the ultimate culprits of unemployment, urban poverty and the informal sector.[9]

This intentionally brief résumé of the reasoning behind the term informal sector in the explanation of poverty and unemployment is clearly only a caricature of much more complex theoretical arguments, most of which, to a certain extent at least, can be defended on empirical grounds.[10] However, the simpler, dominant ideas are the ones that stick; they are the ones that most easily find practical applications. The following extract, one of many that could be quoted, illustrates the way in which the generalized interpretation of the informal sector in Mexico[11] has inherited most of the theoretical power of marginality for describing and/or explaining a whole series of not necessarily related employment situations associated with low incomes. The quotation is taken from a much publicized event when academics, public and private functionaries, members of the official party and other interested persons expounded their ideas on the subject of employment, training and productivity to the then future president, in January 1982.

The development model of the last decades propitiated the transfer of rural poverty to urban marginality, thus creating large population groups lacking every kind of public service and with deficient economies. These groups have been termed urban informal sector, from the point of view of their employment and they are constituted by people whose activities are characterized by: low income levels, lack of indirect wages (*prestaciones*), no social security, low productivity, low occupational stability, almost exclusive use of physical labour, low information levels used in production and, in many cases, lack of organization. (García Ogalde, IEPES 1982).

It is remarkable that most of the axioms which define informal as an empirical phenomenon, do so in negative terms; it is not legal, its members are not educated, it is not productive, it is not formal and it is not modern. [12] By common logic, this negative definition presupposes that a whole series of positive axioms might be construed about the formal sector. If informal occupation means low incomes then, one supposes, work in the formal sector is paid highly; or if the labour laws are not enforced within the informal sector, then all employers in the modern, dynamic and highly productive industries must be law-abiding in this respect.

From this, although the ultimate causes of the informal sector are, as we have seen, emphatically understood to be imperialism, demographic explosions, over-urbanization, misguided economic policies and so forth, the poverty situations implied by informality are immediately explained by their lack of formality; they are not integrated into the modern sector, even though their contribution to it is generally recognized. [13] In this way, the informal sector terminology not only reinforces the mutually exclusive dichotomy between modern progress and wealth on the one hand and traditional backwardness and poverty on the other, it also diverts attention from the immediate causes of poverty from the modern sector to the non-modern sector. In essence, the informal sector concept does not substantially modify the economic philosophy which inspired Joan Robinson to write in 1959: 'As we see nowadays in South-East Asia or the Carribean, the misery of being exploited by capitalists is nothing compared to the misery of not being exploited at all.' (Robinson 1964: 46 quoted in Galbraith 1982). This was reproduced in marginality theory, ten years later: 'The problem of '*los marginados*' is not that they are exploited, but rather, that they are not even exploited.' (Lessa 1970).

Informal sector in Mexican political discourse

An illustration of the way in which this kind of reasoning behind the words marginality, underemployment and informal sector is eclectically drawn upon to mystify the causes of poverty, especially in moments of economic optimism, can be found in the policy declarations of the Mexican Government.

During the euphoric and ephemeral petro-boom of 1980–1, there was a considerable increase in the demand for labour. Proud announcements of the rising employment rates made it clear that these triumphs were also victories in the battle against underemployment which, of course, is equated with poverty and backwardness.[14] Less attention was paid to the impact of this unprecedented increase in the 'supply of jobs' on the general and minimum wage level, which in fact continued to drop throughout the period of maximum economic growth and concurrent increase in the labour demand.[15] No attention at all was paid to the fact that a great many of the jobs created by the 'boom' belonged precisely to those employment categories which are considered to be informal or disguised unemployment.

Perhaps the most outstanding example of this is in the construction industry, one of the sectors most affected by the great spending spree on public works. There is absolutely no evidence to suggest that the subsequent increase in the demand for construction workers, which lead at certain times to a relative shortage of this type of labour, gave rise to a generalized improvement of the employment conditions in this industry. Nor did the construction companies try to substitute labour by capital investment in technology and machinery.[16] Instead, in the case of public works undertaken in Mexico City, large contingents of unskilled labourers were recruited directly from the villages, and for work on the heavy infrastructure projects for the oil industries and port complexes in the south-east from Guatemala or Salvador. This kind of worker, hired for short periods on a piecework or day-rate basis, would be classified as informal under any of the usual criteria, as would those temporarily incorporated into the outwork domestic production system, the Northern border 'maquila' industry and the traffic in contraband video equipment in Tepito (for which there was an inordinate demand from the higher- and middle-income groups whose real incomes *had* risen considerably).[17] Nevertheless their labour conditions clearly do not arise out of unemployment but out of the expansion of employment and economic development.

The issue of worker-training provides another example of how the underemployment-informal syndrome is used to disguise government actions which essentially respond to capital's demands in the form of social welfare policies. In the context of the productivity campaign launched by López Portillo in the late 1970s, private- and public-sector industry made vociferous complaints about shortages of adequately trained labour. The immediate response to this was a much publicized reform introduced in the Federal Labour Law in 1979, whereby employers were obliged to provide training for their personnel. This possibly was not what private enterprise had in mind, as it immediately declared itself incapable of fulfilling such a task, while at the same time reiterated the problem of lack of training as a bottle-neck for national development. There followed an open confrontation between the private sector and the Labour Secretariat in May 1981, after which the question of training continued to occupy the press and public discussion. This time, however, less emphasis was placed on training as a productivity factor but rather lack of training as a cause for underemployment; an idea strongly supported by all those studies which show that low educational levels result in marginal occupations (e.g. Muñoz et al. 1977). This reasoning was expressed in catchy aphorisms coined by the Labour Secretariat like 'There is no such thing as unemployment, only lack of training', or 'Training is everybody's welfare' and supported by declarations such as 'what we need is training', expressed by a street vendor in a lengthy article on underemployment. Meanwhile, the press stopped reporting the private sector's non-compliance with the new labour law and filled the space with accounts of government expenditure on specific training programmes.

At a more general level, reference to the informal sector concept indirectly reinforced the developmentalist doctrine in the policy declarations regarding the administration of the country's unprecedented oil revenues. This policy was clearly articulated in the 1980–2 Global Development Plan, published in April 1980. On the one hand, the dominant emphasis was on the need to modernize, on promoting capital goods and export-orientated industries, on overcoming productivity bottle-necks and on inefficiency in the 'strategic' sectors. In these terms, justification was provided for the materialized policies already underway, in which the lion's share of the oil revenues and heavy overseas borrowing financed ambitious public investment programmes in certain decentralized, concentrated 'growth poles': the Northern border area, the oil regions and their adjacent industrial ports, basic industries in the para-State sector and high-price tourist centres. Against this, a fair amount of space in the Global Plan was taken up with employment and social welfare problems, for which the solutions indicated were of an entirely different nature. Regarding public investment, the case for promoting the backward economic sectors is argued, together with the need for increased government involvement in the commercialization of essential consumption goods, especially foodstuffs. Programmes along these lines were also being implemented. Prominent among these were those attributed to the newly created COPLAMAR (Coordinación General del Plan Nacional de Zonas Deprimidas y Grupos Marginados), which participated with municipal, State and central authorities in providing items such as schools and medical services in marginal areas, in exchange for voluntary labour from the inhabitants for road-building and other public works. In the same vein, the Global Development Plan also made some not so specific proposals about developing the 'traditional economic activities' in both the rural and the urban marginal areas. This would take the form of selective aids to labour-intensive activities using 'adequate' technologies, e.g. the promotion of co-operatives to produce or distribute low-priced basic foods and 'self-build' housing projects. None of this materialized to any significant extent in practice, though further research into the informal sector was financed, especially with a view to developing ideas on how this could achieve autonomous growth with the aid of alternative, labour-intensive technologies and the identification of its requirements in the field of training, information and organizational aids. This last item closely coincides with the policy recommendations made by the PREALC team (PREALC 1981: 314).

It would seem therefore that in an economic context in which private and public capital achieves high profit rates which spill over into unprecedented consumption levels in the middle- and upper-income brackets, the usefulness of the informal sector concept for the State in legitimizing its economic and social policies is two-fold. Primarily, the massive subsidies channelled towards certain dynamic sectors (oil, exports, capital goods and the 'maquila' industry) is justified *vis-à-vis* the less favoured sectors and continued rural and urban poverty. Here the equation 'informal sector = unemployment' is used to argue the case for modern development as a panacea to unproductive backwardness. When possible, productive expenditure (or social investment, to use O'Connor's terminology) is disguised as social expenses, as in the case of the training programmes. At a secondary level, increased emphasis on welfare expenditure (whether this be real or rhetorical) needs to be justified to private enterprise. In this case, the usefulness or functionality of a possibly autonomous informal sector is referred to, especially in relation to the production of basic consumer goods and services and housing and also as a way of coping with unemployment.

What happens when the dollars rush out of the fools' paradise and the economy is dragged into an almost paralytic depression?

Contrary to what seems to be the case in Europe and the USA, interest in the informal sector has waned considerably as the crisis has advanced, and so has its application in government (or any other) discourse. An intermediate phase may be discerned when the cracks began to appear; e.g. the first half of 1982 when the peso had suffered 70 per cent devaluation, profits were falling and factories were closing, and the upper- and middle-income groups, alarmed by their loss in purchasing power, were buying up dollars (but when the effective minimum wage was just achieving its highest level since 1977). At this time, and also in the pre-boom recovery period of 1978–9, the informal sector was still present in public discourse, but was not depicted in such an optimistic light, or even as a disguised form of unemployment. Instead, its backwardness and low productivity were emphasized, leading to arguments that the traditional activities should be modernized or replaced by other types of economic organization.

When the screws really began to tighten leading to a second devaluation in August and another in December, the imposition of currency restrictions, an inflation rate of over 100 per cent for 1982 (to be superseded in 1982) and massive lay offs in virtually all sectors of the economy, the informal sector, along with its prime exponents, COPLAMAR and the Continuous Survey on Employment, disappeared from the public vocabulary. The question of underemployment gave way to an alarmed concern with open and undisguised unemployment, seen both as a social problem and as a waste of productive capacity. Every government programme began to be portrayed as job-creating, while investment in the labour-intensive construction industry was given high priority.[18] Informal sector, as an economic category, was substituted by 'small industry and commerce'; how small is not specified but this was often shown to be the beneficiary of the emergency subsidy programmes to bail out the indebted firms.

On the other hand, some of the connotations of the European and North American 'informal sector' may be making headway: a recent newspaper leader referred to 'certain sectors of the economy which have 'sunk' beneath the line of possible fiscalization' (Unomasuno, 19 April 1983, p. 7). Reference to the informal sector as an occupational group is limited to the 'mass of non-salaried workers' who are unprotected by the Labour Laws. These are invoked by those opposing a generalized increase in the minimum and industrial wage level, which, they argue, would not benefit the non-wage-earning population as their incomes are not determined by the legal minimum wage and, at the same time, would be prejudiced by the resulting increase in inflation.

This disappearance of the informal sector from political announcements and from public opinion in general may be partly attributed to the presidential change-over in December, a process which frequently involves a substitution of keywords and slogans. However, a more important factor is probably the shift in the ligitimizing needs of the State. These are now orientated primarily towards the struggling national industries, the middle classes (who can no longer go to Disneyland for weekends) and organized labour, whose continued support for the IMF-dictated, belt-tightening measures must be wooed and bargained for with extreme care. None of these groups are particularly interested at present in the informal sector. Above all, it might be hazarded that at times like these of acute recession *there is no need for informal sector discourse*. A more obvious and less compromising cause may be held responsible for impoverishment and low wages — the crisis — which naturally is not the fault of the national economic structure (except perhaps, for the consequences of certain policy errors committed by the previous administration). On the contrary, the country as a whole is depicted as the hapless victim of the global capitalist system and the international bankers.

The Informal Sector and Empirical Research

The underlying assumptions behind the informal sector as an applied concept previously described in this chapter are clearly not lacking supportive evidence from empirical research (e.g. the PREALC studies already mentioned). However, as the selection and interpretation of data are largely determined by a theoretical framework based on the accumulation of previous research, the same basic premises tend to be reproduced and reiterated. Many of these are derived from studies which are not necessarily representative of the wide variety of contexts to which they are applied. For instance, it is possible that many of the assumptions about marginality and the informal sector, derived from observations of the Argentinian *villas miserias* or Lima's *barriadas* in the 1960s still bear a strong influence in the interpretation of urban poverty in Sao Paulo or Mexico City today. The following section questions some of these basic assumptions and their application in the practical definitions of informal in Mexico, in the light of recent statistical material and research findings.

Some myths and half truths: marginality, terciarization
and the non-wage earners

One recurrent idea which still lurks behind the association between informal sector and poverty is the already much discredited correlation of occupational and ecological marginality. The belief that the inhabitants of the precarious squatter settlements which surround Latin American cities constitute an excessive relative surplus population which has not been absorbed by the capitalist labour market was widely accepted in the late 1960s and early 1970s (Castells 1973; Quijano 1971). Moreover, this conviction proved stronger than empirical evidences to the contrary. A revision of 15 socio-economic monographic studies, undertaken between 1968 and 1978, has shown that the survey results have little bearing on many of the conclusions arrived at (Centro de la Vivienda y Estudios Urbanos 1981) e.g. in situations where 40 to 50 per cent of household heads are industrial workers, there is an insistence on the predominating 'underemployment' or 'insertion in non-capitalist production relations'. By the mid 1960s, however, the preponderance of marginal occupations in marginal settlements was conclusively disproved for the case of the *favelas* in Brazil (Kowarick 1977; Perlman 1976), giving way to a general consensus regarding the heterogeneous nature of the occupational structure and thus the social class of these peripheral urbanizations (Castells 1981a:84) Later studies in Mexico (Moctezuma 1981; CENVI 1981) tended to emphasize the fact that the inhabitants of the *colonias populares* make up the major part of the active and productive labour force.

In spite of these more recent research findings, the idea that economic marginality is the cause for precarious housing conditions still persists: graphical demonstration that the so-called marginal areas of Mexico City house a population which is economically active in industry still causes surprise. The fact that productive workers in the modern sector might be living in shanty areas is not easily accepted, as can be seen in the following quotation, a comment from the Partido Socialista Unificado de México (PSUM) on the miserable housing conditions in the industrial north of Mexico City:

> The living conditions of its inhabitants presents a strong contrast to the great wealth created in the industrial zone Azcapotzalco-Vallejo. For example, in relation to the housing problem, there is an average of 6 persons per dwelling . . . 20% of the houses lack drainage . . . and 60% of the households earn less than $2,500 a month. It should be explained that most of the industrial workers earn higher wages than this, *but they do not live in this area.* (*Revista Dí*, 2 March 1982, p. 13).

This kind of statement may be partially due to an unjustified confidence in official or unofficial income data. The truth of the matter is that if the wages declared in the census and other surveys remotely approximated actual incomes, the essential reproduction of the population concerned, in terms of daily calorific intake, would scarcely be accomplished.[19] The logical assumption that declared incomes in the region of 'less than half the minimum wage' must necessarily imply the extralegal, underemployed, informal syndrome should at least be questioned. At the same time, the realities of the housing market tend to be ignored in this type of analysis: to say that 'industrial workers live somewhere else' assumes that there is a corresponding supply of non-marginal housing. Such housing does not exist, or only in small quantities and at prices which are not accessible to average industrial wage-earners.

Closely related to the assumption that the poorly housed must somehow belong to the marginal or informal occupational structure, is the hypothesis that the increase in tertiary employment is

over-represented among the lowest-income population. This idea
has led some researchers to ignore the results of their exceptional
time-series data on the employment structure of a particular *colonia
popular* (which show a constant proportion of terciary employment,
in spite of a general tendency for older people to switch from
industrial jobs to set up their own small businesses as their sons and
daughters enter the job market) and try to prove the terciarization
hypothesis by other means (Alonso 1980: 165). However, for
Mexico City and other industrial centres this is difficult: although
there are contradictory statistical sources on this matter, the
increase in service employment would seem to be no greater than
that in industry, while commercial employment diminishes.[20]

Another corner-stone of the excessive tertiarization theory is the
idea that the hordes of rural immigrants swell the ranks of the
(underemployed, marginal or informal) service population. This has
been recently disproved for Mexico City by de Oliveira and others,
who show that on the contrary 'from the forties to the sixties, the
incorporation of the immigrant labour force was principally into
industrial work' (de Oliveira 1976).

Finally, the supposed correlation between tertiary employment
and low incomes should be questioned. When the inhabitants of
Mexico City are stratified by average incomes of the area they live
in, the opposite has been shown to be true: the rich and middle-
income residential areas are inhabited almost exclusively by people
working in tertiary activities, while the impoverished periphery
houses the highest concentrations of industrial workers. Only in the
commercially dense central localities do you find both low income
and tertiary employment. It is true that at the level of individual
workers census data confirms the covariation between low incomes
and tertiary activities. However, surveys in *colonias populares* have
shown that in these areas the highest earnings are almost exclusively
achieved by commercial occupations, especially independent small
businesses, and some of the service employees; middle income
largely corresponds to industrial workers, while the lowest income
bracket is comprised of construction, domestic employment and
other service jobs, self-employed salesmen and, to a lesser extent,
salaried industrial workers. On this kind of evidence, it is difficult
to construe an informal sector out of non-productive labour, in the
common usage of the word.

With respect to the Marxist definition of productive labour and
its influence in the conceptualization of the informal sector, in
terms of non-capitalist social production relations, it must be

admitted that in nearly all statistical data available, the self-employed and some of the small or family businesses constitute an important contingent of the lowest-income working population.[21] They also constitute those kinds of occupations which tend to provide the most underestimated answers to questions about income in census and other surveys; among other reasons, because their earnings are the most variable and unpredictable. They also embrace a wide variety of employment situations, including disguised wage relations and a disproportionate amount of part-time workers, especially women, a condition which is seldom taken into account in income data. It should be remembered also that the 'self-employed' and independent small businesses are a minority among the urban working population in Mexico – roughly 20 per cent according to the SPP survey on urban employment in 1976–7, a similar percentage to that found in the CENVI study (21 per cent) directed exclusively at the *colonias populares* inhabitants.

Informal workers as an empirical group

The above considerations cause some doubts to be cast about the basic assumptions which define the informal sector as an empirically observable group. At the same time, it must be recognized that low income has been found to correlate with most of the other characteristics attributed to informality. At least this is the motivating premise behind the project which put informal sector onto the Mexican statistical map: the Continuous Household Employment Survey of 1976–7. Apart from providing a comprehensive insight into the employment situation in urban areas, one of the major aims of this survey was to explore the nature of informal occupations. For this, *previously* determined criteria, based largely on the results of the PREALC studies, were used to identify informality among the working population. Essentially, these criteria consist of the overlapping of the *first* and two or more of the following attributes (the percentages in brackets denote the proportion of informal workers in relation to the total number of workers registering each attribute, which gives some idea of the degree of internal correlation among all these variables):

1 income of less than 1.1 the legal minimum wage (58.5 per cent), the indispensable defining attribute;
2 absence of medical coverage (82.4 per cent);
3 absence of other labour benefits (81.9 per cent);
4 instability of employment (74.1 per cent); and

5 absence of union affiliation (49.8 per cent).

For self-employed workers, the following attributes are also included:

6 absence of medical services (68 per cent);
7 non-affiliation to any labour or trade organization (69 per cent);
8 operating without a licence (77.6 per cent); and
9 not having access to credit (72 per cent).

Apart from these defining variables, low educational and training levels (53.6 per cent and 69.4 per cent for wage-earners and self-employed respectively) and various attributes relating to the place of work (such as being private, occupying precarious buildings, employing less than six people, and lacking hierarchical internal organization and specialized services) were also considered as supplementary, though not defining, characteristics of informality (*Secretaria de Programacion y Presupuesto* 1979: 73–104).

It can be seen that apart from the basic income factor and union affiliation, which are less than convincing, the construction of a sub-group of informal workers on the basis of shared empirical attributes may be allowed some justification.

But once defined, what is the informal sector?

Proving the existence of a sub-group of employment situations which show a reasonably high proportion of shared characteristics does not, however, overcome the theoretical muddle which inspired the selection of these characteristics. The lack of a coherent conceptual base is manifest in the semantic problems which arise in the interpretation of the results of the survey: we are told, for example, that 'while 68.5 per cent of the informal workers are employed in informal establishments, the remaining 31.5 per cent are employed in establishments which are, to a greater or lesser extent, formal' (SPP 1979: 82). It might have been more meaningful to state the point in these terms: at least 30 per cent of the unprotected, less-than-minimum wage earners work in legally established firms employing more than five workers and having organized division of labour; this does not include the 40 per cent of non-informal, less-than-minimum wage earners.

The fallacy of identifying inferior labour conditions with a particular type of production relations becomes all the more clear

Table 2.1   Concentration of informal
occupations for women by branch of activity in
the metropolitan area of Mexico City, 1976–1977

Women by branch of activity	Total		Informal		% of informal occupations
	(thousands)	(%)	(thousands)	(%)	
Total	1,384	100.0	603	100.0	43.6
Agriculture, etc.	4	0.3	2	0.4	54.8
Industry	291	21.0	119	19.7	40.8
Food	28	2.0	13	2.1	45.2
Textiles	20	1.5	8	1.3	40.1
Clothing	90	6.5	51	8.4	56.7
Other industries	153	11.1	47	7.8	30.8
Construction	12	0.8	5	0.8	44.1
Commercial	257	18.6	151	25.0	58.7
Services	701	50.6	319	52.9	45.5
Selling prepared food	70	5.0	47	7.7	66.7
Cleaning	17	1.2	10	1.7	58.8
Domestic service	282	20.4	216	35.8	76.5
Other services	332	24.0	49	8.2	14.9
Transport	17	1.2	2	0.3	11.0
Government and public administration	92	6.7	6	0.9	6.0
Other activities	10	0.7	–	–	–

Source: Sría de Programación y Presupuesto (1979) *La Occupación Informal en Áreas Urbanas*. Mexico City.

when the occupational categories designated as informal are crossed with economic activities (tables 2.1 and 2.2). What emerges is not an informal sector comprised of a wide variety of activities which operate under similar production relations but on the contrary, a relatively limited number of activities clearly differentiated with respect to their production relations. In fact, it would be difficult to derive any common characteristic, apart from unfavourable labour conditions, from which an overall theoretical categorization could be construed.

In the first place, when the data is differentiated by sex, it appears that almost everything that has been said about the informal sector might well be applied to female employment: in nearly all

Table 2.2 Concentration of informal occupations
for men by branch of activity in the metropolitan
area of Mexico City, 1976–1977

Men by branch of activity	Total		Informal		% of informal occupations
	(thousands)	(%)	(thousands)	(%)	
Total	2,700	100.0	798	100.0	29.5
Agriculture, etc.	42	1.5	25	3.1	59.7
Industry	892	33.0	206	25.9	23.1
Food	96	3.5	28	3.6	29.7
Clothing	62	2.3	28	3.6	45.7
Footwear and leather	25	0.9	12	1.5	47.8
Timber and cork	18	0.7	10	1.3	58.1
Metal furniture	42	1.6	20	2.5	47.9
Other industries	649	24.0	107	13.4	16.5
Construction	208	7.7	117	14.7	56.3
Commercial	453	16.8	207	26.0	45.8
Services	640	23.7	189	22.7	28.2
Selling prepared food	62	2.3	24	3.0	38.3
Motor-car repair	64	2.4	32	4.0	49.3
Machinery repair	32	1.2	19	2.4	55.4
Cleaning	39	1.4	21	2.6	53.4
Domestic service	20	0.7	13	1.7	65.5
Other services	422	15.6	72	9.0	17.1
Transport	175	6.5	42	6.1	27.6
Government and public administration	236	8.7	12	1.5	4.9
Other activities	55	2.1	–	–	–

Source: as for table 2.1.

the economic sectors, the proportion of women classified as informal is twice that of men. Moreover, these female workers are fairly highly concentrated in relatively few specific occupations. Domestic service, for instance, not only accounts for 36 per cent of all informal female employment in Mexico City, it also constitutes 20 per cent of all economically active women and 15 per cent of the total informal sector. This numerical weight implies that many of the characteristics imputed to informality refer in fact to domestic service. The other sectors where female informal workers are concentrated are commerce, the garment industry and prepared foods: those economic activities traditionally assigned to women. It may be noted that it is precisely in these economic categories that we also find a high concentration of male workers classified as informal. All this suggests a possible line of enquiry which could substitute the informal sector approach: the historical cultural and ideological.determinants of women's work, and how these might explain the way certain economic activities have developed (or survive), on the basis of highly exploitive specific types of labour processes.

It would not, however, be possible to explain all of the empirically constituted informal sector in terms of the particular nature of women's work. At least 30 per cent of the male labour force also appears to work under extralegal conditions or is self-employed and many of these job situations bear no relation to the above mentioned female-dominated activities. Although these informal male jobs are more widely dispersed than the female ones, there is a certain degree of concentration in some sectors, which should be analysed separately.

This is the case for construction, which exhibits practically all the characteristics attributed to informality – highly exploitive, labour-intensive production conditions, discontinuous production, low productivity, use of unskilled manual labour, etc. The resulting labour conditions would appear to share many features with other kinds of unstable occupations, domestic service or ambulant selling for instance, and it is significant that all these tend to constitute a gateway into the urban employment market for immigrants. However, construction differs from these other casual-work situations in that it cannot provide fallback jobs for the unemployed in times of recession. It is well known that construction is particularly sensitive to the economic cycle (and the tentative efforts to create jobs by the much publicized minor public works programmes do little to offset the massive redundancies caused by the recurrent paralysis of public and private investment in construction).[22] This cyclic dependence and relative backwardness of the construction industry, arising out of the peculiar nature of buildings as commodities, combined with the private property of land, is the logic behind the vast army of informal wage-earners in this industry (Connolly 1977). It could also be argued that the inexhaustible supply of cheap labour generated in rural areas is also a contributive factor in the development or rather, underdevelopment, of construction; this is an hypothesis which might find some parallels in the sectors which rely on predominantly female labour. There could also be other examples of specific employment situations qualified as informal, such as the wide range of activities orbiting the motor-car and domestic hardware industries, which need to be explained by the interrelationship between the development of production forces within the sector concerned and the availability of cheap labour. However, until further advances are made along these lines, at the level of each particular economic sector, it would be difficult to propose a general hypothesis which could embrace all the badly paid, extralegal and self-employed occupational situations for the purposes of reconstituting the informal sector as a theoretical category.

Perhaps the most significant implication of this rejection of informal as a category concerns its complementary opposite, the formal sector. For this must also be rejected as an ideal type which presupposes a correspondence between certain production relations and good employment conditions. This means obliterating the vision of the modern-sector labour force comprised exclusively of highly trained, unionized workers who, after spending eight hours a day in some vast shining industrial complex, look forward to paid holidays, social security and medical coverage and a Corbusian dream machine for living in. This is not the kind of worker who, in countries like Mexico, has created most of the four decades worth of economic growth in import substitution and the industrialization of the internal production base. However, the kind of labour force which *has* been responsible for this industrial expansion, or rather its inexpensive living conditions, is exactly what many branches of global capitalist economy are increasingly dependent on. At least, the recent tendencies of the international division of labour would seem to point in this direction: towards decentralized and volatile production processes and organizational and geographical separation of the different phases of production, parts of which are being located in countries where labour is cheap, taxes are minimal and living standards are correspondingly low (György 1975: 91–2; Michalet 1976: 149–62; Minian 1981).

It is therefore in the light of the dominant trends in the global economy that explanations of poverty, unemployment and the diverse manifestations of over-exploitive labour conditions may be found. This necessarily diverts attention away from actual conditions in themselves, conceived as a kind of underworld or exceptional state, and focuses the analysis fairly and squarely on the dynamics of capital accumulation, both at an aggregate level and in terms of specific branches of the economy.

Recent Theoretical Substitutes to the Informal Sector

Important steps have already been made in this direction by some recent critiques which, from different standpoints, begin to conceptualize the informal syndrome as an integral part of capitalist development. At the risk of oversimplification, these new trends may be classified into four or five types of theoretical approach which have been resonant in Mexico in the past few years.

Back to Marx: the informal sector as the industrial reserve army

The first approach arises out of a frontal reaction to marginality theory and seeks to re-establish the Marxist category of relative surplus population/industrial reserve army within the 'law of population under capital' (Navarro & Moctezuma 1980a,b). Influential in this reformation was the discovery that the so-called marginal housing areas were inhabited by a majority of industrial workers, as was the political standpoint which sees contemporary, popular urban movements as part of the proletarian struggle. From this viewpoint, the population working in informal-type conditions are not conceived as a separate group but rather as an integral part of the working class, independently of whether it is actively exploited by capital or not.

One important methodological implication of this approach is the need to analyse the ebb and flow of this reserve army population: the mechanisms by which labour is incorporated into and expelled from productive activities, according to the overall and particular economic cycles. Theoretically, the restoration of the industrial reserve army should throw light on the dynamics of unemployment in itself, as this would no longer be considered as an independent variable or an underlying premise which 'explains' a distinct phenomenon − the informal sector for instance. However, in practice, this potential has hardly been explored.[23] In all events, on its own, the dynamics of unemployment cannot sufficiently explain the specific social roles of the various kinds of work carried out by the population while it is in reserve. If other considerations are not taken into account, there is a danger that the substitution of informal sector for industrial reserve army at best throws the baby out with the bathwater, by denying all unproductive labour any serious economic function in society, apart from providing a relative surplus population; at worst, all that is achieved is a Marxian synonym for marginality or informal occupation in their earlier and least imaginative formulations – by no means unheard of in current usage.

Curiously enough, the more penetrating insights 'beyond the informal sector' have not emerged out of this kind of attempt to discredit or substitute informal altogether but rather are either derived from within the informal sector theory itself or are completely independent of it.

Informal sector's direct contribution to capital accumulation

The second approach evolved from the analysis of the direct economic functions attributable to certain activities considered as belonging to the informal sector. In particular, attention is directed to the mechanisms whereby value is directly transferred from small productive units upwards and the subsumption of 'hybrid' production relations by capital. Possibly, the major advance in this direction has been theoretical, based on a reconsideration of Marx's texts on 'traditional' and 'hybrid' forms (1976: 595–601) and 'formal subsumption' (Marx 1976: 1019–38), as well as the application of the 'unequal exchange' concept.[24] However, recent empirical studies, using anthropological methods, have substantiated these ideas, by exposing typical situations of wage-labour disguised as self-employment or small businesses (Alonso 1980). For example, it has been shown how carpenters' shops and other small productive concerns are virtually over-exploited wage-labour for their suppliers, to whom they are permanently indebted and who are essentially in control of the production. Similar situations are found in small retailers, chemist shops and ambulant salesmen, whose major income takes the form of commissions from the sale of industrialized commodities, paid directly by the producers, these being, as often as not, international firms such as General Foods, Coca Cola and the major drug companies.

Within this line of thinking, we have developed some proposals derived from the CENVI study on the production and consumption of the urban environment. Here, the role of unpaid work by users, self-employed construction workers and specialists and small master builders are considered in relation to the production of the *colonias populares*. These areas, which make up about 65 per cent of Mexico City, are conceived as part of social fixed capital in as much that all built environment is a vital material support for the reproduction of capital, especially in the circulation sphere (and not just for the reproduction of the labour force). Thus, all these various types of apparently unproductive labour (in the Marxist sense) create value which contributes directly to the general and specific productivity levels achieved by capitalist production relations. The means (and the proof) of this value transfer is fundamentally the appropriation of the land rents which are generated in this production process CENVI 1981).

Informal sector in the reproduction of the labour force

Very much related to the 'economic-function' approach, a third line of research emphasizes the role of informal activities in the reproduction of the active labour force (Kowarick 1977; Margulis 1980). This kind of analysis concerns both paid labour which produces major basic consumption goods and services, such as prepared food, clothing and housing, and unpaid work for individual or collective auto-consumption. While owing a lot to certain analysts of 'peasant economies' (Lehman 1980; Meillasoux 1980), this approach in the urban context responds more to a general theoretical position and is firmly rooted in the tradition which regards the city basically as a means of reproduction of the labour force (Castells 1976; Topalov 1979).

Informal sector in the production of the labour force

A fourth line of study, which should be seen in combination with the previous group and with the analysis of the industrial reserve army, focuses its attention on the relation between family and occupational structures. This approach goes beyond the survival strategy interpretation of the informal sector by recognizing the importance of the division of labour inside the domestic unit, not only for the subsistence or reproduction of the work-force function, but in direct reference to the way this work-force is produced. García, Muñoz and de Oliveira, for example, re-examine their 1970 survey under the hypothesis that the domestic unit is 'an instance which filters the demand and regulates the supply of labour in the market.' By this, they have demonstrated the relevance of socio-demographic characteristics such as kinship, the family's stage in the life cycle, the age and sex of the major income contributors, etc., in determining the way the different members of the family relate to the labour market (García et al. 1982).

Similar results were obtained in my study (the data for which was collected ten years after the previous example) on the employment

structure in Mexico City's *colonias populares*. The stage in the reproductive cycle or age of the primary couple were found to have a decisive
influence on their occupational situation, basically because of the
changes provoked by the integration of wives and children into the
labour market. A family with young children tends to be nuclear and
with high economic dependency ratios based on the husband's salary.
At this stage, he tends to be a wage-earner, with a higher-than-average
income and a longer-than-average working day. When the economic responsibility begins to be distributed among other members of
the family or when there are other adults living in the same
household, individual incomes diminish and the main wage-earner
works fewer hours or switches to a less intensive job or self-
employed work. It is at this stage that some people manage to fulfill
their dream of setting up their own business, in which the wife's
and children's labour generally play a fundamental role. Otherwise,
the wife and older children enter the job market, usually part time
and under disfavourable employment conditions. It is in this more
mature kind of domestic unit that a higher incidence of some of the
employment categories labelled as informal may be found: less-
than-minimum wages, part-time or self-employed work, unpaid
family labour and women's employment. This tendency towards
more non-wage labour in the family as it ages not only applies to
remunerative occupations; these families also tend to be the
principal self-builders of their houses and supply the most unpaid
labour in neighbourhood organizations and improvement projects (CENVI 1981). This 'family-cycle model (whose derivation is
essentially commonsensical but might suggest a rereading of
Chayanov) provided the most adequate explanation of the data
obtained in the study. However, it is clearly only an ideal type of
much more complex and varied situations which need further
analysis.

This emphasis on the family structure does, in all events, have
important implications for the informal sector debate. It suggests
that people involved in radically different types of production
relations not only collectively consume (and produce) their neighbourhood or *colonia* but also share the same table and are often
represented in the same individual. This makes nonsense of
attempting to associate the various types of workers classified as
informal with a specific population group and points towards more
careful studies of the various functions of non-wage labour, both in
the production and/or reproduction of the labour force and in the
determination of its value.

Informal sector and women's work

An issue which is raised by the previous discussion of the role of the family is clearly the implication of being female with respect to employment conditions. The incorporation of women in the informal sector discussion is due to the observation that female workers make up a disproportionate part of the empirically iden-tified informal occupations; a fact that has been paid little attention until recently. Since this connection has been made however (and due to the international boom in 'women's studies'), interest in female labour in Mexico has multiplied.[25] The informal sector concept here has now been injected with new content, derived from a wide diversity of studies on women and work: from housework and domestic service (de Barbeieri 1978), female labour and domestic production in specific branches of the economy such as the garment, toy and electronic industries (Alonso J.A. 1979, 1981; Alonso J. 1980) to more general research on women's position in the labour market (de Leonardo & Guerra 1978; Pedrero & Rendón 1982; de Riz 1975). In the CENVI study, attention was also focused on the differences between the way men and women relate to their work, especially in the subjective, and thus economic, evaluation of their job skills.[26] Undoubtedly, by far the most articulated body of research has been directed towards the labour conditions of women working in the *maquila* industries in the border cities, within a conceptual framework dominated by a preoccupation with the internationalization of capital and the global division of labour (see Carrillo & Hernández 1981 for an extensive bibliography on this). More recently, there has been a widespread interest in unpaid female work, especially that concerning the consolidation of irregular settlements and the role of women in the popular urban movement.

This line of analysis, related to the specific situation of women and gender differentiation, may begin to explain important areas of highly exploitive employment situations, the dynamics of the labour supply and the devaluation of labour in general. More especially, this approach opens up the otherwise highly controver-sial possibility of seriously reconsidering the cultural, ideological and biological aspects behind the production of the labour force as a determinant factor in the way that capital accumulation is achieved, without falling into the demographic explosion – 'demand for jobs' model. However, the female condition on its own, at most, can only provide one half of the answers to poverty, unemployment and economic development and therefore can only be considered as a partial substitute to informal sector discourse.

Informal sector and social movements

Most of the previous theoretical positions regarding the social role of the non-wage earners and the over-exploited have been formulated or applied in the context of large industrial cities. Their logical consequences point towards a progressive abandoning of the search for *an* informal sector as a population group, as the occupational categories and work processes are proved to be more and more inextricably linked with capital accumulation, at a local level and on an international scale; the workers involved either turn out to be the active labour force directly exploited by capital or they contribute in various ways to the creation of the general conditions which make this possible. In short, the informal workers are becoming increasingly classed as proletarian. This progression is clearly reflected in a related area of theoretical inquiry and political practice − the characterization of urban social movements.

Whereas in 1980, in a manner which is reminiscent of marginality theory at its hey-day, the Urban Popular Movement defined itself as that sector of the working class: 'integrated by *colonos,* petty tradesmen, tenants, the unemployed, the underemployed, drivers, loaders & carriers, ambulant salesmen, shoe shiners, etc., whose *own particular struggle* (respectively) is for a piece of land to live on and the provision of services, against paying taxes and permits, against evictions and rent increases, etc.' (CONAMUP 1980), more recent announcements depict this movement as 'the urban struggle of the proletariat' and 'the response of the proletariat and the people to their needs in the realm of consumption' (CONAMUP 1982; Moctezuma 1981).

In the light of this tendency, it is worth mentioning a new Mexican proposition which, on the basis of arguments which are essentially similar to all that has been discussed so far, would appear to point in the diametricaly opposite direction: the re-establishment of a newly baptized informal sector, virtually as a social class − TRADIFAS. Taking as a point of departure a penetrating criticism of the marginality concept, especially for its reliance on negative definitions, Esteva (1983a,b) attempts a reconceptualization of these human groups in more positive terms. Drawing on the concept of modern society as a 'social factory which produces for its own reproduction' (Cleaver 1983), the peasants, together with what amounts to the empirically defined urban informal sector are defined

as a single human group whose activities are primarily concerned
with that part of the social factory not realized in capitalist
industries (Esteva 1983a: 746–9). In other words, they are responsible for their own reproduction and, in this, have found a way
towards their own auto-valorization (Cleaver 1983). Notwithstanding the logical, not to mention practical, difficulties involved
in identifying an actual human group in these terms, a more
promising part of this argument is when this essentially economic
definition is seen as a motivation for mass mobilization, out of
which specific forms of social cohesion are generated; a potential
capsulated in precautionary slogans such as 'the TRADIFAS are
coming' and 'it's the hour of the TRADIFAS.' Here, the role of the
struggle for land in Mexican history is evoked and the occupation of
urban areas by 'rural immigrants' is regarded as a continuation
of the peasant tradition. This coincides certainly with many of
the ideas expressed by *colonos'* movements of cities in Northern
Mexico (Torreón, Monterry, Durango) which did arise out of
organized land invasions. However, in other areas of Mexico,
especially in the capital, land occupation has generally been on an
individual basis and controlled by the official party political
machinery; the independent organizations tend to emerge in the
consolidation phase after a rupture with the previous 'leaders' has
been achieved.

Although criticisms of the specific arguments put forward in the
TRADIFA hypothesis could be raised, it contains an important
consideration which deserves further thought. This is the mobiliz-
ing potential of different economic and ecological relations outside
the direct wage relationship: a change of focus from the various
functions for global capital accumulation (which surely may be
proved in relation to virtually any contemporary economic
phenomenon) to the socio-political effects of such economic organization. It is undeniable that particular human groups are mobilized on the basis of certain (but by no means all) economic activities
which have been labelled informal or associated with marginality.
The *colonos'* movements, in the struggle to build their urban
habitat, are not the only example. Many neighbourhood organizations, especially those of tenants in central areas, are consciously
defending not only their housing but also their territorially
prescribed petty trade and production interests: not only where and
how they live but also the integration of their habitat to where and
how they work. At the same time, other territorially based
self-employed occupations – rubbish sorting, shoe-shining, organ-

grinding, newspaper-selling, taxi-driving, or even land-invading –
have, in Mexico, been nominally organized and largely incorporated
into the government party machinery for a long time. 'Popular
movements' can, therefore, offer no substitute for informal sector as
a general classification of population groups. The incorporation of
their analysis to the post-informal sector debate could, however,
open up alternative and maybe more optimistic theoretical avenues
for future research.

Concluding Remarks

It was stated in the introduction that the arguments presented in
this chapter were not intended as a contribution to the theoretical
debate on informal sector but rather as an attempt to evaluate the
theoretical production on this topic, from the point of view of its
practical implications. On the whole, this balance is negative. As
far as the analysis of employment structures is concerned, very little
is gained by grouping a whole series of economic activities under
one conceptual category, and a great deal is lost. Infravalorization of
wage labour is confused with small enterprise and non-commodity
production or with illegal *modus vivendi*; the specific nature of gender
exploitation is lost as women's work is associated with unskilled
manual labour; any badly paid job is disguised as unemployment and,
lastly, no distinction is admitted between brutal, alienating labour
relations and potentially autonomous, creative forms of production.
Any generalizing category, whatever its name, which tries to reduce
these multiple realities into an overall explanation of poverty and unemployment can only amount to an apologetic and mystifying discourse.
    Beyond this assessment of the informal sector concept itself, it is
hoped that some light has been thrown on the intense ideological
undertones which are inevitable in any discussion touching on the
problem of employment and poverty. The basic issue here is how
wealth is produced and why the majority of the population lack
access to it. Whatever interpretation is given to this phenomenon,
it will necessarily be conditioned by a particular vision of an
alternative future. This makes it extremely difficult, in the context
of the present chapter, to conclude with facile proposals for future
lines of research. It is clear that the new avenues of inquiry are
inspired by differing political models. Those who envisage urban
popular movements as part of the proletarian struggle, or are
involved in organizations who see themselves as such, will naturally

try to relate as many occupational situations as possible to capital accumulation, whether this be in the form of the industrial reserve army, via the direct transfer of value upwards, or for the reproduction of the labour force. Those who, on the other hand, begin to question the proletariat's historic mission in the construction of the New Society will contemplate these same activities with a view to their revolutionary potential as alternative forms of social organization. For those who are more concerned with women's struggle against male domination, the specific role of female labour, the family and women's consciousness becomes the central question. For those who have no commitment towards any social transformation, and for those whose primary interest is making the most of the way things are, further developments in and around the informal sector concept are to be highly recommended.

Notes

1   Centro de la Vivienda y Estudios Urbanos a.c. (CENVI), *El Trabajo no Asalariado en la Producción y el Consumo del Espacio Urbano*. A research project on the occupational structure within families and the division of labour between the sexes and age groups in relation to non-wage labour in house-building and in the promotion and consolidation of the *colonia* or neighbourhood. The study included surveys of 600 domestic units and 60 in-depth interviews in six *colonias populares* in Mexico City in 1981.

2   In the USA: Feige 1980; Gutmann 1979b; in Spain: Martínez Vázquez 1981; Moltocalvo 1980; and in other European countries: Sauvy 1980.

3   Some authors use the grade of illegality as a criteria for classifying activities within the informal sector (e.g. Lafuente Félez 1980).

4   Moser (1978) goes a long way in clearing up many confusions created by the informal–formal dualism, suggesting instead the importance of analysing the 'structural linkages and relationships between different production and distribution systems' (p. 1061). However, I am not sure that the alternative overall framework she proposes (the continuum of economic activities) fully overcomes the fundamental problem of the backward-impoverished–modern-rich dichotomy. Like Redfield's 'continuum', this one necessarily needs a pole at each end. (To my knowledge, Moser's article has not been translated into Spanish).

5   These ambiguities refer more to the Spanish word *eventual* than to the English casual. However, the lack of precision often survives translation, either by non-translation, or by the use of the incomplete casual. It should be noted that *eventual* without further

qualification, is a census category in Mexico and is widely used in surveys.

6   Another term that defies translation.
7   The whole idea of subemployment as disguised unemployment owes a great deal to Myrdal's early economic philosophy of underdevelopment: 'an underdeveloped country is also characterized by the fact that a large portion of its working force is unemployed or eking out a bare subsistance through various forms of disguised unemployment.' (Myrdal 1957: 97.) See Castells (1981a: 38) for an emphatic reiteration of the same theme: 'Paradoxically we can say that the only occupational situation which does not exist in a dependent society is unemployment . . . In Venezuela, Mexico, Chile, Peru, one cannot live without working.' One wonders what kind of interpretation is given to the declared unemployment rates of up to ten per cent (people out of work and actively looking for a job) which have been registered in Mexico in official and unofficial censuses and surveys.
8   This confusion has been discussed in more detail by Singer (1979: 53).
9   In Mexico, the problem of 'imperialism' and the world economic system is widely assimilated into public discourse and educational programmes at all levels. In addition, 'social imbalances' are also attributed to erroneous development models of previous governments. This kind of explanation, generally based on critical research findings, tends to appear at the beginning of each presidential sexenium.
10 Not all theorists see fit to do so; a task that is also complicated because by definition data on the informal sector is scarce. The most empirically convalidated informal sector seems to be that defined by the PREALC/OIT studies. On the other hand, most of the structuralist hypotheses arising out of the CEPAL research, have been recently corroborated with 1970 and 1975 census data for Mexico (Lustig 1981).
11 The category informal employment, defined more or less in the above terms and under the guidance of the PNUD/OIT programme, was institutionalized in Mexico by the late 1970s, when it was incorporated into the design and processing of the continuous survey on employment in urban areas. The publication of the results of this by SPP has contributed largely to the use of informal sector terminology in general discourse on development, employment and poverty.
12 In the SPP survey this negative definition is made explicit in the methodology applied, in which informal workers are selected by their lack of attributes (SPP 1979: 75).
13 The economic functions of the marginal occupations are explicitly recognized in the official definition of marginal: 'as those groups which have been excluded (*al margen*) from national development and

the wealth generated, but not necessarily absent (*al margen*) from the generation of this wealth, nor still less from the creation of the conditions which make this possible.' (COPLAMAR 1979 p. 1)

14   One such announcement was:

> Today, the anguish of recession, of increasing unemployment, of extreme injustice, of the insecurity and the pessimism of desperation have been overcome. The goal of generating sufficient employment for the population which demands an adequate *modus vivendi* was reached for the third consecutive year as 700 thousand jobs were created in 1980. This will allow a continued reduction in unemployment and underemployment. (Miguel de la Madrid, Minister for Programming and Budget, speaking at the IV Reunion of the Republic, 5 November 1981).

The private sector expressed similar opinions. J.L. Coindreaux, President of the Confederación Patronal de la República Mexicana announced an unprecedented 'supply of jobs':

> 'With the highest private investment ever, it will be possible to maintain for the fourth consecutive year the generation of employment rate' although he admitted to the persistence of margination in the country. He explained that this rise in employment is 'proof of the undeniable development of the country, because, with the creation of 700,000 jobs since 1979, not only has the demand of the unemployed population been covered, but also, the supply of jobs has extended towards part of the 8 million underemployed, which make up 40% of the population in condition and of age to work.'

15   Real minimum wage index, national average 1977–83:

	1977	1978	1979	1980	1981	1982	1983
January	112.0	107.0	104.2	102.8	109.4	112.0	92.0
April	106.1	103.2	100.4	96.8	102.3	128.5	
July	102.7	100.0	96.8	90.8	97.7	110.1	
October	98.1	95.9	92.6	86.7	91.9	90.6	

July 1978 = 100
Minimum wages are revised in January and there was an emergency 30 per cent rise in March 1982.
Source: Banco de México, *Indicadores Económicos*. 1983.

16   Data is only available on this subject up to 1980. However, around this time and in previous times of construction boom, wages in the construction industry did not rise over and above the annual average industrial wage increase and continued to represent about 70–80 per cent of this. Fixed capital investment in the construction industry

remained constant throughout 1970–80.
17 After the crisis, the Tepito sellers went back to the second-hand clothes business.
18 After moderation of public expenditure, employment protection occupied second place in the government's ten-point Programme for Economic Reordering. The emergency programme for employment protection included four fundamental lines of action:

1 Employment creation in rural areas by normal public works programmes aimed at multiplying the number of jobs created per peso invested.
2 Employment creation in depressed (*deprimidas*) zones in the principal urban areas, with the aim of providing income for the population and simultaneously producing works of collective benefit.
3 Employment creation for *pasantes*, to cater for young graduates.
4 Programmes to protect the industrial plant, which aimed at maintaining existing employment levels and avoiding a deterioration of unemployment. This included public purchasing in the internal market and subsidies to supply national goods to the border areas and financial guarantees and finance to help firms with overseas debts. A certain selectivity for these programmes was envisaged but not specified. (Informe sobe la Situación Económica. [April 1983] *Acciones y Resultados del Primer Trimestre de 1983*)

19 In CENVI's experience, working as adviser to neighbourhood organizations, the declared income levels go up in every successive socio-economic survey, as confidence increases and the purpose of the data collecting is clarified, e.g. to organize a demand for housing finance, where it is convenient to be able to prove more, rather than less, economic resources. Even so, the underestimation of real incomes has been shown to be considerable.
20 Distribution (in percentages) of the EAP in the metropolitan zone (City and State of Mexico) by economic activity for 1950 and 1970.

	Agri-culture	Oil and mining	Indus-try	Const-ruction	Elec-tricity	Trans-port	Com-merce	Ser-vices	Govern-ment	Other
1950	2.9	0.8	26.5	5.8	0.7	4.9	15.9	25.3	7.9	9.5
1970	2.6	0.8	31.1	5.9	0.7	4.2	13.6	30.2	6.4	4.5

Source: census data processed by the Colegio de México, quoted in Negrete et al. 1982.

21 In the SPP continuous survey on employment of 1976, in urban

areas, 71 per cent of self-employed workers declared less than 1.2 the minimum wage, compared to 55 per cent of the wage-earners. In the CENVI survey, which only concerns *colonia popular* inhabitants, the difference was found to be greater: 70 per cent of the independent workers declared the minimum wage or less, compared to 57 per cent of the small-business owners and 41 per cent of the wage-earners.

22 In Mexico, construction is not only dependent on short and medium economic cycles but also on the presidential sexennium cycle which determines investment in public works (60 per cent of all investment in construction). See Connolly (1977).

23 With the exception of some work undertaken by the Grupo Asesor del Movimiento Popular Urbano (GAMPO) (CONAMUP 1982).

24 See Singer (1980: 187–92) for a discussion of this.

25 Two official publications in Mexico are symptomatic of this sudden interest in women: *Estadística Sobre la Mujer,* a recompilation of various statistical sources, and *Estudios Sobre la Mujer,* an anthology comprised mainly of translated articles published abroad (SPP 1982).

26 When asked about their job skills, women whose employment was cooking (in commercial quantities), seamstressing, 'running the shop', etc., considered that these were unskilled occupations and, as such, they were paid accordingly. The ability to do all these tasks is not thought of as an acquired skill but some sort of innate female attribute. Men, on the other hand, thought that practically every job they did, except perhaps those involving brute muscular force, needed some kind of training or learning process, even those (such as taco preparation) which are identical to the women's 'unskilled' activities. It was also noticeable that many women had difficulty in connecting the work they did, even if paid, to questions on employment, showing a marked underestimation of their role as workers or even certain shame of owning to the fact that they were employed.

3

The Contested Domain:
Gender, Accumulation and the Labour Process

Nanneke Redclift

The area of social reality which we commonly refer to as 'domestic', previously seen as the special province of anthropology, or confined within the boundaries of the sociology of the family, has emerged in the last decade as the focus of theoretical attention. One aspect of this has been to argue that we cannot trivialize the personal by seeing it simply as a matter of individual, rather than of social or political concern. Another aspect has been to question the adequacy of concepts derived from formal institutional structures, economic or political, and to argue that a specific set of processes in the 'private' household sphere can be distinguished. For some authors these even constitute a separate domestic 'mode' based on its own principles. This mode has been said to characterize types of society (Meillasoux 1981; Sahlins 1974), or to form a distinct yet essential adjunct to capitalism (Delphy 1977; Lipton 1980; Meillasoux 1981). Recent Marxist analysis has also attempted to move away from a 'productionist' orientation and has directed attention to the 'mode of reproduction', which is seen as separate from, but determined by, the mode of production (Gimenez 1982). This discussion has its roots in the nineteenth century, as shown by the recent revival of interest in Engels' account of the relationship between the family and the State. However, in the intervening lapse of time the debate has been modified and transformed by the current preoccupations of late capitalism. Within this, three separate lines of thought can be identified.

In developing, or less industrialized economies, the persistence of 'pre-capitalist' subsistence production based on the household has raised questions about the nature of capitalist penetration. Despite widespread destruction by the gradual, but inexorable, process of commoditization, self-provisioning and petty commodity production has shown unexpected resilience in both urban and rural economies. The household economy has had little specific place in Marxist analyses of development (Long & Richardson 1978; Safa 1982), but the controversy over the conditions leading to the conservation or dissolution of these forms has implicitly placed the domestic domain at the centre of theories of underdevelopment. This argument reaches its apotheosis in the work of Meillasoux, who sees the continuing exploitation of the domestic economy as fundamental to capitalist development itself, and the family under capitalism as the direct successor of the domestic agrarian community.

The paradox Meillasoux defends, following Luxembourg, is that the domestic mode is simultaneously maintained and destroyed by the penetration of capitalism. His implication is that a set of specifically 'domestic relations' can be identified that are constant and enduring and form 'the basis on which all other economies are built' (Meillasoux 1981). The similarities between this argument and that over the role of domestic labour for capitalism are clear. Unfortunately, however, the contradictions of his paradox effectively beg the very questions about the historical nature of this transformation that we need to ask. What is it about the domestic community that survives; what aspects provide this supposed continuity? Despite the wealth of empirical evidence demonstrating the variety of forms subsumed under the rubric of the domestic sphere, theoretical analyses still tend to assume that the concept has some natural or transhistorical validity (Harris 1981; Yanagisako 1979).

Under advanced industrialism, on the other hand, restructuring and the decline of full employment have also revealed the importance of economic processes that are not encompassed by commodity relationships or by accepted definitions of the capitalist mode of production. Goods and services that are privately consumed may be produced domestically, as well as through public institutions and social insurance and the private capital employed in the household economy may increase in importance so that a process of *de*commodification can be discerned, even as commoditization persists in other areas. Innovations in information technology provide the opportunity to relocate work in the household that was previously centralized (Gershuny this volume). It is even possible that the separation of home and workplace that occurred in the industrialized countries during the nineteenth century may come to be seen as a historical shift of limited duration. Ultimately, these trends suggest that accounts of class and the labour process under capitalism require reconsideration. We need to reflect on the permanence and ubiquity of the division between production for the market and production for use, the 'formal' and 'informal' economies, the 'public' and 'private' domain.

A major stimulus for this analysis has come from the feminist critique, which has emphasized the limitations of definitions of the economic which exclude the production of use values and the reproduction of labour power, processes that lie at the core of conceptions of the household and domestic sphere. Although such activities have been ignored in previous androcentric analyses, many commentators would argue that they have always provided the crucial conditions of existence for the creation of surplus value. Thus, the household production of subsistence is not only character-istic of underdevelopment but must be set within a comparative analysis of the sexual division of labour. The element of continuity hidden behind Meillasoux's account of the persistence of the domestic economy would therefore appear to lie in the appropria-tion of unpaid female labour, through the domestic bonds of kinship (Delphy 1977).

However, the generalization of a universal set of domestic rela-tions, in which women share an ahistorical, acultural similarity, conceals more than it reveals. It should lead us to a concrete examination of the relationships between paid and unpaid labour, domestic and social production within any given context. Although the *form* taken by household labour, and the nature of its appropria-tion, are historically specific, and may vary from the direct production of use values to the transformation of the wage, an analysis of the relationship between the family and the labour process must be central to any account of the mode of production as a whole.

Several, sometimes conflicting, trends have therefore directed attention to the changing relationship between waged work, conceptualized as statistically visible, taxable and accountable, and 'other' forms of work, not directly organized by capital, whose productivity is less easily measurable and which seem to lie 'outside' capitalist relations of production. A variety of concepts − the informal sector, the household economy, subsistence production, the domestic domain – have been invoked to encompass and locate these diverse activities. Although they are are often misleadingly conflated, the referents of these ideas are different. However, they have in common the delimitation of a separate sphere, where consumption and individual livelihoods are shaped through personal bonds, existing in dualistic opposition to the 'public' world of production and accumulation, yet articulated with it in certain not very clearly specified ways, and defined principally by the absence of those qualities which are thought to characterize economy, polity and society as a whole. Thus, despite competing accounts of its nature and status, the household and the domestic domain have emerged not merely as the incidental location of the workers' natural instinct for self-preservation, in Marx's famous phrase, which can be safely ignored while the serious business of production takes place, but as fundamental to the analysis of the economic system.

The question remains: how is this analysis to be carried out? The common sense of everyday usage makes the domestic domain an elusive concept. Its location seems obvious, yet this privileged terrain keeps changing its ground when we examine it more closely. As the debate on informal economies,[1] of both Third- and First-World varieties has shown, sectors and spheres lose their separate reality and analytic usefulness when we attempt a dynamic interpretation of their perpetuation or demise. The attempt to explain the continuing existence of pre-capitalist modes has questioned the validity of dualistic models and directed the inquiry from the articulation of separate and bounded 'modes' to the subsumption of all forms under capitalism (Banaji 1977; Bernstein 1979; Goodman & Redclift 1981). Difficulties nevertheless remain in conceptualizing labour outside value (Bradby 1982), such as that typified by household subsistence production. Such labour cannot be located outside the circuit of capital, yet as Bernstein (1979) points out it exists 'in conditions less determinate than those of the proletariat'. It is 'not subject to complete expropriation nor to the particular modes of regulation and discipline of labour exercised within the capitalist production process'. Thus it is subsumed, yet it obeys a different 'logic'. Such formulations remain ambiguous. Furthermore, the feminist critique has undermined the unitary nature of conventional concepts and has suggested that women's relationship to these processes must be seen as specific and distinctive.

Nanneke Redclift

The purpose of this chapter is therefore to explore a variety of approaches to these ideas and to discuss some of the difficulties involved in developing a historical account of this special domain where self-preservation and the means of existence are defended. To do this a number of issues are reviewed: the relationship between gender and work, the role of 'non-capitalist' forms in the accumulation process, the connections between the international and sexual division of labour and the significance of the concept of reproduction. However, first it is necessary to examine in more detail some of the conceptual and methodological issues involved.

'Problematic Unities'

Despite the recognition of the need to link historically specific patterns of capital accumulation to forms of social organization, the precise definition of the problem has been far from unanimous and has subtly shifted according to disciplinary perspective. A number of related concepts have appeared as objects of analysis and the reification of these as empirical categories has made it difficult to unravel the areas of overlap between them or to develop a coherent theoretical framework. The continual imprecision of the terms 'informal', 'domestic', 'subsistence', 'black' or 'underground', etc., in the discussion of economic processes, focuses attention on categorical or definitional issues, at the expense of understanding the total process in which they are inscribed. They can all too easily be isolated as self-contained compartments making it more difficult to capture the important inter-relationships between them.

A particular confusion is that these terms are frequently used as if they refer to sets of activities. The analytic problems this raises in the context of the debate on the informal economy in the Third World have already been discussed (Moser 1978). A more fruitful approach is to see them as defined by different types of relationship. Thus, black work describes a relation with the State, 'secondary' work describes the relationship of activities *within* a domestic group. The 'second economy' on the other hand describes relationships within the economic system as does the term informal economy, while the domestic economy describes the relationships which organize the reproduction of subsistence, particularly the provision and consumption of food, daily maintenance activities and child-bearing and rearing, sometimes but not necessarily based on ties of kinship. Though these significant differences can be identified, however, there are also points of congruence. The domestic economy, for example, is subsumed by the concept of informality though the reverse is not the case. The production of use values and the reproduction of labour are central to most conceptions of the domestic domain, yet are an example of the tautology to which the inquiry is prone: are the processes to be defined by the fact that they occur in a particular place, 'the home', or is our idea of what constitutes the domestic defined as the site of certain specific processes?

A further problem is that these concepts are often treated as self-contained and mutually exclusive, or are misleadingly correlated with spatial, residential or marital criteria. They have a complex relationship with the dichotomies established between 'inside' and 'outside', 'private' and 'public', 'natural' and 'social', 'productive' and 'reproductive'. Some of these categories, or the relationships between them, are culturally specific, and such dualistic aproaches can be very misleading if they are applied uncritically from one context to another. The correlation between the production of use values and the activities which go on inside the home is not necessarily applicable to the work of many women in developing countries who are not merely producing use values in the household (as opposed to male producton of exchange values outside), but are producing exchange values domestically (ILO 1980). In developing economies use values are frequently transformed into exchange values at times of crisis, or women may secretly sell tiny surpluses saved from their stores, process a little extra food for cash or lend grain for interest or money (Abdulla & Zeidenstein 1981). What is important is not whether activities themselves are productive or unproductive and generative of use or exchange values, since the same tasks can be either or none of these at different times but, rather, the relationships through which the work is carried out are critical (see also Harris & Young 1981). Cooking might be seen as 'reproductive' when provided for family maintenance but enters into the sphere of exchange if prepared food is sold on the streets. As Moser (1981) points out, the tasks of preparation and production are sometimes done by the woman, in her capacity as unpaid family labourer, while the transaction is often controlled by the husband as the vendor. In other cases women both produce and trade. The distinction between them as categories is therefore far from clear-cut.

We need new ways of thinking about these patterns which transcend the static dichotomies that have already been the subject of lengthy reanalysis in the literature on developing economies (Bromley & Gerry 1979; Moser 1978; Tokman 1979). Moser herself suggests that we should replace sectoral dualism with the idea of a continuum of productive activities and argues convincingly that the concept of petty commodity production has more analytic weight than the amorphous descriptiveness of informality. Her revaluation has been important and influential. Nevertheless, the substitution of a continuum model may serve to neutralize and mask the relations of appropriation that her own ethnography successfully demonstrates. O'Laughlin's discussion of the Mbum Kpau is illustrative here. She argues that to see the sexual division of labour merely in terms of participation in particular activities conceals inequalities in access to means of production, control of labour and distribution of the product which are much more fundamental features of the mode of production (O'Laughlin 1974).

Clarifying these terminological problems, however, is only part of the problem. Greater precision in the use of concepts (e.g. specifying that the referent of the family is kinship while that of the household is propinquity), avoids inaccurate conflation of terms but still leaves us with the question of explaining diversity of form and historical change within these frames of reference (Yanagisako 1979). We cannot attach explanatory weight to concepts we cannot accurately define; we cannot describe historical change unless we can specify what it is that is being transformed. Yet relationships which appear genealogically or structurally similar do not necessarily have the same meaning across cultures, and the universalism implied in the notion of the domestic and the household has already been questioned (Coward 1983; Harris 1981; Yanagisako 1979).

Not only must these forms be seen as historically specific but it cannot be assumed that they are monolithic units confronting the formal economic system.[2] Several feminist commentators have pointed out that the terms of discussion themselves are frequently treated as 'unproblematic unities' and conceal unfounded assumptions about gender relations (Harris & Young 1980). The usage of domestic, household, family, informal and subsistence frequently ignores or naturalizes gender differentiation. Thus 'family labour' is often a synonym for the unpaid work of women and children and serves to mask rather than to illuminate crucial aspects of the relations of production. The domestic is not merely the location of alternative economic practices as some authors have implied (Lipton 1980; Szelenyi 1981). Men and women are incorporated into the labour process in different and unequal ways and although the sexual division of labour is not static the evidence for a widespread convergence of roles has still to be produced. The nature of market incorporation may be changing but it is not changing in the same way for both sexes. Szelenyi (1981) has noted the 'subcontracting of certain processes to smaller units which are often domestic in scale'. In reality these are often sweat-shops staffed by female labour working for low wages and lying outside the realm of employment protection and regulation (Phizaclea 1981). Utopian and alternative accounts of the domestic as an escape from alienation often ignore such invisible exploitation. In the analysis of the household it is therefore important to give adequate weight to differentiation by gender, both in market and non-market relations.

The attempt to provide an explanation for the sources of gender differentiation must therefore be essentially a comparative exercise. Many feminist anthropologists have been justly critical of the search for 'origins' in the sense of pin-pointing a moment in time or a set of ecological or technological determinants. Theoretical frameworks derived from the experience of white Western women are also prob-lematic. However, even if we reject simplistic monocausal accounts, identifying the preconditions for variation in sexual inequality remains central to the development of a theory of gender relations.

Yet is the logical outcome of the insistence on historical specificity and the identification of the culturally meaningful domains in each context the relegation of the concept to purely descriptive usage? Can we develop general explanations which have historical validity (Coward 1983)? In her review of anthropological studies of the family and households, Yanagisako suggests that the problems stem not so much from the lack of unambiguous and precise terminology, but from 'the conviction that we can construct a precise, reduced definition for . . . complex multifunctional institutions imbued with a diverse array of cultural principles and meanings'. If this is the case must we logically accept, as she does, that household, family, marriage, kinship, etc., are merely descrip-tive terms and useless as tools for analysis and comparison (Harris & Young 1981)? To give this question concrete form the next section considers the example of recent theoretical approaches to the sexual division of labour which have suggested a causal link between the nature of the family or household, the sexual segregation of the labour market and the development of capitalism. I then consider to what extent these models are applicable outside the frame of reference of the advanced industrial economies and ask to what extent their experience is being repeated under peripheral capitalist

development. Is the 'domestication' of women a common component of different paths of transition (Rogers 1980)?

Gender and Work: The Problem of Universals

Discussion of these issues has so far been pursued in three separate,
and to some extent, self-contained debates. First, there has been the
lengthy exploration of the significance of domestic labour as a
special form of work, in which the focus has been on the productive
or non-productive character of household work and the extent of its
autonomy from the capitalist mode of production (Delphy 1977;
Gardiner 1975; Harrison 1973; Himmelweit & Mohun 1977;
Molyneux 1979; Seccombe 1974).

A separate area of discussion has been the sexual segregation of
the labour market, the particular characteristics of women as wage
labourers and the role of a reserve army (Amsden 1980; Anthias
1980; Beechey 1977, 1978; Bruegel 1979; West 1982). Occupational stereotyping, low pay, dual labour markets and deskilling
have been central issues here, and there has been considerable
historical investigation of the role of gender in the development of
specific aspects of the labour process. Both these themes have been
examined in the context of advanced industrial societies.

Meanwhile, a third body of literature has considered the changing nature of the economic roles of the sexes in developing and
non-Western societies, the consequences of capital penetration for
the sexual division of labour and the survival or destruction of
subsistence economies. The so-called 'women in development'
literature has revealed a variety of forms of incorporation of the
household and the differential impact of economic change on the
work of women and men[3] (Ahmed 1980; Beneria 1978; Beneria &
Sen 1981; Benholdt-Thomsen 1981; Boserup 1970; Deere 1976;
Deere & Leon de Leal 1982; Harris & Young 1981; ILO 1980;
Loutfi 1980; Mies 1980; Nelson 1980; Pala 1977; Palmer 1977,
1979; Papanek 1977; Remy 1975; Tinker 1976; Young 1978).

As Molyneux has pointed out (1979), feminist analysis of
women's work under advanced capitalism has tended to treat
household and wage-work as separate topics for investigation, thus
precluding a discussion of the full-range and interrelationship of
women's economic and non-economic activities, and the development of a 'comprehensive theory of the political economy of
women'. A comprehensive theory may still elude us; it is neverthe-

less important to examine some of the contradictory hypotheses that have emerged from the discussion of womens' work. To do this not only housework and wage-work but also the diverse accounts generated in advanced industrial and in developing economies need to be brought to bear more closely on each other.[4]

The issue of value has been central in these debates, whether or not in explicitly Marxist form. As Bradby asks, 'How could one maintain a labour theory of value in face of the recognition that the labour of half the world did not take the form of value . . . the use value of labour power, the capacity to work is itself the appropriation of unpaid female labour' (Bradby 1982: 1–25). The undervalorization of women's work relative to men's is one feature to be identified with apparent consistency. They are paid less for comparable tasks or concentrated in low-pay activities, or hired on a different contractual basis, such as piecework, which works to depress the wage in relation to male earnings. More importantly, a large proportion of their daily activities are unpaid. This includes both work that is strictly for the maintenance and reproduction of the domestic unit and production that ultimately enters the market in which unpaid family labour makes a significant contribution, either as part of peasant production or as an element of a wage-labour relation in which it is the male who is formally contracted.

Notable among the attempts to provide a general explanation of this phenomenon is Beechey's explanation of the characteristics of women's employment, which argues that it is the relationship between the family and the productive system that accounts for the conditions of female participation (Beechey 1977). Her paper is part of the wider body of feminist literature which has sought an explanation for gender role ideology in terms of the historical changes in the economic function of the household within capitalist production. Beechey locates the explanation for women's low wages outside the labour process itself, within the economic exchanges of the household. Thus her basis for an analysis of the position of women under capitalism is the separation of the family from the means of production in the course of capitalist accumulation. She maintains, however, that this disjunction is largely illusory, in that the family appears separated but is 'actually only divorced from the labour process'. The central task, as she sees it, is therefore to analyse the relationship between the family and organization of production as capitalist accumulation develops.

This useful point is somewhat undermined by a rather mechanistic connection between the household and the productive process. Drawing a direct analogy between 'married women workers' and the semi-proletarianized migrant labourers on the periphery, she argues that both can be paid below the value of labour power because of the secondary nature of their wage and the availability of subsidies external to their own wage relationship.

Beechey thus bases her analysis on a specific form of the family, in which the household consists of a woman married to a man who is earning the primary wage. Men are bread-winners and women are dependents.[5] It is evident from her account that she sees this not merely as an ideal model of family roles but as a statement of fact. Only at one point does she use the words 'on the assumption that'; the precise form of words chosen in the rest of her paper suggest that she believes that it is because all women workers *are* members of households with male bread-winners that women can be paid below the value of labour power.[6] Her explanation therefore rests on empirical reality, not on the existence of ideological mystification.

At one point in her paper she counters the obvious criticism that her theory deals inadequately with single women. Here she argues that they are dependent in exactly the same way as married women on their families of origin. In other words, that daughters are dependent on fathers. Again this is presented as a statement of fact and exceptions (women without husbands or families of origin to subsidize their costs, living in households that are not formed around kinship or marriage) are seen only to prove the rule, in that they are unable to cover the costs of their own reproduction adequately and, as she puts it, 'are depressed into poverty'. A generalization that implies that poverty is somehow an aberration from the normal workings of the capitalist system.

There are thus several problems with this kind of approach. First, if the terms 'female labour' and 'married women's labour' are conflated and confused, it becomes difficult to apply the model to an analysis of specific categories of women. Beechey writes as if she assumes that female wage earners actually are married to male bread-winners. Those who are not are merely an exception to the underlying logic of her argument. The labour process is not only gender specific but is also often marital-status specific, a fact that Beechey's hypothesis cannot explain.

Second, whether married or single, the model assumes women's dependency on a male wage. Several recent articles have questioned the validity of this as a generalization based on statistical evidence of household income sources. While it appears that in terms of national averages, for example, women in the UK contribute a smaller proportion of total household income than men do,[7] one could equally well argue that this was the result rather than the cause of women's low pay. More significantly for Beechey's argument, however, is the fact that it is clear that even if women do not cover the entire costs of their reproduction nor do many low-income earning men. In the Third World, the wage has never been a 'family wage' and the abundant supply of labour has always undercut the value of labour power. What exactly does 'dependent' mean in terms of percentages? The man who is dependent on a wife to provide one-third of total household costs is rather less dependent than the wife who is dependent on the husband's contribution of two-thirds of those costs but her income may nonetheless be crucial. Quantitive measures are not at issue, however. The point is that it is tautological to argue that women are economically advantageous to capitalism because they are economically dependent, while at the same time they are economically dependent because they are low paid. Low pay for men has not been analysed in this way. The 'presumed' dependence of women and their ideological construction as 'housewives' (Mies 1980) may be extremely significant but this is a different issue.

Third, Beechey makes the important point that 'the existence of the family must be presupposed if Marx's implicit arguments about the advantages of female wage labour are to constitute a satisfactory explanation'. However, she then goes on to presuppose not only the *form* of the family, which she treats unproblematically as a constant, but also the nature of the distribution of income within it.[8] The end result of her own account is an analysis in which changing forms of the family, the experience of other ethnic groups, and the changing relationship between households and the productive process cannot be explained.

A somewhat different approach is offered in Barrett and McIntosh's discussion of the family wage (1981). They are concerned with 'a description of the means by which the reproduction of the working class has in fact been accomplished'. Unlike Beechey, they emphasize that the notion of the male chief bread-winner is ideological. It has been an expectation or a moral prescription emanating from the social construction of women's subordinate role and reproductive obligations rather than a reality, since many working-class households have always covered the costs of their reproduction from multiple sources. They see the *idea* of the family wage as the *outcome* of a historical process in which male predomi-

nance in the labour process is a distinctive feature of the development of British capitalism, and they link this with the need for
better conditions of reproduction for the working class. They stress
that this was both an aspect of working class struggle and congruent
with the needs of capitalism. On this point, their conclusions about
the *source* of the idea of the family wage are somewhat contradictory.
Was it the result of the logic of capitalist development or the
outcome of working class struggles? If both, what was the precise
relationship between them?[9] The strength of Barrett and McIntosh's
article is their discussion of the evolution of the notion of the male
bread-winner as an aspect of labour history, and their account of the
complex play of interests involved in the emergence of the family
wage as ideology. Ultimately, however, such explanations are
teleological, since the basic supposition is that 'Women's wage-
labour can be explained through its economic advantages (to
capitalism) and it is these economic advantages that structure the
forms of that labour.' (Anthias 1980: 51). By treating capital as an
homogeneous category, one must logically suppose that the costs of
the male wage are met within the same system; therefore no real
reduction of costs to collective capital can be made. Beechey's direct
analogy with migrant labour is not a valid one, since implicit in
that argument is the existence of a pre-capitalist or non-capitalist
mode of production. Since she had explicitly stated that the
separation of the family from the production process is more
apparent than real, she cannot argue for a domestic mode of
production that is analytically separable from the capitalist system.

    In summary, Beechey argues that women are paid low wages
because they are enmeshed in a family structure in which they are
dependents. Therefore, the value of their labour power actually *is*
less, because the costs of their reproduction *are* less, being partially
met through male wages. The wages of all women are assumed to be
covered by this general formulation, since all women are regarded as
economically dependent on a male, whether husband or father.
Barrett and McIntosh, however, emphasize that there may be no
necessary congruence between the 'expectation' of women's economic dependence as ideology and the reality of income distribution.
They nevertheless remain ambiguous as to the sources of this
ideology. Thus, a somewhat inconsistent account of women's waged
work emerges from these two papers. On the one hand, the 'needs'
of capitalism are served by cheap female labour, on the other they
are served by paying men enough to keep women at home. To say
that capitalism will attempt to pursue the most profitable labour

strategy is a *post hoc* argument that cannot explain why certain categories of worker should be more exploitable than others at particular times or why particular combinations of domestic and/or factory production should be optimal at any given moment. Ideological forces and the requirements of political control are also important in this contradictory process in which the family both shapes and is shaped by the process of accumulation (Stolcke 1981).

Forms of Incorporation and the Value of Labour Power

Capitalism is not only interested in labour power as an abstract commodity. It is interested in cheap labour. However, there are various ways in which production may be related to reproduction to obtain this. In some contexts, male migrant labour that retains a foothold in some rural area may be drawn on, in others, whole families labour under a male contract, in others, female, part-time or homeworking labour will be incorporated. As yet, we know little about the determinants of these patterns.

Thus, the concrete manifestations of capitalism and patriarchy give rise to diverse outcomes which are the results of a series of interactions between economic forms and between ideological representations and productive systems. While many of the characteristics of female labour, such as labour intensivity, low productivity, 'ghettoization' in specific sectors of production and differential wage rates, appear to be widespread, the explanations of these patterns developed in a European context do not necessarily hold good for peripheral capitalist economies where the capitalist transition and the nature of women's economic participation takes different forms.

As we have seen, functionalist explanations relating the nature of women's labour to the needs of capitalism have been prevalent in these debates. They provide conflicting accounts which are difficult to reconcile with cultural or historical variations in women's economic roles. There has been a tendency to draw generalizations about the relationship of gender to capitalism on the basis of an experience which should be seen as historically specific. The articulation of capitalism with the sexual division of labour cannot be assumed to be uniform, but is a matter for concrete investigation. As Deere has pointed out:

To the extent that capitalist expansion engenders a process of underdevelopment in the periphery, the economic participation of women in the Third World differs significantly from women's economic participation within the centre of the world capitalist system.

On the one hand, capitalist development in centre economies has required greater labour force participation, while, on the other, capitalist expansion in the periphery has often intensified women's economic participation in non-capitalist modes of production, particularly in rural areas where women's work is geared to subsistence agricultural production and petty commodity production and circulation (1976: 9).

It is precisely because the concepts of housework and waged-work have often been treated as universals and applied uncritically across time and space that the 'problem' for women in the non-Western world was initially defined as one of *lack* of integration in development. Because women commonly work as unpaid family labour, the economic significance of their role in food-crop production was often ignored, rendering women and their activities invisible (Boserup 1970).

Several writers have subsequently criticized the 'integrationist' position, documenting the wide range of economic activities, both remunerated and unremunerated performed by women, whether as unpaid family-subsistence producers, agricultural wage labourers, independent artisan producers, subcontracted homeworkers, petty-commodity producers, or small traders in the informal sector. They have noted the inadequacy of a simple dichotomy between wage-labourers and the self-employed in peripheral economies (MacEwan Scott 1979). These studies have made clear that women are already fully integrated into the economy, whether as domestic or extradomestic labour, and have emphasized that the problem lies rather in the exploitative nature of their integration (Roberts 1979).

Clearly, considerable variation exists in the forms of women's participation, even among countries at a similar level of economic development, and there are substantial differences in the response of the female labour force to this process (Youssef 1974). The class-based nature of this response has been noted in several ethnographies (Stoler 1977; Young 1978). Beneria and Sen (1981) have also drawn attention to the inaccuracy apparent in Boserup's original characterization of Africa and India as female and male farming systems respectively, pointing to the crucial significance of landless women wage labourers in Indian agriculture and stressing the relevance of major underlying differences between the two continents historically in terms of social stratification, access to land and relations of production.

While giving full recognition to this diversity, three points can nevertheless be stressed in the comparison between the Western European experience and that of currently developing countries.

First, the wage sector absorbs fewer people and pays them less for comparable tasks in peripheral as opposed to core economies. Thus, full employment and a family wage have never been options for more than a minority of the labour force and women's contribution, through both waged and unwaged work, has always been crucial for the reproduction of the family.

Second, because of the smaller proportion that formal wage employment represents in the overall economy, we cannot assume that the relationship of the family to the means of production is necessarily the same as that which obtained during the expansion of capitalism in Europe, since the continuance of subsistence production and the production of use values assumes greater importance. Countries like Bangladesh, for example, remain largely subsistence economies, in which 73 per cent of the consumption of rural people is made up of food and 14 per cent is taken up by housing (Abdullah & Zeidenstein 1981).[10] Post-harvest food processing, the boundary beyond which statistical measurement virtually ceases, is an area of crucial economic importance and a central aspect of women's activity. Merely to render some foodstuffs edible can take as much as four times as long as the time expended in their cultivation (Abdullah & Zeidenstein 1981). Given the division into male semi-proletarians and female subsistence producers that has been identified for some regions (Deere 1976), it may not be helpful to consider the family as a unit in its relationship to the means of production. Differentiation by gender within it may be of greater importance.

We must also consider family structure itself. Female-headed households are now estimated to represent between one-quarter and one-third of all households world-wide, and in Latin America and the Caribbean the trend is particularly marked. It is statistically very difficult to document the difference between 'stable' and 'unstable' consensual unions. What has emerged from recent microstudies, however, is the importance of the pattern in which the stable unit is the matrifocal household of women and children, in which male partners come and go (Phizaclea 1981). The explanation offered for this is precisely the reverse of that suggested by the British case, since it is argued that this is an economic strategy that is adaptive to highly unstable employment opportunities for men and women, when labour market conditions as a whole preclude the existence of male bread-winners. Under such circumstances, it has been argued that women can sometimes 'make out' better on scarce resources on their own (Stack 1974).

Third, within the overall population redistribution that is a crucial feature of many developing economies, sex-specific migration is of continuing importance. In some areas males are selected, leaving women responsible for the provision of daily subsistence, as they have always been in many parts of Africa for instance, but also leaving them with cash-crop responsibilities and the need to generate income for other necessities (Hanger & Moris 1973). In other areas, such as Latin America, female migration remains significant. Young (1978) documents this clearly for the Mexican state of Oaxaca, where migration was also highly age specific, and where sex and age specific outmigration had wide local ramifications in terms of the reduction of unpaid family and domestic labour.

> Girls were the principal victims of population redistribution: in the 1940's, 50's and 60's never less than 40% of female migrants between 10 and 29 were under 20 years of age, the majority were under 15 and had neither completed their schooling nor gained any specific skills . . . only 28% of male migrants between 10 and 29 were under 20 years of age. (142)

This pattern is reflected also in the age structure of the female work-force. In most Latin American countries, for example, peak activity in the non-agricultural labour force occurs between 20 and 25 years old, and as Youssef (1974) has pointed out: 'The propelling factor in the growth of the female labour force came in the form of an influx of single women into the labour market.'

We should note, too, that the limited development of the internal market in most developing economies and the corresponding lack of commoditization means that the woman's role as consumption agent is much less significant than in the central economies.[11] In rural areas of developing countries where there are fewer commodities to 'administer', the physical fabric of the dwelling, or the lack of it, allows for little fetishism. The domestication of women around commodity management is less pronounced, even though it may permeate as ideology or status marker. Housework in this sense of the term occupies less time;

however, the production and transformation of primary subsistence and the acquisition of basic resources (water, fuel, etc.) remains paramount and occupies considerable amounts of time (as much as 16 hours daily in some cases). The generation of additional cash to buy in food that is no longer produced locally is also increasingly important in many areas.

Lastly, the process of proletarianization takes different forms for men and for women, and one of the outcomes frequently commented on for women has been increasing conflict between their productive and reproductive roles. Young's account of the changing sexual division of labour in Oaxaca, for example, describes a process in which the introduction of coffee as a cash crop, a consequent narrowing of other economic opportunities and the resulting out-migration, lead to a decline in inter-family labour exchange and in increased emphasis on the fertility of the individual family, reflected in higher birth rates. Young stresses that women from each stratum of local society were differently circumscribed by the customary division of labour and that the impact of capitalism on them is cross-cut by their class position. However, she sees a basic contradiction between their insertion in the labour force and the cultural norms that constitute their subordination. Since each married couple is now more dependent on producing the labour it needs, women's reproductive role is reinforced, thus creating a basic contradiction between the women's need to produce labour and to sell labour. Poor households are dependent for their survival on women's labour, which means, she argues, that they are less dependent on their husbands economically. However, as she points out: 'the cultural prescription that a woman's place is in the home ensures that those who have to work outside it derive no social benefit from it.' (151) Thus, in this account, women's low pay derives not from economic dependence, since they are vital both to the reproduction and maintenance of labour, but from their 'specialization in reproduction' or the expectations surrounding it. She concludes: 'Their labour can thus be devalued both because of their 'real' role, and because this role itself places constraints on the type of work they can undertake.' (153)

It is interesting to compare this account with Stolcke's (1983) discussion of coffee cultivation in Brazil in which changing labour needs lead to an increasing emphasis on a matrifocal household unit. Although in some cases urban indistrialization may have tended to reinforce the nuclear-family pattern in others it has encouraged the proliferation of a wider range of kin ties. The spread of capitalism into the periphery has also led to the break-up of the traditional family as the location for reproduction. Mies (1981) states: 'Often the men find difficult to make enough money to send to their wives in the village. Therefore, the women, often without any means of production turn to begging, to prostitution, or to employment for less than the minimum wage. In any case, they become the main bread-winners of the broken family.' (10)

As Chen and Guznavi (1979) found in their account of 'Food for work' programmes in Bangladesh, rural, male unemployment, out-migration and increasing landlessness have reduced many female-headed households particularly those of widows, to destitution. Many women are forced by economic necessity to forgo social acceptability and contravene cultural norms of female seclusion entirely in order to survive.

Thus, class and sexual polarization intersect, and a contradictory pattern may emerge in which the upper strata of rural women may become domesticated and removed from agricultural production altogether. At the same time many small peasant households become increasingly indebted, lose their land and are forced to seek wage employment which may often take them out of the rural economy entirely. Women from the poorest strata may thus be forced to seek gang work on construction projects and public-works schemes, and far from becoming domesticated, become literally 'defeminized', in the sense that in order to exist they must often abandon the norms around which their sexuality was constructed. Whatever the nature of these norms may be, relinquishing them under circumstances in which they remain the dominant model merely reinforces their exclusion.

It is evident, then, that the differing paths of transition to capitalism give rise to varying forms of relationship between the family and the productive system, and that these themselves are influenced by the precise configuration of the local labour market and its insertion in the national and international economy. [12]

Patterns of Accumulation and the Sexual Division of Labour

The relationship between the international and sexual division of labour has so far been approached through the interesting but limited case of the so-called world market factories, the multinational assembly operations established within free trade zones in several newly industrializing countries, such as Mexico and Malaysia, which draw heavily on cheap female labour (Cardosa-Khoo & Khoo 1978; Fernandez-Kelly 1978; Heyzer 1981; Lim 1978; Pearson & Elson 1981). This case has attracted attention as a 'new' type of wage employment for women, in which the connections between the internationalization of capital and the employment of a gender-specific labour force are particularly clear. Pearson and Elson (1981) point out that although the capitalist labour process is not gender ascriptive, it is the bearer of gender, and women enter with a predefined status as inferior bearers of labour. Thus, while employment may offer them certain advantages, it does not necessarily provide a challenge to traditional patterns of authority and can 'intensify', 'decompose' and 'recompose' existing forms of subordination.

The focus of their valuable study is on the 'need to evaluate world market factories from the point of view of the new possibilities and new problems which they raise for the women who work in them'. In doing this they provide an important counterbalance to earlier accounts which had concentrated on the structural determinants of production (Fröbel et al. 1980). In emphasizing the experiential aspects, however, it is important not to lose sight of the fact that this new process is new chiefly for its visibility, for the fact that it is characterized by the mobility of capital rather than labour, and for the physical relocation of parts of the production process, made possible by the combined effects of communications technology, deskilling and fragmentation (Braverman 1974). However, the significance of cheap female labour for international patterns of accumulation is not new, as Safa (1981) has shown in her historical account of labour intensive industries in the USA. Nor is it confined to the wage-labour relationship alone. It is merely the latest stage in a constant search for cheap labour, each of which has drawn on a different type of female labour; in the case Safa describes this has been rural, migrant and non-Western in turn.

Bridging the conceptual gap between the international and the 'domestic' economy is a difficult task. However, some recent steps have been taken towards this (Deere & de Janvry 1978; Meillasoux 1981; Portes 1978). Portes, for instance, has argued in the context of the informal economy debate that the apparently micro-level relationships which characterize it are fundamental to the understanding of the operations of capitalism as a world system, and provide the 'missing element' in current models of the relationship between core and peripheral economies. He too suggests that the

informal economy is more than 'an exercise in self-preservation' but
is a basic element in maintaining the disparities between core and
peripheral wages, stemming the falling rate of profit and preventing
downturns in core economies, through its ability to provide cheap
goods to a low-paid work-force.

As we have seen, the informal economy is a gender-neutral term
which covers the work of both sexes but which conceals an internal
sexual division of labour (Moser 1980). Women's subsistence and
petty commodity production forms an important element of these
activities and, as Moser points out, men and women occupy
different economic 'spaces' in which their work is interdependent.
Similar arguments have been put forward about the continuing role
of 'subsistence agriculture', also used in a gender-neutral sense. It is
clear that fully proletarianized wage labour is not the only link that
can be established between women's work and the evolution of the
international economy; various aspects of self-provisioning and
domestic labour, i.e. subsistence reproduction, can also be seen in
this light.

There is now a large literature, both empirical and theoretical, on
the penetration of capital in developing economies. This has given
rise to two different accounts, which identify different roles and
outcomes for women. The first, which might be called the 'subsidy
thesis', stresses the role of subsistence reproduction in the general
process of accumulation. It argues the necessity for the continued
recreation of pre-capitalist modes of production, following
Rosa Luxembourg's interpretation of the need for ongoing primitive
accumulation for the extraction of surplus labour and surplus
product:

> In the central economy the freeing of labour serves a double
> purpose: it lowers the cost of labour by giving to the employer
> flexibility in hiring and firing, and simultaneously it increases
> the size of the market. It implies the destruction of the
> subsistence economies, and complete proletarianization of the
> workers. In the periphery the cost of labour is also reduced
> through its freeing, but there is no rationality of market
> expansion though proletarianization. Hence, wherever possi-
> ble, as in agriculture, the subsistence economies will be
> maintained. This will permit further lowering of labour costs
> since it allows for the indirect exploitation of family labour
> occupied in the production of use values and petty commod-

ities that cover part of the subsistence of the workers. (de Janvry & Garramon 1977: 210)

In many accounts family, household and domestic are synonyms for female and child labour. As de Janvry writes: 'Surplus value is increased . . . by collapsing the price of agricultural labour by an amount equal to the production of use values by the worker's family in the subsistence plot. In this way subsistence agriculture supplies cheap labour to commercial agriculture which in turn supplies cheap food to the urban sector where it sustains low wages.' The subsidy hypothesis has been influential both in the debate about the nature of capitalist transition itself and, as we have seen, in explanations of women's work in advanced and in peripheral capitalism. The concept of domestic economy has often been used as a generalizable category applicable to both. Yet the economic content of women's roles is very different, and the production of subsistence or the transformation of commodities implies a different relationship with the capitalist system.

The precise nature of the linkages that are thought to exist between households/domestic economies/pre-capitalist forms and capitalism proper is therefore far from clear. These forms pre-date capitalism, implying that they have a certain autonomy, yet they cannot be seen as entirely distinct modes of production. To the extent that capitalism penetrates a particular region, they become 'subsumed', yet they are not 'directly' integrated in that the relations that obtain within them are different from capitalist labour relations.

The terms of these relationships are themselves influenced by the coexistence of capitalist relations and the exchanges that are established between them. These exchanges are themselves seen as unequal, with capitalist relations comprising the 'structure in dominance' to which other relationships are subservient. However, the form of this articulation and the exchanges involved have recently been the subject of much debate (Banaji 1977; de Janvry 1977; Vergopoulos 1978). While it is argued that capitalist enterprises in the periphery shift replacement and welfare costs of their work-force onto the subsistence sector, it has also been suggested that remittances from migrant workers are crucial in the continuance of some subsistence economies (Arizpe 1982; Busta-mante 1979). To take the case of Mexico, for example, migrants to the US are said to provide remittances of between three and four billion dollars annually, and it has been estimated that as many as

21 per cent of Mexican households, particularly in rural areas, may be partially supported by migrant incomes. A simple one-way model of subsidies from one to the other thus seems hardly adequate to describe the complexities of the transfers that occur.

While proponents of the subsidy thesis have provided a theoretical model to explain the persistence of subsistence production and the role of the domestic economy, other writers have provided empirical accounts of local conditions of change which stress the *decline* in women's economic roles, their loss of control of productive activities and/or the decline in the economic importance of those activities (Boserup 1970). Several studies have documented the way in which the development of export-oriented crops undermines domestic production, stimulates the cultivation of a limited product mix dominated by male labour and restructures local economies, creating increased differentiation along both class and sex lines (Beneria 1979; Chambers & Moris 1973; Loutfi 1980; Mies 1980; Palmer 1977; Rogers 1980). The principal outcome of this process is seen as the decline in overall importance of women's handicraft and subsistence production, and increasing reliance on income from wage labour. The precise mechanics of this 'simple reproduction squeeze', as Bernstein (1979) has called it are complex, but common elements reported for a number of cases can be identified. These include:

increasing commitment of labour *time* to cash crops, especially in traditionally female work such as weeding. (This is particularly acute in the case of high yielding 'green revolution' varieties which allow multiple cropping and thus greatly increase women's already heavy work burden, allowing less time for subsistence production.)

expansion of cash crops into land formerly used for food crops

relegation of food crop land to less fertile areas

increasing distance of food crop land from dwelling

absolute loss of household plot due to indebtedness, expropriation or resettlement

control by men of new technologies and agricultural inputs (through their greater access to credit and information, and the assumption by extension agencies that household heads are males, and that males are the principal cultivators)

control by men of new sources of income

alienation of women from their customary land rights, through land registration or land reform policies which recognize males only as family heads

increasing need for cash to buy food no longer produced domestically, competing needs for available income and possible decline in family nutritional standards and women's control over resources.

In this model the squeeze occurs both in women's available labour time and in their resource base, and it is argued that cash incomes remain inadequate to counterbalance this tendency. Moreover, not only do women lose food-production capacity but they often lose previous income sources of their own. Examples of this have been noted in the technological impact on women's food processing. Case studies have shown that rice huskers, tortilla machines, mechanized looms, sago processors and grinding mills of various kinds have often been introduced and taken over by men to the detriment of women. Women's loss of control over distributional systems has also been documented, e.g. where increased scale ousts the smaller traders (Dixon 1978; Mies 1980), where capitalist marketing penetrates indigenous market systems (Mies 1980; Young 1978) or where new organizational forms, such as co-operatives, are introduced as intermediaries.

It is important to stress that though many writers have talked about the increasing limitations on economic access for women, in the sense that the subsistence economy becomes increasingly marginalized or even disintegrates, it does not follow that women then become economically inactive, as is sometimes implied. As we have seen, a sharp distinction between the subsistence and wage-earning sectors is largely inaccurate and women may be pushed into an intermediate position in which their subsistence base is reduced but their ability to earn income is fragmentary and intermittent. Often they are seasonal and part-time workers, sometimes contracted through male household members as auxiliaries, and they frequently build up meagre incomes from multiple sources that remain unrecorded.

Can we reconcile the contradictions of these two positions, both of which have been put forward as generalizable processes or universal theoretical models of the relationship between capitalist development and the sexual division of labour? The available empirical evidence suggests that both patterns occur under different circumstances. If this is the case, however, the theoretical logic of necessity in the subsidy model is severely weakened.

Proponents of the 'necessity' view in discussions of the family wage similarly argued that the 'requirement of reproduction of the working class' made a family wage essential. It has not proved essential in the Third World, and the continuing 'super-exploitation' of women and children has been central to the development process (Leacock 1981). As we have seen, supporters of the exclusion thesis would argue that the ability to produce subsistence is under threat in many areas. As Sen (1981) has shown in his study of the Bangladesh, Sahel and Ethiopian famines, natural resource crises played a much smaller part in mass starvation than failures of purchasing power to buy in high-priced foodstuffs that could not be produced by landless labourers. Sometimes this is a problem of landlessness *per se* but frequently it is gender related, in that men become semi-proletarianized while women's subsistence base is eroded.

Clearly, these variations reflect specific regional patterns. Deere (1976), for example, drawing on Columbian material, argues that male semi-proletarianization at low wages is facilitated by the *continuance of* the female subsistence base. Hanger and Moris (1973), however, in their account of the Mwea rice scheme in Kenya have argued that the introduction of rice as a cash crop, coupled with the resettlement of a peasant population, *decreased* the land available for subsistence and introduced time constraints that made it impossible for women to produce enough food for family consumption. Males were increasingly pulled into wage labour elsewhere but cash incomes were too low to buy in enough staple foodstuffs or fuel. Nutritional levels reportedly declined dramatically and family poverty increased. Thus the conditions which in nineteenth century England gave rise to a family wage ideology and the domestication of women are being repeated in the periphery, but given the different nature of the capitalist transition, a frequent outome is inequality of distribution between classes and genders and increasing pauperization. It is clear that contradictory patterns are found between regions, suggesting once again the dangers of regarding 'the penetration of capitalism' as a homogeneous process or assuming that the response to it will be everywhere the same.

Reproduction and Domestic Practices

The concept of the costs of reproduction has been central to the attempt to explain sexual inequality in the economy. Many Marxists and Marxist feminists have used the concept in its broadest sense in order to develop a theoretical account of the relationship between the family/household and the wider society, which does not necessarily prejudice the notion of the family as a locus of contradiction and which is based on process rather than on bounded units of analysis. Yet reproduction has also proved to be an elusive and confusing notion.

Harris and Young (1981) suggest that reproduction is a concept which allows for the discussion of the complex variety of relationships between the genders. They go on to indicate three separate levels of analysis at which the concept operates, usefully breaking down its unitary nature and showing that it encompasses several processes, which may even be in conflict. As in their previous articles, they are justly critical of the use of the term 'women' as a universal category. They reject a simplistic association of reproduction with women, and emphasise the significance of their productive roles. Nonetheless, at each level of their analysis they see reproduction 'as the field within which women's positioning is defined', suggesting that they should, in fact, be equated. They are also concerned throughout to specify the relationship between women and various aspects of reproduction in which they 'occupy clearly defined and significant positions'. For social reproduction, for example, they ask how crucial certain forms of control over women's reproductive powers are for the creation of the conditions of existence for production and the reproduction of the system. For the reproduction of labour, they are concerned to demonstrate the connections between women and various aspects of the process, such as allocation to specific class positions, ideology, early socialization and material reproduction (daily care and maintenance). For human, or biological, reproduction they are interested in how different patterns of fertility give males greater or lesser power over women. Thus, on the one hand, they oppose unitary notions of reproduction and support substantivist positions, arguing throughout for the specificity of pre-capitalist modes of production. On the other, despite initial disavowal, their paper is devoted to showing aspects of the connection between women and reproduction. They conclude by suggesting that the need to control women's generative powers is a universal feature that overrides differences, not because the needs of reproduction are unchanging but 'precisely because of differences over time in the requirements of human groups *vis-à-vis* biological reproduction'.

The link between the control of women's reproductive capacities, including their capacity to reproduce labour (which is sociologically rather than biologically given) and their subordination, by means of marriage exchange, regulation of sexuality, limitation of access to resources, etc., has been debated in a variety of forms. However, of itself 'control' tells us very little about the gender relations that result. Harris and Young, in contrast to Engels for example, phrase the problem in terms of the 'requirements of human groups' rather than the requirements of individual property-owning males. The difference is surely important, for the perennial question is, of course, why women are not controlling their own reproductive powers, exchanging men in marriage, regulating male sexuality, etc. As some anthropological accounts of women's alternative power have suggested, in some contexts perhaps they are. As far as the eventual outcomes for women are concerned it is the *forms* of control which are crucial. In a society such as the Trobriands, so compellingly described by Annette Weiner, where women's reproductive powers are fundamental to positive evaluations of their self-hood and to the regeneration of society as a whole, we get a very different reading of the consequences of group requirements, one which is far removed from suggestions of passivity and oppression (Weiner 1979). On this point, Deere and Leon de Leal (1982) are surely correct to argue that women's role in reproduction cannot fully explain the sexual division of labour since the former is relatively constant, while the latter is very varied.

Harris and Young leave till last the question of the relationship between production and reproduction and the degree of autonomy of the latter. They note that various feminists have posited a separate set of structures for the social relations of human reproduction and they find this separation of production and reproduction appealing. They regard as too simplistic the orthodox Marxist approach that sees them as a single system with the mode of production determinate in the last instance (Gimenez 1977). Certainly it is possible to find similar modes of production in which gender relations are significantly different. Though how we assess 'difference' and 'similarity' is not always very clear, and there are obvious difficulties in establishing criteria by which the gender relations of societies could be ranked on some sort of a sliding scale. Young's own work, cited earlier, does however suggest that even if there is no absolute functional fit or strong line of determinancy, the sexual division of labour, domestic practices and reproductive strategies do indeed vary significantly with changing relations of production.

A final problem lies in the conceptualization of change and the definition of what is necessary for a system to continue to exist in a defined form. Various authors have criticized the concept of reproduction for implying that a given mode of production exists to reproduce itself and can, of itself, assure the conditions of its own existence. They have argued that the conditions of existence for social formations, such as that described by Meillasoux for instance, lie beyond their own boundaries, a fact that must be central to any theory of imperialism. Reproduction is commonly held to entail the 'adequate' provision of the material means of survival, but how is adequacy to be defined? It is not only a question of culturally specific requirements, as defined by Marx. Inequalities in adequacy are fundamental to stratified societies, and any model of reproduction must be able to capture the dynamics of unequal entitlements in which some groups are perpetually reproduced less adequately than others. The central issue in the analysis of the penetration of capitalism and its effects on social groups must be the differential levels of reproduction that are created in the process. Levels and styles of reproduction are the markers of class and to blanket them all by the assumption of some absolute standard of need is to confuse the issue.

In general, then, it seems hard to escape a return to dualism in these models. The difficulties of empirically separating production from reproduction are evident; they must be rooted in their material base, yet to see either one as determinate seems problematic. Rather they form a unity in which the possibilities for contradiction and some degree of autonomy for the relations of reproduction must be included. Nor can we automatically correlate them with gender differences, although the reproduction of labour on a daily basis and overtime is characteristically women's work in a wide variety of contexts. We have widespread evidence of the descriptive fact that women are particularly associated with a set of processes that we label 'reproductive', over-represented in the informal sector, yet not exclusive to it, and exhibit certain characteristics in relation to the valorization of their labour. However, regularities are not the same as explanations and it can be argued that the difficulties outlined above suggest that we are posing the question in the wrong way. It may be more fruitful to see a totality in which each is enmeshed in the other, to see determination as lying in the process of interaction itself and to examine the relationship between the way systems are reproduced and the gender relations which constitute them.

Production and reproduction are a unity, but of an often contradictory rather than a functional kind. They are neither independent, determined nor determinate in any simple mechanical way. Nor is an explanation of one necessarily to be found in the other; rather their intersection shapes the form of the whole at any given time. Dualism and the concept of 'articulation' serves to reinforce the notion of separate spheres. The conditions for the reproduction of the household lie partly outside itself, and the reproduction of capitalism is premised upon unpaid domestic labour. Each is embedded in the other. Just as the reproduction of labour has seldom been guaranteed by the wage alone, so capitalist relations are 'engendered' (Harris & Young 1981) in that they are based on covert but crucial assumptions about gender and reproduction. Relations of appropriation are concealed by ideas about what is natural, biological or institutional, concealed behind the idea of a timeless domestic relationship. However, as Weiner (1979) points out: 'The system of reproduction is never in equilibrium, it is always in flux, in movement, containing points of limitation and points of possible expansion which demand continual attention.'

Conclusion

Several strands of argument have been considered in this chapter. One has to do with structural changes in advanced industrial capitalism which lead to the reduction of employment and the increasing importance of forms of work based on other activities, usually considered 'non-economic'. The problems in defining these 'other' activities as 'non-capitalist' have been mentioned, but some way of handling their distinctiveness must still be preserved, while emphasizing their interdependence with capitalist relations proper. The terms household, domestic and informal present problems both because they tend to bound units too firmly, which are themselves changing in response to the process of restructuring, and because they conceal internal sexual divisions and gender inequalities. As in wage relations, women tend to be clustered in the activities of lowest returns to labour and to predominate in labour-intensive areas of work. At a very general level, women's greater responsibility for the reproduction of basic subsistence can be identified as a common element. However, what it means to subsist in different socio-economic environments produces very different outcomes for women. Thinking about these economic processes in terms of types of activity is also misleading since the same task can have very different meanings when done by different sexes, and whether it is valorized or non-valorized, visible or invisible, esteemed or not esteemed, will depend as much on the sex of the performer as on the job itself and the relationship within which it is done. Thus the sexual and domestic divisions of labour do show an element of cross-cultural consistency but they also show important historical and cultural variations which need to be taken into account in the development of general theoretical explanations.

It proved difficult to apply explanations of these characteristics based on women's actual economic dependency to many non-Western settings, though the *ideology* of dependency and the secondary nature of women's 'non-reproductive' work remain a powerful influence. Functionalist accounts based on the needs of capitalism also left many things unexplained. Why should it be in the interests of capital to domesticate some women at some times or to proletarianize them at others, to pay some groups of workers a family wage or to rely at other times on the self-provisioning of women and children to make up deficiencies? The political power of groups of workers, the size of the relative surplus population, the nature of the subsistence base in terms of products and landholding, the type and extent of capitalist and/or multinational penetration, all have an important bearing on the patterns of reproductive and productive relations that develop.

At an international level the search for profitability can also have diverse outcomes. As Aranda and Arizpe (1981) put it, the 'comparative advantage' of women's 'disadvantage' is a powerful incentive: in many areas of developing countries, a deteriorating rural economic situation, increasing needs for income and high rates of male unemployment make available a young, cheap, female pool of labour which may be incorporated in various ways; or it may be excluded; or, yet again, included in invisible ways as when women are compelled to invest more time in specific tasks in cash-crop production, such as weeding, yet remain categorized as unpaid family labour.

The variety of these patterns make it hard to see the subsidy function as an adequate general explanation of the persistence or expansion of subsistence production. It cannot capture the complexities of the transfers taking place at different levels of the system, nor can it encompass the chronic erosion of the subsistence base that is occurring in many regions. As Mies argues, the process of accumulation appears to create an expanding mass of relative surplus population, which will never be absorbed into the formal wage-labour pool, who will remain structurally non-wage labourers and who are forced to produce their own survival in various forms.

This chapter began by re-examining the categories which pervade the debate about production, reproduction and gender roles. It argued that a number of separate debates, on urban informal economies, on the importance of agrarian subsistence production and on the contribution of domestic labour to capitalism, could be seen as different facets of the same problematic. Their underlying concern is with the connections between seemingly separate spheres of social and economic life and with a renewal of interest in the production of the 'means of existence'. Often these processes have, as in classical Marxism, been regarded as natural, physiological or instinctual, masking internal contradictions. Informality, use-value production, reproduction, kinship arrangements, etc., have been seen either as 'given' or 'determined' by capitalism. The revival of interest in them has sometimes been couched in individualistic and voluntaristic terms, as in much of the literature on household strategies. My argument has been that the identification of common patterns does not necessarily justify universalistic, ethnocentric or monocausal explanations. The subsidy thesis, a common thread uniting these debates, provides a partial account but not a total explanation for the persistence of forms or relationships outside capitalism. Such dualistic separation reflects pervasive Western ideology and masks a continuing tension between the process of accumulation and the reproduction of individual and household subsistence. This could not be adequately represented either as merely subordinate to capitalist accumulation or functional to it, as recent historical and cross-cultural analysis has shown. The contest for the domestic domain is played out in a variety of different ways as part of the expansion and contraction of capitalism.

Notes

This chapter was presented at the World Congress of Sociology, Mexico City 1982. I would like to thank members of the Women's Studies M.A. at the University of Kent for their stimulation and encouragement. I am also grateful to Peter Fitzpatrick, to Brian Roberts for excellent editorial advice and to Michael Redclift for helpful comments on the final draft.

1   For a concise account of this literature see Moser (1978).
2   Whitehead (1981) defines the domestic domain as 'a producing and

consuming collectivity bound by ideologies of sharing'. These ideologies are not necessarily unitary and may operate on a number of different levels, or even be contested internally. Who shares what, with whom, creating what lines of cleavage and dependency, under what changing circumstances, is, as Roldán points out in this volume, precisely the point at issue.

3   The term 'development' is sometimes misleadingly used as if it referred to 'development projects' (i.e. the impact of planned change, which has often been directed at men to the detriment of women), rather than the wider processes of economic change.

4   As Norma Chinchilla noted in her study of Guatemalan industrialization:

> it gives an incomplete understanding to study occupational structures or industrial growth independently of an international context of investment, production and control . . . The fate of women, the way they carry out their daily tasks and the view of the world they derive from these experiences depends . . . not so much on the policies of their governments, or the enlightenment of the men around them as on the function that the economy of which they are a part serves in the world system. (1977: 39)

The implication here is that the experience of women is merely a dependent variable, derivative of the macro-economic system, and the writer gives greater priority to the impact of monopoly capitalism than to the interaction between capitalism and forms of patriarchy. Despite the functionalism of this approach it nevertheless underlines the necessity of developing a conceptual framework which encompasses the national and international economic context within which women's productive activities are located (Ifeka-Moller 1975; Pala 1977; Remy 1975) and it is this issue which will be taken up here. The question of the autonomy of patriarchy versus the historical and cultural specificity of gender subordination remains a central theme for feminists (Beechey 1979). Less attention has, however, been given to the North–South dimension of forms of capitalist oppression, the problem which has polarized the international feminist movement.

5   For example, Beechey writes of women workers:

> It is their dependence on male wages within the family for part of the cost of the production and reproduction of labour power which accounts for the possibility of individual capitals paying wages which are below the value of labour power. The married woman does not therefore have to pay for the entire cost of reproducing her labour power nor for that of her children who will become the next generation of wage labourers and domestic labourers.

6   In a later article (1983) Beechey substantially modifies her argument, emphasizing the importance of the construction of gender divisions within the production process itself. Unfortunately this was not available at the time of writing this chapter.

7   In 1980 this was at least 25 per cent or, for the USA a decade earlier, 36.8 per cent, if a woman worked full time all year, according to Rowntree and Rowntree 1970.

8   This is somewhat surprising, since Beechey explicitly states that it is important to transcend an approach such as that offered by Engels, in which the family form is presumed to change as a mechanical result of changes in the organization of production.

9   Certainly it was a demand that found support mainly among bourgeois reformers and the upper strata of male workers. On the other hand, the bitter opposition of many employers to the factory legislation and even more to its implementation suggests that individual capitalists did not favour the exclusion of women from the factories. Yet it seems clear that the collective interests of capital as a whole, as eventually articulated in State Policy, lay in establishing the principle if not the practice of the male bread-winner. (Barrett and McIntosh 1981: 56)

10 The sharp rise in landless labourers has nevertheless meant that increasing numbers of rural peasants cannot produce their own subsistence and are forced to buy in food.

11 This role has been described thus by Galbraith:

Without women to administer it, the possibility of increasing consumption would be sharply circumscribed. With women assuming the tasks of administration, consumption can be more or less indefinitely increased. In very high income households, this administration becomes an onerous task. But even here expansion is still possible: at those income levels women tend to be better educated and better administrators. And the greater availability of divorce allows a measure of trial and error to obtain the best (*sic*). Thus it is women in their crypto-servant role of administrators who make an indefinitely increasing consumption possible. As matters now stand . . . it is their supreme contribution to the modern economy.(1974: 34)

12 This micro-level data can be statistically supported, for some areas. In India, for instance, a drop has been noted in the female participation rate in all categories of employment except transport (Mitra 1977). Between 1911 and 1971 the ratio of women to men in the work force declined from 525 per 1,000 males to 210 per 1,000 males. Between 1951 and 1971 the number of women workers in agriculture declined from 31 to 25 million. The total number of female workers suffered a decline of 12 per cent, while male workers

increased by 27 per cent (Indian Council of Social Science Research).

> Whereas, the number of female cultivators dropped by 52%, the number of male cultivators increased by 6%. This is a clear indication of the fact that women are losing control over land as a means of production, i.e. they are gradually becoming pauperized. Similarly, the female agricultural workers increased by 43%, whereas the male agricultural workers increased by more than double that rate to 88%, women are also not becoming proletarianized at the same rate as men. (Mies 1980: 4)

In Latin America, on the other hand, the trend is different, and rates of labour-force participation are increasing more rapidly for women than for men. Although statistical measures of women's work are among the most unreliable data yet collected (Beneria 1979), they do indicate broad regional differences in the incorporation of the female labour force, and in the balance between unpaid, unenumerated family labour and some form of wage-labour.

Part II

The Reproduction of the Household:
Strategies and Contradictions

4

Economic Development and Change in the Mode of Provision of Services
J.I. Gershuny

Socio-technical Change and Extra-economic Production

Economic development involves two different sorts of changes in household behaviour. The first of these is widely recognized: the tendency for households, as they become richer, to change their pattern of expenditure proportionately away from basic necessities and towards luxuries. Initially applied to the transfer of expenditure from food to manufactured goods, Engel's Law (named after the nineteenth-century German statistician who pioneered the empirical analysis of household budgets) has in later useage been extended to include the similar proportionate transfer of expenditure from manufactures to services. Underneath this empirical observation of economic behaviour lies a psychological hypothesis, that of the 'hierarchy of needs', according to which individuals strive first to achieve the fundamentals of physical security and nutrition, and only subsequently to achieve the less fundamental requirements for comfort, association and amusement. As societies become richer, they can satisfy a wider range of needs for a larger proportion of their populations, and this is reflected in the change in the sorts of commodities demanded by households: from basic commodities, such as food and fuel, to manufactured goods, and from manufactures to 'luxury' services.

The second sort of change, which has been much less widely recognized, qualifies the first. The connection between psychological needs and economic demands is not in fact a direct one; it is mediated by technology (the term is used here in its broadest sense to include both physical techniques and the social organization which surrounds them). As time passes, the means by which particular needs are satisfied may change and hence alter the correspondence between a household's needs and its demands for commodities. The same, or at least closely analogous, needs that are satisfied by domestic servants, train tickets and theatre seats are met later by domestic machinery, motor cars and video recorders. This category of change in the provision of services will be denoted in the following paragraphs by the term 'socio-technical innovation' (though only one particular sort of socio-technical innovation, involving the diffusion of changes in the modes of provision for household needs, will be discussed). It is a major influence in the process of economic development and an important explanatory variable for the pattern of development of both economic and social structure. On one hand, new modes of provision for particular needs require new sorts of inputs from the money economy, so it has a determining effect on economic structure through *final demand*. On the other hand, new modes of provision involve change in the organization of time use (with respect to paid and unpaid work, and to non-work time) and so it affects social structure through its consequences for individual and household *activity patterns*.

This second category of change has substantial implications for sociology as an academic discipline. It suggests that to understand the nature and processes of development of industrial societies we must look outside 'the economy'. We must look at the 'informal economy', which is of course not a separate economy at all, but an integral part of the system by which work, paid and unpaid, satisfies human needs.

We must look at the development of household work strategies – the processes of inheritance of values, adaptation to changed circumstances, and decision making, which determine both how households get the things they need and how work responsibilities are allocated among household members. These fields of enquiry have been traditionally occupied by sociologists concerned with the *consequences* of economic development; they have traditionally been ignored by economists. The arguments that follow suggest that the phenomena studied in these apparently 'extra-economic' areas may be, if not unique determinants, at least contributory *causal* factors for economic structure. These sorts of sociological analysis may in the future become more central to the study of the nature of developed economies.

This chapter will attempt to make some empirical sense of these propositions. It will show how, starting from statistics on final expenditure, which are themselves in part derived from household (money) budgetary studies, we can use the concept of innovation in the mode of service provision to explain change in patterns of paid employment. It will also show how this concept may be used to explain patterns of change displayed by time-budget data. A general model of innovation in the provision of final service functions is outlined here. The process involves elements of subdivision of tasks, capital itensification and pursuit of economies of scale, which are characteristic of the conventional view of the nineteenth-century innovations in manufacturing production. We can view the process as the industrialization of service production, with an important part of the final production displaced outside the formal economy.

The innovative process has four crucial elements:

1 investment in equipment (and purchase of necessary materials), typically by the individual or household seeking the service (e.g. motor cars, television, petrol);
2 collective investment in material ('hardware') infrastructure (e.g. roads, broadcasting networks);
3 collective investment in non-material ('software') activities and infrastructure (e.g. television programme); and
4 unpaid 'informal' labour, using the first three elements to produce the final service functions (e.g. driving a private motor car).

These four elements may be viewed as factors of production, which in varying proportions are combined to produce the final service functions. In this process of innovation, the outputs of manufacturing, construction, utilities and tertiary industries are used in a further production process, outside the money economy, whose output supplements or replaces the outputs of final service industries. What follows is not intended as an exhaustive treatment of an empirical argument (much more lengthy and careful discussions of this evidence will be found elsewhere [Gershuny 1983; Gershuny & Thomas 1984; Gershuny & Miles 1983]) but as a demonstration of the significance of changes in household service provision, both for explaining the past and for exploring the future of developed economies.

The Mode of Service Provision and Engel's Law

The two different sorts of change in household budgetary behaviour interact over time; during a given historical period there may be *both* a change in the proportion of household expenditure devoted to each particular need *and* a change in the distribution of expenditure on commodities to satisfy each category of need. If, therefore, we wish to track the dual effects of Engel's Law and socio-technical innovation, we will need to adopt a new procedure for the analysis of final expenditure. Instead of considering final expenditure as a single vector, an ordered list of commodities, we will have to think of it as being classified along two different dimensions. Each item of final expenditure will have to be classified by the *sort* of need it satisfies. It must also be classified according to the *manner* in which it satisfies that need – in the very crudest possible version, classified as either a final service which is produced by the 'formal', money economy and directly consumed by the purchaser, or as a good or material which is not consumed directly by the purchaser but used in a further informal production process within the household in order to provide the ultimate 'service function' which is actually consumed.

To illustrate, a particular set of expenditures may be classified as satisfying 'transport' needs: of these, some (e.g. payments for bus or taxi trips) are obviously payments for commodities which are final services in themselves, while others (e.g. payments for petrol, motor cars or garage services) are payments for intermediate commodities which are subsequently combined (with informal labour in the form of driving) to produce an approximately equivalent, transport final service function. Once our expenditure data is appropriately classified, over a period such as the 1950s and 1960s we would expect to see two distinct sorts of change. Societies were becoming richer over this period. In this historical context transport might be considered to be a luxury need, so we would expect that the proportion of all household expenditure devoted to transport to rise, as a result of Engel's Law effect. We also know that over this period the mode of provision of transport services (or more precisely, the 'modal split', the distribution of provision between alternative modes) was changing, so we would expect the proportion of expenditure on the transport function devoted to purchasing final transport services to decline and that devoted to transport-related goods, materials and intermediate services to rise.

Table 4.1 Distribution of household and government final expenditure, classified by function and type of commodity

Function classification	Commodity classification		
	Primary and manufactured goods	Marketed services	Non-marketed services
Food, drink, tobacco	Food, drink, tobacco (D1)	–	–
Shelter, clothing	Rent, fuel and power, clothing and footwear (D2, D3)	Personal care and effects (D81)	Housing and community amenities (sewers, etc.) (G6)
Domestic functions	Furniture, furnishings, appliances, utensils and repairs to these (D41 to D44)	Household operation and domestic services (D45, D46)	Social security and welfare services (G5)
Entertainment	Equipment, accessories, and repairs to these, books, etc. (D71, D73)	Entertainment, recreation, cultural, hotels, cafes, etc. package tours (D72, D83, D84)	Recreational, cultural and religious services (G7)
Transport, communications	Personal transport equipment and operation (D61, D62)	Purchased transport and communications services (D63, D64)	Roads, waterways, communications, and their administration subsidies (G8.5, G8.6, G8.7)

Function classification	Commodity classification		
	Primary and manufactured goods	Marketed services	Non-marketed services
Education	–	Purchased education (D74)	Public education (G3)
Medical functions	Medical and pharmaceutical products and appliances (D51, D52)	Purchased medical services, medical insurance service charges (D53, D54, D55)	Public health services (G4)
Other government functions	–	–	General public services, and economic services excluding transport and communications (G1, G8.1 to G8.4, G8.8)
Defence		–	Defence (G2)
Functions NES	Goods NES (D82)	Services NES (D85, D86)	Other public services NES (G9)

References in parentheses to classifications of the European Systems of Integrated Economic Accounts (ESA).

Sources: ESA classifications and coding of the purposes of final consumption of households (ESA 1979, tables 7 and 8; the same as SNA, UN, New York 1968, tables 6.1 and 5.3 respectively).

J. I. Gershuny

Table 4.2   Distribution of all final consumption by
function of households and governments in five European countries
in the early and late 1970s

(a)   Proportions

| | West Germany | | | | | |
| | Early 1970s | | | Late 1970s | | |
Function	Household	Government	Total	Household	Government	Total
Food	21.4	–	21.4	19.7	–	19.7
Shelter	13.4	0.6	14.0	12.5	0.5	13.0
Domestic	9.7	1.1	10.8	9.6	1.0	10.6
Entertainment	11.2	0.5	11.7	11.5	0.6	11.9
Transport	11.4		11.4	12.1	1.1	13.2
Education	–	5.2	5.2	–	5.8	5.8
Medicine	8.6	1.2	9.8	11.0	1.1	12.1
Other governmental	–	7.6	7.6	–	6.0	6.0
Defence	–	5.2	5.2	–	4.5	4.5
Other	2.9	0.0	2.9	3.2	0.0	3.2
Total	78.6	21.4	100.0	79.4	20.6	100.0

| | The Netherlands | | | | | |
| | Early 1970s | | | Late 1970s | | |
Function	Household	Government	Total	Household	Government	Total
Food	20.0	–	20.0	19.2	–	19.2
Shelter	13.6	–	13.6	11.6	–	11.6
Domestic	9.7	0.9	10.6	8.1	0.9	9.0
Entertainment	8.2	–	8.2	10.0	–	10.0
Transport	7.5	–	7.5	10.2	–	10.2
Education	0.0	9.6	9.6	0.1	9.8	9.9
Medicine	8.8	–	8.8	8.9	–	8.9
Other governmental	–	–	–	–	–	–
Defence	–	5.6	5.6	–	4.2	4.2
Other	5.0	11.1	16.1	6.1	10.9	17.0
Total	72.8	27.2	100.0	74.2	25.8	100.0

UK

Function	Early 1970s			Late 1970s		
	Household	Government	Total	Household	Government	Total
Food	21.8	–	21.8	19.4	–	19.4
Shelter	12.2	0.3	13.0	12.3	0.8	13.1
Domestic	6.2	1.4	7.6	6.3	1.9	8.2
Entertainment	15.6	0.5	16.1	16.3	0.6	16.9
Transport	11.1	1.0	12.1	11.8	0.9	12.7
Education	2.1	5.7	7.8	1.8	6.1	7.9
Medicine	0.7	5.7	6.4	0.6	6.2	6.8
Other governmental	–	4.6	4.6	–	4.7	4.7
Defence	–	7.5	7.5	–	6.7	6.7
Other	2.3	0.8	3.1	2.8	0.9	3.7
Total	72.0	28.0	100.0	71.3	28.7	100.0

Belgium

Function	Early 1970s			Late 1970s		
	Household	Government	Total	Household	Government	Total
Food	23.7	–	23.7	19.8	–	19.8
Shelter	13.7	0.0	13.7	13.9	–	13.9
Domestic	10.2	1.7	11.9	10.4	2.0	12.4
Entertainment	11.3	0.4	11.7	11.1	0.3	11.4
Transport	9.5	1.3	10.8	10.1	1.2	11.3
Education	–	8.6	8.6	–	9.8	9.8
Medicine	6.1	0.3	6.4	8.0	0.2	8.2
Other governmental	–	4.3	4.3	–	4.1	4.1
Defence	–	5.6	5.6	–	5.1	5.1
Other	2.8	0.5	3.3	3.4	0.6	4.0
Total	77.3	22.7	100.0	76.7	23.3	100.0

Italy

Function	Early 1970s			Late 1970s		
	Household	Government	Total	Household	Government	Total
Food	33.4	–	33.4	30.5	–	30.5
Shelter	13.6	0.6	14.2	13.4	0.7	14.1
Domestic	5.8	1.4	7.2	6.0	1.4	7.4
Entertainment	12.2	0.1	12.3	13.3	0.2	13.5
Transport	9.0	0.8	9.8	9.5	0.7	10.2
Education	0.4	6.2	6.6	0.4	7.0	7.4
Medicine	3.3	1.3	4.6	4.5	1.1	5.6
Other governmental	–	6.7	6.7	–	6.4	6.4
Defence	–	3.2	3.2	–	2.9	2.9
Other	1.9	0.1	2.0	1.9	0.1	2.0
Total	79.6	20.4	100.0	79.5	20.5	100.0

Table 4.2(b)   Changes in total consumption

Function	West Germany	The Netherlands	Italy	UK	Belgium	Row counts −	0	+
Food	−1.7	−0.8	−2.9	−2.4	−3.9	5	0	0
Shelter	−1.0	−2.0	−0.1	−0.1	+0.2	4	0	1
Domestic	−0.2	−1.6	+0.2	+0.6	+0.5	2	0	3
Entertainment	+0.2	+1.8	+1.2	+0.8	−0.3	1	0	4
Transport	+1.8	+2.7	+0.4	+0.6	+0.5	0	0	5
Education	+0.6	+0.3	+0.8	+0.1	+1.2	0	0	5
Medicine	+2.3	+0.1	+1.0	+0.4	+1.8	0	0	5
Other governmental	−1.5	(−)	−0.3	+0.1	−0.2	3	1	1
Defence	−0.2	−1.4	−0.3	−0.8	−0.5	5	0	0
Other	+0.3	+0.9	0	+0.6	+0.7	0	1	4

Sources: EEC (1981) *National Accounts, ESA: Detailed Tables by Branch 1970–1979*. EEC, Brussels, Tables 5; EEC (1981) *General Government Accounts and Statistics 1971–1978*, EEC, Brussels.

This sort of final expenditure accountancy can actually be implemented within some national accounting systems (the UK system is not particularly suitable, but the UN and EEC systems, which embody the sort of functional classification suggested here, are appropriate for this purpose). Table 4.1 gives an example of such a system of accounting definitions, developed from the European System of National Accounts. It identifies ten separate categories of need or final service function. The list is of course arbitrary; the classification might be made either more or less aggregated according to the particular purpose it is to be put to. It identifies three different sorts of commodity: primary and manufactured (in which are included intermediate services purchased by households), marketed services (final services directly purchased by households) and non-marketed services (those final services provided to households, in the main part without any direct payment, by government or charitable agencies). Once again, this categorization, though appropriate for the present purposes, might be very considerably disaggregated. To continue with our example, those expenditures classified by the European System of Accounts as 'personal transport equipment' and 'operation' fall into the transport/primary and manufactured goods category, purchased transport services into the transport/marketed Services category and public expenditure on roads, etc., into transport/non-marketed Services. Unfortunately, the European System of Accounts has only published statistics for the 1970s but this data is sufficient to allow us to demonstrate our two effects.

Let us consider first the more conventional Engel's Law effect, by summing the categories in each row of table 4.1, to give us the total expenditure on each function. Table 4.2 shows the change in the distributions of all final expenditure for five European countries during the 1970s.[1] A quite clear pattern of change emerges. In spite of the relatively slow economic growth of the 1970s, expenditure in all of the five countries for which data are available show a decline in proportional expenditure on shelter; by contrast, four out of five show an increase in proportional expenditure on entertainment, and all increase their expenditure on transport. The more 'basic' categories are substituted for by the more 'luxury'. Similarly, the traditional 'basic' public services of defence and public administration proportionately decline, while the new luxuries of education and medicine grow. This is exactly the pattern of development we would expect from Engel's Law.

However, this does not tell us the whole story; we must also look at changes in patterns of expenditure within each final service function. Table 4.3 shows the change in the split between household expenditure on goods and on services during the 1970s. No very clear pattern of change emerges for the more basic food and shelter categories (largely as a matter of definition, the very great majority of all expenditure on these categories is necessarily on goods and materials) but in the next three categories, domestic, entertainment and transport functions, the split preponderantly shifts away from the purchase of final services and towards the purchase of goods. This shift is an indicator of the change in household provision; it involves people buying less finished services from the formal economy and instead buying goods as inputs to the informal provision of services. We might note that this data covers the 1970s, by which time markets for most of the basic goods meeting these three functions (e.g. cars, washing machines, televisions) were approaching saturation in Europe. It seems reasonable to presume that data for the 1950s and 1960s would show much larger changes in the same direction. The remaining functional categories show no regular patterns. We shall return, in a later section, to suggest why innovation may be concentrated in particular functions over particular historical periods; for the present, it will suffice to say that the available technologies and social and material infrastructure have been, until this decade, inappropriate for socio-technical change outside these areas.

Table 4.3(a) Modal split in household provisions of service functions (percentages) in eight European countries, 1970 and 1979

		Belgium		Denmark		France		West Germany		The Netherlands		Ireland		Italy		UK	
		Goods	Services	Goods	Services	Goods	Services	Goods	Services	Goods	Services	Goods	Services	Goods	Services	Goods	Services
Basic needs																	
Food	1970	100	0	100	0	100	0	–	–	100	0	100	0	100	0	100	0
	1979	100	0	100	0	100	0	–	–	100	0	100	0	100	0	100	0
Shelter	1970	92	8	94	6	95	5	–	–	95	8	97	3	89	11	95	5
	1979	93	7	96	4	94	6	–	–	95	5	94	6	89	11	95	5
Focus of European social innovations 1950–1980																	
Domestic	1970	67	33	67	33	68	32	–	–	82	18	70	30	61	39	74	26
	1979	74	26	75	25	75	25	–	–	82	18	74	26	62	38	74	26
Entertainment	1970	27	73	45	55	33	77	–	–	58	42	49	51	29	71	24	76
	1979	37	63	54	46	39	61	–	–	66	34	52	48	35	65	28	72
Non-catering	1970	74	26	74	26	75	25	–	–	83	17	63	37	58	42	63	37
	1979	76	24	79	21	75	25	–	–	84	18	63	37	67	33	63	37
Catering	1970	0	100	0	100	0	100	–	–	0	100	0	100	0	100	0	100
	1979	0	100	0	100	0	100	–	–	0	100	0	100	0	100	0	100
Transport	1970	77	23	75	25	81	19	73	27	74	26	74	26	73	27	66	34
	1979	83	17	71	29	78	22	74	26	76	24	82	18	73	27	66	34
Predominantly public provision																	
Education	1970	–	–	0	100	0	100	–	–	0	100	0	100	0	100	0	100
	1979	–	–	0	100	0	100	–	–	0	100	0	100	0	100	0	100
Medicine	1970	27	73	35	65	22	78	–	–	8	92	62	38	50	50	63	37
	1979	27	73	36	64	21	79	–	–	13	87	62	38	41	59	57	43

Table 4.3(b)   Change in modal split 1970–1979

Shift to goods	Belgium	Denmark	France	West Germany	The Netherlands	Ireland	Italy	UK	Row counts −	0	+
Food	0	0	0	−	0	0	0	0	0	7	0
Shelter	+11	+2	−1	−	0	−3	0	0	2	3	2
Domestic	+ 7	+8	+7	−	0	+4	+1	0	0	1	5
Entertainment	+10	+9	+6	−	+8	+3	+6	+4	0	0	7
Non-catering	+ 2	+5	0	−	+1	0	+9	0	0	3	4
Catering	0	0	0	−	0	0	0	0	0	7	0
Transport	+ 6	−4	−3	+1	+2	+8	0	0	2	2	4
Education	−	−	0	−	0	0	0	0	0	5	0
Medicine	0	+1	−1	−	+5	0	−9	−5	3	2	2

Sources: As for table 4.2, excluding government expenditure.

Even in a period of relatively low economic growth, therefore, we can find evidence of both sorts of effect on patterns of final expenditure. What is the aggregate consequence of Engel's Law and socio-technical innovation on the distribution of final expenditure? Table 4.4, which is constructed by summing the categories in the columns of table 4.1 (and also separating primary from manufactured products) shows a rather unexpected pattern of change over the 1970s. In four of the seven countries for which the data is available, final expenditure on marketed services *fell* as a proportion of all final expenditure, while the proportion devoted to manufactured products rose in six countries and fell in none; it is almost the reverse of the pattern of development that would be expected from the Engel's Law relationship.

Mode of Service Provision and Employment

This decline in final expenditure on marketed services leaves us with something of a problem. We know that employment in the service industries has been growing; table 4.5 shows a regular pattern of growth of employment both in marketed and in non-marketed service industries in Europe during the 1970s; similar patterns are to be found throughout the developed world from the early 1960s. How can we reconcile the discrepancies between the patterns of change in final expenditure and the industrial distribution of employment?

There are two different sorts of possible explanation. The first rests on the observation that there is no one-to-one correspondence

Table 4.4 Distribution of all final consumption by commodity for eight European countries, 1970 and 1979

Commodity	Belgium 1970	1979	Change	Denmark 1970	1979	Change	France 1970	1979	Change	West Germany 1970	1979	Change
Primary	35.6	32.7	−2.9	23.0	29.3	−3.7	34.2	29.8	−4.4			
Manufactures	30.1	23.0	+2.9	20.6	20.6	0.0	22.2	25.0	−2.8		(Insufficient data)	
Marketed services	21.6	20.9	−0.7	15.1	13.5	−1.6	21.8	24.5	+3.7			
Non-marketed services	22.7	23.4	+0.7	31.3	36.6	+5.3	21.8	20.7	−1.1			

Commodity	The Netherlands 1970	1979	Change	Ireland 1970	1979	Change	Italy 1970	1979	Change	UK 1970	1979	Change
Primary	32.5	29.7	−2.8	50.8	45.5	−5.3	44.4	41.6	−2.8	32.7	30.5	−2.2
Manufactures	20.4	23.2	+2.8	16.1	19.0	+2.9	15.9	18.3	+2.4	17.1	18.6	+1.5
Marketed services	20.1	21.3	+1.2	13.6	12.4	−1.2	19.6	19.5	−0.1	22.1	22.2	+0.1
Non-marketed services	27.0	25.8	−1.2	19.5	23.1	+3.6	20.1	20.5	+0.4	28.1	28.8	+0.7

Row counts

	−	0	+
Primary	7	0	0
Manufactures	0	1	6
Marketed services	4	0	3
Non-marketed services	2	0	5

Table 4.5   Changing distribution (%) of employment by sector in six European
countries, 1970–1979

Sector	Belgium			The Netherlands			France			West Germany		
	1970	1979	Change	1970	1979	Change	1970	1979	Change	1970	1979	Change
Agriculture	4.9	3.3	−1.6	7.0	5.9	−1.6	13.2	9.0	−4.2	8.5	6.0	−2.5
Fuel and power	2.1	1.6	−0.5	1.5	1.3	−0.2	1.6	1.4	−0.2	2.0	1.8	−0.2
Manufacturing	30.4	24.1	−6.3	25.5	20.4	−5.1	26.4	25.3	−1.1	36.8	33.6	−3.2
Construction	8.5	8.2	−0.3	10.8	9.7	−1.1	9.6	8.5	−1.1	8.1	7.5	−0.6
Market services	36.8	42.4	+5.8	41.2	46.2	+5.0	32.8	37.9	+5.1	31.0	33.4	+2.4
Non-market services	17.3	20.4	+3.1	14.1	16.5	+2.4	16.5	18.0	+1.5	13.6	17.7	+4.1

Sector	Italy			UK			Row counts		
	1970	1979	Change	1970	1979	Change	−	0	+
Agriculture	18.3	13.8	−4.5	2.8	2.6	−0.2	6	0	0
Fuel and power	0.9	0.9	0.0	2.6	2.4	−0.2	5	1	0
Manufacturing	27.8	27.3	−0.5	30.3	27.6	−2.7	6	0	0
Construction	10.3	8.3	−2.0	7.3	6.9	−0.4	6	0	0
Market services	28.6	32.2	+3.6	37.2	39.1	+1.9	0	0	6
Non-market services	14.2	17.5	+3.5	19.7	21.4	+1.7	0	0	6

Source: EEC (1981) *National Accounts, ESA: Detailed Tables by Branch 1970–1979.* EEC, Brussels, Table 4.

between the output of a particular industry and the final consumption of a particular sort of commodity. Simply, the commodities produced by some industries never reach final consumers directly but are used as intermediate inputs to further production processes. Households seldom buy industrial lathes or semi-finished car bodies, even though these are the outputs of particular industries; rather, households buy the final commodities that they have been used to produce. Just as some manufacturing industries produce commodities which are not directly sold to final consumers, so some marketed service industries produce 'intermediate' outputs. Engineering consultancies and contract cleaning companies, for example, produce services and are counted within the marketed services sector, yet sell their output predominantly to firms in the manufacturing sector rather than to households. We actually consume their products indirectly, as embodied in manufactured goods. Less obviously, we very seldom pay directly for the services produced by the retail distribution industry; the cost of sales services are bundled

Table 4.6   Simple input/output matrix for a closed economy

		Commodities		
	Primary, Manufactures	*Marketed services*	*Non-marketed services*	*Total value added*[a]
INDUSTRIES				
Primary, manufacturing	27[c]	5	5	37
Marketed services	23	17	8	48
Non-marketed services	0	0	15	15
Total household consumption[a,b]	50	22	28	100

[a] Total value added and total household consumption are distributed in proportions as in the UK in 1979.
[b] Total household consumption includes governmental direct (i.e. non-transfer payment) expenditure in the 'non-marketed services' category.
[c] Co-efficients within the I/O matrix are hypothetical.

up in the price paid by the consumer for the manufactured good; again, though in a slightly different way, these are intermediate services embodied in manufactures.

We can put this more concretely in terms of the simple input/output matrix in table 4.6. In the UK in 1979, primary and manufacturing industries accounted for about 37 per cent of all value added (i.e. net output), marketed services accounted for about 48 per cent and non-marketed service industries about 15 per cent. By contrast, about 50 per cent of all expenditure by households was on manufactures and 22 per cent went to purchase marketed services. We can only account for the differences between the proportions by assuming the pattern of intermediate inputs from industries to final commodities is something like that suggested in table 4.6. (The coefficients inside the matrix in table 4.6 are only estimates; since the published UK I/O matrices treat investment goods conventionally as final output, the inter-industry flow of investment products is obscured.) While perhaps three-quarters of the net output of manufacturing and primary industry is consumed as final manufactured commodities, with the remaining quarter going as intermediate inputs to service production, perhaps only one-third of the total output of marketed service industries is finally embodied in marketed services directly purchased by households, and half of this total output may be embodied in goods.

Hence, we have a category of marketed service industries (we shall refer to them collectively as 'producer services', a term originated by Greenfield [1966]) which do not provide services for final consumption. These, clearly, provide one possible explanation for the discrepancy between the growth of marketed service consumption and employment; the growth in employment *could* be accounted for by a growth in the producer service industries. Table 4.7 shows that for those European countries for which statistics are available, value added by market service industries is about twice as large as final expenditure on final marketed services; the implication is that about half of the output of the marketed services sector consists of producer services. It is also clear from table 4.7 that the producer service proportion of output from marketed services has, in most cases, been growing faster than the final service proportion: a small part of the discrepancy between final demand for services and employment in services is certainly explained in this way. Nevertheless this is by no means the whole story.

The second sort of explanation that is available to us relates to the labour productivity levels of the individual industries. Obviously, if

Table 4.7   Distributions of value added compared
with distributions of final consumption by sector
for five European countries

Sector	Belgium				France			
	Consumption		Value added		Consumption		Value added	
	1970	1979	1970	1979	1970	1979	1970	1979
Primary, manufacturing and construction	55.7	55.7	46.7	47.0	56.4	54.8	49.5	44.9
Marketed services	21.6	20.9	41.5	40.7	21.8	24.5	39.9	44.9
Non-marketed services	22.7	23.4	11.8	12.3	21.8	20.7	11.6	10.2

Sector	The Netherlands				Italy			
	Consumption		Value added		Consumption		Value added	
	1970	1979	1970	1979	1970	1979	1970	1979
Primary, manufacturing and construction	52.9	52.9	47.3	45.7	60.3	58.9	50.7	49.0
Market services	20.1	21.3	39.2	41.7	19.6	19.5	38.2	40.2
Non-marketed services	27.0	25.8	13.5	12.6	20.1	20.5	11.1	10.8

Sector	UK			
	Consumption		Value added	
	1970	1979	1970	1979
Primary, manufacturing and construction	49.8	49.1	39.8	37.4
Marketed services	22.1	22.2	46.8	47.7
Non-marketed services	28.1	28.8	13.4	14.9

Source: EEC (1981) *National Accounts, ESA: Detailed Tables by Branch 1970–1979*
EEC, Brussels, Table 2; constant prices expressed as percentage of total
value added.

productivity in manufacturing industry is growing faster than
productivity in service industry, then a rising proportional expenditure on goods relative to service is perfectly consistent with a rising
proportion of employment in services relative to employment in
manufacturing industry. Table 4.8 demonstrates that labour
productivity growth in the services is indeed substantially lower
than that in other sectors. The contrast between the evolution of

Table 4.8 Labour productivity growth by sector as proportion of national average of six European countries

Sector	Belgium	The Netherlands	France	West Germany	Italy	UK	Below average	Average	Above average
Agriculture	1.18	1.28	1.12	1.24	1.14	1.13	0	0	0
Fuel and power	1.59	1.79	1.15	1.09	0.94	1.06	1	0	5
Manufacturing	1.30	1.18	1.03	1.04	1.09	1.04	0	0	6
Construction	0.93	0.78	0.88	1.02	0.92	0.94	5	0	1
Market services	0.86	0.95	0.97	1.00	0.93	0.97	5	1	0
Non-market services	0.88	0.81	0.80	0.79	0.80	1.04	5	0	1
National average for 1970s	1.32	–	1.36	1.35	1.25	1.02			

final demand for marketed services and the evolution of employment in marketed service industries is explained in part by the development of the producer services and in part by the relatively low labour productivity growth rate in the service sector.

This 'productivity gap' between the services and manufacturing industry is quite crucial to our argument. One of the main reasons that over this period we tended increasingly to drive private cars rather than paying for 'finished' transport services is simply that private motoring, on the whole, became cheaper relative to travelling on public transport. One reason for this is precisely the productivity gap: motor manufacturers tend to become more efficient in their use of labour, whereas public transport systems have in the past shown a tendency not to do so. In general, final service prices tend to rise relative to others because of service industries' historically low potential for innovation (Skolka 1976). In other words, the effect of the productivity gap on employment works in two ways: it increases the employment generated by a given proportion of final expenditure on marketed services; but it decreases that expenditure insofar as it encourages change in the mode of household service provision.

We might speculate that a rather similar process applies to non-marketed services. These also show relatively low labour productivity growth; though we do not pay directly for each item, we do pay indirectly for the whole basket of public services through our taxes. Low productivity growth in non-marketed services mean that extra taxes go disproportionately to pay for higher real wages for unchanged jobs (i.e. maintaining wages relative to similar occupations in industries with higher productivity growth). So given levels of non-marketed service provision become increasingly expensive as time passes. It could be that these continuously rising effective prices of public services are part of the explanation for the increasing apparent unpopularity of welfare spending. Social innovations that enable alternative modes of provision for the sorts of services produced on a collective basis may have been, in the past, difficult to find (though, as we shall see, this situation may change in the future). Nevertheless, the fact that increments of expenditure on non-marketed services are as likely to go to increase service workers' real wages without increasing service output as they are to raise the level of service provision, must act as something of a disincentive to the growth of the non-market service sector. (We should, however, bear in mind that whatever the real facts about the evolution of output and productivity in the public service sector, the 'tax revolts' that have, in one form or another, been an ubiquitous phenomenon throughout the developed world, are orchestrated in the main by politicians ill-disposed towards the welfare state. So it would perhaps be appropriately cautious to give this particular part of the argument the status of an unproven hypothesis.)

In general, however, the arguments in this section do seem an adequate basis for a plausible general description of the linkages

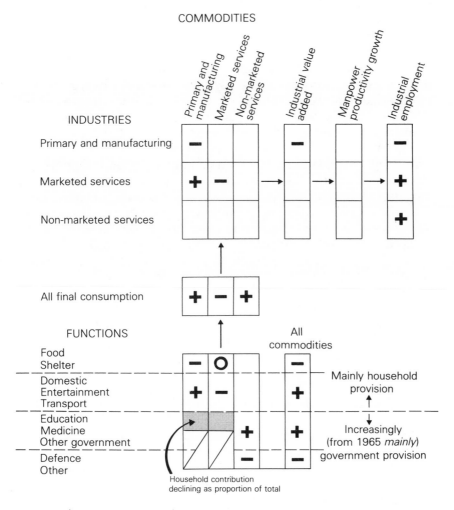

Figure 4.1 Summary of the major economic changes in Europe, 1950–1980

between Engel's Law, socio-technical innovation and the structure of employment. Though our data covers only the 1970s, figure 4.1 provides a summary of the sorts of changes experienced by developed economies over the past three decades. In accordance with Engel's Law, the proportion of total expenditure devoted to non-basic functions – domestic, entertainment, transport, public welfare services – has increased. Within those functions that are predominantly provided by households there has been a shift away from purchase of finished services towards the purchase of manufactured goods and materials. This has meant that the final expenditure on marketed services has declined as a proportion of the total, while proportional expenditure on manufactures and non-marketed services has grown. The proportional decline in expenditure on final marketed services has been partially compensated for by a growth in intermediate marketed 'producer' services, so that the marketed service industries may overall have maintained their proportion of total industrial value added. By contrast, in the latter part of the period at least, a large part of the growth in the value of final demand for manufactures has been accounted for by the growth in value added contributed by producer services, so the growth in manufacturing output has been slower than might have been expected. Finally, the low productivity growth in the services, which fuels the social innovation, also has the effect of increasing the proportion of employment in both service sectors.

We should note, at this point, the importance of the 'self-service' changes described here for generating economic growth. They do more than just displace paid service labour, they also enable the development of new markets for manufactured goods. The vast new European markets for consumer durables and motor cars in the 1950s and 1960s were, in effect, *generated,* or, perhaps more properly, *facilitated* by such changes. Arguably, these new markets were the economic foundation of the growth and prosperity of the post-war period. Thus, changing household behaviour may have very significant consequences for the process of economic development.

As it stands, this argument leaves us with a perhaps rather pessimistic view of our future prospects. The growth of employment in marketed services is threatened by its relatively low productivity growth, and the demand for manufactures induced by the innovations we have discussed generates a decreasing demand for labour, precisely because of manufacturing industry's relatively high productivity growth (and for countries like the UK because of its poor performance relative to foreign competition). An increase in public expenditure on services seems in general to be ruled out because of political opposition. So where are new jobs to come from? There may in fact be a more optimistic view of the future emerging from the arguments so far discussed but before we consider this, let us turn for a moment from the effects of socio-technical change on economic structure, to its effects on household and individual behaviour.

The Use of Time

We started our discussion by considering the error in our understanding of the consequences of economic growth for economic structure that arises when we make inferences from cross-sectional data to longitudinal. Engel's Law gives us a misleading view of the evolution of economic structure because it fails to take account of technological change, more specifically, because it ignores the particular sort of technological change that we have identified in household service provision. This section will consider some rather similar errors that would result from generalizations from cross-sectional studies of time use to historical change. We shall consider two examples concerning respectively housework and leisure patterns.

The housewives' day

Robinson et al. (1972), in their analysis of the 1960s multinational time-budget survey, consider that 'there might well be a fully counter-intuitive relationship between the efficiency of household technology and amounts of time given over to household obligations' (p. 125), i.e. the more domestic gadgets, the more domestic work time. If we convert this cross-sectional observation to a longitudinal prediction, we would expect that, as societies become richer and households acquire more domestic technology, hours of housework would increase. Indeed, such a pattern of changes has been suggested for the USA. Robinson and Converse (1972) report (on a longitudinal comparison which they stress is somewhat unreliable): 'The time spent on chores associated with the upkeep and management of a home and family including care of children and shopping for food . . . is remarkably higher in our 1965/66 data than in the studies from the 1930s' (p. 48). They do, however, suggest that part of the explanation may be the preponderance of 'affluent' households in their 1930s samples, which might be expected to overestimate the effect of domestic servants on the average American household of the period. The results of another US study (Vanek 1974), which probably does not suffer from an overestimation of paid domestic services, are summarized as follows: 'In 1924 (non-employed women) spent about 52 hours per week in housework. The figure differs little (and in an unexpected direction) from the 55 hours per week for non-employed women in the 1970s (p. 116).

Is a positive relationship between ownership of 'domestic capital goods' and time spent in housework necessarily counter-intuitive? Even if we were to find a society in which households with a scarcity of gadgets did less housework than otherwise equivalent households with a plenitude of gadgets, we could still argue as follows: gadgets make housework more productive, therefore it is rational to transfer labour time to capital-intensive domestic activities, i.e. households with washing machines wash more shirts, with good kitchen equipment spend more time cooking, and so on. As long as the increase in the output of household services is larger than the increase in the efficiency in the use of time arising from the presence of the gadget, the total amount of time devoted to the activity will increase. The USA data we have cited *could* be consistent with such a process of 'rational choice' of time use. As we shall see, however, when we look more closely at the data, this sort of explanation is insufficient and we have to introduce the notion of change in service provision.

Let us start by considering the longitudinal data. Vanek (1974) shows an increase from 52 to 55 weekly hours of work for the average American housewife between the 1920s and 1960s. Data for a similar group in the UK shows what is, all things considered, a remarkably similar pattern of change, from 47.5 hours to 52 hours between 1937 and 1961. Do we conclude that domestic technology has increased housework time? The original manuscript diaries from 1937 (collected by Mass Observation) still exist,[3] which means that we can look at the data in some detail. When we consider it broken down by social class (and also weighting the 1937 sample to give the same proportions in each social class and with children as in 1961) an alternative explanation emerges with some clarity. Figure 4.2 summarizes these results; there are clearly two quite separate processes in train. In the first place, household work for working-class housewives shows a pretty continuous decline, from 66 hours per week in 1937, to 52 hours per week in 1961, to 40.5 hours per week in 1974–5. In part, this may reflect declining family size and,

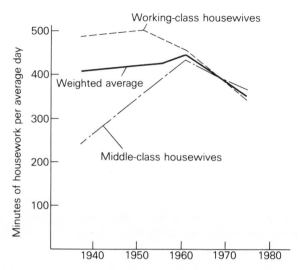

Figure 4.2   Housewives' domestic work (non-employed or part-time-employed women)

Sources: 1937, Mass Observation manuscript diaries (Gershuny & Thomas 1983); 1951, Mass Observation Limited, *The Housewives' Day* (working class only); 1956, Mass Observation Limited, *The Housewives' Day* (middle and working class averaged); 1961 and 1974/5, BBC Audience Research Department data (Gershuny & Thomas 1983).

in part, the increasing participation of housewives in part-time employment (though the data for wholly non-employed women show identical trends), but in general, it would seem perverse to refuse to ascribe a substantial part of the reduction to the diffusion of domestic technology. Second, middle-class housewives *increased* their housework between 1937 and 1961, from which point their housework time allocation remains pretty similar to working-class housewives.

The reason for the middle-class rise in housework between 1937 and 1961 is quite clear. The few middle-class housewives without servants in our 1937 sample do, if anything, rather more housework than their working-class equivalents (the result of keeping up appearances?). Servants were almost universal in middle-class households in 1937 but very rare in 1961. It is therefore very likely that the increase in domestic work is the result of the loss of servants. It seems quite possible that the rise in average domestic work time between the 1920s and the 1960s in the USA stems from the same source.

We can extend our previous economic arguments to take account of these more sociological issues. During the 1950s and 1960s particularly, we had a growing proportion of total final expenditure being devoted to the 'domestic service function' – an Engel's Law effect. To a considerable extent, the extra resources were devoted to buying consumer durables which increased the ease and efficiency of domestic work; in particular they were 'labour-saving' in the sense that they increased service outputs per unit of time input. The increase in domestic productivity in effect makes particular domestic services cheaper, with the result that we wish to consume more of them. If the size of the resulting increase in output is greater than the increase in domestic productivity, then by definition, domestic work time must increase; if however the increase in productivity is greater than the increase in output, then domestic work time will decline. Hence, we have no general ahistorical prediction of the trends of domestic work.

We do however have some empirical evidence. Working-class housewives' domestic work time has declined dramatically. We would certainly not wish to argue that the material circumstances of working-class households have declined since the 1930s; assuming for a moment that they have remained unchanged, that in the terms of our argument output is constant, the time-budget evidence of falling domestic work time therefore implies a very substantial increase in domestic productivity. If, as seems very probable, the material circumstances of working-class households has improved over the last 40 years, then we would infer that this particular period falls into the category in which domestic output grows, but at a slower rate than the growth of domestic productivity.

Middle-class households during the first part of this period underwent a change in the mode of provision of domestic services. The proportion of middle-class households' domestic services derived from paid servants decreased and the proportion provided on a self-service basis increased. As the general level of incomes rose, so did the cost of employing servants and middle-class housewives switched to an alternative mode of production of services, one much more demanding of their own time for housework.

It should be stressed that this argument is only partly dependent on the time-budget data. We are required, in addition, to make wholly unsupported assumptions about the material output of domestic services within households and empirically untested assumptions about the extent of the use of consumer durables. We cannot take the above description of the evolution of domestic work in Britain as being in any sense a *proven* one. Our intention here is slightly less ambitious: to provide a structure of argument within which this issue may be considered.

Our argument suggests three different sorts of effects that economic growth may have on housework time. First, it enables the purchase of consumer durables which increase domestic work efficiency and hence reduce the time required per task. Second, in increasing efficiency and lowering effective cost, it may induce increased demand for 'domestic service functions'. Third, in association with narrowing income differentials and with technical advance in the design of consumer durables and reduction in their cost, it induces social innovation. On the evidence presented here it seems likely that the net consequences of these effects in Britain over the last four decades has been to reduce the work time of working-class housewives and add to the burden of work on middle-class housewives, so eliminating entirely a very striking class inequity.

Leisure hours

We can deal with the second example of time use more briefly. How would we expect leisure patterns to change as societies become richer? It is obviously very tempting to adopt an 'embourgoisement' model, such that the *differences* between better- and worse-off groups are taken as predictors of likely *changes* in the behaviours of the worse-off groups as their economic position improves. We might notice that the middle classes are more frequent participants in 'out-of-home' entertainments, such as cinema or theatre, and in sports activities than the working class, and spend less time in 'passive' leisure pursuits, such as watching television or listening to the radio. Obviously there are some high-status, high-income activities, and some low-status, low-income activities. As the society as a whole becomes richer, we might be tempted to expect that activity patterns shift proportionately towards the high-status categories – a sociological equivalent to Engel's Law.

We can see from figure 4.3 that this general description does have *some* virtue, but it certainly only tells a small part of the story. Some of the cross-sectional characteristics are present at each of the time points. Passive leisure activities in the home, for example, take up in each case more time for working-class people than for middle-class; the 'other away from home' leisure activities category accounts for a larger part of middle-class than working class time. The cross-sectional relationships are *preserved* over time but they do not in any sense *predict* changes over time.

J. I. Gershuny

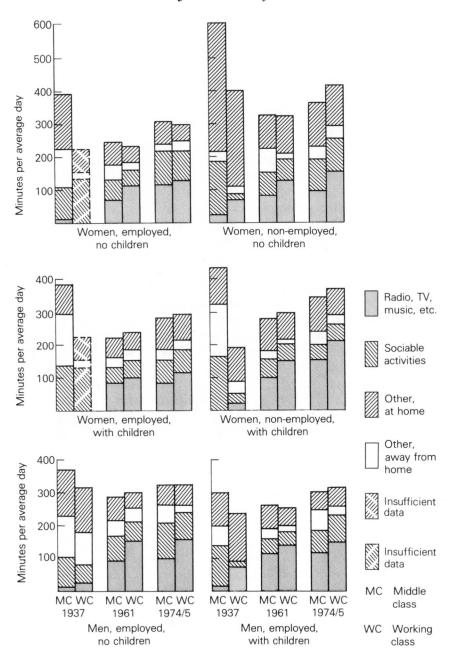

Figure 4.3   Changing distribution of leisure time for people aged 25–45

There is in fact no necessary correspondence between cross-sectional differences and longitudinal changes. In some cases the working-class time allocation to the activities such as (meeting friends, eating out, parties, dances) and the 'other away from home' category does grow over time in the way that would be predicted by the embourgoisement hypothesis. (We might note that the middle-class total of time spent in these categories was reduced between 1937 and 1961.) However, in the case of passive leisure the trend seems to correspond to a 'proletarianization' model, the lower-status activity growing for both classes over time even though the cross-sectional difference between classes is maintained.

It appears that we have the same two processes recurring. We have, on one hand, the Engel's Law changes, whereby desirable categories of activities grow proportionately as budgets (in this case leisure-time budgets) grow, and on the other, we have socio-technical innovation whereby change in the mode of provision of particular services (in this context change in the techniques and organization of leisure production) in turn changes the nature of an individual's participation in leisure activities.

Table 4.9   Classification of leisure activities

Type of activity	Mode of provision	
	Self-serviced	*Serviced*
Spectator	Television, radio	Cinema, theatre, sports
Sociable	Seeing friends, party, dance, etc.	Restaurants, pubs, clubs, church, etc.
Other at home	Reading, hobbies, etc.	

We can demonstrate the latter effect by classifying leisure-time budget in a way analogous to the classification of money budgets in table 4.1. Table 4.9 has three classes of leisure activity and two alternative modes of provision. Table 4.10 gives some illustrative data classified according to this scheme for various different social groups, and table 4.11 summarizes the changes in time allocation over the period 1937–75. It becomes immediately obvious that in the 'spectator' leisure category, the 'self-serviced' mode of provision has grown much faster than the 'serviced'. In the case of the

J. I. Gershuny

Table 4.10 Allocation of leisure time, excluding leisure travel, in minutes per average day for people aged 25–45, in 1937, 1961 and 1975

		Middle class			Working class		
		Self-serviced	Serviced	Total	Self-serviced	Serviced	Total
Employed men, with children							
Spectator	1937	19	31	50	76	17	93
	1961	118	23	141	144	10	155
	1975	120	18	138	151	18	169
Sociable	1937	95	24	119	7	7	14
	1961	32	10	42	25	13	38
	1975	46	18	64	49	30	79
Other	1937	–	–	94	–	–	126
	1961	–	–	67	–	–	52
	1975	–	–	79	–	–	53
Employed men, no children							
Spectator	1937	11	71	82	26	55	81
	1961	95	18	113	155	27	182
	1975	98	26	124	161	12	173
Sociable	1937	56	38	94	12	43	55
	1961	49	24	73	43	17	60
	1975	65	47	112	56	23	79
Other	1937	–	–	141	–	–	132
	1961	–	–	65	–	–	42
	1975	–	–	54	–	–	55
Non-employed women, with children							
Spectator	1937	1	64	65	24	27	51
	1961	103	12	115	156	8	164
	1975	120	14	134	167	10	177
Sociable	1937	63	104	167	27	3	30
	1961	46	11	57	44	7	51
	1975	67	11	78	87	11	98
Other	1937	–	–	114	–	–	94
	1961	–	–	100	–	–	77
	1975	–	–	100	–	–	79

'sociable' leisure category the trend is not quite so clear. However, the two cases (middle-class men, with and without children) which do not conform to the general pattern in which growth of time in the 'self-serviced' category outstrips the 'serviced' categories, both had very high allocations of time to 'meeting friends' in 1937. While the cross-sectional relationships do not provide very much of an explanation of the pattern of change in leisure activities over

Table 4.11   Change in leisure activities in minutes
per day 1937–1975

	Middle class			Working class		
	Self-serviced	Serviced	Total	Self-serviced	Serviced	Total
Men, employed, with children						
Spectator	+101	−23	+88	+ 72	+ 1	+ 76
Sociable	− 49	− 6	−55	+ 42	+13	+ 65
Other			−15			− 73
			+18			+ 68
Men, employed, no children						
Spectator	+ 87	−45	+42	+135	−43	+ 92
Sociable	+ 9	+ 9	+18	+ 44	−20	+ 24
Other			−87			− 67
			−27			+ 49
Women, non-employed, with children						
Spectator	+119	−50	+69	+143	−17	+126
Sociable	+ 4	−93	−89	+60	+ 8	+ 68
Other			−10			− 15
			−30			+179

time, it is clear that at least in the rather general way it is formulated the process whereby serviced leisure activities lose ground relative to 'self-serviced' leisure, does provide at least part of an explanation.

The Informatics Revolution

Innovation in service production

The pattern of service innovation that we have introduced has its effect, not just on the service sector, but on the economy as a whole. It transforms the manufacturing and construction sectors, possibly even to a greater extent than the service industries. Indeed, since by our definition, all commodities are ultimately transformed into service functions, we would argue that service innovations, broadly understood, are perhaps the most important source of change in the overall industrial structure.

The long-term economic development of a society can be understood in terms of its changing techniques for the provision and distribution of services. The economies of the Western world during the 1950s and 1960s were dominated by the consequences of a wave of innovation in the modes of provision for a particular range of service functions – transport, domestic services and entertainment. The manufacturing industries (vehicle engineering, consumer durables, electronics) that provided the equipment for these service functions were important motors of economic growth over this period. A 'cluster' of related innovations provided the technical means which combined with the available material infrastructure and informal labour skills to meet the specific characteristics of particular service functions. Cheaper mass-produced motor cars, together with metalled roads, and not very demanding skill requirements for the private driver, combined to enable the transport innovation. A regular electricity supply, electronic valves and later, transistors, combined with, in the mass, shared tastes, enabled the innovation of public broadcast entertainment. Electric motors and pre-existent housework skills enabled changes in the mode of domestic service provision. Certainly these innovations were not all there was to the post-war boom but they were certainly far from negligible factors.

This interpretation of recent economic history can be brought to bear on the end of the boom and the subsequent problems of the Western industrial economy. By the 1970s this particular line of service innovations was beginning to falter. As the switch from serviced to self-serviced modes of provision for particular domestic, entertainment and transport functions is completed, so markets for the corresponding consumer goods become saturated. Increasingly, technological change reduces the production costs, and hence labour requirements, of existing products, so new purchases of durables generate less employment than formerly. This particular wave of innovations has reached the shore; the range of potential functions that can be met by electro-mechanical technologies and their associated infrastructures has come close to being effectively exhausted.

Of course, there are new products (e.g. video recorders, home computers) which do sell buoyantly but these products will not in themselves generate new markets and new employment to compare with the markets and employment associated with motor cars or consumer durables in the 1950s and 1960s. In part this is because they are produced in a very capital-intensive way but also it is because they are not currently part of service innovations. They do not really provide, as the 1950s innovations did, an opportunity for the substantially more efficient provision of particular service functions. They could do so however. The new technologies, together with the new infrastructure, could allow innovations in the more complex service functions which were not affected by the 1950s wave: in education, in more varied and personalized entertainment and in the provision of medical advice. Cheap computing and information-storage technologies mean that much more demanding and interactive functions can now, in principle, be met by less-skilled, final-service workers, relying more on stored software supplied by skilled, intermediate-service workers.

Some examples of innovations which have already been proposed can be listed (in many cases these are already at the stage of working demonstrations):

(1) In *domestic services*, we can construct systems for automatic, centralized monitoring and control of a range of household functions (heating, lighting, safety); these household systems can themselves be linked to local security or safety services. In addition we might imagine information packages giving advice on household operations.

(2) In *entertainment*, there are already operational 'home box-offices' and analagous systems, giving households the option of access (via cables) to a much wider and more varied range of entertainment material than could be provided on a mass broadcast basis. By a simple extension, we could imagine subscription schemes, using such systems to promote new films, plays and musical performances which would otherwise not find a market either in theatres or in broadcasting.

(3) In the *transport/communications* area, the same infrastructure and domestic equipment could enable electronic funds transfer and 'remote shopping'., There would also presumably be facilities available for video telephones and other sophistications of the current telephone system (such as computed switching to enable a conversation not with any one specified individual but with anyone who wished to talk about some specified topic).

(4) In *education*, we could imagine the proliferation of packages for remote and, if necessary, interactive education or training.

(5)   In *medicine,* we might foresee continuous remote monitoring of chronic disorders, enabling more home care. Similarly we might perhaps develop systems for remote diagnosis. Certainly interactive packages for medical and other counselling would be a sensible use of the available facilities.

Considering each of these as individual innovations, certainly the costs, particularly the infrastructure costs, would be prohibitively high (though some, particularly the entertainment examples, may well turn out to be viable in isolation). We could not justify a 'wired city' infrastructure on the basis of, say, potential educational innovations. If the infrastructure costs of various of these services were to be shared however, their economics become rather more plausible. Once the infrastructure is built, the marginal costs of most of these examples amount to little more than the software they require. It does appear that the same basic infrastructure could be designed to serve all the examples we have quoted. Of course there are probably many more sorts of services that could be provided in this way.

In order to apply our model to exploring the implications of these sorts of innovation for economic structure, it is helpful to identify separately a new class of final consumption commodity – software. Consumption of this sort of product was not particularly substantial through the 1950s wave; the only category of final consumption that would really fall into this category would be television, radio programmes and recorded music. However, as our brief discussion will have made clear, this will be a crucially important and perhaps, in growth terms, the dominant commodity in the potential 1980s wave.

It may also be helpful to identify separately the industrial sector which produces this software for domestic consumption as the 'intermediate consumer services' sector. (It would also include all those professionally involved in maintenance of domestic machinery.) Just as actors who moved from the theatre stage to the television studio could be classed as transferring from a final to an intermediate service industry, so we would classify those doctors, teachers or firemen who write algorithms or record video programmes for use in these innovative modes of provision as 'intermediate consumer service workers'. This new software sector includes much more than just computer programmers; it covers any productive activity which involves the embodiment of skills in an information storage device, such that those skills may be used subsequently, and

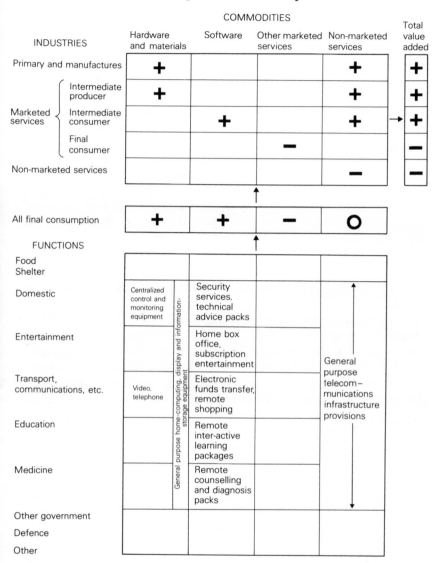

Figure 4.4 Technologically feasible changes in final consumption patterns and their consequences for industrial value added

elsewhere, for the provision of some final service function.

Figure 4.4 shows the possible impact of the sorts of innovations we have outlined for the structure of industrial value added. We would expect the innovations, initially at least, to stimulate manufacturing production (just as in the first part of the 1950s wave). Certainly there would be very considerable growth in the construction industry during the initial installation of the infrastructure. Both sorts of intermediate service industry might be assumed to benefit, while the marketed final consumer sector would have an accelerated rate of decline. Even if government expenditure were to rise, in this model most of the growth would be concentrated in manufacturing, construction and the intermediate services, so value added in the non-marketed service sector itself would also probably decline. This is, of course, the very vaguest of possible outlines but it is not the function of this chapter to develop a less coarse-grained picture. The point is simply to suggest that the analysis of household consumption patterns provides us with a framework for thinking about the structure of the 'information economy.'

Conclusion: The Usefulness of the Concept

Socio-technical innovation, as it has been considered in this chapter, is useful in a number of different ways. It offers an improvement on the conventional explanations for the changes in economic structure that result from economic growth. In combination with Engel's Law, it yields a quite rich and revealing description of the processes whereby the sectors of developed economies interact with each other. It is also an integrating concept, giving a common explanation for changes in patterns of behaviour of interest both to economists (e.g. employment patterns) and to sociologists (time-use patterns).

The concept might be objected to as being overly individualistic and economic. The foregoing arguments might be read as suggesting that individuals or households in some sense *choose* to adopt some particular mode of provision of services whereas in fact these choices may be predisposed by some collective decision (e.g. governmental decisions to build roads rather than subsidise public transport) or by other sorts of corporate activity (advertising, trades-union action). The arguments have also been presented in a way that suggests that the maximization of material output of a basket of service functions is the ultimate human objective whereas, in fact, we seek much less easily quantifiable objectives, to the satisfaction of which service functions are merely means. A mode of service provision which uses resources with less than optimal economic efficiency may be nevertheless preferable to alternatives because of its benefits in terms of sociability or personal autonomy.

The essential point of the argument is simply that modes of provision of services do change over time. For different purposes we might wish to explain the process of change in different ways. The more 'economic' models of diffusion of alternative modes of provision may be most helpful as a basis for assessing the consequences of particular technological developments. To the extent that these are found to be politically or sociologically insensitive, there is no reason that we should not develop models derived from, say, political economy or social psychology. The process of social innovation may itself be explained by many other factors than the conventional economic ones.

The most important application of these ideas may however be prospective; they give us a useful perspective on the determinants of future economic and social structure. We are too often given a rather cataclysmic view of the 1980s and 1990s. We are told to expect the rapid growth of quite new and unprecedented sectors of our economies ('quaternary' and 'quinary' economies) to exceed in importance the traditional trilogy of primary, manufacturing and service industries – often without any very clear picture of exactly what these sectors are to produce.

Certainly the new telematics technologies will enable innovations in areas of service provision which have not in the past been subject to much change and certainly, as we argued above (p. 158), there is a temporal discontinuity between the past wave and the one coming (partly caused by the inadequacy of the current telecommunication infrastructure for the needs of the information economy).

Nevertheless, the next wave is likely to follow the same underlying model of service innovation as the last did. There is no reason to suppose that the scale of social and economic consequences will necessarily be any larger or more unmanageable than the last. An understanding of changes in service provision at the household level gives us a basis for speculation about what the nature of these consequences might be.

Notes

This chapter is a revised version of 'Social Innovation', *Futures*, December 1982/June 1983.

1   Expenditures are deflated by the appropriate price indices provided by the ESA and expressed as proportions of total household and direct (i.e. non-transfer-payment) government expenditures.
2   Calculated here by dividing each sector's change in value added at constant prices by change in numbers of employees.
3   As far as we, and the archivist of the Mass Observation Archive, are aware, this is the first time that this collection of diaries has been used in systematic sociological analysis.

5

Local Exchange and State Intervention

Didier Cornuel and Bruno Duriez

It has become customary to make a distinction between types of exchange in industrial societies. On the one hand, there is the formal or official economy where exchange takes place within the framework of market or State organizations and, on the other, there is the informal or underground economy which is the source of invisible wealth (Rosanvallon 1980) and which eludes statistical and/or legal investigation.

Certain authors go beyond this dualistic vision of the economy. In particular, Gershuny (1979) and Pahl (1980) identify two sectors within the informal economy: the 'underground economy' and the 'household economy' which function according to different logics. Mendras (1980) also employs this triad in his account.

The informal sector is not very amenable to economic analysis. This is particularly so in attempts to quantify the production of *travail noir* (black work), which give very divergent results. The same applies to the evaluation of domestic production which, unlike black work, does not involve money. In this case, the value of the work is measured by the time expended (Chadeau & Fouquet 1981). Estimates in this area are equally problematic. Apart from the obvious difficulties of data collection in the case of black work, the very conceptualization and normal categories of economic measurement are being questioned.

The economic crisis has done much to stimulate discourse about the informal economy. Whether the subject is black work (which is sometimes decried as unfair competition and sometimes made a candidate for 'whitening' because it can give the market greater flexibility) or whether it is that of domestic and community exchange (involving a revaluation of 'DIY' and 'small is beautiful' [Schumacher 1973]), the boundaries are challenged.

The scientific approach is not impervious to the fashions of political discourse. However, the attention which has been paid for some time to the informal sector does not have to be seen simply as a conjunctural effect. What is actually involved is the question of how the field of economic activity should be defined and the underlying assumptions of the economic approach which is adopted (particularly where the opposition between the substantivist and formalist definitions of the economy is concerned). It is also a question of the relationships between consumption and production and the implications of applying the analytic schemas for capitalist production to domestic and community production (Bourgeois et al. 1978). On a broader level the issue is one of the relationship between the production of goods and the social structure.

Analysis of the existence of different sectors of production and exchange of goods and services and their evolution relative to each other can be reduced to an economic analysis and, more precisely, to analysis of the relative labour costs in each of the sectors. However, some have related the existence of these various sectors to different social structures (particularly those inspired by the concept of the domestic mode of production in Sahlins 1972) and others have gone so far as to treat certain activities in the informal sector as irrational from the economic point of view and to deny them any significance except in terms of sociability or social identity (Tievant 1982).

We are not adopting this latter point of view. We aim to show that the two types of explanation can be employed simultaneously, not just in a complementary way or in opposition to each other. We have applied this double analysis using observation of informal exchanges in a village on the urban periphery in the north of France, which we have called Ervelinghem. The choice of village was not based on the rural–urban distinction. Analogous observations could have been made in an urban district. The choice was made for reasons of convenience, in particular the limited size and relatively circumscribed local area which contribute to the creation of a fairly well-defined and bounded area. It also involves a group with a common past and hence a series of common references to collective life. Finally, the fact that the village is on the urban periphery made it possible to study the exchanges born of the encounter between an old population and a new population of urban origin.

First we will attempt to draw out the economic logic of the

informal exchanges and then show how these exchanges constitute the local social structure.

The Economic Logic of Informal Exchanges

Our aim is to show that informal exchanges follow a logic which is no different from the one which is at work in formal exchanges, namely a logic of cost minimization. In other words, informal activities are those which cost less in this sector than they would in the formal sector, and vice versa. We will look at the different cost elements which work in favour of the informal sector before considering those which hinder its extension.

The first element of costs which gives the informal sector an advantage is the absence of obligatory deductions, taxes and social security contributions. In the case of domestic production this absence of deductions is legal. Housework, child rearing, gardening, etc., are not subject to Social Security contributions, value added tax or taxation of the revenue in kind created by this labour. This situation means that production for oneself is less onerous, for work of equal value, than making use of an opportunity provided by the formal market.

The lack of deductions can also be the result of fraud; in which case one is dealing with black work. Several cases were identified in Ervelinghem. Thus, Monsieur Six, age 26, a worker in a construction company, has had an undeclared contract with a private individual for two years. He is renovating a cottage on Saturdays for 50F an hour or about 1600F per month. If the deal had been done through his firm his work would have been billed at 80F per hour, including taxes. His client saves 30F, which is the VAT, overheads and the entrepreneur's net profit. Monsieur Six earns about 20F on top of his usual wage. In addition he saves income tax of 5F.

The non-payment of social security contributions and taxes is only of interest if one continues to benefit from the provisions financed by these deductions. As far as public services are concerned, they are provided independently of the payment of taxes, so there is nothing but gain in avoiding the financing of these public services. On the other hand, with social security, one only benefits from the provisions if payment has been made previously. Monsieur Six is only interested in doing black work because he has a primary occupation which gives both him and his family cover against the risks of illness.

Similarly, it is in the interests of the housewives of Ervelinghem who only work for a few hours per week not to declare this because the number of hours they work is not sufficient in itself to bring the benefits of Social Security although both they and their employers would be paying contributions. Besides, if their husband is in employment they benefit from Social Security as the spouse of one who is 'socially insured'. One can see that the circumstances in which workers gain their income exclusively for opportunities for black work are uncommon: at Ervelinghem it involves spouses or children of those who are socially insured doing domestic work, cooking, organizing banquets or minding children.

The second element which keeps the costs of the informal sector to a minimum is the absence of work regulation. In the formal sector there is a high degree of regulation in the labour market in terms of price and quantity. In terms of quantity, regulation sets the maximum daily hours of work and there are further regulations if these limits are exceeded. Thus, Monsieur Six who puts in additional hours of black work would probably find this opportunity denied him in the formal market for labour. In any event, they would cost the employer up to 100 per cent more than the hourly wage for the 39 hours. Similarly, there is a minimum salary. People whose capacities are reduced because of age or infirmity who are considered by employers as inferior to workers on the minimum wage (SMIC)[1] are excluded from the labour market. Thus, Monsieur Carmaux who is 79 and does gardening would clearly be unable to find a job at the level of SMIC because his age prevents him from achieving the productivity which corresponds to this level of earnings. One could think of his wage of 6F an hour as being an extrapolation of the earnings curve of manual workers which declines after the age of 50.

It is the same for evening baby-sitters. In Ervelinghem, the wage for this work is 10F an hour which is clearly less than the SMIC. However, it could also be said that when this activity is simply restricted to supervision without the need to give children meals or put them to bed, it is not worth the SMIC. Indeed, it is interesting to note that the State has institutionalized a wage lower than the SMIC for recognized child minders. An 'assistante maternelle', a label bestowed by institutionalization, can care for a maximum of three children and receives for each child at least the equivalent of two hours of the SMIC for 8 hours of care. In other words, it has been necessary to relax a rigidity in the labour market so as to allow a hitherto informal activity to become institutionalized.

The third element which operates in favour of the informal sector is its capacity to make provisions of a quality which the formal sector is unable to supply at the same cost. One example of the formal sector's inability to provide a certain level of quality is that of transport. Ervelinghem is served by train and bus but the time-tables and the journey times are such that the transport service which they provide is not of sufficient quality to satisfy the inhabitants of Ervelinghem. It is very clear in the case of the transport of secondary-school children who make no use of the 'scholar's pass', i.e. children who do not attend the schools they would normally be assigned to on the grounds of their place of residence and who therefore do not benefit from the school pick-up. The parents of these children have organized a variety of informal school transport among neighbours. A similar service could be provided by taxi but at a significantly higher cost.

Another example of the informal sector's capacity to make provision of a certain quality concerns the education of children. It is well known that, despite compulsory schooling, children's social milieu remains fundamental to their upbringing. This means that the time spent by a parent from a middle-class milieu is worth more economically than when the parent is from a working-class milieu because the middle-class child is educated to become a *cadre* (an executive) whose income is higher than that of a manual worker. This fact rules out simply using the number of hours to measure the value of domestic production, as is usually done (Chadeau & Fouquet 1981; Hawrylyshyn 1976; Hawrylyshyn & Adler 1978).

Allotments are another area where taking quality into account makes sense of the domestic production of vegetables which, at formal market prices, would be uneconomic. This applies to Monsieur Roux, a worker who cultivates his allotment with his son and who considers this to be an economic activity when the quality of the produce is taken into account. The same argument is often put forward to justify the purchase of vegetables from the growers in the village instead of commercial growers from the surrounding area: 'at least you know what you're getting with them'.

One of the reasons for the lower cost of informal sector provisions compared with the formal sector is the absence of fixed costs due to the low level of informal production. This is the central problem of the transition from an informal to a formal activity. What is required is sufficiently large volume of production to cover these fixed costs. Thus, Monsieur Six, who does black work on Saturdays, has thought seriously about starting his own business but, he says, 'it's not viable to be self-employed, you need to reach quite a size.' He estimates that he would have needed 80,000F to set himself up as a small builder.

Similarly, Monsieur Dubreucq, a technician, had thought of starting a cycle shop and repair workshop instead of 'rendering service' on demand. However, he regards the operation as uneconomic because in a shop in Lille, which he knows well from the jobs he does for them, the income from repair work just covers his wages with nothing to spare.

Likewise it is the comparison with wages in the labour market which is the basis for the division within the family between domestic tasks and paid activities.

The fourth element of costs which helps to explain informal activities is the opportunity cost. This is the cost one shoulders in doing an activity oneself instead of having recourse to the market. It is clear that one is only going to produce for oneself if the opportunity cost is lower than the market price. There is proof of this in Ervelinghem with the allotment keepers. The majority of inhabitants have a garden but only a handful have an allotment. If one estimates for a family of four a saving of 300F per month on vegetables due to the allotment, and gardening time of one hour per day, the maximum opportunity cost is in the order of 10F per hour. This explains why, setting aside the question of the quality of the vegetables, it is basically those in retirement who keep gardens because their opportunity cost is low considering the level of pensions. Thus, the garden belonging to Monsieur Smagghe, a 34-year-old teacher, is maintained by his father-in-law, and Monsieur Carmaux, a retired manual worker of 79, produces vegetables for his daughter and son-in-law. In contrast, the previously mentioned Monsieur Six's garden lies fallow. He explains the alternatives with great clarity. For him, the choice is very simply between black work in building or the cultivation of his garden, and the former is by far the most profitable.

The theory of opportunity costs (Becker 1965; Lemennicier 1980) also provides an explanation of the division of tasks within the household between men and women. The spouse who will carry out more domestic activities is the one with the lowest opportunity cost. One can actually check for France as a whole (INSEE 1978) that the activity rates for wives decrease with the husband's income because women's wages are lower than their husband's, and that the couples for whom tasks are least differentiated are those in which the occupational earnings of each are most similar. Ervelinghem is no exception to this general rule.

Opposed to these factors which work in favour of the informal sector, there are two elements of cost which are a hindrance to informal activities: the cost of risk and the cost of networks.

The cost of risk

The risks run in informal activities are of two types. The first involves the risk of suffering injury. The possibilities are numerous, with accidents being the most common. An event of this nature can occur in black work (e.g. Monsieur Carmaux was injured while gardening, Monsieur Six just escaped a falling beam), domestic activities (e.g. DIY on Sundays brings self-inflicted wounds, amateur gardeners have accidents with their lawn-mowers) or communal activities (e.g. an accident involving a child supervized by an unqualified holiday camp leader). To these risks of accident must be added those of bad workmanship or the non-receipt of anticipated payments.

All these risks are covered in the formal system by obligatory deductions. These obligatory deductions serve to finance the monitoring organizations which minimize all these risks (e.g. work inspection and health and social inspection) and the judicial system which allows the possibility of redress against those responsible and eventually the indemnification of the victim (e.g. work accident pension and indemnities paid by compulsory insurance). To all intents and purposes, the informal sector lacks all of these systems. The risk of accident is low but the injuries suffered can be important and the means for dealing with them can be very onerous.

Nevertheless, there are certain procedures for obtaining cover from the formal sector for some of these risks. An example of this is '*brocantes*', an expression used in Northern France to describe black activities. Thus a small businessman may agree to consider one of his employees who is doing black work on his own account as working for him at the time of the accident.

In addition to this risk of sustaining injury there is the risk of discovery in the case of illegal activities. Although the inherent risks in the law of 11 July 1972 on the suppression of clandestine work are low (cf. Choain & Jacquemart 1982) the penalties incurred under the tax laws and Social Security are serious enough to make certain individuals keep away from black work. It is an argument which is often put forward in Ervelinghem. Monsieur and Madam Crespin employ a woman who does housework and minds their child. She declares her earnings because it is wiser to declare 'so as to

be safe'. Madame Roux, the domestic help, turned down offers of
extra hours 'on the black' because 'if you're a lucky sort of person its
alright, if not you get found out. A girl who did hairdressing on the
side had to stop.' Madame Cordonnier refuses to do black work in
Ervelinghem because it would be known and it would cause her
problems.

An even more obvious example of the importance of the risk of
discovery is the study of the unemployed by Foudi et al. (1982) in
the Denain area. It shows that the risk run by the unemployed
doing black work is greater than for the employed. In fact the
employed risk no more than the fines whereas the unemployed run
the risk of losing their employment benefit which is already a
reduced income compared with their previous situation.

The cost of networks

Formal exchanges operate in structures like enterprises, administra-
tions and commercial organisations whose constitution and functioning have a cost independent of the production of goods and services.
The same applies in the informal sector. Exchanges or production
require structures which include neighbours, friends and the family –
in short, the relationships, necessary for these informal activities to
take place. These relationships, which involve two or more persons
and which have a certain degree of stability, form networks. In this
sense the conjugal family can also be considered a network. These
relationships are self-maintaining, which in practice means the
expenditure of time. The fact that this time can be pleasurable does
not prevent it from being a cost, for the simple reason that it
prevents other activities. Furthermore, the effectiveness of the
network presupposes a degree of permanence in the relationship and
this acts as a constraint.

The conjugal couple with or without children represents the most
important network in terms of the economic value of the products
which it generates. The cost of the constitution or reinforcement of
the network helps to explain what appears to be a certain economic
irrationality. The Roussels, for example, gave up their house to
their daughter and son-in-law and had another house built for
themselves 40 metres away. The daughter and son-in-law rejoined
the firm where Madam Roussel used to work. The son-in-law paid
for the new job with a loss of seniority. However, the close
proximity allows the small children to be cared for either by the
grandmother or by the great-aunt who also lives close by. The same
situation exists with the Six family. Monsieur Six arranged for his

brother-in-law to be taken on in the building firm although he had no skills in construction. He works with him as a team so that he is able to keep his job. This occurred at the time when the brother-in-law had just moved house to be closer to his wife's family in Ervelinghem. This is consistent with the observations of Segalen (1980a, 1980b) at Saint-Jean Trolimon where 'parents provide mutual aid to keep their children on the spot.'

The cost of the network can therefore extend to a drop in income derived from the formal sector but to counter this there are benefits in the more or less long term. For young households these are the services which come from the free time which parents have in retirement; for the parents it is the assurance of not being left in isolation. In economic terms, the establishment and evolution of the network can be regarded as an investment which gradually realizes profits.

It is obviously still more profitable if a pre-existing network can be used for the conduct of informal activities. This is the case with the occupational network which, by definition, exists independently of the informal sector. This network is undoubtedly the primary source of contacts for the exercise of black or communal activities. It is the case with Monsieur Cordonnier, who does bricklaying work for his workmates or their acquaintances even though this is not his trade. It is the case with the self-employed worker who made an approach to a lawyer for legal services and received an offer to prepare his documents as a black activity. It is also the case with the employees of a rapid-repair garage who make use of their contacts with customers to create their own clientele. Conversely, this role of the occupational network helps to explain the reduction in black activities on the part of some of the unemployed (Foudi et al. 1982). In losing their formal activity they simultaneously lose contact with potential clients and the possibilities for borrowing material from their firm. This helps to make black work an extension of formal activity.

On the whole, one finds the same economic rationale in formal and informal activities, namely, minimum cost for a given quality and level of production, taking into account the existence or absence of obligatory deductions.

This explains the importance of domestic production, estimated at 50 per cent of Gross Domestic Product (Chadeau & Fouquet 1981). It is due both to the lower opportunity cost of women and the level of obligatory deductions in the formal market. It explains the phenomenon analysed by Gershuny (1978) – the development of the self-service economy which limits the extension of formal tertiary activities.

It also explains why black work and communal production are marginal activities. The first reason is that these activities often only exist because they cannot be carried out in the formal market for reasons of cost, quality and the level of production. If these activities represented a significant volume, the formal sector would tend to produce them. The second reason is that one can only avoid Social Security deductions at the cost of a marginal existence. If one wishes to continue to benefit from the payments financed by these deductions it is necessary to have a main job in the formal sector or benefit from these payments as the spouse or child of a socially insured person.

Finally, it is not possible to deduce from these observations the direction of evolution of the division between formal and informal activities. The rare data which do exist for domestic production suggest that its volume in relation to GDP is relatively stable (Harwrylyshyn 1976). The same cost elements can continue to contribute to the development of formal production by the extension of mass production and the division of labour. Other factors can also work in this direction. The development of the midday meal eaten outside the home for example, is the counterpart in the formal sector to the increased duration of the informal sector activity of travel from home to work. Similarly, the development of domestic production is not expressed simply in the spending of time on travelling but also in the use of material objects (e.g. freezer, washing-machine, electric drill) which are products of the formal sector.

This means that an improved knowledge of the future development of formal and informal activities will depend on the differentiation of these activities according to their function (e.g. education, catering, home maintenance, caring) because each of these functions requires a specific combination of capital and labour. A view of how the functions evolved is a prerequisite to any understanding of informal sector activities as a whole.

If the observed phenomena of informal exchange are susceptible to the same economic analysis as informal exchanges, are they also capable of analysis from a point of view other than the economic? Do they not contribute to the constitution or perpetuation of a certain type of sociability, distinct from or at variance with that of the formal sector? This is what we will attempt to show in the following section.

Informal Exchanges and Local Social Structure

Economic analysis explains the choice between formal and informal by cost differences. Decisions which at first sight appear to be irrational are rendered explicable when placed in a longer time-scale (e.g. patrimonial logic or deferred debts). However, exchanges which occur within the village, especially those which are not formalized by the institutions of the global society, and the State in particular, can be analysed from another point of view; this distinguishes them from the formal exchanges which each individual or group participates in outside this collectivity. In each case, they are experienced differently by the inhabitants of the village. In fact, social intercourse involves constant reference to the mythical reality of the lost village community. However, the meaning of informal exchange is not limited to the villagers' subjective appraisal.

Relationships between villagers tend to obscure the distinctions which stem from capitalism, whether they be class differences, specialized exchanges (e.g. economic, political) or spatial specialization (e.g. place of work, place of residence). Informal exchanges, many of which do not have great economic value, create and reinforce social cohesion between the inhabitants. At the level of social relationships in the nation as a whole, the specialization of networks according to economic, political and other functions leaves the State with the main responsibility for ensuring the cohesion of the national community. If informal exchanges are similarly inscribed in the logic of social cohesion, then their main competitor, if not opponent, must be the State. Thus the informal sector is more anti-State than anti-economic.

Competition between the formal and the informal sector will become apparent in disputes between the two sectors over the provision of services. The dominant tendency is the progressive statization of informal exchanges, i.e. direct take over within the framework of public services or regulation and control by the State. However, in certain areas of activity, informal exchanges have a continuing existence. They show the persistence, even predominance, of a type of social relation and form of social organization among the members of the collectivity which is distinct from the solidarity organized by the State and may even be opposed to it.

It is in an area like education that statization is most manifest. Since the introduction of compulsory schooling, State control of children's education has never ceased to expand towards ever younger age groups and towards increasingly advanced studies. In Ervelinghem, it was to be seen in the extension of enrolment to include younger children and it found its first expression in the creation of a private infants school. The fact that it was a local initiative, not integrated into the system of State education, gives it a certain informal character. Thus, it was the parents who played a major role in the construction of the school buildings, through their financial contributions but also, quite directly, through their labour. The infants school which originated as a pre-school nursery is staffed by nuns. The overlap between the life of the school and the life of the group of nuns is close. The municipality, as the local apparatus of the State, established a public infants school several years later, where the struggle for secularity increased the State's involvement.

The same extension of State control was evident in the provision of care for pre-school children. The most widespread form of care in Ervelinghem remains informal: it involves care by the mother, grandmother or a non-registered minder. This system of infant care became the object of legislation, which had the effect of helping to black a hitherto unregulated phenomenon. Those involved in child minding had to meet certain conditions, including a limit on the number of children they were allowed to mind. Of course, child minders had to declare the income received to the Inland Revenue and the parents of the children had to pay Social Security contributions. In the face of general hostility towards these deductions, the law allowed the income derived from child minding to be exempt from tax up to a certain ceiling and compensated for the costs of Social Security by an allowance. The logic of institutionalization which is at work here is not primarily to increase tax revenues since the public intervention is neutral on this point; rather, it is a logic of control over the form of education of small children. Child minders have to respect certain norms in matters of hygiene, comfort and presentation. Moreover, these norms are more or less explicit and dependent to a large extent on the representatives of the Caisse d' Allocations Familiales (CAF) responsible for paying family allowance, who visit the child-minders. The relationship between the parents and the minder of their children (almost exclusively women) is no longer the same. It is now the State which guarantees that the children will be well cared for.

Aside from any opposition to deductions, the informal method of child minding continues to persist. There are even cases of declared minders who cannot find any children to mind. Even when children are looked after by someone who is not declared to the CAF, the preference is to give them to a member of the family, even a distant relative, rather than to a stranger. This is proof that the informal sector can fulfil the function of control of competence which the State is tending to assume. For recent incomers to the village the guarantee is provided by the person who puts the parent in touch with the minder, whether this intermediary wishes it or not. In the end the best guarantee is that provided by ties of kinship.

The regularity of provision leads to different choices. For example Madam Potier, a teacher, did not wish to rely on her family for the care of her children: 'It would have been a misuse of my mother-in-law to entrust my children to her on a continuous basis.' She therefore asked a lady to come and mind her children: 'It was quite amusing because this lady had coffee with my mother-in-law who understood perfectly the distance I was creating there.' In this case it would have been impossible to compensate the regularity of the service provided by the mother-in-law with a payment. In contrast, Madame Tison, a clerical worker, paid her aunt for looking after her son. There was no obligation to do so but the debt would eventually have become too great to be discharged.

In Ervelinghem the fertile capacity of the informal sector to provide infant care even brought to a halt a more developed form of institutionalization – the day nursery. Some of the recent incomers who, for this reason, were poorly integrated into the network of village relationships, had called for the creation of a nursery for children after school hours. This nursery never saw the light of day because this service, all the more costly for being regimented (e.g. in premises and with qualified staff) is also guaranteed by the grandmother, neighbour or friend. There is remuneration in some cases but not in others.

Still within the realm of education, the *colonies de vacances* (childrens's summer camps) are increasingly controlled by the administration. The *colonie* at Ervelinghem was created 20 years ago by the parish priest. It accommodates 150 children. To ensure safety, the director of the *colonie* must now be qualified, but institutionalization has brought disaffection among the village monitors: 'Its no longer our show'. This is because qualification is synonymous with professionalization and remuneration. If public intervention is not expressed directly in deductions, it leads to the monetarization of an activity which was hitherto outside the realm of monetary exchange. There have been important changes in this area in recent years (regulation, financing, professionalization, certification, etc.) and they are still under way. Witness a recent decision of the Conseil d'Etat (23 April 1982) confirming a judgement of the administrative tribunal of Toulouse which endorsed the claim of two leaders of a holiday and leisure centre demanding that the municipality make up the difference between their wages and the SMIC. Reporting this, *Le Monde* newspaper underlined the fact that the decision 'threatens to pose a number of financial problems for these centres and perhaps to inhibit what is left of the spirit of voluntary service among the helpers. Therefore, legal intervention to conciliate between these two contradictory imperatives should not be ruled out' (25 April 1982). Thus the problem is rather similar to that which was posed in the professionalization of infant care.

The same kind of evolution is apparent in help for the aged. In place of mutual aid, there has been the creation of public aid financed by the Caisses d'Allocations Familiales which is made available in the form of hours of labour performed by 'home helps'. Until now, care of the elderly was provided thanks to cohabitation by three or even four generations, which in turn helped to solve the problem of the care of young children.

Previously, one rendered service and, with increasing age, service was rendered in return. Informal aid was an exchange of services, albeit differentiated in time and generalized (e.g. it could be the children of those you gave service to who gave you their help).

The single example of Madam Joly, a widow, provides a negative summary of all the differences between the informal and institutional solutions to the problem of old people. Her only son had left the village, so 'they advised me to go into one of the small houses for old people, but I didn't want to . . . You try to help people all your life and then look what happens to you!' The institutional solution involves living in a *beguinage,* (a group of houses for the elderly) situated right in the centre of the village, at a short distance from her present accommodation. The removal would not therefore be important as far as she is concerned and she could benefit from the specific help provided for the elderly. However, she perceives this way of life as a penal sentence and unhappily relates her son's and her son's family's refusal to live with her as she had once accepted living with her mother-in-law and old uncle. Institutionalization implies specialization of exchanges, just as it involves specialization of places; place of work and place of residence but also places for infants, young people and the old.

The reasons behind the transition from informal to institutional help are to be found in changes of residence among the inhabitants of Ervelinghem. As far as Madame Joly is concerned, it was her son who should have been the first provider of help but he, like so many others, had left Ervelinghem. This means that there was no longer the continuity of residence among the inhabitants which gave authorization of credit in the exchange of services. One can no longer place confidence in people, not because they fail to merit confidence, but because life chances in the formal sector create uncertainty about the duration of relationships and therefore prevent all trust. The State becomes the only reliable structure because of its permanence. One subscribes, pays taxes, and therefore receives benefits.

These, then, are the characteristics of social life in the industrial system (credibility, even instability) which give rise to the need for a specialized provider of benefit in the form of collective services, namely the State. Thus Pitrou (1978) notes that unskilled workers, a mobile population, are those who make most claim on the local social assistance to resolve their various problems. Skilled workers, however, are more integrated into the old neighbourhood or kinship networks. This is also one of the observations made by Foudi et al. (1982) concerning the survival of the unemployed. The family is their primary source of help. The unemployed who are isolated from their families eventually become clients of the Bureau d'Aide Sociale and other forms of public assistance. The installation in Ervelinghem in mid 1981 of an office for the area *Assistante sociale* (social worker) is a further sign of statization.

For some, the myriad of small services between inhabitants and kin, or more important types of production and exchange, are the way to cross the threshold of survival and independence from the services of the State. They are also indicative of the contrast in the mode of social indentification between industrial society, which proposes a single alternative between work and social assistance, and village society where each person is known through several reltionships and implicated in multiple exchanges. This complex mutual knowledge makes for significantly greater continuity.

There is an example of this in collective security. In the town it is provided by the police but in Ervelinghem there is a further corporate guarantee. Everybody knows everybody else. When we were waiting at a front door, a lady called out to us: 'Monsieur X, he was in the garden a moment ago. I can see everything from my house.' Young people in particular have cause to resent this; a

17-year-old boy explains: 'If I do something at one end of the village, my parents know immediately.' Teenagers 'going steady' for example, acquire a semi-official status. Although it is not institutionalized like an engagement this status imposes certain rules of behaviour.

The possibility of controlling children is explained by Monsieur Pinon as being directly tied to the habitat: 'now they're going to build HLMs[2] at Ervelinghem. I'm against it. My children are going to meet the children of those people at school. They'll be contaminated.' The HLMs are therefore seen as a place of slackness and indiscipline, whereas the village provides the means to ensure a certain upbringing for children. This is not a class reaction, since Monsieur Pinon is from a working-class background and Ervelinghem is not as bourgeois as some of the neighbouring villages. (In 1975, 36 per cent of the active population was manual working class, a figure close to the French national average.)

Within this framework, black activities are perfectly understood but denunciation is reserved exclusively for those who do not play the game – 'the stranger', the person who attempts to achieve as much as he can from services rendered and whose isolation makes it impossible to make demands in turn. The only way to regulate the conflict is via the State. Conversely, 'strangers' are accused of being involved in reporting illegal work practices. The depersonalization of exchange relationships tends to increase reliance on the State, which in turn contributes to reinforcing the statization of exchange. However, village life and the specificity of exchange in the village continue to be valorized.

The persistence of the informal sector in spite of statization, which is the dominant phenomenon, can be explained by the continuing need to maintain social cohesion in the local collective. The State ensures this at the national level, while in the village it is ensured in and through the organization of exchanges and discourse. The way the organization protects exchanges is by making a sharp distinction between internal and external exchanges. This is the case with '*brocantes*'. There are two types of black work: *brocantes* within the village and *brocantes* outside. A deal within the village appears as a free helping hand: one does a service for a friend or a relation. The majority of these services are not paid for, being inscribed in the cycle of exchanges and obligations which will one day be fulfilled, but some of them are paid (because of the regularity of the provision or the importance of certain kinds of work). However, even in such cases they are inscribed in a friendship or kinship relation. This finding coincides with the results of extensive studies of black work. The researchers at SEDES (Le Bars et al. 1980) note that in many cases the contact between the worker and the supplier of work is direct and that it generally involves friends or family members. Relations between the client and the worker extend over a long period so that if they were not friends at the outset, the relationship becomes one of friendship. In this system of personalized relationships there is no desire to compete with the skilled worker from the village who has to make a living: Monsieur Tison, who has the requisite skills, installs windows or doors 'for friends'. The statement 'there isn't any black work in Ervelinghem' is often heard. It does not mean that there are no undeclared exchanges of goods and services (e.g. domestic work, carpet-laying, gardening, sale of poultry or eggs, bricklaying) but rather that these are not experienced as specialized occupational relationships with a monetary aim.

In contrast, those wishing to do *brocantes* will go outside the village to do them. This is so in the case of Monsieur Cordonnier who acquired building skills in fitting out his house and began to do *brocantes* to finance the improvements. He does these outside the village and avoids it becoming general knowledge. One of his friends in the village asked him to do a job but he keeps postponing it. If the work is done in order to bring in a good return, as a means to acquire money, it has to be done elsewhere.

The same situation exists among the skilled tradesmen based in the village. The conduct of their activity along capitalist lines is hard to imagine in the village. After-sales service or odd jobs in passing cannot be turned down. The skilled workers do a fair number of jobs for villagers but only with reluctance and, when this happens, the relationship becomes one of mutual service. Monsieur Roussel, an unskilled manual worker, on his wife's insistence because she feared having to wait for ever if he did the job himself, asked for estimates for refurbishing the exterior of the house. The village tradesman was much cheaper than the others but gave no date saying: 'I'll do it when I've got a gap.' The tradesmen are unable to do 'good deals' and there is dislike for anyone who is seen to be too grasping.

The distinction between internal and external exchanges can even be found within the family itself. Monsieur Six gets paid for the work he does for his uncles for 'there are no ties' but in contrast he receives no payment for the work he does for his wife's uncles. In this case 'it's a lend for something in return.' It is no accident that they chose to live close to his wife's family. On the one hand there are formal relationships and calculated exchanges: 'When we go to my mother's we have been invited or at least given warning. She won't accept giving us an improvized meal.' On the other hand there is a permanent relationship which constitutes the community: 'When I go to my mother-in-law's she asks me if I've eaten. If I haven't, she puts a plate on the table.' The difference between the two families is quite clear.

Exchanges therefore take place within kinship networks but also amongst all the villagers: these exchanges are complex and they frequently have little economic value. A lady takes soup to a sick neighbour; Monsieur Carmaux opens a neighbour's shutters every morning; the cafe in the square is always full, a place where people talk about everything and nothing, where information circulates; Monsieur Demon has been shooting and offers the pigeons to his friends ('It brings pleasure'); the lettuces in his garden are for whoever wants them. Examples could be given *ad infinitum*. 'Repairing lawn-mowers is a way of talking to your neighbours', says Monsieur Turpin, a mechanic. These gifts of small items and services allow 79-year-old Monsieur Carmaux to be recognized socially. The price of the provision therefore bears no relationship to its economic value, e.g. Monsieur Dubreucq occasionally repairs bicycles for children and parents offer him a bar of chocolate in return. The debt is acknowledged, it is not discharged completely. The sequence of exchanges and therefore relationships is not severed. One does not exchange in order to obtain immediate benefit. At the boundary, some of these informal exchanges result in economic disadvantage. This applies to exchanges on pretext, like that of the lady who went to buy her eggs from a farmer's wife she helped during a family crisis; this small-value purchase involves her in a journey to the very edge of the village but she does it 'to keep in touch'. It applies to the farmer who still obtains his fertilizer from the wholesaler his father used for making his purchases, even though the co-operative would give him better terms. He is waiting for the wholesaler's impending retirement before changing his supplier. These are the ways in which exchange relationships proceed according to a logic other than economic logic.

These exchanges are thus a way of 'keeping in touch', which ultimately means reinforcing social proximity and hence social cohesion. They may actually run counter to an economic logic. This occurs when the exchange entails a surcharge but it is most evident when there is not an exchange but a gift, the village fairs being a particularly good example.

The organization of the village fair is in the hands of a group of people each of whom knows 'what is to be done', which is the same thing every year. The members of the group give up their time to set up the hall (at the Catholic Association's fair it is an agricultural building belonging to one of the big Ervelinghem farms, prepared by several of the farmers), others borrow materials or give or sell primary produce at a low price (potatoes are supplied by the farmers, the butcher supplies meat at a special price) and some give their time and produce (Madam Vansteene supplies the ingredients for the pastries which she prepares with other ladies). On the day of the fair, the roles intermingle. Madame Smagghe prepares the chips and when her husband, her son and his family arrive for their meal, she comes to sit at the table with them. The person who has made the pastries will come to eat them, paying for them in the price of her meal.

Participation in the fair is a symbol of the integration of the village. It also creates the opportunity and the requirement for each person to maintain their position. For some, this participation is experienced as an explicit obligation: 'I would prefer to put my money on the table and not have to go', says Madame Potier, a teacher. However, not to attend the fair is to opt out of the collective life of the village. The other side of the coin is explained by Madame Martin who, not having an occupational position (her husband is an engineer), is somewhat outside the village and has friends in the nearby town. She does not go to the fair, she says, because 'its more for the village folk.'

For the organizers of the fair, the financial aims are insufficient to justify the event, so that meeting tends to become the explicit object. The same applies to the officials of various sporting associations (e.g. shooting, clay pigeon shooting, cycle touring, tennis, football.) Their action proceeds from a voluntary project of reinforcing the village community. The teacher, Monsieur Breton, is a club secretary who wants 'people to be less inward-looking' and believes that 'they should be promoters or at least participants.' This sometimes gives rise to misunderstandings, even conflicts, between different categories of members; between those for whom the encounter and the well-being are more important than the activity and those for whom the club exists to provide services which allow them to engage in their favourite leisure activity. A conflict arose within the cycle-touring club, between those who wanted to ride and win and some officials who wanted the greatest possible participation at outings. Similarly, at the football club, the idea of the game varies between the middle-class members and working-class youths.

Freely provided services are likewise a non-economic alternative – power. This power takes the form of 'noteworthiness' for the people who are the most dedicated, which leads quite naturally to the exercise of local institutional political power. The leader bases his authority on his generosity. The role of associative life in the constitution of political power is demonstrated negatively by the example of one of the leading opponents to the present mayor in the 1977 municipal elections; this person was the leader of an association which he had helped to found. Having been soundly beaten in the elections, he appeared disappointed by the lack of recognition by the voters and gave up his association responsibilities. On the other side, we were told 'if the mayor is elected, it's because he is helpful to people.' To a certain extent, this makes the municipality the expression of village solidarity, but it is an expression distorted by the capacity of the communal institution and the national modes of political expression. In other words, the cleavages between political parties are still to be found, albeit in attenuated form.

Of course, social distinctions are not totally unlike those which pertain outside the village. Differences of income and occupational status are firmly entrenched, as are contrasts of political opinion. However, relationships in the village are confused by the multiplicity of relationships through which the inhabitants are known to each other. The cleavages imposed by occupational hierarchies come after identification in terms of kin-group membership. Even new arrivals without any previous links with the village, provided they give tokens of membership of the collective, will be given recognition in terms of multiple and criss-crossing identifications. The formula 'he's not proud' summarizes both acceptance of the new arrival by the collective and the obscuring of differences which could threaten its cohesion. Madame Tison (a clerical worker like her husband) speaks of his friends like this: 'Perhaps we do have affinities. We get on really well with them. The two couples we know as friends have a higher social position than we do. We feel at ease with them perhaps because of the sport aspect, very straightforward people, we get on very well together . . . they aren't trapped in their surroundings.' There is also a saying in Ervelinghem that 'the workers are not real workers' because of their rural origins, although the village has long since grown accustomed to those who work elsewhere.

This means that social cohesion does not depend solely on

proximity of status between the members of the collective but also on the more or less compulsory affirmation of its necessity. The unanimity of the villages has to be stated and repeated with increasing frequency as the frameworks of solidarity disappear and are replaced by the apparatuses of the State. The same applies to the factors leading to fragmentation. The village 'excludes' those who do not recognize this. A gift or a service is more a sign of belonging than an economic reality. The ones who are excluded are those who do not recognize this symbol. This is evoked by Monsieur Valdon: 'When someone refuses, they're never asked again.' To refuse to render a service or accept a service is to make oneself a stranger. One can certainly continue to live, and even live well, in the village, but as a stranger, apart from local relationships.

The village would therefore appear to be like a community which creates and perpetuates itself through local exchanges. It is through these exchanges that the hierarchies of prestige and local differentiation are constituted. In this respect, the village appears to its inhabitants as the locus of meaning. Local exchanges, whether formal or informal matters little, involve material production which is not always very voluminous but which invariably carries great symbolic weight. The distinction frequently evoked by villagers between 'those who say hello' and 'those who don't say hello' is one of many signs which marks the boundary between the inside and outside of the community.

This outside signifies the threat of the breakdown of cohesion. It implies the transfer of the guarantee of solidarity to the State. The local society defends itself by maintaining the local forms of guarantee of social cohesion and sometimes by opposing State intervention very explicitly. Ervelinghem municipality's rejection of a *Plan d'Occupation des Sols* (Land Use Plan) can be interpreted in this way. Statization is nevertheless the dominant phenomenon. The social hierarchy is increasingly traced along the lines of external occupational or national political hierarchies. The maintenance of local forms of social cohesion tends to be a consequence of discourse or to occur in imported institutions like clubs. 'Participation' or 'conviviality' become the explicit objectives of these structures of regrouping.

The concrete reality of the village, and one could add the suburb or any other collective, involves overlap between the various types of exchange so that State control merges with local collective restraints; hence the misunderstandings between different categories of inhabitants, misunderstandings which do not present a common life but which sometimes lead to conflicts. Is the myth of the village as a classless society anything more than the ideology which allows certain fractions of the middle class to ensure their local hegemony? Is not the more or less explicit anti-Statism both the condition for another form of solidarity and the price paid to the State for the local concession which then allows certain fractions of classes to intervene by delegation? The need, therefore, is to examine more closely the practices of those who do not 'play the game' – who do not say hello in the street, who refuse to provide services, who reject family identity, who only play football to kick the ball or to beat the opposition and subsequently win money and who prefer night spots outside the village to their own fair – such attitudes clearly spell the end of village society and its absorption by the system of formal exchange and the apparatus of the State.

Conclusion

From the economic point of view, the opposition between the formal and informal sector is not justified: the rule of efficiency applies equally to both. Division of labour and specialization are just as manifest in the couple or between friends as in industrial production. If the informal–formal distinction and hence the question of relationships or the transition between the two sectors has any meaning, it can only be by reference to the State. The formal sector is organized by the State, whose intervention consists of statutory deductions from income but also in activities of organizational control or prevention. The State can ensure that risks are covered, guarantee the satisfactory completion of exchanges and present itself as the arbiter and place of appeal in cases of conflict. To define the informal sector exclusively as the opposite of the formal sector is corrrect insofar as the State is absent. However, such a definition lacks precision to the extent that it allows one to suppose that control, organization and guarantees do not exist in this sector. These functions are also fulfilled in the informal sector but by other means, e.g. it is the personalized and non-specialized knowledge of the participants which provides guarantees for exchange, in particular through the role of kinship or the local collectivity.

Similarly, as far as the symbolic significance of exchange is concerned, the same rationality is present in the formal and informal sector. The social cohesion of the collective is at stake.

Exchanges ensure this cohesion, whilst at the same time cohesion makes it possible for them to occur. If not, there is conflict. In this reading, moreover, it is the State which divides the shares between the two sectors. Indeed, there are two types of social regulation; on the one side, the State and the law, on the other, kinship and the constraints of proximity. Conflicts can certainly arise but it is the regulation of these conflicts which differs. Instances of social regulation are guarantees of social cohesion *vis à vis* the exterior, with which exchanges are possible (only they are of a different type) and within the interior of the collectivity itself.

Certainly in reality there are few situations in which the activities can be assigned strictly to one or the other sector. To classify the activity of enterprises in the formal sector and domestic activities in the informal sector is no more than a repetition of commonsense categories which lead to the belief that they obey different rationalities a priori. The reality is ambivalent. Thus, the muncipal institution functions in the formal and the informal. The commune can clearly be assigned to the formal sector because it is a State apparatus but politics tends to make it function not simply according to institutional dispositions but also within the framework of the local exchange of services and client relationships.

In this sense, the village is certainly the ideal place for the informal sector, a type of social relationship which is distinct from capitalist relations of production and political relationships organized within the apparatus of the State. However, in the real village, State regulation and local regulation are intertwined.

The question, therefore, comes down to economic and political explanation of State intervention (Rosanvallon 1981).

Statization gaining ground over other types of regulation appears to be occurring. The extension of the large apparatuses of production involves specialization, individualization and hence reinforcement of general systems of guarantee and State constraints on solidarity. The informal sector (if the use of this terminology may still be allowed) is thoroughly dominated by the formal State sector. Only with difficulty can it be analysed independently of this relationship. Can it still claim any kind of specific organization? Is the general movement towards statization irresistible? Are the practices which continue to fall outside this process a form of resistance to the domination of certain kinds of social relationship or are they simply the consequence of the ever-increasing disjunction between State regulation and provisions? Could not statization in its turn be bounded by the internationalization of exchange and organizations?

A reply to these questions must first involve a break with certain current taxonomies. How can one explain the development of certain practices, e.g. DIY, and the growing attraction of these types of question for researchers? The skilled practices which are now classed as informal, self-production, mutual aid and family sector are by no means new, especially to the working class and, naturally to agricultural workers. Why should they be innovative or the medium of a transformation when it is certain fractions of the middle class who are fending for themselves or creating certain forms of community action? Does not the choice of analytic categories itself depend on this domination by the formal State sector? Perhaps one can find here an explanation of why social and cultural phenomena often appear as residues of the economic approach and thus come to be defined according to its contours.

Survival, accommodation or the beginning of a reverse movement: the informal sector can be all three at the same time. The question of the State and statization can only be posed with great difficulty when it is put so frequently from the point of view of the State. When it is the State which valorizes the informal sector, it is essential to see it as something more than a paradox.

Notes

The reflections presented in this chapter derive from research carried out under the auspices of the ATP of the CNRS, *Observation du Changement Social et Culturel,* during 1981, in collaboration with Marc Foudrignier. The chapter was translated by Howard H. Davis.

1   SMIC (Salaire Minimum Interprofessionel de Croissance) was 19.03F on 1 May 1982.
2   HLM (*Habitations à loyer modéré*): low-rent public housing blocks.

6

Household Work Strategies in Economic Recession
R.E. Pahl and Claire Wallace

Post-industrial Society, De-industrialization and Domestic Production

Speculation about the future of industrial society was encouraged by the observation, widely made in the 1960s, that the motor of industrial development could be maintained with fewer workers. This led to a focus on the shift in the *nature* of employment: jobs in the manufacturing sector may decline, but many considered that the service sector would then expand to take up the slack. For a time this indeed seemed likely. The expansion of education, health and welfare in the 1960s encouraged commentators to extrapolate such an expansion of employment to other new spheres: whole new sectors of service employment were envisaged. This shift from manufacturing to the service sector was compared with the shift from the primary, mainly agricultural, sector into the secondary or manufacturing sector at an earlier period. However, it was thought that the transition might be painful – particularly for individuals – as it seemed unlikely that displaced male factory workers could be readily retrained as office workers or computer programmers. One of the most convincing and widely noticed accounts of this process was provided by Daniel Bell in his book *The Coming of Post-Industrial Society*. Basically optimistic in tone, Bell foresaw the development of a new, creative, knowledge society, which would be 'better' in many important respects than the traditional industrial society which it displaced:

A post-industrial society is based on services. Hence, it is a game between persons. What counts is not raw muscle power, or energy, but information. The central person is the professional, for he is equipped, by his education and training, to provide the kinds of skills which are increasingly demanded in the post-industrial society. If an industrial society is defined by the quantity of goods as marking a standard of living, the post-industrial society is defined by the quality of life as measured by the services and amenities — health, education and the arts — which are now deemed desirable and possible for everyone. (Bell 1973: 127)

The concept of post-industrial society stimulated considerable debate (Kumar 1978), which in a very few years became increasingly irrelevant. The shift from a focus on post-industrial society as a liberation to a concern with deindustrialization as a burden took place in the mid 1970s. Few saw deindustrialization as a game: as the basic industries in certain traditional industrial areas of Britain collapsed, a fear developed that the global processes of capital accumulation would harm disproportionately whole nations, of which Britain seemed well set to be the best example. The rise and fall of regional prosperity was a well-documented and almost acceptable aspect of the economic history of most industrial nations. The possibility that what had, in the past, been seen as a 'regional problem' would now be a national problem had alarming implications (Blackaby 1979; Jenkins & Sherman 1979). Most economists and politicians responded by suggesting practical and pragmatic ways in which employment in manufacturing could be maintained or shifted to new growth industries, like micro-electronics.

Clearly there was a need for some fresh thinking and one of the lively contributors to the next wave of scholarly debate was Gershuny, who directly took issue with Bell, vigorously arguing that the service economy was a myth. He claimed that time-series data relating to certain expenditure categories showed that the trend was moving away from expenditure on services to expenditure on goods (Gershuny 1977). He later developed this argument in detail in *After Industrial Society?* (1978). Gershuny claimed that people were spending more on manufactured goods in order to produce services for themselves. He cited national data to demonstrate, for example, the decline of public-transport expenditure contrasted with the increase in expenditure on private cars. Whilst it is possible to argue that such calculations are not entirely free from ambiguities of interpretation (e.g. how does one calculate the expenditure on motorways – is it more for public or private transport?), Gershuny certainly presented a powerful case. If people were using goods to produce their own services in their own time and in their own homes, reports about the death of British industry were, perhaps, much exaggerated. However, it did not, of course, follow that it would necessarily be *British* industry which would supply the cars, washing machines, television sets, video recorders and electric drills which would keep people so busily occupied. Nor, of course, does it follow that people's capacity to acquire such goods would continue to expand indefinitely.

The model developed by Gershuny did provide hope for industrial societies caught in stagflation in the late 1970s. However, he was not simply concerned to provide a more critical analysis of production and consumption; he also recognized that the final production of many services, and indeed goods, was increasingly taking place in the home, which would inevitably alter social relations. He suggested that there would be 'a change from a society of masters and servants (both in personal consumption and in the manner of provision for that consumption), to a society of consumers – still unequal in the quantity of consumption, perhaps, but increasingly equal in the way in which the consumption is provided' (Gershuny 1977: 113). With appropriate caution, Gershuny recognized that what he was describing was 'only a trend'. He suggested that 'a new sort of class structure' would develop, based on a technocratic elite controlling a largely undifferentiated mass 'almost entirely separated from the wider economic system, being involved principally in the production of final services, by direct labour (i.e. by the final consumer) in their own homes'.

Whilst we would not disagree with the emphasis placed upon the domestic production of goods and services based on the private ownership of domestic capital equipment, the *sociological* implications need to be explored with some caution. More recently, Saunders has put forward another model based on the provision of consumption facilities. The sectoral divisions he discerns in the sphere of consumption are between those who own their homes, cars and domestic equipment and those who rent or are dependent on public provision. Saunders suggests that the privatization of the means of consumption which began with the mass ownership of private cars has now extended to dwellings, now owned by more than 50 per cent of households, and is likely to apply to health and welfare services too as unions take out policies with BUPA on behalf of their members (Saunders 1983). Clearly, Gershuny's emphasis on the private, domestic provision of goods and services has theoretical implications in other directions from those which he himself developed. Indeed, his initial model was to be further refined.

From an emphasis on the home as a unit of production (which followed very closely a position developed by Burns [1977]), Gershuny took his argument a stage further by postulating a third arena of service production, namely the 'informal' or 'underground' economy. He extended the concept of 'the home' to include the household or communal economy and he suggested that a conventional view of economic development, passing from primary production through manufacturing to services in a one-way line of progress, was 'wholly misleading' (1979: 9). Rather, he claimed 'that technical innovations, combined to produce a rather less tidy pattern of development'. He suggested that there were six possible transitions of production between the three economies he had formulated (figure 6.1).

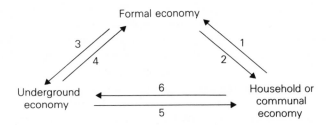

Figure 6.1   The six transformations

Gershuny used this highly simplified model to demonstrate that at *specific* times and under *specific* circumstances (of technology, labour supply and public regulation and organization) which pertain to the production of any commodity, certain sorts of transformations will develop. Overall, of course, household/communal production has been in decline as activities and functions have been taken over by the market or the State welfare system, but there is no a priori reason why such a decline should necessarily continue. He was also careful to say that the growth of household production of services was merely *inferred* from the growth of household ownership of domestic capital goods. People might own power tools, but, at that stage, Gershuny was not in a position to demonstrate that they actually used them. His later work on time budgets allowed him to argue the point with greater confidence. Work on time budgets is obviously less likely to provide information on the question of the informal provision of goods and services and it was evident that Gershuny had considerable problems in moving from his aggregated analysis of consumer behaviour to the more specific analysis of households differentially placed in the social structure. He seemed more concerned to argue at a general level that substantial productive activity was taking place outside the formal economy and, hence, was unmeasured.

Perhaps the unmeasured was growing in a way which would off-set the manifest decline of the measured. It was an appealing prospect which shifted the focus from the macro concerns of the economist to the more locally grounded work of sociologists, social anthropologists and the more empirically-minded students of local labour markets.[1] In 1979, Gershuny and Pahl extended the notion of transformations between the three spheres as ways of showing shifts in the manner of the provision of services to ways of getting work done. They argued that it was necessary 'to enlarge our notion of work to embrace a much wider set of activities than are usually considered in this context' (1979:128).

This focus on the notion of work was a radical departure from the line of thinking which Gershuny had been developing. The authors of the joint paper emphasized that work took place in other spheres than simply the formal economy:

> Evidently the permutations between the three spheres for different members of a household over time can get very complex. But it is this very complexity that has to be explored and in which new mixes or choices have to be created. Job-sharing, seen in this light, means much more than just shorter hours in the formal economy; *which* work in *which* economy for *which* member of the household for *how long* are basically the questions at issue. (1979:134).

The authors concluded that: 'We cannot segregate work in the different spheres to different categories of people'. Concerned with these other forms of work, Pahl suggested that 'a man with his own tools, his own time and a long-stop income in the form of unemployment pay may not be in such a vulnerable position' in the 1980s as his unemployed counterpart might have been 50 years earlier. Somewhat rashly, he went on to suggest that 'his *work* identity can still be maintained even if his employment identity is in abeyance' (1980:5). Two case studies elaborated in that contribution seemed to confirm the notion that there were a variety of ways of getting by and that what in one case was clearly a coping strategy of the poor could, in another case, be a voluntary choice, allowing a greater flexibility in the use of time and labour and a greater feeling of satisfaction through the greater personal control of the labour process.

In what follows, we want to take issue with much of the foregoing, which, in the light both of changing trends and more detailed empirical research, seems less compelling. Much of the work in the late 1970s was grounded in a very weak empirical base: we are now able to report on much more wide-ranging and also more detailed empirical research.

Attempts at a more macro level to measure the 'hidden economy' have indicated that, if it is growing at all, it is growing in a patchy and erratic way. Indeed, there is some indication that it has passed its peak, its size being associated with the amount of cash available for redistribution (O'Higgins 1980). Gershuny has argued that he is not presenting a unilinear or evolutionary model but is concerned with the consequences of the interaction of processes at given conjunctures, although there is perhaps an unintended evolutionary tone to his work. He was certainly right to emphasize the privatization of consumption and this was an important point of departure for further work, but there were unstated assumptions in his model which should perhaps be made explicit. In particular, much of his analysis is in a highly aggregated form, hiding important differences. He also avoids specifying any *essential* motor of change, although we infer that technological innovation is more important than distributions of capital and politico-legal arrangements in producing distinctive forms of service provision. There tends to be an implicit optimism in his work, which assumes a benign State and limitless economic growth and expansion. It is important to disaggregate technological innovation: the domestic washing machine is equated as just another piece of domestic technology, to be seen in the same way as a gadget to allow blip games to be played on the television screen. There is surely an analytical distinction of some value between a piece of technology which enables what has to be done to be done more efficiently or even more cheaply and a piece of technology which occupies the mind whilst one's wits go wool-gathering in front of a television screen. It is surely necessary to know who buys and who uses the domestic gadgetry and the distributional consequences of whatever benefits they may produce.

Burns and Gershuny in their detailed documentation of work done in the household or 'domestic economy' unwittingly, perhaps, suggest that a common set of processes produce a similar result – mass consumers, as Gershuny describes them. This is too generalized. We show in detail that privatized consumption can be created by both increasing affluence *and* increasing poverty: richer people may be spending more time in the domestic environment with their electronic gadgetry but poorer people may be privatized for opposite reasons. They cannot afford to buy services from the formal economy should they wish to do so. A conflation of processes of both choice and constraint would be confusing and would suggest an implausible consensus on goals and values. The motor of change in the way services are provided will depend on class relations and on values as much as on the factors Gershuny adduces. It may, indeed, be more economical, for example, to buy meat in bulk and fruit and vegetables in season to put in a deep-freeze, but this implies not just the resources to acquire capital equipment but also the flexible cash flow required to run it effectively. The logic of higher productivity in the service sector may lead to self-service stores with lower prices rather than corner shops which allow credit, provide social supports and sanctions for saving through Christmas clubs and similar schemes. It is commonplace to note that innovations and more profitable ways of doing things are not universally progressive in their effects. The distributional effects of the self-service economy, postulated by Gershuny, need to be worked through very carefully.

There are alternative ways of providing services or in getting work done and people may be just as 'rationalistic' or 'economistic' in their diverse courses of action. The differences are based on their distinctive value systems and it cannot be claimed without argument that one is equivocally better than another. We are not making this point in a purely negative sense: our emphasis on values is at the heart of the position we wish to develop. It seems not unfair to characterize the work of Burns, Gershuny and others during the 1970s and early 1980s as more narrowly economistic than many would now accept. It did, however, serve the valuable function of prompting questions about the different values of different social groups and about the patterns and consequences of distinctive household work strategies. There was a real danger, evident in Pahl's paper of 1980, that unemployment would be misperceived as liberating people in order to trap them in their homes. This was because the focus of that earlier research was on the detailed and precise mechanisms of how people were coping, or getting by, under difficult economic circumstances. It was based on highly selective case studies from which it was not possible to generalize to larger populations.

Curiously, this limited view of the role of informal work can also be found in some Marxist analysis, which attempts to relate it to the overall process of capital accumulation. Such Marxists argue that informal work is largely a response by people reeling from the results of the universal and homogenous process of the restructuring of capital. We cannot accept such a simple deterministic model. Our understanding of the process of capital restructuring is that it is very uneven in its effects and certain categories of people are able to improve their material conditions substantially. Indeed, some can improve their living standards through engaging in informal work precisely because they are also benefiting from the restructuring process. Similarly, the Marxist–functionalist notion of capitalism's 'needs', a conveniently catch-all phrase, is also too narrow. Capitalism 'needs' a cheap work-force but it also 'needs' consumers with sufficient wages to fuel profits. Capitalism in the advanced societies is certainly not a system where most of the people are losing most of the time. Informal work can both lower the cost of the work-force and can also fuel expansion if people have more needs through engaging or wishing to engage in informal work, but this is not a particularly Marxist argument.

To conclude this initial introduction to our argument, we may note that two main themes stimulated our work; namely, the decline of manufacturing employment and an understanding of the complexities of forms of service provision, particularly as this relates to activities of household members within their local areas. Evidently, the growth of domestic technology is a new and significant trend which deserves careful analysis, both for its implications for class and gender relations and for its impact on forms of employment. The imputed growth of unpaid work of household members in the home can be seen to be related both to affluence and to the recession and the growth of a pauperized unemployed element. Any notion of 'the' household acting in a universal and distinctive way is surely hard to sustain, but without detailed analyses of specific household work practices, the argument could not be developed. This encouraged us to develop a deeper understanding of all forms of work in context, by focusing on the specific work practices of a sample of households in a given labour market.

The Retreat from the 'Three Economies'

When 20 per cent of all manufacturing output is lost in three years, it hardly has to be demonstrated that the economy is undergoing some kind of fundamental change. The fact that the same or a greater number of motor cars can be produced with substantially fewer workers or can be imported much more cheaply than they can be made in Britain, is not a comfort to those without employment. Without an earned income, people are evidently unable to enjoy economic benefits, whether self-provided or otherwise.

Early in our research we discarded the notion of a separate, so-called informal economy and we cannot rehearse all our arguments for doing so here (Pahl 1984a, 1984b). However, we may mention that we focused on the social relations of work and argued that the fact that an employer in not fully declaring his income or not fulfilling his obligations under Employment Protection legislation certainly modifies the relationship between capital and wage labour but does not, in essence, change those social relations in any fundamental way and certainly does not put them in a separate economy. Similarly, whether the self-employed do or do not declare all their income to the Inland Revenue does not determine whether they are in one economy or another. Once the unexceptional point is made that not all domestic activity is counted or analysed by economists, there is little more analytical value in the term informal economy. We do, nevertheless, distinguish three kinds of work which we relate to three distinctive spheres.

In the first sphere, the social relations of work are determined by the way the formal demand for labour is constructed or determined: wage-labour may be recorded or unrecorded, protected or unprotected and the social relations of wage-labour may be more or less modified or moderated by the actions of the State. Where wages and salaries are exchanged for labour, we argue that the nature of work is intrinsically the same whether or not that work is formally recorded in the national accounts. Within this sphere there may be petty-commodity production with its distinctive social relations of work and which again has its undeclared, darker side or shadow. How far this 'shadow' wage-labour and *a fortiori* petty-commodity production is accurately recorded in national accounts is to a degree arbitrary, depending on the State policies at the time.

In the second sphere of domestic work, we refer to all the production and consumption of goods and services undertaken by members of the household within the household for themselves, irrespective of the pattern of motivations determining these activities and the pattern of constraints under which they may or may not be done. Here the emphasis is on who does the work and where it is done. This is essentially the sphere of self-provisioning.

The third sphere refers to all those activities carried out by members of other households, whether or not they are related to them. By and large this work does not depend on payment, or, if it does, the payment is not based on strictly market principles. More likely, goods and services are exchanged according to norms of reciprocity, which may, in particular localities, be extremely forceful and binding. However, again, we are concerned with all this activity, irrespective of the pattern of motivation or the pattern of constraints under which the work may or may not be done. Here the work is defined by the distinctive social relationships and local context in which it is embedded.

These three spheres are emphatically not necessarily mutually exclusive, nor should they be considered to relate to distinct physical contexts. Evidently petty commodity production very often takes place in the household and reciprocal exchanges can take place at the formal workplace. However, the analytical distinctions between these three spheres are important as means of understanding more clearly all forms of work taking place in distinct territories. The intention is to understand how these three spheres of work interrelate and how the whole assemblage of work in distinctive milieux relate to the restructuring of capital and the current economic recession.

We began by expecting to be able to document the shifts between these distinctive spheres of work as households developed more ways of getting by under difficult circumstances. As will be explained below, this expectation was not validated.

It is important to avoid too mechanistic an approach. People's work practices differ substantially – even under broadly the same material conditions. Evidently, what people do is as much dependent on their cultural values as on the exigencies of the local labour market, the current practices of the political system or the opportunities presented by technological innovation. Happily, people do not respond uniformly and puppet-like to oscillations in the cycles of capital accumulation or to Kondratieff cycles of product innovation and development. On the other hand, patterns of behaviour are not entirely voluntaristic and independent of material conditions. This dialectical interaction is the essence of the process that structures social formations. A realistic research strategy demands some simplification and our present position is to disaggregate household work practices into specific tasks done by members of specific households in specific contexts. In this way we ground our theoretical argument in detailed empirical observation and analysis. The work practices of households are perhaps too frequently disaggregated into the economic activity of individuals, as if the social relations of the household and the context in which households live were of little importance.

The Context for Household Work Strategies

A concern with the self-provisioning work undertaken by households without putting those households in context may well produce generalizations which mask crucial variations. As we remarked above, one of the inevitable weaknesses of the aggregated data is that households are plucked out of context, or the context has to be aggregated up to a level at which important local differences cease to have significance.

Whilst each household is in some way unique in the way it allocates its time and resources to get work done, distinctive patterns emerge, dominated, of course, by the need to get money from land (rent), capital (interest), labour (wages) or the State (benefits and allowances). Hence the markets for land, labour and capital and the nature, range and style of State intervention and provision crucially determine the potential for household work strategies. Furthermore, these factors change in emphasis and importance over time: the changing market for land and the changing availability of skilled labour may be crucially important in, as it were, 'allowing' a given style of household work strategy to emerge. Once a given pattern has emerged with its distinctive practices, this in turn helps to reflect back upon and partially create the material conditions for a later period. However, it should be emphasized that the centrality of the household work strategy is not intended to imply that the actions of households are the central determinants of economic and social life. It is simply that we see the actual *practices* of households as being a useful tracer of the effects of the restructuring of capital in specific milieux. The same process of investment can have different consequences in different milieux and this is both revealed in and caused by household work strategies.

In order to put our detailed knowledge of household behaviour into its material context, we made parallel studies of the local context, the Isle of Sheppey in Kent, a detailed account of which would be complex and lengthy.[2] The Island presents a distinctive pattern of opportunities and constraints and it is to this that households must accommodate more or less passively.

Different layers of investment on the Isle of Sheppey took place at different historical periods and in different sectors of the local economy. The interaction of these flows of capital into land, housing and industry created a distinctive local political economy based on distinct social milieux in different parts of the Island. The involvement of the State in directing capital and providing infrastructure is also important.

During the eighteenth and early nineteenth centuries, Sheppey consisted of a collection of agricultural villages with the ancient Borough of Queenborough established as a military fortification to defend the strategic site where the Thames and the Medway meet (Daly 1904). Further along the coast, where the water was deeper at Sheerness, ships had been manufactured for the Royal Navy since the seventeenth century, but most of this part of the Island had been plagued with malaria and was still largely uninhabitable. Early dockyard workers lived on hulks moored in the estuary. From 1826, the Admiralty reconstructed the dockyard at Sheerness (Buck 1981), the nearby marshes were drained and the first houses were constructed from materials said to have been removed unofficially from the dockyard itself. Later periods of expansion in the dockyard, such as in the 1850s and later in the 1900s, brought an influx of low-paid workers with a large measure of security of tenure. Most of the housing in Sheerness was built at these periods to satisfy a growing demand for privately rented accommodation: in the middle of the nineteenth century, up to 69 per cent of the work-force was employed in the dockyard. When steam ships were introduced into the British Navy in the 1850s, new skilled workers came to the Island and new hierarchies within the dockyard were mirrored by the size of houses that were built. Sheerness began as a site to house dockyard employees and as a military garrison but gradually its importance as a servicing centre continued to evolve so that by the end of the nineteenth century, at the height of British imperialism, it was a prosperous commercial township.

The investment of the State had encouraged the expansion of the dockyard with a town alongside and provided scope for speculation in private housing development, but by the early twentieth century, with the investment of commercial and service capital,

Sheerness had become a town with a dockyard alongside it.

In other parts of the Island, patterns of settlement followed different imperatives. An earlier phase of capitalist restructuring in the primary sector produced a collapse in the market for home-produced food, creating an agricultural depression in the latter years of the nineteenth century; land prices depreciated and the small villages and hamlets in the east of the Island began their decline. Marginal agricultural land, such as that on Sheppey and also in other areas of South and East England, was purchased by specula-tors, who endeavoured to sell it for residential development in the form of small plots of land (Hardy & Ward, forthcoming). This process was produced by a combination of factors, which included improved transportation, particularly rail, the new prosperity of the lower-middle-class artisans and traders (who were nevertheless in a marginal position between the private rented sector and owner occupation in London), the continued growth of the holiday industry and, finally, the ideology of independence through proper-ty ownership, all of which helped to provide a market for the new speculators to exploit. A modest injection of petty bourgeois capital into land was a pretty thin layer of investment and most of it did not turn into housing until the 1960s. This fragmentation of land into small plots with many different owners shaped the pattern of land speculation and development in a later period and allowed the possibility of a distinctive self-building household work strategy.

Thus, there were three waves of investment: State investment in the dockyard, private capital investment in new industries and investment in communications, housing and land. A fourth flow of capital to affect the Island was associated with the holiday trade. During the 1920s and 1930s, there was some development of the most far-flung stretches of land at Leysdown into caravan and camping sites for summer visitors. These sites were developed after the Second World War by entrepreneurs with greater capital resources into holiday camps and became a popular resort for the working class of London in the 1950s.

It was this interweaving of layers of capital investment in different sectors since the nineteenth century which produced the geography of a distinctive local political economy and has provided the setting within which distinctive household work strategies emerged at specific conjunctures. In terms of present-day employ-ment, it is clear that a heavy dependence on manufacturing and a poorly developed service and small business sector makes the Island acutely dependent on the fluctuating market for its manufactured products. In 1983, the level of unemployment was hovering around 20 per cent. A survey of its main employers in 1981 had demonstrated that their vulnerability was likely to continue: if economic conditions improved, employers were likely to put in more capital equipment in the hope of maintaining jobless growth in productivity, and if the economic climate did not improve, many saw the likelihood of closure or of moving their plants overseas. By and large, wage rates were very modest: skilled manual workers were earning around £120 a week and semi-skilled workers around £85 a week at the time of the survey in 1981. Twenty per cent of the jobs in the largest twenty-five employers of labour were done by women. Increasingly, employers in manufacturing industries prefer to employ female factory workers: they receive lower rates of pay, being classified as semi-skilled workers no matter how objectively skilled the work they do may be, and they are also more likely to be employed on a part-time basis with the greater insecurity that this implies. Insofar as one can generalize about typical households of ordinary working people, it does seem that not only does the local labour market depend increasingly on female labour in the factories, but households are increasingly dependent on the extra income provided by a further earner.

We may summarize the position for the workers of the Isle of Sheppey as being extremely precarious. Low wages and the need for multiple earners for households to get by puts an added squeeze on those without employment. Most people on the Island find employment through friends and relatives. Evidently that is easier if members of the household are already in employment, since they are much more likely to find or to hear of employment for their partners or older children than those who are unemployed. Employment tends to generate further employment; unemployment tends to generate further unemployment. Wives of the unemployed tend to find it not worth their while to carry on working when their earnings are offset against the unemployment and/or supplementary benefits to their husbands.

The particular characteristics of the local employment situation make it extremely difficult for young people to find work. With no office development and an underdeveloped service sector, job opportunities are limited and most employers prefer to employ a married woman part time than what may unfairly seem to be an untried and risky school-leaver. Hence, few young people are likely to be able to afford to establish their own household for many years after leaving school. Many are, therefore, forced to stay at home and play some part in the work strategy of their parents' household.

The local labour market, therefore, encourages multiple-earner households by the levels of wages, the opportunities for employment for married women and the lack of long-term job prospects for young people. In certain male occupations, such as stevedores, which are highly paid but which make less demands in terms of time and physical effort, more time and energy are available for other activities. This provides a distinctive type of household headed by a manual worker with time, resources and very often craft skills: it is perhaps unsurprising that when these households have multiple earners they are particularly well-placed to engage in a wide range of domestic activities.

There are other aspects of the local context which should also be emphasized. House prices on the Island are substantially lower than on the mainland.[3] The differential in house prices is greater than the differential in wages. Furthermore, there is an existing stock of dwellings available for owner-occupation due to the construction of housing for dockyard workers already described A programme of private refurbishing, making use of what grants were available, enabled people to get better accommodation for a given expenditure than was possible at that level of income in other contexts. In this sense, dwellings in less adequate condition can be seen as a resource to be exploited by households to improve both their existing living conditions and their capacity for capital accumulation.

There has also been a tradition on the Island since the early years of the century, as has been indicated, for people to acquire land and to build their own dwellings, either with their own labour, with the help of colleagues or by commissioning a local builder to do it for them (Pahl & Wallace 1982). Sometimes ownership was ambiguous: determined or devious people could get access to land in a way not normally possible in many localities. Public services and facilities were often rudimentary: sewerage and street lighting were slow in coming and the roads are still not all made up. It is evident that this is very fertile ground for the development of a flourishing petty bourgeois ideology of domesticity and an inward-looking privatization, where members of the household looked to their own particular dwelling to provide themselves with what Giddens (1981), following Laing, refers to as a sense of ontological security.

As a result of these and other factors, the Island has a singularly high level of home ownership. In addition, the local authority is supporting a policy of sale of its own stock of dwellings to individual households. It is perhaps therefore not surprising that seven out of ten households on the Island have their own homes: there will inevitably be substantial home refurbishing and mainte-nance. The material and ideological encouragement for such activity is substantial: Sheppey is a frontier of privatization.

There is also very strong material encouragement for the private acquisition of the means of transport. The Island is not well served by public transport. Most of the services are centred in Sheerness at the north-west tip of the Island. However, the hospital is at Minster in the centre of the Island and, in the summer, the beaches at Leysdown at the east end of the Island are the focus for discos and various forms of live entertainment. Elderly people tend to retire to Minster or to the east end of the Island and this creates a further demand for transport. There is only one combined road and rail bridge connecting the Island with the mainland and this inflexibil-ity, coupled with a poor rail and bus service, makes car ownership highly desirable, if not essential. Travel to mainland towns for entertainment and shopping is possible but inconvenient by public transport and attendance for specialist medical treatment at the larger and better equipped hospitals is almost impossible by public transport from the more scattered settlements away from the main train stations at Queenborough and Sheerness. The lack of State or public provision forces people to private provision.

Overall, the class composition of the Island is much the same as that for the country as a whole, but that is more an artefact of the Registrar-General's system of classifying occupations. There are very few top managers or professionals on the Island, but there are enough relatively senior people in business and industry for the higher class categories to be proportionately similar to the national average.

The Local and the National

We did not do our detailed empirical investigation on the Isle of Sheppey because we felt that it was in any sense typical or a microcosm of a larger whole. Rather, we argued that specific practices must be seen in context and this context needs to be meaningful and salient to the people concerned. Every area is to some degree distinctive and it was relatively easier to isolate this distinctiveness by choosing an island. Now we need to consider not whether Sheppey is distinct from a more general pattern, but rather to ask how far trends and tendencies we have detected on the Isle of

Sheppey are also found at a national level. We refer briefly to the national pattern of unemployment and of self-provisioning work by households.

The growth of unemployment

The decline of job opportunities in the formal economy is, unhappily, too well-known to require much documentation. The national level is a number of percentage points below Sheppey, but all the indications are that the national unemployment rate is approaching that of Sheppey rather than the other way round.

Deindustrialization in Britain continues at a steady rate. One and a half million jobs were lost in the manufacturing sector between September 1979 and December 1982, a fall of 22 per cent. Jobs have also been lost in the service sector, but at a much lower rate – only a third of a million over the same period. Service industries most affected by job losses have been in transport, communications and the distributive trades. Those least affected have been insurance, banking, finance and business services, public administration and defence (Manpower Services Commission 1983). Unemployment rose from 5 per cent when the present Government took office in 1979 to 11.8 per cent at the end of 1982. These figures exclude school-leavers. Unemployment rates are expected to continue to rise. No region of the country has, as a region, such a high level of unemployment as the Isle of Sheppey. The Northern Region had a seasonally adjusted rate of 16.7 per cent in January 1983 and this was some three percentage points below that of Sheppey at that time. However, there are, of course, smaller, isolated parts of Britain's depressed cities and regions where the rate is substantially above that of Sheppey. As the MSC *Labour Market Quarterly Report* laconically puts it: 'The economic outlook continues to look uncertain and a continuation of the current fall in employment looks likely.' (MSC 1983: 1.)

The growth of work by households for themselves in their own homes

There is certainly evidence that do-it-yourself (DIY) has grown substantially in recent years. *The Economist* calculated that DIY is the fastest growing sector of the building industry: maintenance and repair grew by 16.5 per cent from 1978 to 1979, whereas the construction industry as a whole grew by only 4.5 per cent over the same period.[4] Another estimate, relating to the same period, suggested that DIY had increased by 25 per cent over the period, accounting for £1000 million of trade by 1979.[5] Evidence from the National Readership Survey on the readership of DIY magazines in 1974 (unfortunately the most recent available) shows that those households most likely to read these magazines are couples in their twenties and thirties who have completed their full-time education at the minimum age or very soon after. They are likely to be low-grade white-collar workers and skilled manual workers. These categories are well-represented on Sheppey.

Work Outside Employment on Sheppey

In the spring and summer of 1981, a one in nine sample survey of the Island produced information on 730 households. This sought to document all the forms of work undertaken by all household members. Involvement in formal employment was relatively straightforward to document, although attempts to get information on job history – particularly in terms of self-employment and periods of unemployment – added complexity. Men and women were interviewed alternately to avoid any discrimination or bias by gender. Gathering precise information on informal work and self-provisioning was obviously more difficult. We adopted a variety of strategies and in the case of self-provisioning carefully selected some 41 specific tasks and activities and asked those households that did the task, how frequently it was done (if appropriate), who did it (if it was done by a household member) and, if it was done outside the household, whether it was done formally or informally, paid or unpaid. This provided extremely detailed information, not only about the distribution of household work between the three spheres, but also about the domestic division of labour between men and women. Furthermore, we are able to relate a household's particular mix of work between the three spheres and the division of labour in self-provisioning alone. In this way we are able to discuss how the balance of all forms of work is changing.

In the summer of 1982, a selected proportion of the sample of households was contacted again for one, or sometimes two, further interviews. This part of the research programme yielded extremely rich qualitative data to set beside the more quantitative material deriving from the survey. It also enabled a more detailed and in-depth exploration of norms, values and attitudes of the selected households.

It is important to emphasize that we were not content to ask simply, as those doing similar work frequently do, 'who does the housework?'. Rather, this and all other spheres of activity were disaggregated into specific tasks and questions were asked about these, even though they might later be presented in an aggregated form, as we illustrate below.

Owing to limited space, we shall disregard the effects of changing household work strategies upon the relationships between genders. Findings related to this are reported in chapter 10 of *Divisions of Labour* (Pahl 1984a, in collaboration with S. Missiakoulis). In the following we shall proceed from a simplified – and certainly unrealistic – consensual model of the household.

So returning to the household as our unit of analysis, our first conclusion certainly supports the arguments of Burns & Gershuny: households do indeed carry out a remarkable amount of work for themselves in spheres where one might reasonable expect the task to be provided by a formal contractor. Table 6.1 shows that four out of five of all 730 households do their own painting and a quarter do plastering or fix the brakes on the car themselves. Perhaps more astonishingly, 56 households put in a reinforced steel joist (RSJ)

Table 6.1 Four tasks by the sphere of work in which they are done

| Task | Households which do the task (%) | Sphere in which task is done by households (%) | | | |
| | | Within household | Informally outside household | | In formal sector [a] |
			Paid	Unpaid	
Painting	96.7	83	6	3	7
Plastering	49.7	51	9	8	31
Mending broken window	52.9	53	9	3	34
Fixing brakes on car	54.5	46	8	5	40

[a] We have had to assume that the answer 'landlord', 'builder', or 'firm' implies that the work was done 'officially' with all VAT, Inland Revenue and other obligations appropriately observed.

themselves – more than those who arranged for the job to be done by a contractor (31) or informally through neighbours or kin (12).[6]

The tasks listed in table 6.1 were carefully selected to explore the putative shifts between the formal, informal and communal spheres. They were among the most likely activities that could be paid for informally, whether or not in cash, to people outside the household, but not in their formal capacities. If there *was* evidence of a shift to informal provision in the black economy, we would expect it to be reflected here. In the event, we could not show that this was happening.

Turning now to informal work outside the household, respondents were asked an open question about all the other unpaid, informal work they might do for friends and neighbours.[7] This covered a very wide range of activities from voluntary work to baby-sitting, and we were reassured to discover that there was no important task which members of one household might do for another which we had not asked about more precisely on the interview schedule. A quarter of our sample claimed to do at least one other informal task outside the household.[8]

Further questions were asked, designed to elicit information about other informal work that was paid. In response to the question: 'Do you do any own-account work for extra money?', four per cent of the sample replied in the affirmative; a further one per cent of our respondents acknowledged that they did other work for an employer or firm for which they got paid (presumably in cash or some other informal way). Analytically this is what we term 'shadow wage labour': i.e. payments may or may not be declared to the Inland Revenue. Our respondents were alternately male and female, as we have said, and when we analysed the 27 respondents who acknowledged that they earned extra money informally, some striking contrasts emerged. Of the eleven men, ten were in full-time employment and the other was unemployed. He appears to be the single 'honest scrounger' on the Island! Furthermore, of the ten male full-time workers, five were in households earning more than £150 per week in 1981. By contrast, of the 16 women, half were full-time housewives and ten were in households earning less than £80 per week in 1981. Clearly, the relationship between economic circumstances and paid informal work seems to be sharply differentiated by gender.

Returning to the one in four of the sample who engaged in unpaid informal work outside the household, it is interesting that broadly the same proportion of each social class reported doing some form of informal work. As we shall document below, greater class differences emerge when focusing on informal work done by members inside the household. Whilst engaging in informal work is fairly randomly spread across our sample, there appears to be a division based on gender in the *kinds* of work that is done. Women are more likely to do routine domestic work (e.g. shopping, housework and washing), presumably largely for elderly dependants. Men, on the other hand, are more likely to do improvement and maintenance work for others (e.g. gardening, decorating, repairs and carpentry). Women are also more likely to help with local activities and more structured voluntary work, to provide personal services for others (e.g. hair-care and dressmaking) and to care for people and animals in other people's households. Unpaid, informal work outside the household is therefore highly gender-specific.

It is frequently asserted that the unemployed are more likely to be doing unpaid informal work than those in full-time employment. We therefore explored this point in more detail. Table 6.2 indicates that those who are unemployed are no more likely to be doing informal work than those who are employed. Indeed, if the sexual division of labour in informal work is taken into account, it is

Table 6.2 Economic activity of the respondent, by whether he/she engages in unpaid informal work outside the household, by sex of respondent

Economic activity of respondent	Men			Women			Total (N)
	Yes (%)	No (%)	Total (N)	Yes (%)	No (%)	Total (N)	
Full-time work	31	69	206	21	79	81	287
Part-time work	40	60	5	21	79	76	81
Unemployed	19	81	26	38	63	16	42
Retired	21	79	63	22	78	85	148
Full-time housework	–	100	1	23	77	168	169
Other/did not answer	–	–	1	–	–	–	1
All %	28	72		23	77		
All N	84	218	302	96	330	426	728[a]

The question on the interview schedule was: 'Are there any jobs that you do *outside* your home, for other people?'

[a] Two respondents failed to give information.

clear from table 6.2 that men who are in employment are more likely to be doing extra work than any other male category and that unemployed men do least. This pattern is reversed for women, reflecting again the division of labour in unpaid informal work by gender. Men need tools and materials for their work; women more often simply need energy and some capacity to care for others.

This relationship between male economic activity and involvement in informal work does not accord with conventional wisdom. It is possible that as unemployment increases, the possibilities for informal work decline. It is perhaps when the unemployed with skills are surrounded by people in full-time employment that most opportunities for earning extra money for doing odd jobs for others, sometimes on a reciprocal basis, exist.[9] More research on the interaction between different kinds of work on a longitudinal basis is needed.

Our sample survey of households provided an unequivocal answer to the question of who does what work outside the formal economy: *members of households do it for themselves.* They do not do it for other households, or only to a very minor extent. Reciprocal exchanges between households seem very poorly developed, according to our data. Similarly, attempts to elicit information about second informal jobs, work for cash and all other possible ways of exploring participation in the so-called black economy produced remarkably few cases.[10] Some households engage in informal work outside the household on a reciprocal basis for others; a very few engage in such work for cash but these are a very small minority. Most informal, unpaid work is being done by household members for themselves and other members of the household. It is to a detailed analysis of this type of self-provisioning that we now turn.

Self-provisioning: Patterns of Work in the Domestic Sphere

We referred above to only four specific tasks, whereas we systematically gathered information on 41 tasks. We now turn to that complete set of tasks to show the relative balance of work between the household and other spheres, grouping the 41 tasks into six categories.

These data are included in table 6.3 which indicates clearly that, overall, the household in the most important sphere: of all tasks, if they are done at all, 84 per cent are done by household members in the household. The table also demonstrates the crucial importance of income in relation to the amount of work that is done: by and large, the more income, the more tasks are done *within* the household. However, these results relate to the whole sample of 730 households and so one reason for, say, less routine housework amongst those on low incomes may almost certainly be explained by the fact that elderly, single people may be unable to do certain tasks for themselves. Hence the results show the effects of age as much as of income.

It is clear, therefore, that analysis of the 41 tasks at this aggregated level can only be taken so far. Households which do their own home maintenance, for example, may be newly married couples getting their house in order, whereas those growing their own vegetables may be middle-aged, working class men who may or may not be living in dwellings that they own. For this reason, we shifted our analysis from the total number of tasks to measure the spread of activities of the same household across a broad spectrum of tasks. Thus, we are not concerned here with whether a household is able to do its own plastering and painting and glazing, but whether it has the capacity to do one of these activities as well as vegetable growing and a car-maintenance task, and so on. We devised a six-point scale based on distinct spheres of household or domestic tasks which could be done by household members, but which could equally well be bought in the market. People can buy vegetables, cakes and jerseys; they do not have to dig, bake and knit. These six tasks produced a Self-Provisioning Scale (SPS).[11] The problem was to discover which households scored highly on such a range. It was by no means self-evident that, for example, the most affluent households would do their own car maintenance, beer brewing, etc. These households are presumably the best placed to pay for goods and services. By contrast, it would seem unlikely that the poorest would be able to score highly, since they would not be able to afford a car, would not be owning their own homes and would not be able to afford the materials for domestic refurbishing and maintenance.

The 730 households of the complete sample were distributed on SPS as shown in table 6.4. It will be seen that households with a male and female partner scored most highly at points 5 and 6 of the scale. Indeed, if we dichotomize the SPS into 'low' (2–4) and 'high' (5–6), it will be noted that one-half of couple households (55.3 per cent) scored high on the scale. This is a better basis for our assertion that substantial domestic work by households does take place, since it avoids the

Table 6.3 The distribution of tasks by household income

Domestic task by function[a]	Household income	Households in which task is done (%)	Where task is done, whether it is done:					N
			Within household	Outside household Paid	Unpaid	Formally	Other	
Home maintenance	Less than £70 pw	60	53	12	7	28	n	244
	£70–149 pw	69	73	7	3	16	1	267
	More than £150 pw	71	74	5	3	18	n	138
House improvement and renovation	Less than £70· pw	15	42	7	5	46	n	244
	£70–149 pw	16	34	2	2	61	n	267
	More than £150 pw	22	39	4	3	54	0	138
Routine housework	Less than £70 pw	83	90	4	3	1	2	244
	£70–149 pw	90	96	1	3	n	n	267
	More than £150 pw	93	98	0	2	0	n	138
Domestic production	Less than £70 pw	44	89	7	n	n	3	244
	£70–149 pw	57	88	7	n	n	5	267
	More than £150 pw	58	93	2	n	1	3	138
Car maintenance	Less than £70 pw	24	67	11	2	19	1	244
	£70–149 pw	66	71	6	2	21	n	267
	More than £150 pw	84	70	1	2	27	0	138

				Where task is done, whether it is done:				
Domestic task by function[a]	Household income	Households in which task is done (%)	Within household	Outside household Paid	Outside household Unpaid	Formally	Other	N
Child care	Less than £70 pw	14	75	3	n	11	10	224
	£70–149 pw	47	78	1	n	12	8	267
	More than £150 pw	41	75	2	0	13	10	138
Overall	Less than £70 pw	45	81	6	3	8	2	244
	£70–149 pw	60	84	3	2	8	2	267
	More than £150 pw	63	85	1	2	10	2	138
	All households	55	84	4	2	8	2	730

Percentages 0.5 and above have been rounded up; below 0.5 given as 'n'. Eighty-one respondents declined to divulge information about household income.

[a] Forty-one domestic tasks were classified as follows:

Home maintenance: indoor painting, plastering, mending a broken window.

House improvement and renovation: putting in an RSJ, double glazing, bathroom, central heating, building a garage, extension, converting an attic.

Routine housework: washing dishes, tidying, hoovering, cleaning windows outside, cooking family meals, fetching take-away meals, preparing packed lunches, main food shopping, washing and ironing clothes, washing and ironing sheets.

Domestic production: making and repairing clothes, knitting, baking cakes, making jam, bread, wine or beer, gardening.

Car maintenance: washing and cleaning car, checking oil level, tuning engine, doing work on brakes.

Child care: bathing child, changing nappies, looking after sick child, collecting child from school, seeing teacher, taking child to doctor, cutting child's hair.

Table 6.4   Household type by self-provisioning scale

Household type	1	2	3	SPS(%) 4	5	6	N
Couple	–	3.0	13.3	28.3	39.7	15.6	526
Other male-headed	–	12.5	37.5	30.0	17.5	2.5	40
Other female-headed	–	31.1	31.1	28.0	9.1	0.6	164
All	–	9.9	18.6	28.4	31.6	11.5	730

problems posed by certain tasks being appropriate only at certain stages of the life cycle: particularistic circumstances are ironed out by using the scale.[12]

The first issue to be explored, following our earlier discussion, is how far involvement in the formal economy affects the household's capacity to score highly on the SPS. To make the analysis simpler, we limited ourselves to 'low' SPS and 'high' SPS. Table 6.5 shows the direct relationship between formal employment and high SPS. It demonstrates that more self-provisioning is done in households where the chief male is employed than where he is unemployed. If we select only those households where the male is in full-time employment and focus on his partner's economic activity, it appears that 'high' SPS is also directly related to her economic activity.

Table 6.5   Economic activity of males in couple
households by the dichotomized
self-provisioning scale

Male	Low SPS %	N	High SPS %	N
Full-time employed	40	152	60	223
Unemployed	56	18	44	14
Retired	62	59	38	36
Other	–	6	–	8
All	44.7	229	55.3	292

Thus, where both partners are in full-time employment, 65 per cent of couples score 'high' on the SPS, whereas when the female partner is retired, the proportion falls to 50 per cent. Pursuing this line of analysis a stage further, we focused on those 65 households with more than two earners employed in the formal economy. Of the 65, 45 (or 69 per cent) scored 'high' on the SPS. Finally, we selected those households where both partners were in full-time employment but at least one of the partners was on shift work: this pushed the proportion scoring 'high' on the SPS to 74 per cent. When male shift-workers had a non-employed partner as a housewife, the proportion scoring 'high' on the SPS dropped to 43 per cent.

Table 6.6 Class of head-of-household by
dichotomized self-provisioning scale

Class of head-of-household	Low SPS		High SPS	
	%	N	%	N
1	36	31	64	55
2	41	73	59	107
3	50	122	50	124
Other	64	9	36	5
All	45	235	55	291

This is a significant finding: *employment and self-provisioning go together, rather than one being a substitute for another.* One might have expected that those earning more or in a higher social class would be more likely to pay others and to do less self-provisioning themselves. If anything, the reverse was the case: households were categorized on the basis of the Registrar General's socio-economic groups into three classes.[13] Table 6.6 shows that there is a slight tendency for higher-class categories to do more self-provisioning in the dwelling. This must, of course, be partly a function of the higher incidence of car and home ownership in higher-class categories, but it still does not follow that these households should necessarily do so much for themselves. There is an indication that people actually *choose* to do this domestic work.

In recent discussions relating social class to social attitudes and behaviour, attention has been directed to the social status of the marital partner in modifying the pattern produced by the socio-economic characteristics of the male chief earner alone (Britten & Heath 1982). With such considerations in mind, we created a class scale based on the class of both partners, so that Class 1 became 1.1, 1.2, 1.3, etc. We did find that this significantly altered the pattern. Thus, when Class 1 males are married to Class 3 females, the proportion scoring 'high' on the SPS rises to 70 per cent. Similarly, when Class 3 males are married to higher-status females, their scores rise substantially: when married to Class 3 females, the proportion scoring high on SPS amounts to 43 per cent, but when married to class 2 or 1 females. This proportion rises to 65 and 63 per cent respectively.

These appear to be discrepant findings, but one possibility is that status inconsistency between partners is possibly a source of tension or of complex feelings of guilt which generates a distinct dynamic element into a household work strategy. Lower-status men and women may compensate to their partners by doing more gender-linked tasks. Hence, lower-status men may do more decorating or car maintenance and lower-status women more of the female gender-specific tasks. It is important, therefore, to recognize that the internal dynamics of the couple relationship modifies the otherwise direct, linear relationship between higher class and higher SPS scores.

Finally, we focused on household income, stage in the domestic cycle and number of workers in the household. These variables all affected to some degree the amount of domestic work that is done. However, it is evident that whilst some correlation between single variables can be demonstrated, we are faced with a pattern of activities related to a number of variables, and teasing out the exact weight of each variable, whilst providing some statistical accuracy, does not necessarily improve understanding. Single-factor analysis may be better for provoking questions than for providing answers. Thus, there was evidently some relationship between household income and domestic work but not a directly linear one. House-holds earning £80–£99, £125–£149 and more than £200 per week all had about the same proportion in SPS 5 and 6 (10–12 per cent). Those earning £100–124 or £150–£199 per week, on the other hand, had higher proportions at those levels of the scale (17–18 per cent). A more distinctly linear relationship was, however, discern-able when the employment status of partners was taken into account. This suggests that a domestic life-cycle variable comes into play, since, as we have shown, households with unemployed female partners score lower on the self-provisioning scale. It should be recognized that since child-care work does not appear on the scale, women who are largely preoccupied with this activity perhaps do less of other kinds of domestic work. Couples with children were *overall* likely to score higher on SPS than couples with no children (60 per cent compared to 47 per cent). However, the very highest score (78 per cent) is for couples where the woman is over 35, the youngest child is still between 5 and 15, but there is the strong likelihood of older children still living at home, contributing not only extra money to the household but also extra working capacity. Evidently, level of household income on its own is less important in determining the household work strategy, which emphasizes a broad range of domestic work carried out by household members in and around the home.

Since we are concerned with a range of activities in the SPS, it is perhaps not surprising that the more adults there are in the household, the higher the score. In a phrase, households do more and a wider range of activities in and around the house if they have access to land, labour and capital. Growing their own vegetables requires access to a garden or allotment, and coping with activities as diverse as knitting, jam-making, repairing the car and painting the house requires a gender-divided pool of hands to do the work. Finally, unless households have the capital equipment of a car and, of course, the house itself, they are unable to score on all the points of the scale. Nevertheless, it does not follow that people's behaviour is mechanistically determined by the ownership of property and consumer durables. It is simply not the case that households with a given mix of the factors of production will *necessarily* do such work in their dwellings. More affluent households could pay for the task to be done in a garage or by a building contractor or painter and decorator and many items of self-provisioning can be obtained more cheaply by buying them in the shops, e.g. jams or jerseys.

Single-variable analysis, as we have seen, can be confusing: differences in class, for example, may be masked by multiple earners in lower-status households reducing the class gap in household incomes.[14] Yet, whatever the precise statistical measures to account for the differences, the differences themselves are overwhelmingly apparent. There appears to be a *process of polarization.* This produces at one pole busy households with many workers, some of which are in employment, where a wide range of domestic tasks are done; they own their own homes and cars and have the money to maintain and service them. At the other pole are the households with only one or no earner, which do not own a house or a car or, if they do, do not have the resources for the materials to maintain them adequately.

Polarization, Self-provisioning and Privatization

In the previous sections we have discussed three kinds of informal work: the production of goods and services for consumption within the household; doing work for cash for others on one's own account or for an employer; and unpaid informal or communal work outside the household for non-household members. We have demonstrated that in global terms the first of these is far the most important. For the reasons we have outlined, we focused our analysis on the households doing a range of tasks and showed that a majority of couple-based households scored positions 5 and 6 on a six-point scale measuring the range of self-provisioning tasks. Thus, much of our analysis concentrated on those households ranked 'high' on the dichotomized self-provisioning scale.

We have demonstrated with our empirical data that certain types of household score consistently highly, whereas others score consistently low: households with more income, either because of the size of individual incomes, the number of individual earners or a combination of the two, are likely to score most highly on the SPS. The more adults in a relatively affluent household, the more work will be done. Households of higher status not only do more work for themselves, they are also more likely to get others to do work for them. Such households produce more and consume more, formally and informally. Hence, employment status is the key to participation in *all* forms of work, not simply to the formal economy. Put negatively, unemployed men are more likely to be in households scoring low on the SPS and do very little or no informal work outside the household themselves. Hence, we argue that on a number of frequently overlapping dimensions, there is a process of *polarization* between the busy, highly work-motivated households, generally well-off with multiple earners and potential household workers, and others who are at the opposite end of the scale.

This process of polarization is partially supported and encouraged by the distinctive mix of opportunities and constraints provided by the local labour market. It is here that the possibilities for given household work strategies are embedded. Polarization in the sphere of production is achieved through the distinctive earning capacities of household members; polarization in the sphere of consumption is achieved through multiple adults in the household. In a different context, no doubt, households would adopt different strategies to 'get by'. In Sheppey, the relatively low wages, coupled with relatively easy access to home ownership, have produced both polarization and high levels of self-provisioning.

Self-provisioning is the production of goods and services outside the market by household members for their own use and enjoyment. *Domestication* is the product of a value system which puts home-centred activities as the central focus of a distinctive life-style. Household members may *choose* to maintain their own car, even though they could afford to have it serviced in a garage, or they may be *obliged* to do such work for themselves because they cannot afford the market price. The same process may, therefore, be produced as much by choice as by constraint, and households in different objective situations may end up equally domesticated. *Privatization*, on the other hand, relates to the market provision of goods and services which had previously been or could now be provided publicly. Here again there is an element of both constraint and choice. A household may choose to provide its own means of transport by buying a car, even though public transport may be perfectly adequate; or, on the other hand, a household may be obliged to run a car simply in order to reach employment and basic services. Such a constraint operates over much of the Isle of Sheppey, where public transport is poor and the population not living in Sheerness is relatively scattered. Evidently, increasing privatization can encourage increased self-provisioning, and people's values can influence the degree to which they decide to buy private transport, health, housing and education. We return to this theme below. Our point here is that people may choose to do more self-provisioning than they, as it were, objectively have to.

Self-provisioning flows largely but not entirely from a home-centred value-orientation. Households may choose to pay others to do work such as painting, decorating and gardening or they may choose or be obliged to do it themselves. The level at which they are satisfied again varies according to the value orientations of the household. However the work is done, and to whatever standard, the element which unites many households in self-provisioning sees the house and home as a central defining and determining feature of a life-style and as a symbolic and material expression of success in life. Very often, households make very precise calculations about the balance of work between that which is paid for and that which they do themselves. Given the goal of achieving a predetermined standard of domestic comfort and style, households work out the best means of achieving it. Hence it is very hard to say in a given case whether a household is working for itelf, either according to one kind of rationality by which it is calculated that it is 'cheaper' (in a limited economic sense) or according to another kind of rationality which supports the activity in terms of other satisfactions – overall higher standards achieved, more work done or the self-fulfulment from seeing a job well done. This produces a mixture of rationalities (for which we see little point in providing labels) which is inevitably complex and in some cases would be impossible to disaggregate. People know that they have mixed motives and, if they are encouraged to concede a reduction of salience to one form of rationality, they will simply 'top up' with another in an unconcernedly pragmatic way. Exploration of this matter is best done by extremely detailed, in-depth study of specific cases.

The self-provisioning households of Sheppey make sure that their homes are well decorated and often extend or modify them in various ways to make them more comfortable. They grow their own vegetables and 73 per cent of our sample had a deep-freeze, compared with the national figure of 47 per cent as a whole.[15] Women in employment augmented the resources of the household, but then very often used these same resources to do more of other forms of work in the household. Here again we meet problems. Households may choose to own their own dwelling and a private car and then find that they are obliged to maintain them, becoming, as it were, reluctantly self-provisioning. Whilst the mixture of rationalities suggested above enables some households to aim higher by extending the potential for household work, there may also be a ratchet effect on other households, who feel obliged to keep up to the standards of their local milieu, even though their household resources barely allow them to do so. What is 'choice' and what is 'constraint' under these circumstances is as hard to disentangle as is the mixture of rationalities. Indeed, the modes of rationalization and the awareness of the contextual constraints in which such justifications are grounded are clearly interrelated. Households in the same material circumstances may choose to use these resources in fundamentally different ways, whereas those in different material circumstances, but with similar goals and values, may work to achieve similar outcomes and life styles. Whilst we do not have space to discuss the issue in detail, we must emphasize that the current trend to the privatization of housing and other services and facilities is a powerful support to the growth of self-provisioning which we have described. However, both self-provisioning and privatization can be highly divisive, especially within the working class. Lower-income households, that cannot get the resources to provide services and facilities for themselves, will become increasingly isolated, politically impotent and socially invisible. Forced to rent because they cannot afford to buy and maintain their homes, forced to use a declining public transport because they cannot afford to own, tax and maintain a private car and increasingly unable to retrieve their position through their own efforts, such households are likely to make the process of polarization more acute in the years ahead, as the labour market continues to contract and privatization continues as the policy of the Government.

In this respect our account of informal work in this chapter is dramatically different from that in other contexts, particularly in the Third World. There is nothing in our findings to suggest that the work outside employment on the Isle of Sheppey generates much growth or provides communal support and benefits. All the work is private, inward-looking and concerned with domestic comfort. However, it is not enough to echo Galbraith by emphasizing private affluence and public squalor. What we are describing is a polarization between a precarious household work strategy, entirely dependent on the wages of multiple earners in a declining labour market, and those households cut off from even that modest security. Indeed, it is arguable that those doing well now would suffer the more if their income was drastically reduced through redundancy. Our interviews have documented the despair of men living in their own homes, with their own tools, with time on their hands and with urgent decorating jobs staring them in the face, but without the money to buy the paint.

Faced with their powerlessness in the face of economic realities, households are clearly in a more secure position when owning their dwelling outright, keeping it in good repair and also owning a car and other domestic consumer goods. Those who desire such a modest degree of security and are unable to achieve it seem even more excluded. It is difficult to say how much this desire for a modest self-sufficiency is at all widely shared, although we did find some evidence amongst certain households we interviewed. There may be more security to be found in the sphere of consumption than in the sphere of production. An inward-looking concern with private comforts might be one way of coping with the consequences of global processes of capital accumulation. Another way might be to drink oneself silly: a pattern more common in vodka-drinking lands. This point is not entirely frivolous. Alcohol is one escape from circumstances over which one has no control. Enormous quantities of beer are drunk on the Isle of Sheppey: there are over 140 licensed premises on the Island.[16] Evidently there are alternative ways of coping with conditions in a context. It would be wrong to postulate a value consensus on the Island. Indeed, we were struck as much by the diversity of values as by the polarization in practices of self-provisioning on which we have focused here.

Work in a Wider Context

At the level of larger-scale analysis, we suggest that the Isle of Sheppey is not an atypical, unusual spatial context in the declining periphery of one of the core capitalist countries. Rather, it is typical of those parts of the country experiencing deindustrialization and the restructuring of capital. Over half the main employment on the Island is controlled by foreign capital – German, French, Canadian, Japanese and American and so on. Substantial profits leave the Island and substantial investment comes in. A new factory recently opened by Klippons (a German-based, electrical components manufacturing company) produced 12 new jobs for an investment of £1.4 million.[17] By and large, however, most companies are contracting and our survey of employers suggests that this will continue.

There is very little that ordinary people can do about their position in the local labour market. Militant trades-union activity is likely to be counter-productive. Investment decisions are taken off the Island, more likely in another country. Multinational companies are, if anything, more paternalistic than smaller, local companies and are likely to take greater care of fewer people. A sound, pragmatic strategy for such people, concerned to get by as comfortably as possible, is to put their resources of time, energy and skill into making their domestic world more secure. At least in that sphere they have some control.

Our initial hypothesis that extra-household informal work would play an important part in household work strategies has been shown to be mistaken. Very little extra work is done for others, even though there might be a logic in the reciprocal exchange of specialist skills or in certain economies of scale. The only co-operative venture which we could document in detail was connected with growing vegetables. The Sheppey Horticultural Society buys fertilizer, garden tools and equipment in bulk and sells at favourable rates to members.

What reciprocal work there was between neighbours and the generations was related to the domestic cycle. Parents helped children substantially when setting up home and children visited elderly parents to do their shopping or decorating. Even baby-sitting was more likely to be done by members of the same family at different stages of the domestic cycle rather than by neighbours at the same stage. From the experience of five years fieldwork on the Island, we would judge that if working-class, married women in employment required help and support looking after their young children, this would typically be provided by a 'nan'. Three out of four Class 3 couple households had another relative living on the Island and even 60 per cent of Class 1 households did so. The emphasis by Gershuny and others on separate economic spheres distracts attention from the continuing importance of family and kinship. When times are hard, people may feel the obligations of kin become stronger, but this is a question which we are still exploring. We have already mentioned the importance of kin for finding employment.

We must conclude by adopting a more cautious acceptance of the argument put forward by Gershuny. Much work is certainly being done by some households for themselves but this is for many precariously dependent on multiple earners. Household work strategies take place in specific contexts and reflect distinctive value systems. The material conditions provide the frame, but how and what people consume is fundamentally determined by their values.

Our analysis suggests a tragic precariousness at the centre of people's lives and in this we take issue with the optimism implicit in the analyses of both Bell and Gershuny. The households which we are able to describe cannot achieve any real independence from market services in their nest-centred life-style. A few fortunate ones, perhaps, do achieve a remarkably close approximation to self-sufficiency and resent having to own a car or to have a telephone but these are exceptional. About the rest, with all their ideological eggs in the domestic basket and more heavily dependent than they are perhaps aware on the fragile basis for gaining income in a declining labour market, we are inclined to be pessimistic. We feel that we are describing a *dependent* domesticity: the more capital goods and equipment they own, the more they are dependent on market services to maintain them. The ontological security associated with home-ownership and a high commitment to work for self-provisioning can be shattered overnight with an unexpected redundancy. The overwhelming dependence of all forms of informal work, including self-provisioning, on the money from formal employment is the basic fact underlining our polarization thesis. The very detailed survey material on household work strategies of which we are providing some preliminary analysis here sharply undermines the more optimistic scenarios of those like Burns, who see people being able to liberate themselves from the tyrannies of markets, exchange values and the capitalist relations of production to something more productive and satisfying in the cocoon of the so-called 'domestic economy'. The whole burden of our argument rests on the reality that there is only one economy and that a household's position in that is fundamental in determining its positions in other economic spheres. Whilst we have sympathy with those who seek to find a better society 'after industrial society' and 'beyond employment', we cannot offer much comfort or support. On the Isle of Sheppey, beyond employment most likely means poverty, isolation, little opportunity for informal work, involuntarily home-centred, with deteriorating dwellings and capital goods. Multiple earners bring prosperity, however short-lived: no earner brings a downward spiral of economic and social detachment. We find no way of disguising the fact that, in present circumtances, the self-provisioning households on Sheppey would face a very bleak future beyond employment.

Notes

We are very pleased to acknowledge that the research on which this chapter is based is funded by the Social Science Research Council (Grant No. G00230035). All the officers of the Council who have been concerned with our project over the past three years have been unfailingly helpful and supportive. We also acknowledge the very considerable help we have received from Jane Dennett in preparing this chapter. As research assistant, project administrator and typist of the various drafts and final version, she has been meticulous in everything she has done and has remained the firm rock around which the discussions between us have swirled. We would also like to acknowledge the comments on an earlier draft by the editors who took on a thankless task under considerable pressure.

1 The Social Science Research Council encouraged the production of a bibliography surveying the existing work in this field in 1980.

2   Surveys were made of the local employment situation (Pahl & Dennett 1981) and the local housing situation (Wallace & Pahl 1981); there was also a study in historical demography (Buck 1981) on which future research could be based. See also Pahl 1984a.

3   An analysis of similar houses in Sheppey and in the nearest towns on the mainland, advertized in the same paper on the same day, revealed that in July 1981 ordinary terraced housing or bungalows were 20 to 40 per cent cheaper in Sheppey and the cost of a small plot of land was less than half the price.

4   *The Economist,* 13 January 1979.

5   *British Business,* Department of Trade, 1980.

6   Putting in an RSJ is important in the local context where many small terraced houses can be improved by making the two downstairs rooms into one by knocking down the intervening wall and building on a kitchen at the rear.

7   Much of the work outside employment which we discuss in this chapter is referred to as informal. This carries no analytical weight.

8   Since the 730 households included many elderly and single-person households, we focused much of the analysis of the tasks on those households with couples.

9   Anecdotes about this kind of activity provide the main support for popular speculation for the so-called informal economy.

10 In order to be sure that this was not simply the understandable caution of respondents who might be reluctant to reveal all their activities to an anonymous interviewer on the doorstep, we carefully selected 30 households for more detailed in-depth interviews. In some cases these households were interviewed more than once by each of us in turn. Furthermore, we have knowledge of families on the Island stretching over a period of five years and we are confident that our assessment is correct.

11 The SPS was devised to measure the production of goods and services by households themselves which could be purchased formally. Therefore, we selected tasks from our questionnaire which were sometimes purchased formally and sometimes done within the household; individual households were ranked according to the number of such tasks which they performed. The SPS therefore gives a measure of the tasks performed by a given household, whereas our other tables illustrate the number of households doing a given task. It was decided that it would be more accurate if the SPS measured the *range* of tasks done by a household rather than the gross number of such tasks, since the tasks covered such distinct areas of activity. Thus, we wanted to discover not just whether a household did a great many housing repairs but whether it repaired the car, grew vegetables and provided personal goods such as clothes as well. Hence the tasks were divided into six clusters and the household could score one SPS point if it did just one task within each cluster,

up to a maximum of six points for all the clusters. Tasks of a fairly routine nature were only included in the SPS if they were performed with some frequency but the major tasks were included if they had been performed at any time at all. The clusters of tasks for the SPS are as follows:

SPS 1 Vegetable growing at any time.

SPS 2 Painting, plastering or mending a broken window in the last year.

SPS 3 Checking the oil level, tuning the engine or doing work on the brakes of a car at any time.

SPS 4 Putting in an RSJ, double glazing or central heating or building a bathroom or an extension or converting an attic at any time.

SPS 5 Making jam or, beer or wine either fortnightly or regularly.

SPS 6 Making clothes or knitting at any time.

12 For present purposes we are excluding non-couple households from the analysis, simply because single-parent households and single-retired-person households have special and distinctive problems and we have problems enough in accounting for variations between couple households.

13 These social classes have been condensed from socio-economic groups 1–17 as follows:

Class 1 = SEGs 1, 2, 3, 4, 13 (i.e. professional and managerial).

Class 2 = SEGs 5, 6, 8, 12, 14, 16 (i.e. junior and intermediate non-manual, foremen, own-account workers, farmers and armed forces).

Class 3 = SEGs 7, 9, 10, 11, 15 (i.e. all manual workers, personal service workers).

The fourth class, which we do not mention here, comprises those in SEG 17 (unclassifiable) and those who have never had paid employment.

14 In an attempt to get a more precise measure of what seemed to be the three main variables affecting households' position on the SPS multiple-regression analysis was used for couple households. The variables taken were the social class of the male chief earner (defined as in footnote 13), the number of adults in the household and an income variable dividing households into those with incomes under £100 a week and those with £100 or more. These three independent variables were described as ClassM, Adults and Povline respectively and the dependent variable in the equation was the SPS described in footnote 11. The three coefficients were highly significant, the coefficients for ClassM and Adults being almost precisely the same and the Povline coefficient being slightly more significant. The full equation is as follows:

$$SPS = 18.7 - 0.108 \text{ (ClassM)} + 0.100 \text{ (Adults)} + 0.13 \text{ (Povline)}$$
$$(-0.07) \qquad\qquad (0.08) \qquad\qquad (0.03)$$

15 *Social Trends,* 1983.
16 We have documented many other styles of 'getting by' or household work strategies than those which are the focus of discussion here. These included styles based on short term opportunism, the communal pub-centred style and various other idiosyncratic styles. For a fuller discussion see C.D. Wallace and R.E. Pahl, 'Polarisation, unemployment and all forms of work', in Sheila Allen et al. (eds), *The Experience of Unemployment,* forthcoming 1985.
17 *Sheerness Times-Guardian,* 11 March 1983.

7

Informalization and Social Resistance: The Case of Naples

Gabriella Pinnarò and Enrico Pugliese

Premise

Processes of informalization within the economic system have different origins and characteristics in diverse contexts. They have frequently been interpreted as an attempt to evade market rules or seen as a means of escaping the obligations and organizational forms imposed by the State.

Analyses such as these emphasize a *subjective* element, i.e. the expression of an individual desire for self-affirmation in the face of externally imposed constraints arising from excessive institutionalization and formalization of relationships. New social impulses and new expressions of subjectivity are seen to give rise to processes of informalization[1] which run counter to the historically established tendency toward the regulation of social relationships. Thus, according to Gallino (1982): 'A large collective movement of escape from universalistic regulation (*normazione*) . . . and a resumption of particularistic values and behaviours . . . is reflected in the informal economy.' This 'collective escape' is thought to be caused by the increasing costs that universalistic regulation implies. This view reflects a large body of international literature that sees informalization processes as the results of a free and voluntary choice.

However, the question is more complicated in those contexts where the process of consolidation of universalistic regulation has never fully developed. In interpretations of Third World economies, for example, the informal sector is often understood as an area of subsistence production that lowers the costs of reproduction of the labour force and maintains the surplus population (Portes and Walton 1981). Interpretations of this kind are less relevant to advanced industrial societies and the analyses developed with reference to Third World countries are only partly applicable to the area of our study (Naples) where, as we shall see, the existence of an urban subsistence economy is mainly a phenomenon of the past. However, the situation of Third World countries – and the different aspects and characteristics that the informal sector presents in different social contexts – is relevant for discussion of some peculiarities of the informal economy at the local level and we shall outline them here.

The inadequacy of the concept informal economy has been widely debated. As has been frequently pointed out, it would be more appropriate to talk about informal productive structures since there is only one economy. Moreover, as many scholars have emphasized, the informal and the formal (institutional) sector of the economy are in close and functional relations. The term informal has only recently been adopted in the Italian literature. Other expressions such as '*economia sommersa*' (submerged economy), '*economia parallela*' (parallel economy) or '*occupazione occulta*' (hidden employment) have been more common in the past. Our own choice of the term does not imply that we attribute to it a greater heuristic value but reflects its common currency in the international literature on the subject.

This chapter presents a case study that contrasts with the interpretation now dominant in the relevant literature: a situation of unequivocal social resistance to the conditions of work and livelihood in the informal sector.[2] It may seem paradoxical to speak of *resistance* to involvement in the informal sector. In literature on the subject, informalization processes – the persistence of productive structures of an informal type – are often understood as a *resistance* to commodification, to the pervasive extension of market mechanisms, and to the domination of market rules in the field of production and reproduction. In other words, very often *informalization* is identified with *decommodification*. Decommodification is certainly one of the dimensions of the process of informalization. However, another dimension should not be ignored, i.e. the attempt to evade the regulation of productive and reproductive activities imposed by the State. A subjective element can be identified in this tendency that expresses itself in various contradictory ways. Therefore, in the analysis of the development, persist-

ence and *resistance* to the informal sector three poles can be identified: the social actor, the State and the market. The way in
which these three poles interact gives rise to the various outcomes of
the process and to the various connotations of the informal
economy.

As this chapter will indicate, resistance to the informal sector
derives from the fact that there has been a deep-rooted tradition
of informal productive activities in Naples. These informal productive structures were established in the inner-city areas (*centro
storico*) and employed large sectors of the local working population.
We refer to the so-called '*economia del vicolo*' (street-corner economy)
widely publicized in literature on Naples in the 1950s and 1960s, a
reality with closed boundaries and traditional rules, where market
penetration was limited and public regulation obviously absent, but
also a reality of backwardness and misery, experienced and rejected.
In many respects therefore the 'informal' in Naples is a past and not
a future perspective.

Resistance or lack of adaptation to the informal sector expresses
itself as an increase in the officially unemployed labour force.
Contrary to the common view of the phenomenon, a situation
whereby fewer jobs and less employment go together can be
observed. The conditions offered by the informal sector are too
unattractive. The lack of labour demand in the institutional sector,
particularly the stagnating demand in the industrial sector, coupled
with resistance to the informal sector, give rise to the characteristics
of local unemployment.

As we shall show, the well-known mobilizations of the Neapolitan
unemployed are not only the effect of high rates of official
unemployment (107,014 registered unemployed out of a popul-
tion of 1,210,503 inhabitants) but of the social and political
characteristics of the unemployed and their attitudes towards
occupational solutions in the informal sector. The informal economy in the form of the street-corner economy is hence well known
in Naples. Its connotations have been the object of analysis in the
literature. Before discussing these in more detail it is useful to make
a brief theoretical digression which presents some relevant implications for empirical analysis.

Formal–informal dualism is a fashionable issue in the studies
concerning the Italian South. In the past, however, another
dualism, that between advanced and backward sectors, or between
modern and traditional sectors, has been the object of debate in the
literature. In both cases, the problem has been conceptualized in

terms of sectors of the economy both responding to the rules of the market and subject to general set of norms that the State considered necessary.

In previous debate the relations between modern and backward sectors were considered in much the same way as the relations identified today between the formal and informal sector. The same variables were employed to partially distinguish the two sectors. The prevailing size of the firm, the degree of development and technology, the more or less labour-intensive character of the labour process, the relations between the firm and labour force (the percentage of self-employed workers), the degree of trade unionization and the rate of self-consumption have been the most important factors used to distinguish the modern sector from the backward one, and in large part they have also become important in the debate on the informal sector, though the problem is clearly different. In the analysis of the relations between modern and backward sectors the specific character of the backward sector (self-employment, self-consumption, labour-intensive technology, etc.) has been considered a heritage of the past, which would be eliminated in the further development process. The trends towards informalization, however, are recent ones whose motivations and origins have been variously interpreted and generally seen as a new evolution of productive structures.

A full discussion of the distinction to be drawn between backward and informal sectors is beyond the scope of this chapter, but we should emphasize that the backward sector and the informal one are not the same thing although they may be overlapping empirical realities. In other words, it would be wrong to continue to speak about the traditional sector as it has been identified and described in the past, and then rename it, for example, informal or underground. This is exactly what has been done by some authors who have discovered the persistence in Naples of the street-corner economy and interpreted the present reality of Naples by reference to this fact.

Our own definition of informal refers to *those productive activities generally but not necessarily done by the self-employed, that are labour intensive, with a strong tendency to elude the State and union rules of work conditions with a high degree of self-consumption and/or alternative commercialization and with evasion of taxation.* Using this definition of informality we now consider its characteristics and contradictions in Naples and in Southern Italy more generally.

The Question of Informal Economy in the Italian Context

The interpretation of Italian economic development has been traditionally based on dualistic models. The existence of forms of economic dualism between advanced and backward sectors was coupled with the existence of regional dualism between the 'industrial' North and the 'agrarian' South. In the 1970s, however, the development of regional analysis and increasing evidence of the relevance of regional phenomena to the Italian economy led to the identification of a third regional dimension – *the Third Italy* (Bagnasco 1977; Calza Bini 1977; Paci 1980).

The late 1960s and 1970s have witnessed a decrease in employment in large-scale industry in Italy. Conversely, employment in small-scale industry has been observed everywhere in the country, particularly in the North-eastern regions (Veneto, Marche, Umbria, Emilia Romagna, etc.). The increase in registered employment in small-scale industries has been correctly understood as the 'emerging edge' of a phenomenon of greater relevance – of increasing employment in the informal sector. Small manufacturing industry (in textiles, but also in metal, leather and footwear, and even in the electronic sector) showed an increase in employment, both at the official and unofficial (*sommerso*) level. Development of the *'economia sommersa'* and changing economic and social role of the Third Italy have been identified in the Italian debate.

Although employment in small industrial units has also increased in Southern Italy, a phenomenon of similar relevance cannot be observed in the South or in the city of Naples itself. This does not imply that there is no informal employment in Southern regions but implies rather – as Mingione's detailed analysis of other areas of the South has clearly pointed out – that informal work and employment have different characteristics than those assumed for regions of peripheral industrialization. We believe that in this respect the main difference is due to the particular mixture/connection with the traditional backward sector of the economy. Street-corner activities and black work in the building industries have always been part of the backward sector and remain diffused in the South but they are not all typical of the diffused peripheral/informal industrialization which has developed in the Third Italy. Confusion has remained because the main elements of the analysis of the backward economy have been mechanically transposed in the analysis of the informalization processes of recent decades.

Small-scale industry and cottage work and illegal and precarious employment, have traditionally been considered conditions of backwardness in Italy. The resurgence of these types of economic structure and forms of employment in the late 1960s has also been interpreted in a very traditional way. In studies focused on the decentralization of production, the development of small and very small firms was considered to be a localization of productive activities in geographic areas characterized by weak unions and flexibility in the use of the labour force. It was no accident that the new forms of cottage work were referred to as black work, a primitive form of exploitation of the female work-force (Brusco et al. 1980; Leon 1980). The emphasis was placed on the 'perverse' character of the new organization of labour and technology and related precarious and irregular forms of employment. Needless to say, this interpretation was accompanied by a critical denouncement of its social implications, which had as its targets the firms and capitalist development in general.

Analysis of specific territorial characteristics and attention to the social organization of production have subsequently cast doubt upon the validity of this entirely negative interpretation. In fact, investigation of permissive conditions on the part of labour supply has revealed the existence of some advantages that are not only economic. Thus, it is clear that in certain conditions, a smaller and more flexible (and also more informalized) industrial organization can become more profitable and consequently advantageous for the industrialist.[3] This idea differs very much from the assertion that 'small is beautiful', as espoused by Schumacher (1973), in some cases extended to produce the affirmation that 'informal is beautiful', as argued by Szelenyi (1981). In this second case, small and informal are seen as general strategies of survival, reducing exploitation and control, and leading to more freedom for the individuals and households, rather than the opposite. This interpretation is consequently based on the assumption that the small or informal which is beautiful is also a free option and not a superimposition, aimed at achieving increased exploitation or self-exploitation, or the only possible solution to survival on a very low income or in an uncertain precarious situation (as is the case in the Mezzogiorno or in underdeveloped areas).

Atomized and dispersed production as the driving force of a basically different economic structure, 'rugged micro-entrepreneurship' as a lever for free market activity outside the sphere of legal and union regulations, flexibility of the labour force as a capacity for interstitial adaptation – these are the principal ideas being investigated, but they result in interpretations that are as unilateral and schematic as the preceding ones.

The very terms of reference have been changed and watered down, with more neutral accents added to their 'dark', 'perversely submerged' and 'illegal' aspects. Terms such as 'informal', 'parallel' and 'invisible' are not merely alternative definitions but represent different approaches to the subject.

Approaches referring to a model of different social structure of informal economy have been generalized and applied to a different territorial context – Southern Italy and Naples. The reference models are both Italian and foreign, relating to regions where informal economic structures are more widespread and better documented. However, these models do not apply very well because informality here is characterized by persistence of a long-term, precarious artisan and commercial productive structure, typical of the traditional sector of the economy. In many respects these forms of informalization have been updated, but not in such a way as to be more progressive and humane.

Naples: Formal and Informal Economy

The industrial situation of Naples presents many particularities and contradictions. Two of these deserve to be singled out: (1) a dichotomy between large-scale industries, mainly in the modern manufacturing branches, and small-scale industries, mainly in the traditional branches; and (2) the social and political relevance of the labour force employed in the large-scale industries, notwithstanding its relatively low numeric weight.

Another peculiarity is that with 156,433 persons employed in manufacturing industries, the province of Naples rates among the first Italian industrial provinces, on the basis of the absolute number of the industrial labour force; however, taking industrial employment as a percentage of the total population, the figures are very low (table 7.1).

According to official data, the percentage of population employed in manufacturing industries is 4.8 per cent in the province and 5.2 per cent in the city (while for the country as a whole the same percentage is 10.2 per cent). In addition, the general rate of employment appears to be very low if compared with the national figures.

Table 7.1 Official Figures (1981) for employment and unemployment
in Naples and Italy

	Naples	Naples Metropolitan Area (province)	Italy
Population	1,210,503	2,947,982	56,243,000
Official employment in manufacturing industries	58,539	156,433	5,731,264
Official employment in manufacturing industries as percentage of population	4.8	5.2	10.2
Total employment in industry	77,070	189,240	7,140,326
Total employment in industry as percentage of population	6.4	6.4	12.7
Total official employment according to 1981 Census	307,109	586,362	16,623,141
Total official employment according to 1981 Census as percentage of population	25.0	19.0	29.0
Registered unemployment	107,014	227,492	—
Unemployment as percentage of population	9.0	7.7	—

Sources: Censimento Generale della Popolazione, 1981; Censimento Generale dell'Industria, Commercio, Artigianato e Servizi 1981; Ufficio Provinciale del Lavoro, Naples.

It is not surprising then to find extremely high rates of unemployment. The total number of registered unemployed is now 107,014 in the city and 227,492 in the province. The percentage of registered unemployed of the total population is 9 per cent in the city and 7.7 per cent in the province (official figures). (These percentages are based on the *total* population and not, as is usual, on the *active* population.)

The industrial dualism of this area is demonstrated by the following data: 45 per cent of the 156,433 persons employed in manufacturing industries in the province are concentrated in 35 industries of large size (over 500 employees) and 14 per cent (22,978 persons) are employed in 14,159 small- and medium-sized industries (with less than nine employees). Very often these 'industries' are constituted by the self-employed artisan with no employees at all.

The industrial history of Naples has always been marked by a considerable turnover in industrial structure; a phenomenon which official data fail to register. The general outcome of such fluctuating processes and of their interconnection is a high unemployment rate, resulting in a population with an industrial background, who have no occupational chances outside marginal activities. Many of the unemployed in Naples have been industrial workers in the past. The flow of investments in the industrial sector which took place in the 1960s and early 1970s has created additional employment but has also changed the structure of the industrial working population. Clearly, the official figures given so far underestimate real employment in manufacturing industries. Recent surveys, such as that by Becchi Collidà for IRES-CGIL (1981), suggest higher rates of employment in various manufacturing branches (particularly the footwear and leather industry and the textile industry) and at the same time points out the role of industrial delocation and of '*lavoro a domicilio*' (cottage industry) in these manufacturing branches. Informal employment is estimated to be high, but no precise figures are available. Small-scale, submerged industries, employing black, unofficial workers are seen as specific to the inner-city sections of Naples.

The industrial structure, the presence of informal industrial activities and the resistance to the work and living conditions of the informal sector place Naples in a special situation in the general context of the Italian South.

Naples is more industrial than the other Southern metropolitan areas. In particular it benefited from the flow of industrial investments towards Southern Italy in the late 1960s. These investments have led to the creation of larger industrial plants and the formation of a modern industrial working class. In the meantime, despite the huge success and failure rates of small, industrial plants, small traditional industry has been able both to employ a large number of workers and to socialize a still larger number of population to industrial work. This industrial socialization, coupled with a high rate of structural unemployment, has provided a permissive environment for informal activities in the industrial sector. Hence, it is not surprising that the character and amount of informal activities is somewhat different from that of other urban areas in South, such as Messina, as described by Mingione.

On the other hand the industrial informal sector did not develop in a way that was attractive for the working population. Thus, the industrial and union culture which developed in the city was committed to successive mobilizations against informal working conditions.

A further aspect that we shall describe, related to the older and more traditional reality of Naples, has attracted the attention of such researchers as Allum (1973). Together with a minority working class, Naples has always had its marginal groups. Originally, some of these were engaged in industrial employment, including very small-scale industry, and others were engaged in the street-corner economy. According to Allum:

> Its principal characteristic is that it is both closed and clandestine; it is based on a building or a block of buildings which form an economic 'island'. Capital from various sources (contraband goods, prostitution, petty larceny, etc.) street vending, and the incomes of one or two stably employed persons in the 'island' circulates, passing from hand to hand in a series of petty services by means of which each person tries to procure his immediate needs, or *arrangiarse* . . . In this way, the little capital that enters the 'island' remains within it and enables every member to enjoy a crumb.

In conclusion, Allum adds that 'the importance of this sub-economy lies in the closed and integrated structure that constitutes the basis of the *Gemeinshaft*'. In short, it is a truly emblematic representation of informality. There are no regulations governing relations, no one pays taxes and, there are no work contracts; personal relationships are exactly of the *Gemeinshaft* type.

It is useful to examine some of the characteristics of this process that are not brought out in the passage quoted. The first characteristic is a situation of underconsumption and subsistence. Literature on the subject of the street-corner economy has always referred to a situation in which very small-scale artisan and commercial activity serves to furnish very particular goods and services which are for specifically local consumption. The list of trades in the street-corner economy is too long to go into here.

Ignoring for the moment the strictly illegal aspect of this type of economy (which is related in a discontinuous and vaguely defined manner to other types of activity), we can say that the street-corner economy is a combination of artisan activity and services, of a self-employed nature, with limited invested capital and low income, with outlets restricted to a local level, in a basically closed market and in a situation characterized by underconsumption and subsistence.

It is on this basis that social relationships are created, and the destruction of this reality helps to explain social transformations in the city. The Naples described here is not the symbol of present social reality. It is the Naples of the past, described by a foreign scholar as it was 15 years ago.[4] Little understood by scholars and even less by the media, the street-corner economy is now practically extinct. The fact that a series of activities intended to provide for local consumption exist in the ecological context of a city with high unemployment rates and the presence of marginals in the city centre, indicates merely that the phenomenon persists to a minimal degree. It would be a serious error to confuse these final residues of the street-corner economy with a new type of informal economy.

Some characteristics of the local social fabric can clearly explain the reproduction of the activities of the new informal economy. However, they can also be found in other metropolitan areas and the substitution process was a discontinuous rather than an unbroken one. Based as it was on underconsumption and subsistence, the traditional street-corner economy inevitably faded away in the face of social and civil progress and the influx of income, no matter how meagre. The subsistence situation has now been partially overcome in both rural and urban Southern Italy. Although the territorial distribution of public welfare funds by the welfare state undoubtedly privileges the countryside, a minimum flow of welfare income has also begun to reach the city.

In Naples, distribution processes, income levels and consumption structures have changed so as to have become incompatible with a street-corner economy. Nevertheless, when speaking of Naples, the concept of the street-corner economy is confusingly used as if it were interchangeable with the concept of informal economy. There is, however, an undeniable relationship between the two concepts. Apart from the fact that the two phenomena occurred within a single social setting, there is a relation between the crisis and extinction of the first phenomenon and the difficulties of establishing the second, and the reluctance of the masses to accept it.

The decline of the street-corner economy is the result not only of problems implicit in the market of goods and services that it provided, but also of changes in the work-force that operated in it. We have already discussed the first aspect; now let us turn to the second. As evident in Allum's definition, the income produced by this type of activity was inevitably totally insufficient. It was the only outlet in a situation in which the weight of workers' and unions' political and structural influence was almost non-existent. The street-corner economy suffered a further crisis when industrial investments began to flow into the developing poles of the South, especially into Naples, during the 1960s and the first half of the 1970s, opening up new employment prospects. The change in market structure cut off the street-corner economy's market outlets and the once-desperate supply of manpower that existed in the urban context of historically reproduced marginality dwindled.

In those same years, Naples became not only a working-class city but also a centre of services and activities related principally to the reproduction sector and administered by the State. The labour force, including that part of it from the city's marginal, proletariat neighbourhoods, sought outlets outside the traditional sector and the street-corner economy. The modernization of the city and the industrialization process gave impetus in the same direction. The transformation of the situation must be interpreted also by reference to political as well as structural variables.

This contradiction between 'the old' ('the old' in Naples being the street-corner economy), which is already in decline, and the new, which is not yet established and has not yet created the processes that will lead to increased employment, has had some interesting effects on the labour market. Unemployment begins to spread and becomes characteristic of the situation in Naples. The 1970s were the years of a revival of informal activity under the new form of the submerged economy, but they were also mainly the years of the great extension of explicit unemployment. As we mentioned above, employment rates were quite low, but activity rates were also low. In a discussion of the informal economy this fact could be of little significance or could reflect a strong tendency toward informal employment. Since a characteristic of the informal economy is the difficulty of its statistical measurement, these low levels of explicit employment and low rates of activity must signify a burgeoning hidden economy. This is, in fact common in the media's treatment of the city.

We hold, instead, that the phenomenon is much more complex, and can be interpreted as follows. Conditions exist in Naples that are undeniably permissive as regards the development of informal economy, because employment opportunities in the formal sector are scarce indeed. There is an abundance of manpower, a tradition of labour and there is also that process known as 'manufacturing socialization' which usually explains the marked development of this type of activity. Furthermore, there is a tradition of productive activity in precisely that sector of traditional small enterprise (textiles, shoe manufacturing, etc.) in which the informal economy has reached its greatest levels of development. Given these permissive conditions, a certain degree of development of the informal economy was inevitable. However, on-the-spot investigations demonstrate that it is limited when compared with the effective availability of the labour force.

The definition of informal economy that we have been using so far is restricted: we have been assuming an identity between black work (in the manufacturing and building industries) and informal economy. Of course this does not exhaust the whole range of possibilities of informal occupation. It should be added, that people are often engaged in the informal economy in a second job. But *second jobs*, strictly speaking, presuppose a *first job*. In other words, the same range of occupations carried out in Torino, Ancona, or even Naples as second jobs, may have different characteristics, may have different significance and may give different gratification if carried out as first and only jobs.[5]

We must turn therefore to protagonists of the process of informalization. Basically they represent the most disadvantaged sectors of the labour force: women, young people and, more recently, minors and schoolchildren. One could say that in Naples, outside of the formal and regular employment force, two poles can be identified: on one hand, the labour force registered at the employment office (young and adult males), and on the other women and children employed in the informal/black work economy. The figures at each pole are exaggerated by the fact that some of the women employed in black work are also registered as unemployed, while at the same time the registered unemployed adult males sometimes carry on irregular occupations (informal by definition).

With regard to this last aspect a survey has been carried out on a sample of registered unemployed (Liguori & Veneziano 1982). The results of the survey highlight the absolute precariousness of these jobs – extremely low income and intolerable working conditions. These elements also explain the mass tendency to escape from informality. Widespread registration at the employment office appears to be understood subjectively as a temporary parking situation, in hopes of subsequently entering the formal economy or, better still, formal employment.

Organized Resistance

Very often a strictly inferential conclusion can be found in Italian literature on the subject of informal employment. Given the low rates of occupation and the official low rates of activity, a high level of occupation in the informal sector is often inferred, 'since people must have some kind of job'. This mechanistic and schematic conclusion does not take into account events concerning the recent social and political history of the city, and in particular the war against black work waged by the stronger sectors of the labour force. The mass movement of unemployed which took shape in the second half of the 1970s has to be regarded in this framework. The Movimento dei Disoccupati Organizzati was a unique experience in the context of working-class struggles in Italy for its dimensions, its mass support, its ability to mobilize and, at least at an early stage, for its tendency to relate itself to the organized labour movement and to the unions. Even now, when the movement can be considered largely exhausted, at least as a mass phenomenon, the tendency to escape the trap of informality is evidenced by mass enrolment in the lists of the employment office.

The movement's contradictory development and its crisis in the 1970s were caused by the structural and social transformation of the city. The flow of investments and the strengthening of the local working class had fostered expectations concerning the possibility of entering the 'system of guarantee' and had given great impetus to the war against black work. At the same time the organized labour movement had extended its control over working conditions, trying to limit the extent of black work.

It cannot be denied that there is presently a revival of black work. The few studies carried out in this field show an expansion of black work among schoolchildren (with wages absolutely unacceptable for adults, or even for youngsters). This fact can certainly be related to general world-wide trends towards informalization. On the other hand, these trends are the effects of the decline of investments in the industrial sector (large-scale industries), of a less strongly organized working class, of a less combative workers' movement and of crisis and disintegration of the movement of the unemployed.

Another indication of the tendency to escape occupation in the informal sector (or at least an indication of the fact that it is an involuntary choice) can be found in the physical distribution of black work in the city. The traditional working-class sectors of the city, such as Bagnoli, where Italsider, the great steel mill, is located, have a restricted informal economy. This has implications for the whole metropolitan area. A survey carried out in Pomigliano D'Arco, where the Alfa-Sud automobile works is located, shows that cottage work in the textile industry (which employs a female labour force, officially a 'non-working population') is widespread in the old part of the city but is entirely absent in the new sector, inhabited by the new working class (where women prefer and can afford to remain unemployed instead of working in the informal sector) (Cetro 1977).

But this negative view is not only based on inferential considerations. A number of studies have been carried out in Naples concerning the work conditions and wages in the informal sector. Apart from the construction industry, work in the informal sector is basically done by women and children (mainly in the footwear and leather industry). The best indicator of working conditions is the number of girls that have been victims of *paralisi di collante* (paralysis from glue). Needless to say, the average daily wage is far below the official union rate, and these workers have no union or social-security guarantees (de Marco & Talamo 1976; Pugliese et al. 1976).

More evidence points in the same direction. Naples has benefited from a new flow of state-supported investments in the building sector, intended to favour reconstruction after the 1980 earthquake. It is widely known that the building industry (particularly in situations of less advanced technological development) lends itself readily to black work and non-regular, informal work relations. A noticeable amount of informal work is at present absorbed by the building industry. The structure of the local building sector, coupled with some characteristics of the Social Security structure of the sector, make it even more difficult and even less convenient to respect union and legislative norms. The reason for the prevailing informal norms must be found in the difficulties of unionization and union defence. Working conditions in the building sector are particularly degraded as far as deskilling, low income, bargaining capabilities and precariousness are concerned. In addition to the lack of universal norms and regulations there are other 'regulations' − those imposed by the *camorra* (racket), which exerts a strong control on the building sector (FLC 1982).

One has to bear in mind that at present a large part of the labour demand comes from the building sector and it is understandable that the precarious work chances in this sector are not always refused. Again, it is not a matter of 'free propensity' towards informality on the part of the labour supply. It is not by chance that workers precariously employed in the construction sector still register as unemployed at the labour office, thus being part of the 'official employment' figures.

The processes of formalization (the attempt to extend a system of universal regulation) have been not only instruments for modernization, but also, and above all, a means of improving the conditions of the working population.

Informality here has been coupled with poverty and backward social relations of work. The development of industrial social relations in the city and a greater strength of the working class have influenced the general social context. The political mobilization of the unemployed, influenced by industrial and trade-union values and culture, has contested the conditions of informal work. The mobilization of the unemployed in Naples has been based on the denunciation of the working conditions in the informal sector and by an effort to enter those jobs characterized by the so-called system of guarantees.[6] The major demand of the unemployed − 'a steady and secure job' − on the one hand can be seen as the reflection of a traditional regional cultural value and on the other it represents a rational and mass-supported political demand to elevate the conditions of disadvantaged segments of the working class to those of the more advantaged (those belonging to the system of guarantees). The point to be made here is that this movement has been able to make the local labour supply, or at least a section of it, more rigid and less available for informal activities.

Hence, in Naples prevalent attitudes and behaviour seem to be characterized by an element of flight rather than pursuit as regards informal potential. This is a far cry from the informal as 'cultural stimulus', recently referred to by Sachs (1980). In particular, analysing the causes of the development of informal activity and starting from the observation of the crisis of the apparatus of production and reproduction, Sachs derives the image of a post-materialist reaction taking the form of the development of post-bourgeois values that are centred on self-realization and that lead to an economy of *being* rather than *having*.

The kind of situation recognized by this approach cannot be found in the Southern Italian context; it presupposes different life-styles and cultural models and a different concept of time and its use. Only superficially can *'l'invention du quotidien'* and the fact that *'le quotidien s'invente avec mille manières de braconner'* be related to the daily exercise of expediency as practised in Naples. *L'arte di arrangiarsi* (the art of surviving) is considered one of the main characteristics of the street-corner economy. The *'invention du quotidienne'*, and also the 'coping strategies' illustrated by Pahl, seem to refer to similar phenomena but with a strongly different value judgement. In Naples there exists above all an attempt to adapt bits and pieces of precarious and obsolete work to family and social organization (and, in fact, the profiles that result are those of 'a thousand trades' rather than 'two jobs').

The opening of 'more refined paths in the jungle of functionalist rationality' of which Sachs speaks, may refer instead to different territorial contexts. According to Sachs, this evasion of the market should lead to freedom from the formal and informal fetters of mercantile economy to arrive at the creation of a civil society that would be a third power among State and market. The subjectivity implicit in this context is based on the liberation from routine conditions in a modern organization of production and even more so on the overcoming of those precarious and subaltern situations found in many areas in which the processes of industrialization and bureaucratization of relations have only partly penetrated.

The satisfactions that go with irregular work (relative auton-omy, freedom of choice and control over the time and characteristics of one's work), which Gershuny and Pahl (1981) consider induce-ments to work performed for unaccounted compensation or on one's own behalf, e.g. DIY, are a very general projection of a tendency; they are directly contradictory to the case of Naples, in which we find a much less optimistic picture.

The two authors cite the example of a worker who takes time off from work to paint his own house. A doubt arises in our minds as to whether in Naples, metaphorically speaking, in place of an employed worker and a house to paint we might not find instead the classic unemployed person who paints someone else's house for cash pay, with neither contract nor union assistance. Often the analyses published in international literature tend to present in a positive light the realities of contexts of production and industrial relations that have encountered difficulties as a result of the new capitalist dynamics and a return to forms of early industrialization. Pahl rightly insists on the importance of not disconnecting large-scale industrial development from preceding situations. In this sense, links with traditional peasant activity and certain habits of community life favour the emergence of informal activities.

These aspects are missing from the urban reality of Naples. If, on the basis of the analysis informalization of productive processes and activities in terms of the Italian situation, we regard informalization as the body of mechanisms and operations conducted by workers and/or firms, with the aim of evading the inflexible restraints imposed by State and/or market, we can see that it has two main objectives: (1) to evade institutional regulations (imposed mainly by the union) and fiscal control ('Can I have it in cash?'); and (2) to decommodify a series of productive activities. Thus, we can formulate the hypothesis that in the South, and especially in Naples, the informal economy represents an evasion primarily of union and State controls.

Conclusions

Firstly, in its known and concrete forms informalization does not introduce new social processes of modernization, much less of emancipation; on the production level it represents the perpetuation of traditional forms of black work or subsistence economy, while on the reproduction level it simply betrays the fact that the specialization of roles remains as yet unattained and that public intervention is absent in this sector.

Our second observation refers to the overall concept of development and transformation upheld by workers' organizations. These groups have tended specifically to discourage this type of activity, promoting the extension of a modern network of production characterized by the formalization of relations. Even now, when new situations of black work are emerging in some areas, especially in those treated by this study, unions tend to insist on the need 'to bring the invisible economy into the light of day', i.e. to extend regulation to it.

Third according to our interpretation of the process, the attempt to 'emerge from the informal economy' is not imposed from the outside, as by an institution such as the union, which has been progressively delegitimated by the development of the informal economy, but is rather a necessity widely felt on a mass level. In other words, the often mentioned contradiction between the social subjects who are vital protagonists of the informalization process and the institutions that would continue to impose rules and regulations does not exist.

On the contrary, the entire movement of the *organized unemployed* (Basso 1981; Liguori & Veneziano 1982; Ramondino 1978) (social actors directly involved in informal activities or indirectly influenced by informal activities carried on by their relatives) has aimed at attaining regular work, i.e. formalized work. A series of studies of the problem (some of which were empirical and were based on interviews with the protagonists) reveals the full awareness that the unemployed had of the contradiction between their work in the invisible economy and the 'steady and secure' work that they sought to obtain within the guarantee system.

As a corollary of our second observation, we can observe that the process is largely an imposed one. There is no choice of informalization (as a mass phenomenon); instead there is an imposition of informal conditions that tend to reproduce themselves, according to economic and social circumstances and especially in relation to State intervention policy.

These general observations hold true throughout the South. However, although the characteristics of informalization and the specific nature of the process are similar at least in part throughout the entire region, some notable differences exist between city and country and within the metropolitan areas – between those that are traditionally not industrialized and those that have to some extent undergone the industrialization process.

Notes

A first version of this paper was presented at the Symposium on Informal and Peripheral Economies, World Congress of Sociology, Mexico City, 1982.

1   A critical review of the literature on the subject can be found in Bagnasco (1981).
2   We do not follow here the definition suggested by Stuart Henry (1981) in which a distinction is made between 'informal economy', 'social economy', 'hidden economy' and 'black economy'.
3   This apologetic view can be found in many Italian works, e.g. CENSIS (1978); Saba (1980).
4   For a more recent account see Lay (1982).
5   With regard to Italian studies on double occupation see Institute of Sociology, University of Turin (1977, 1980).
6   This contrasts only superficially with the hypothesis that the system of guarantees is a permissive condition for double working (which is also the result of the research carried out in the Torino area). See Gallino (1982). The difference there is, as has been said, that informal work is coupled with a first regular job, which is not the case here.

8

Industrial Outworking, Struggles for the Reproduction of Working-class Families and Gender Subordination

Martha Roldán

Introduction: The Theoretical Context

This chapter contributes to and extends a body of theory which has developed in opposition to the dualist 'formal – informal sector' approach and examines its implications for the employment-creation policies commonly directed towards women in Third World cities. The theoretical discussion is based upon the results of recent research on industrial outworking and gender subordination, which was undertaken in 1981 and 1982 in the metropolitan area of Mexico City.[1]

It would be superfluous to repeat here the origins and applications of the formal – informal sector dichotomy, which have already been presented by several authors (e.g. Bromley & Gerry 1979; Moser 1978). Nevertheless, it is worthwhile summarizing the broadly accepted content of the informal sector concept: an interlocking complex of economic activities, characterized by their lack of security and/or stability and their low level of income, typically undertaken on an own-account basis or in small enterprises or workshops using family labour and/or small quantities of wage-labour, unrecognized by government agencies and therefore not subject to their protection. During the 1970s the informal sector became the centre of an intense debate, which was conducted at the theoretical, political and policy-related levels. Those who adopted the informal sector terminology and advocated the sector's promotion believed that it constituted 'the key to the solution to the problems of Third World unemployment and economic growth. Sophisticated measurement techniques continued to be developed to enumerate the characteristics of the two sectors, while policy-oriented studies increasingly advocate the direct intervention of the state in implementing reforms and fiscal measures designed to promote informal sector growth' (Moser 1978: 1055).

On the other hand, those who criticized the concept attributed its popularity to the combination of a number of historical and political factors; in Bromley's judgement (1978: 1036) the concept of the informal sector was a clear reflection of the dominant development orthodoxy of its period.

A further point about the informal sector concept is the relevance of its set of associated policy prescriptions (training, credit, simplification of rules and regulations, etc., favouring indigenous, small enterprises and intermediate technologies) to liberal international opinion in the early 1970s. The intellectual validity of the concept was, for many people, secondary to its policy implications. Support of the informal sector appeared to offer the possibility of 'helping the poor without any major threat to the rich', a potential compromise between pressures for the redistribution of income and wealth and the desire for stability on the part of economic and political elites.

The critique of the informal sector approach has already been adequately presented (Bremen 1976; Bromley 1978; Gerry 1974, 1979; LeBrun & Gerry 1975; MacEwan Scott 1979; Moser 1978) but it is worthwhile summarizing these authors' conclusions in order to underline the major disagreements. They believe the type of dualism inherent in the informal sector approach suffers from the following deficiencies. First, the concept of the informal sector, rather than providing an explanation, offers a merely descriptive insight into certain occupational categories. Second, the dualist classification is simplistic since it labels all economic activities as either informal or formal, thereby ignoring the subtle but import-ant differences found between economic activities which might be described as intermediate or transitional. Third, the concept offers no specific criteria which would allow the identification of a particular activity with one, rather than the other, sector (i.e. without defining activities in *one* sector except by reference to their lack of the characteristics exemplifying activities in the *other* sector). The dualist perspective implicit in the informal sector concept assumes that the two sectors are autonomous, when in fact the nature of their interrelationship is one of domination/subordination. Finally, the theoretical perspective of the informal sector approach encourages the formulation of generalized and undifferentiated policies whose impact is either neutral or prejudicial for the majority of individuals and enterprises found in the local informal sector; in fact, membership of this sector extends to several different classes and class-fractions whose interests are neither identical nor necessarily complementary.

The critique of the dualist approach and of the policies which have been derived from it were based upon empirical analyses which revealed the comprehensive network of relations which bind the ostensibly autonomous informal and formal sectors together (Bose 1974; Gerry 1974, 1979; King 1974; MacEwan Scott 1979), all of which gave a strong impetus to the development of an alternative theoretical approach – namely that of petty-commodity production (PCP). The different theoretical components which make up the PCP approach have a common, predominantly Marxist origin; the corresponding theoretical model seeks to explain the reality which has intrigued and confused the dualists, by replacing the formal–informal dichotomy with a model reflecting the articulation of forms and modes of production which are asymmetrically interconnected by relations of domination/subordination. The forms and modes of production characterizing the urban sector are on the one hand, the capitalist mode, embedded in the international economic system and, on the other, a number of non-capitalist or pre-capitalist forms whose reproduction is nevertheless subordinated to the logic of the former's expansion. A continuum of forms of production exists, with, at the one extreme, 'pure' artisanal or PCP and, at the other, capitalist production, each one representing different degrees of subordination of the direct producer to capital, according to the social relations which characterize the production process itself, as well as the nature of the relations between producers and the market. The debate on PCP has raised one crucial question with regard to the objectives of this chapter: Is there a general tendency for non-capitalist forms of production to be (1) dissolved or (2) conserved through their relations with capitalism? The European experience (as analysed by Karl Marx in volumes 1 and 2 of *Capital*) has, until very recently, led to the conclusion that these non-capitalist forms' were transitional. In contrast, the experience from 'the periphery' seems to suggest that the predominant tendency has been that of conservation.

How has the persistence of these subordinate forms of production been explained? For some writers (e.g. McGee 1979), the conservation of such activities is necessary or *functional* for the expanded reproduction of capital. MacEwan Scott (1979) and Gerry (in various versions of his work on the Dakar economy, e.g. 1974, 1979; Gerry & LeBrun 1975) avoid the voluntaristic view of capitalism by offering a dialectical analysis which emphasises the *limitations* imposed upon the indefinite expansion of PCP. According to MacEwan Scott (1979: 127), the most important factors which should be taken into account when assessing the future of small-scale enterprises are: (1) the possibility of market expansion; (2) changes in the rate of rural/urban migration; and (3) the internal dynamic and tendencies of the capitalist sector. The nature of the limitations to the expansion of PCP, identified by MacEwan Scott, are evidence of a somewhat economistic approach.

Gerry stresses that PCP could constitute the basis for a process of proletarianization (which he identifies as the dominant tendency) or for some embryonic capitalist accumulation (a minority trend). Such proletarianization can take a number of forms, amongst which perhaps the commonest are: (1) the subcontracting of petty commodity producers by commercial or industrial capital; (2) the domination of PCP by commercial capital without subcontracting; (3) casual or temporary proletarianization; and (4) the State organization of petty commodity producers. The minority trend towards capital accumulation on the part of petty commodity producers develops via the *gradual replacement of family labour in production by wage labourers* and through the acquisition of new means of production. With regard to the likely future of PCP, Gerry concludes that given the socio-economic and political reality of the country in question (Senegal), there is little likelihood of any real improvement in the conditions of labour and the standard of living of the workers involved (1979: 247). Thus, Gerry's analysis requires, but is also limited to, a detailed examination of the relations between classes and class-fractions in a given social formation.

Of the analyses based upon the articulation of modes and forms of production, the contributions of MacEwan Scott, Gerry, McGee and others offer perhaps the best analytical challenge to the formal–informal sector dichotomy. Nevertheless, they still have a number of limitations. The key concepts of mode of production, form of production (at both the abstract and empirical level), reproduction and articulation, for example, are either too imprecise or are defined differently by the various authors. The concept of 'the articulation of modes of production' (McGee) or of forms and modes of production (MacEwan, Gerry) could easily be understood as being little more than the stable and symbiotic coexistence of different components, rather than the contradictory historical process by which the dominant mode of production[2] subordinates the modes and forms of production which precede it. These two very different formulations (namely the functional and the dialectical approaches) have, of course, very different implications – not only at the theoretical level but also in terms of the formulation of concrete strategies for social change.

The absence of conceptual and theoretical agreement helps to explain why the different forms of subordination of labour to capital and the factors which condition the balance between dissolution and conservation of PCP have so far been inadequately understood. However, the principal obstacle to theoretical clarity and rigour has not been the multiplicity of definitions, but rather the economistic version of Marxism which has characterized to a greater or lesser extent not only the above but also much of contemporary Marxist writing. In brief, this economistic application of Marxism reduces the historical process to the mechanical operation of certain objective laws of material development, a vision which excludes any real consideration of the social factors which temporally and spatially condition the specific characteristics of that historical process.[3]

This reductionism impedes theoretical progress in general, but in particular it allows the concepts of classical Marxism, such as the relations of production and the labour process, to remain insulated and protected from a feminist or any other critique which stresses the undeniable relevance of certain *other* dimensions of domination/subordination, namely those of race or ethnicity, or those relating to national and/or regional distinctions.[4] This is one of the principal reasons why specific strategies for the creation of employment and for the raising of political conscience and struggle will remain so deficient and defective, as long as they refuse to take account of the degree to which inter-class, gender, ethnic and other types of stratification influence the success or failure of such policies.

Excellent examples of this theoretical and policy-oriented myopia can be found not merely among the protagonists of the formal–informal dichotomy but, equally, amongst their Marxist critics.

Both are quick to point to the central role played by unpaid, female family labour in the survival of the small-scale enterprise.[5] Glib references are commonly made to the enormous number of women employed in service activities, in hawking and in the manufacture of clothing, without ever explicitly asking *why* it is that women are so disproportionately represented in those particular activities (Allen 1981; Goddard 1981). It seems that in their eagerness to explain the dissolution–conservation process which PCP experiences at a global level, and in their zeal to point to the weak structural position of *all* sections of the 'marginal masses', many Marxists have treated the sexual division of labour at best as a *secondary* issue and, at worst, as something both divisive and diversionary. It can be much more persuasively argued that, on the contrary, this omission constitutes the great theoretical *weakness* of an approach which, even though it superficially recognizes the role of family relations in the reproduction of the small workshop, enterprise or home-based, industrial outworking activity based upon unpaid family labour, it nevertheless persists in focusing its analytical attentions on the *relatively insignificant incidence* of wage-labour in these activities.

Consequently, it would seem both theoretically unjustifiable and, in practice, extremely dangerous for a theoretical perspective which seeks not only to explain but also to contribute to the transformation of reality, to continue to ignore or downgrade the question of gender. The concentration of women in branches of production and other activities specifically characterized by their partial or total lack of capacity to accumulate (outside the sphere of unpaid family labour) is not accidental, nor can it be treated as a secondary issue. Women workers suffer from widespread material instability, a lack of legal protection, poor education and training and lower incomes in relation to men; in brief, they occupy the lowest positions in an already hierarchical structure of labour and production. In the case of industrial outworking, women work in secrecy, cut off from the rest of the working class. What are the implications for class consciousness and organization of this quasi-proletarianization of women? The theoretical 'lens' of the PCP model finds it almost impossible to focus upon relations of domination which are not directly expressed in terms of class. The PCP approach has not been able to answer questions relating to gender oppression under capitalism, nor has it been able to provide the tools for critically evaluating urban, employment-creation policies aimed at women and yet based upon an *undifferentiated* promotion of the informal sector. Without the central issue of gender being taken into consideration, such policies are more likely to result in the reinforcing of subordinate gender roles for women, than in their progressive elimination.

How is this theoretical and practical impasse to be overcome? An alternative approach, adopted in this study of industrial outworking, focuses on the analysis of the role played by other pre-existing hierarchical relations (gender-based, ethnic, racial, etc.), whether acting as a brake on the process of proletarianization, facilitating an embryonic capital accumulation which would transform the small commodity producer into a small capitalist, or contributing to quasi-proletarianization in the sphere of industrial outworking.

The alternative approach sketched out above provides a means of giving form and content to what would otherwise be a somewhat nebulous and undifferentiated continuum of quasi-proletarianization: at one extreme, there is something approximating to the 'classic' form of PCP (such as in garment outworking); while at the other extreme, there is something almost indistinguishable from the 'typical' proletarianization. Within this continuum the two factors which need to be analysed in order to separate one form of quasi-proletarianization from another are as follows: (1) the degree of control exercized by the capitalist/workshop proprietor/intermediary and the direct producer within the production process (factors related to, for example, the full or partial economic ownership of the means of production, or their mere possession, involving control over the physical means of production, the labour of others, and the market for inputs and the final product); and (2) ascribed gender relations, which either facilitate or inhibit the various forms of quasi-proletarianization.[6]

The individuals and groups studied in the empirical investigation were relatively homogeneous in ethnic/racial terms and the analysis focused upon the roles of daughter, wife, mother and female head-of-household, in the class or classes to which the domestic group belonged, the point reached in its life cycle and the specific age and sexual composition of the family group. Research upon the family (both empirically and theoretically) requires direct reference to be made to other current debates. It requires, for example, an understanding of the way in which the domestic group acts as a mediator between macro-economic and demographic processes and individual behaviour (frequently analysed through the study of 'survival strategies'). Clearly, also, the debate over the nature of the working-class family under capitalism is of considerable importance to the analysis of different forms of women's quasi-proletarianization.

In Latin America in the last few years, a new theme has emerged in the analysis of women's labour. In contrast to the pioneering studies on women in the labour process, which assumed that the supply of female labour could be simply explained by women's individual strategies for economic participation, recent studies have stressed the importance of the household and the domestic milieu as factors which condition women's participation in the labour force.[7] These studies (exemplified by the detailed analysis of Garcia et al. 1982) in their different ways have pushed to the fore the crucial role played by the domestic unit in mediating between macro-structural processes and the incorporation of family members into the labour market. According to Garcia et al. (1982) the domestic unit reformulates the influences of these structural processes with the objective of allowing its constituent members to more readily survive and socially reproduce themselves. This constitutes a significant theoretical advance on previous analyses, which have tended to assume that the aggregate labour supply consisted quite simply of the sum of all individual, isolated labour supplies. Nevertheless, this focus upon the family group suffers from its particular conceptualization of the household, which tends to ignore the asymmetrical character of ascriptive gender roles (husband/wife, father/son or daughter, mother/son or daughter, etc.) and, consequently, the relations of domination reflected in these gender roles.

The view that gender roles are complementary, corresponds to a unitary vision of the family group and remains the predominant ideology in the historical and sociological literature on this theme. This same viewpoint is also expressed in the majority of studies of 'survival strategies' (see e.g. Bilac 1978), in which the family is represented as a unified interest group without internal divisions, a social entity which formulates the rational survival strategies upon which the standard of living of its members is based: such strategies are seen as automatically giving rise to welfare maximization for the family group as a whole and for each one of its members. The different factors manipulated by the family unit in this process of 'rational decision-making' include the sale of labour power of family members, articulated with a given internal domestic division of labour, reproductive behaviour and the control of fertility, the transition from school to employment and reciprocal exchanges of goods and services.

In contrast, Marxist studies of the reproduction of labour power under capitalism (e.g. Margulis 1982; Margulis et al. 1981), while

examining the various processes of social reproduction corresponding to different social classes, have nonetheless given little attention
to the gender-based conflict inherent in such processes. Thus, both
conventional bourgeois *and* orthodox Marxist approaches can, in
their different ways, be accused of androcentrism.

In order to avoid these problems, the research summarized by
this chapter assumes that the working-class family is a fundamentally contradictory institution (Sen 1980; Stolcke 1982), thereby
emphasizing both the consensual components of the family (especially with regard to its 'public' face) and (more importantly) the
'internal' conflictive and contradictory elements which often are
instrumental in the maintenance of the family as an institution.
The domestic group habitually turns both to intradomestic and
extradomestic means to ensure its reproduction, yet this process
which goes on within the family, is an integral part of the reproduction of classes at the aggregate level. It was therefore considered
essential to verify empirically the extent to which the processes of
social reproduction encountered in working-class families involved
acts of solidarity of a rational and egalitarian nature on the part of
some or all family members. Of course, it was also necessary to take
into account that such behaviour patterns within the family would
manifest themselves, in a general way, in the form of relations of
class domination, gender oppression and inter-generational subordination.

This approach, with its roots firmly in feminist theory, helps to
demystify the concept of the household by defining it as a specific
locus of class domination, gender and inter-generational subordination. It also emphasizes the elements within the family which make
an authentic contribution to class struggle and defence of workers'
class interests (Humphries 1977), e.g. the provision of solidarity,
mutual aid and protection in times of crisis. This approach also
shows that the feedback from the domestic sphere to that of the
labour process cannot merely be seen as a functional relationship;
the interaction between the two is and remains potentially conflictive. The incorporation of women into the labour process, under
certain conditions of proletarianization (Roldán 1982), brings with
it the possibility of the erosion of traditional norms of behaviour,
which, together with their access to an independent source of
income, could provide them with the basis for the creation of an
autonomous space.

In this way, the study of the different forms of quasi-
proletarianization found in the sphere of women's industrial out-

working is inevitably connected, both theoretically and practically, to: (1) the analysis of struggles for survival and reproduction in the working-class family; and (2) the relations of class domination/ subordination and relations of gender and generational oppression within and outside the domestic group. In order to illustrate this new analytical approach, this chapter brings together evidence collected in an empirical study of women's industrial outworking in Mexico City, with particular reference to the aspects mentioned above. The presentation of empirical data and the corresponding conclusions are preceded by a brief discussion of the chains of subcontracting which emphasizes the macro-economic framework in which such processes must be set.

Quasi-proletarianization, Subcontracting and Gender Subordination in Women's Industrial Outworking

Several branches of industrial outworking (undertaken by women in their own homes) were investigated in the research,[8] including joinery, plastics finishing, textiles and the 'making-up' of garments, electronic component assembly, metal-sorting and a wide range of miscellaneous activities. According to Beneria (1982), these industrial outworking operations, despite their differences, have a number of common characteristics. The major similarity is that all are industrial rather than artisanal activities, representing a single stage or sub-process in the creation of a final product for the market. This results from a specialized division of labour, made possible by a fragmentation of the labour process which exemplifies modern industrial production.

With the exception of garment outwork, in which workers retained partial ownership of the means of production (sewing machines and accessories), the few tools and minimal equipment used (if any were used at all), as well as the raw materials and components, were supplied by the factory or workshop owner, or an intermediary. Nevertheless, in both cases, the freed or partially freed labour power of the outworker is characterized by relations of dependency on the workshop proprietor, industrialist or commercial intermediary, notwithstanding the fact that partial control over the labour process was retained (duration and rhythm of the working day, intensity of labour, decisions relating to the use of unpaid family labour or, in the case of seamstresses, the use of additional wage workers, paid on the basis of piece-rates or time-rates). In all cases, the work involved intensive manual labour in tasks that were highly specialized and monotonous, which nevertheless required only a minimum of formal qualification (except in the case of seamstresses) and a minimal need for quality control. Payment was characteristically made on a piece-rate basis and at levels lower than the legal minimum wage. Since these activities were undertaken in clandestine conditions, any guarantee of even minimal stability of the earnings of industrial outworkers required a considerable increase in the degree of dependency of such workers on their suppliers. The chains of subcontractual relations into which industrial outworkers are integrated are made up of enterprises of different sizes: multinational corporations producing commodities directly for the market, factories producing these types of final products or components, small workshops, the intermediaries who supply the inputs and finally domestic outworkers. These subcontractual chains show that industrial outworking is an integral part of a total and substantial labour process involving *all* the levels and phases of the capitalist production of a final product for the market.

Beneria's analysis (1982) indicates the inadequacy of the formal–informal dichotomy (implying the autonomy of the two sectors concerned) in any explanation of the substantial degree of interrelationship between home-based industrial outworking and the totality of the capitalist production process. Industrial outworking is located on the lowest rung of this total labour process and, as the same author also shows, relations of gender subordination play an instrumental role in the expansion of that overall process of capitalist production.

Industrial Outworking, Gender Roles and Struggles for the Reproduction of Working-class Families

A number of studies (Bilac 1978; Garcia et al. 1982), focusing upon the survival strategies of family groups, have emphasized the relationship between the head-of-household's class position, the socio-demographic characteristics of the domestic group and the position of family members in the overall employment and production structure. Following on from this, it would seem reasonable to identify the quasi-proletarianization of the female industrial outworkers as being one aspect of the broader struggle of low-income family groups to ensure their social reproduction.[9] I tried, therefore, to identify and specify the socio-economic niche of outworking activities, with particular attention being paid to the following crucial aspects:

1   the incorporation of women industrial outworkers into the labour market, analysed in terms of:
     (a)   type of family group concerned, the socio-biological stage which the family has reached (e.g. young, working couples with dependent infants, well-established couples with working *and* dependent children, etc.) and the ascriptive gender roles played by various members of the family group and;
     (b)   class position and income level of the head-of-household and collective individual participation rates in wage-labour and/or domestic chores and/or other survival strategies;
2   the articulation between wage-labour and unpaid domestic work and;
3   other processes and activities within the domestic sphere, in particular the influence exercised by the ideology of domesticity and women's definition of their roles as mothers/wives.

Family cycle and gender roles

Seventy-six per cent of the 140 outworkers surveyed were wives currently cohabiting with their husbands. Thirteen per cent were female heads-of-household and seven per cent single daughters. Four out of five of the large group of married women belonged to complete nuclear family groups and, of these, over half were in the phase of family expansion. Thus, the typical female outworker is a woman of child-bearing age, living in a nuclear family with her husband and with children aged under seven years. This character-ization clearly indicates the importance of the maternal role as defined in the nuclear family, particularly as there is no possibility of substituting or rotating this role by introducing the labour time of female members of an *extended* family. For the typical woman outworker in the ascendent phase of the family cycle, children are still young and dependent, therefore requiring longer periods of close attention, without there being any assistance available from elder daughters. The importance of this specifically maternal role and the general domestic environment play a significant role in determining how women's labour can be sold on the labour market.

In contrast, the very low income derived from such outworking explains why it is of limited popularity as a survival/subsistence strategy for female heads-of-household, except in the case of those who work exclusively for a manufacturer or sub-contractor, those who depend upon a relatively higher-than-normal amount of family labour, and those working at home (for slightly better wages) in the 'making-up trade' for clothing manufacturers. The few *single* daughters involved in home-based work for industry were all young girls who combined outworking with the continuation of their studies or much older women who appeared to prefer this type of work, because it allowed them either to look after older relatives or to help younger, female relatives with domestic chores. The chronically ill (of whatever age) may also show a preference for this type of work, given their restricted mobility outside the home.

The employment structure mentioned above appears to be the opposite of that characterizing other proletarization processes which have taken women 'outside' the domestic sphere, e.g. into factory work or rural wage-work (Roldán 1981). In the majority of such processes, the predominant groups have been single daughters and female heads-of-households, while married women with very young families have normally been substantially under-represented. The ascriptive gender role which predominates in the case of industrial outworking favours the incorporation of women workers (wives and mothers) who are best able to reconcile wage labour with what could under other circumstances be substantially conflicting conjugal and maternal obligations. Domestic isolation combined with low incomes offers little or no incentive for female heads-of-household or single women to join this section of the labour force.

A number of important personal characteristics are also common to this type of female labour. Almost 45 per cent of those interviewed were aged between 21 and 35. The educational level of women outworkers also tends to be very low: 13 per cent were illiterate, only 36 per cent had three years of primary education or less, while 38 per cent had completed between four and six years of primary education. Forty-three per cent of the sample could be described as well-established migrants (having spent at least ten years in the Federal District of Mexico City, while 38 per cent were actually born in the city). Only five per cent of the women interviewed had been living in Mexico City for five years or less. Thus, we are presented with an essentially young population, born in the city, or at least having spent considerable time there, and with little or no education.

*Class position and income level of heads-of-households, labour-force
participation of family members and other survival struggles of
working-class families*

Women industrial outworkers,[10] as members of family groups, were
further analysed in terms of the head-of-household's class position[11]
and level of earnings. Husbands comprised over 78 per cent of
heads-of-households, while 13 per cent of the women interviewed
were themselves heads of their own households; there were only a
few cases of heads of outworkers' households being mothers,
brothers, or other relatives. Let us consider in some detail the class
position, income level and stability of employment of those
heads-of-households. Sixty-one per cent of them were remunerated
uniquely on the basis of capitalist wage employment (working class
in the strict sense); ten per cent may be considered part of the
working class in a broad sense; nine per cent occupied petty
bourgeois positions, while twelve per cent earned their incomes on
the basis of combined wage employment and non-wage activities.[12]
Looking more closely at the question of income and stability of
employment of the members of the working class in the strict sense,
it is interesting to note that 11 per cent of the male heads-of-
households were earning less than the 1981 legal minimum wage;
41 per cent were paid at rates equal to the legal minimum wage; 27
per cent received wages at a rate between the legal minimum and
double the legal minimum and 10 per cent more than double the
legal minimum wage. In other words, almost 80 per cent of those
male heads-of-households involved exclusively in capitalist wage
relations were paid at wage rates equal or superior to the legal
minimum.

As far as the stability of employment is concerned, almost 80 per
cent of those who worked in the manufacturing sector (60 per cent
of the total) were regarded as permanent employees of their firms
and these households had relatively reliable employment.

In contrast, in the construction sector, none of the heads-of-
households could count on continuous and stable employment and
all described themselves as casual workers. Of those heads-of-
households working in commercial enterprises two-thirds could be
described as permanent,, and one-third as casual. Finally, of those
employed in service enterprises, 90 per cent were casual workers.
However, even though in the establishments concerned (bars,
restaurants, etc.) insecure employment and low basic wage rates are

the norm, earnings are not necessarily low; due to the considerable contributions made by tips, the majority of workers can take home more than double the legal minimum wage.

All those heads-of-households who belonged to the working class in a broad sense (ten per cent of the total) were husbands of the women interviewed, had incomes equal or greater than the minimal legal wage and enjoyed substantial stability of earnings. The petty bourgeois heads-of-households (nine per cent of the total) were all husbands, with the exception of one (a mother of the outworker interviewed). Twenty-five per cent of these heads-of-households earned less than the legal minimum, but 42 per cent of the remaining heads earned between the minimum and double the minimum, or double the legal minimum wage. There are considerable difficulties in calculating the stability of earnings amongst those involved in petty bourgeois activities (or among the self-employed) and, consequently, our estimate that seventy-five per cent of them enjoyed substantial stability of earnings are only approximate.

Finally, there were those heads-of-households who were simultaneously involved in both capitalist and non-capitalist production relations: the male heads-of-households in this category earned, without exception, incomes equal to or in excess of the legal minimum wage. However, the six female heads-of-households who fell into this category earned, without exception, incomes lower than the legal minimum wage. Again, approximately 70 per cent of this category as a whole had employment which could be considered to be stable.

On the basis of the data presented above, what type of family context is most likely to provide female outworkers? First of all, it should be emphasized that the family groups under scrutiny here in no way constitute a *marginalized* population (Lomnitz 1977) for whom income instability, rather than the absolute level of income, constitutes the fundamental characteristic. Stability of earnings was considerable, especially among the heads-of-household working for capitalist manufacturing and commercial enterprises. The husbands of the female industrial outworkers interviewed are predominantly and typically manual wage-workers in capitalist manufacturing, commercial and service enterprises, earning relatively stable incomes equal to or reaching as much as double the 1981 legal minimum wage. Other evidence relating to the non-marginality of the individuals and families studied includes the rate of male and female labour-force participation and the absence of reciprocal exchange and mutual aid between equals (Lomnitz 1977), signalling the importance of unpaid female labour in the reproduction of a particular fraction of the Mexican working class.

Much of the literature on survival strategies in the poor districts of urban Mexico emphasizes one particular rule of thumb common to all resource-poor family groups, i.e. use the available labour power to its maximum. This necessarily involves the establishment of individual sources of income by the maximum number of household members to sustain the social reproduction of the whole group. It will also often require the premature withdrawal of children from school to augment the number of individual income earners and maximize the aggregate, 'pooled' income, so that the risks of occupational instability, low wages, etc., can be reduced.

However, this rule of thumb involving the maximum use of available family labour power, the proliferation of individually remunerated occupations and the subsequent pooling of wages and earnings, was not to be found among women industrial outworkers. On the basis of data collected on the labour-force participation rates among men and women (according to type of production relations and level of earnings), it was possible to express the number of paid workers of 11 years of age or more in the family groups, studied as a proportion of the potentially active family labour-power in the same age range. The calculations show that though the male and female participation rates varied from moderate to high, they never reached a level consistent with the maximization or 'over-utilization' of the available family labour power. In general, this participation rate was higher for men than for women.[13] Clearly, the level of the husband's earnings was a fundamental factor in determining participation rates inside the family; nevertheless, another very significant factor was the importance attached to the education of children. In response to questions concerning the importance of education, it was commonly stated, in particular by the mothers interviewed, that 'we are sending them to school so that they will not be ignorant like us and so that they are not forced to earn their living in the same way that we are'. In general, the sons and daughters of those interviewed remained in school at least until the end of primary education; following this, some secondary education or a shorter period of practical or vocational training was sought. If children worked at all, boys might be employed as 'counter staff' on market stalls and girls in *tortillerias* or petty personal services, but without interrupting school attendance or by reserving such employment specifically for the holidays. Consequently, the sons and daughters of female industrial outworkers are not prematurely thrust into work in order to reduce the amount of consumption which is unaccompanied by new income, due to the fact that the father's occupation and the home-based wage-working of the mother generates enough income to make possible a more protracted period of education for their children than would otherwise be financially sustainable.

Nevertheless, the participation rates mentioned above substantially underestimate the total amount of paid work performed by women in particular, as well as the general female contribution in terms of unpaid family labour assistance in outwork and in the overall routine of domestic chores. There are two reasons for the underestimation of women's real participation in productive and reproductive activities. In the first place, the participation rate in no way reflects the double, or in some cases, triple involvement in work, particularly in the case of women. It was found that of the total number of income earners interviewed (392), 16 per cent (63 individuals: 12 men and 51 women) had double, triple and quadruple occupations. Of the 140 female outworkers interviewed, 34 per cent had incomes in addition to their wages from outworking. Of these nine were heads of their own households, two were heads of subsidiary households and one was a sister. The majority, (75 per cent), however, were working wives. The supplementary activities most commonly associated with industrial outworking were personal services of an intermittent and/or permanent nature (e.g. laundry work, hourly paid domestic work for others, small-scale selling, often by children, of foodstuffs and snacks from the doorstep, small-scale retailing of provisions, etc.). One woman, involved in the domestic assembly of pens, also earned wages from her assembly-work in a construction enterprise, while another sold Avon products and received a small salary plus commission.

The second reason stems from the fact that, for example, in the majority of branches of industrial outworking analysed, help given by family members makes an absolutely indispensible contribution to the meagre wages earned by the principal outworker. This is especially the case in the assembly of toys, plastic flowers, metalware, cardboard boxes, etc. Such help is predominantly female and comes principally from daughters, 60 per cent of whom (of six years and over) gave unpaid assistance to their mothers. Equally, help in the production process is also given by other women — aunts, nieces, grandmothers — some of whom come from outside the nuclear family. Thirty per cent of the husbands of outworkers assisted in the assembly of products: 27 per cent of brothers, 19 per cent of other male family members and 8 per cent of brothers-in-law. In the case of younger sons, unpaid help was more common, with between 40 per cent and 46 per cent of these family members providing unpaid asistance. It should be stressed, however, that in terms of total amount of labour time devoted to this unpaid assistance, female contribution was substantially higher than men's.

In general, it was rare for informal networks of reciprocal exchange of goods and services between equals (otherwise a common form of support in social reproduction in the so-called marginal, low-income settlements) to be used in the sphere of industrial outworking. An exception to this rule was found amongst the poorest female heads-of-household and one or two wives whose husbands had earnings less than the legal minimum wage. In such cases, notably when the husband's contribution to family income was limited by excessive expenditure on alcohol, female industrial outworkers called upon relatives to help in the provision of clothing for children, shoes for the family and educational expenditure. However, this was very much a minority trend among the households studied, confirming the hypothesis put forward by Lomnitz (1977) that such survival strategies (rather than subsistence strategies) characterized the most marginal family groups, whose incomes were unstable rather than merely low.

Finally, it is worth mentioning that subsistence production did not contribute significantly to the overall survival strategies of industrial outworkers' families. In over 84 per cent of cases, no such subsistence production existed; in ten per cent of the cases analysed, the raising of domestic animals (chickens, ducks and pigs) for eventual family consumption constituted the major form of subsistence production.

Having described one aspect of the subsistence struggles of industrial outworkers' families, namely in terms of overall labour-force participation, it would now be appropriate to examine the role played by unpaid domestic labour (based upon the dominant gender-based division of labour) which underpins the incorporation of family labour into the 'external' labour market.

Unpaid domestic labour

The female industrial outworker, either as a cohabiting wife or as an independent female head-of-household, normally undertakes all the tasks involved in the day-to-day and inter-generational reproduction of labour-power: cleaning the house, washing and ironing clothes, cooking, buying provisions, fetching water, mending clothes and general child care. In addition to this, of course, the wife or independent female head-of-household is also involved in the emotional and sexual sphere (Ferguson & Folbre 1981), consisting of the provision of affection and emotional and psychological support, as well as the sexual satisfaction of husbands/partners.

The number of hours devoted to domestic chores is extremely variable, ranging from a minimum of two hours per day to a maximum of 70 hours per week. The variation depends on a number of factors: the type of family group (nuclear family or extended family), the socio-biological stage reached by the family, the number and age of children, other paid employment undertaken by the female industrial outworker, the (non)-availability of assistance from inside or outside the nuclear family and the income of the husband in relation to the type of housing occupied.

The fact that the hours devoted to domestic chores on the one hand and industrial outworking on the other are characterized by considerable variability illustrates the woman's capacity to simultaneously exercise several economic and domestic activities. Outworking can be started, interrupted and recommenced at will and is readily combined with other tasks, such as the supervision of children and food preparation/cooking. If a child falls ill, the industrial outworker can take the child to the clinic to be examined or vaccinated and assembly-work can be put off until the afternoon. Equally, if an urgent order is brought to the industrial outworker by her supplier, household chores can be put off until later, or even until the following day, so as to allow time for completion of the wage work.

The contribution made by different members of the family to housework in general varies from family to family and according to its gender composition. However, irrespective of the type of family group under scrutiny, assistance provided by husbands is minimal and, despite the fact that 80 per cent of husbands provided *some* help, this was normally restricted to certain types of shopping, the payment of bills and a limited amount of child care. The particular balance between these types of male contribution to domestic labour will vary according to the composition of the family and the stage of its development that has been reached. However, the contribution to housework provided by sons and daughters is considerable: 72 per cent of daughters and 51 per cent of sons consistently helped in the house, but there was considerable differentiation not only between the sexes but also according to the age of the children in question. Boys were commonly found running messages and small errands, as well as undertaking minor chores around the house. On the other hand, daughters were much more centrally and heavily involved in housework and child care. Additional help was also provided by other female members of the family (mothers of young outworkers, sisters, etc.) and tended to greatly exceed the contribution made by *male* family members of all types.

Extracts from an interview with Senora S. give a clear illustration of the rapid pace and heavy burden of combined housework and outworking characteristic of the majority of women interviewed:

> I usually wake up between four and five in the morning. Really, I am working like mad most of the time, running here and there, up and down. While I am preparing meals, I am washing the clothes or the dishes. If I am not doing that, then I am sweeping or cleaning. Normally I get up before they all do; I prepare lunch early and put it on a low light, so that I can do other things. If I really have got too much to do, or if I have been ill my husband helps me. If I can manage to get up at 4.00 in the morning, then I am usually able to finish the housework by 7.00. Then I sit down to sew. I will carry on until about 9.00 and then give them breakfast. Sometimes it has to be very quick, because I have to deliver my sewing. By 3.00, I have finished clearing up lunch and I can start on my sewing again. Sometimes, I go on until 9.00 or 10.00 at night and then stop to give my husband something to eat. After that, if I am not too tired, I can carry on sewing until 11.30 or 12.00 at night.

Senora S. worked an average of approximately seven hours a day on household chores, and 70 hours of industrial outworking each week, including weekends.

In summary, the female industrial outworker can rely on a certain amount of help in domestic chores from the rest of the nuclear family. However, the type of tasks performed by male and female family members is distinctive both in terms of intensity, scale and frequency. Even if 80 per cent of husbands, 72 per cent of daughters and 77 per cent of mothers provide such help, there is no comparison whatsoever between the participation of males and females in domestic labour. Husbands and other male members of the family provide help almost exclusively in the sphere of repairs, the payment of bills and certain types of shopping. Female members of the family undertake activities of permanent and continuous nature, related to cleaning, washing, child care, cooking and the sphere of 'sexual services'.

Quasi-proletarianization and the ideology of domesticity

The quasi-proletarianization of women brought about by their involvement in industrial outworking, clearly an important part of the subsistence strategies of the family groups studied, cannot be satisfactorily explained without taking into account the dominant maternal/family ideology and the manner in which the majority of the women interviewed defined their role as wife and mother. A number of open-ended questions were posed in order to gain some impression of the way in which these women viewed the different types of work in which they were involved, and how this related to their own definitions of the roles they played in the family as wives and mothers.

When asked why they had opted for industrial assembly work at home, rather than some other type of work, almost 28 per cent of those interviewed emphasized the importance of child care, not only in terms of the physical attention required by their children but also in terms of their general socialization. When those who answered that industrial outworking was the type of activity most compatible with housework are added to this group, we find that 43 per cent of those interviewed made explicit reference to their role as either mother and/or wife. However, many women made no distinction between these motivations, and when these combined answers are added to those already indicated, the proportion of women referring to the compatibility of their current work with household and/or child care exceeds two-thirds of the sample. The second most important reason suggested by the women interviewed for selecting industrial outworking was either the already-experienced lack of alternative employment and/or a lack of information on alternative job possibilities (approximately 16 per cent of those interviewed).

Second, women were asked whether they would accept factory work and the attitude of husbands to this possibility was also investigated. More than 37 per cent said that they would accept such work, 10 per cent were equivocal and 45 per cent said that they would not. The women who said that they would not accept factory work pointed to domestic and/or maternal responsibilities or their husband's opposition as the principal reasons for rejecting this possibility. Once again the importance of definitions of the domestic/maternal role are evident. In 21 per cent of cases husbands' opposition was due to problems foreseen in care of children or house and in 8 per cent it reflected the conjugal role and was expressed as jealousy.

When asked to compare the situation of women factory workers and women industrial outworkers, almost 60 per cent of those interviewed expressed the opinion that a woman factory worker benefited from better wages, greater stability and often received various social benefits. Those who believed that the industrial outworker was better off (21 per cent of those interviewed) again made reference to the possibility of looking after their children and their house as the principal advantages. Three-quarters of the women interviewed, irrespective of their preference for industrial outworking or industrial wage-working, believed that the wages received for working at home were unjustly low. They nevertheless continued to accept these low wages for a number of reasons: however, many women pointed (either directly or indirectly) to pure economic necessity and the need for self-esteem and independence as their principal motivation for continuing in industrial outworking.

When asked whether they would favour any sort of action to put pressure on employers to pay better wages, 30 per cent of the women interviewed replied that nothing could be done, 20 per cent said that they would not know how to go about improving their wages and 23 per cent pointed to individual initiatives (e.g. talking to the supplier, attempting to convince the factory owner or manager that a pay increase should be made). Less than nine per cent of those interviewed were in favour of any type of collective action; however, they recognized that it would be very difficult to take such an initiative since women industrial outworkers tend not to know one another and, were such a 'rebellion' to take place, the supplier would undoubtedly offer work to other women who were prepared to work for low wages. Thus the possibility of any sort of trade-union action seemed to be very remote. Forty-one per cent of the women interviewed said that they did not know the purpose of trade unions, while ten per cent were opposed to trade unions on the grounds that they defraud and rob their members. Thirty-seven per cent of the women thought more highly of trade unions but accepted that they were only advantageous for workers in factories and similar establishments, and had little or nothing to offer women in industrial outworking.

Women were also asked if they thought it likely that they would continue to work; over 84 per cent of those interviewed said that

they would continue as outworkers, 5 per cent thought that they
would not and 6 per cent were unsure. Many women said that they
would continue working even if their husbands were to receive
better wages themselves (57 per cent of the cases). Seventeen per
cent of the women interviewed said that if their husbands' wages
improved, they themselves would cease working, while a similar
number of women replied that it was hardly likely that their
husbands would receive wage increases.

Tentative Conclusions

So far the quasi-proletarianization brought about by women's
involvement in industrial outworking has been analysed as one
particular dimension of the struggle for survival of families belonging, for the most part, to the working class (either in the strict or in
the broader sense of the term), the heads-of-household of which are
characterized by relative employment stability and earning at least
the equivalent or up to two or three times the minimum legal wage.
Initially, however, we had thought that the outworkers' families
most probably belonged to a particular stratum of the so-called
informal sector, more specifically to some layer of the Mexico City
sub-proletariat. However, quickly and almost inadvertently, this
perspective was transformed into one in which industrial outworking was identified as an important component of the reproduction of
labour power in what is clearly a stable section of the working class,
parallel and complementary to the more familar process of the
reproduction of labour power which is assured by capital itself.
Thus, the insertion of the woman industrial outworker into the
labour force, her multiple occupations, the work undertaken by
other members of the family and the articulation between unpaid
domestic labour and wage-labour came to be analysed not merely as
a subsistence strategy of poor, urban families but also, more
importantly, as a strategy of reproducing labour-power at the level
of the class itself. In other words, the analysis of the above factors
made it possible to identify a source of 'additional benefit' or
'subsidy' for capital. Thus, part of the total cost of maintaining and
reproducing the labour power employed by capital is transferred
from the sphere of responsibility of the capitalist employer to that of
the working-class family itself. The analysis of these mechanisms of
subsistence/survival, seen in the context of the nuclear family,
emphasizes the full extent of the articulation between capital on the

one hand and sectors which are involved in non-capitalist relations on the other. This same analysis also emphasizes the inadequacy of the dualistic conception of the formal and informal sectors, which depends so much on the assumption of their relative mutual autonomy.

Given that industrial outworking constitutes an integral part of social reproduction at the level of the family and at the level of a significant section of the urban working class, can the conclusion be drawn that the struggles for subsistence/survival undertaken by these family groups provide the maximum benefit to each and every member of the households in question? Certainly, when examined from the point of view of the female industrial outworker, the answer to this question must be negative.

First, the analysis of the economic aspect of female industrial outworking, which was carried out by Beneria, showed that the low level of wages, the instability of work and the lack of any 'social aspects' of the wage indicate that outworking, as such, in no way provides the economic foundation for the household. In the vast majority of cases, such earnings were clearly supplementary to the wages brought home by the husband. The female industrial outworker earns her meagre wage under conditions which are clearly detrimental to her health, due to the double or triple working day involved in the combination of unpaid domestic labour, paid industrial outworking and other employment.

Second, industrial outworking serves to further isolate women from social contact (except with members of her own household), which undoubtedly contributes to the incidence of emotional and psychological disorders. Many of the women interviewed were only able to continue to combine housework and wage-work through the use of tranquillizers or had used them in the past. Many women also showed signs of a disproportionate dependence (both psychological and physical) on the continued presence of their daughters in the home.

Third, working at home, these women are also isolated from other women in similar wage-earning activities, thereby contributing to the fragmentation of the working class. The physical isolation and dispersion, inherent in industrial outworking, to a large extent explains the marked lack of any significant class- or trade-union consciousness amongst the women interviewed, despite the fact that many of them were fully aware of the injustice of the situation in which they worked. However, in general the women did not know how to overcome their exploitation, except on an individual basis by competing amongst themselves to obtain better jobs.

Industrial outworking thus constitutes a very good example of the particularly oppressive manner in which quasi-proletarianization can take place, in particular for women. In order to 'benefit' from even the most minimal insertion into the labour force and the wage system, women are forced to collaborate in the reproduction of their subordinate role as wives, mothers and daughters. The reconciliation of productive and reproductive activities, facilitated by the domestic location of industrial outworking, leaves husbands and other male family members free to benefit from a better paid involvement in wage labour and reinforces their conventional lack of responsibility for domestic work. In this way, relations of gender oppression and of class domination are reinforced within the domestic sphere to the benefit of capital and the male segment of the working class.

Having pointed out the limited contribution to be made by industrial outworking to working-class struggles for subsistence and survival, can only pessimistic and negative conclusions be drawn from the above analysis? In order to answer this question fully, further analysis is needed of family interaction and the manner in which the different roles played within the working-class family are viewed and defined by those most closely involved. Such detailed study is undertaken elsewhere (Roldán 1984 forthcoming) but some findings particularly relevant to the problematic of this chapter are summarized below.

The Distribution of Income within the Family and Gender Subordination

As many articles have already shown (Blood & Wolfe 1960); Komarovsky 1967; Rodman 1967; Safilios-Rothschild 1967), access to monetary income constitutes an extremely important potential basis for the exercise of power within the family. Consequently, the analysis of the distribution of monetary income entering the household is a useful way of elucidating the mechanisms whereby gender hierarchies are imposed, reproduced and possibly modified.[14]

However, the relationship between access to monetary income and conjugal power cannot be defined in a simple and mechanical manner (Roldán 1981, 1982). The normative expectations which to some extent determine marital interaction and the pre-existent power inequalities between different members of the family must be rigorously studied in order to establish the relation between the availability of an additional monetary income and the manner in which it is subsequently controlled and distributed within the family. The internal disposition of family incomes cannot be analysed in isolation, for the simple reason that it constitutes only *one* of the very many processes of resource acquisition and distribution within the household sphere. Family members also exchange socio-economic resources of other types: prestige, social mobility, affection (understanding, attention, emotional support, etc.), domestic services such as child care and socialization, sexuality, etc. These transactions are usually unequal because the spouses, according to their position in class and gender hierarchies, maintain differential access to and control of exchangeable as well as 'qualifying' resources, such as conjugal and gender ideologies, coercive means, values, feelings and symbols embedded in each individual's consciousness and culture. The cost involved in the use of specific resources, the relative needs of members of the family and alternative courses of action (Safilios-Rothchild 1967) all constitute elements which, in different ways, further qualify the total picture of marital interaction.

Two allocational patterns were found. In two-thirds of the cases encountered in the study, a type of 'common fund' existed, in which the income of the female industrial outworker was quite simply added to that brought in by the husband and other members of the family. The common fund was used in its totality to pay a series of expenses, upon which the social reproduction of the family depended. This form of distribution and use of incomes tended to characterize those families with lower incomes: in slightly over half the cases, husbands were drawing wages equal to or less than the minimum legal rate. Another indication of the particularly poor economic circumstances of families using the 'common-fund' method was the fact that half of the women in this sub-group had one or even two income-generating activities in addition to their industrial outworking. The most common combination of activities (as indicated in preceding sections) was that of outworking with laundry work and/or domestic service paid by the hour.

A second allocational pattern, that of the 'housekeeping allowance', characterized the remainder of the households studies (33 per cent). Here the husband fulfils the role of main economic provider or bread-winner. He hands over to his wife a portion of his earnings as a housekeeping allowance to cover basic expenditure.

The wife, in turn, uses her earnings to cover expenditures which are above and beyond the minimum standard of living secured by the husband's allowance. This distributional mechanism was encountered in households with higher incomes (in 90 per cent of these cases, the husband earned three or more times the minimum legal wage, and in no case did the husband earn less than this legal minimum). Only 25 per cent of the working wives in this sub-group undertook *other* paid economic activities, apart from industrial outworking.

In both of the above sub-groups it was generally the husbands who decided how the money should be handed over and upon the ratio between the money allocated to basic household expenses and that which they retained for 'personal expenses'. Forty-five per cent of wives in the first group and 55 per cent of those in the second did not know how much their husbands earned. All the women in the first group contributed the entirety of their wages to the common fund, i.e., for the wife, there was no equivalent of the husband's 'pocket money'. Nevertheless, the women's contributions to the common fund were almost always less than that of their husbands, except in four cases in which the husbands earned less than the minimum legal wage. In both sub-groups the women decided whether they would contribute to the common fund or whether they would retain their wage for special expenses. However, they lacked real control over how the fund or allowance was spent, because both *must* be used for basic household expenses. It could be said that they budget, rather than control,[15] different types of resources and expenses and were subject to similar restrictions concerning larger or irregular payments, which are controlled by their husbands. The fundamental difference between those families which relied on the common fund and those in which the wives received a housekeeping allowance was that in the latter case husbands' wages were specifically earmarked for such basic necessities as rent, gas, essential foodstuffs and children's school expenses, while the so-called 'extras' were paid for out of the wages earned by their wives through their industrial outworking.

What is the relationship between the various ways in which monetary income is distributed within the family and the different forms of gender subordination? In order to answer this question normative expectations regulating the 'legitimate' interaction and interchange between spouses were examined as well as other control mechanisms employed when ideological 'norms' break down. The analysis of interviews with women industrial outworkers revealed no evidence of a unique and static 'marriage contract' among working-class families; rather, there existed a continuous process of renegotiating the terms of interaction and exchange between husbands and wives, stretching from the time of marriage to the time in which the interviews were undertaken. In the sample of women interviewed, these 'renegotiations' seemed to be associated with the level of contribution made by the husbands to the common fund and the quality of the husband's attitude and behaviour towards his wife. Renegotiation was also related to the contribution made by the wife to the common fund, to her own subjective view of the matrimonial situation and to her general experience of life and work (whether she was a young, recently married woman or an older and more sceptical wife). The distributional patterns studied may, therefore, be considered as one moment in the unfolding of conjugal interaction.

A concrete example, giving details of this renegotiation, elucidates this process. Let us take those women who made a contribution amounting to more than 40 per cent of the weekly fund but whose husbands also contributed to the requirements of the domestic group, the pooling of resources being necessitated by the fact that the husband's incomes alone did not provide a sufficient basis for the family's subsistence (33 per cent of the common-fund group). Among the most prominent justifications for the contribution made by these wives to basic family expenses was the desire to establish some degree of control over the administration of the budget, thereby eroding to some extent the strict control exercised by the husband over the use of his money for basic expenditure. However, the size of the wife's contribution in this common-fund sub-group did not seem to exercise any influence over the basic forms of household income deployment mentioned above, such as the amount kept by the husband for his personal use, and the form in which his contribution was made.

However, the wives in this sub-group appeared to have more personal decision-making power in *other* family spheres, i.e. in decisions relating to work outside the house and the visiting of relatives and women friends (wives' decision in 33 per cent of cases). As far as the control of fertility was concerned, half of the women decided on the number of children and use of contraceptives. In 40 per cent of cases a joint decision was made. Methods of child care tended to be a fundamental and almost exclusive sphere of responsibility and decision-making for the wife, whereas the disciplining of children was the responsibility of the husband in 45 per cent of the cases and in 30 per cent of the cases a joint decision.

Between those families in which the women contributed less than
40 per cent to the common fund (in addition to the husband's
contribution) and those in which the women's contribution exceeded 40 per cent, there was no differentiation in terms of
decisions concerning the schooling and employment of children.
With regard to sexual relations, there was substantial evidence of a
clear disjuncture between the decision-making ideal and reality: in
70 per cent of the cases women said that sexual relations were
unilaterally imposed by husbands rather than being the result of
mutual consent.

Emerging from this analysis is the existence of a slow renegotiation of areas which had previously been exclusively masculine
spheres of decision-making, e.g. a woman's physical and social
mobility, the extent to which she works outside the house and the
sphere of domestic work, as well as the scope and frequency of her
social visits outside the home. The pressure of economic necessity,
combined with the limited control a husband can exercise over the
'outside' activities of his wife, also contributes to this process of
renegotiation. Wives must still maintain standards of personal
behaviour consistent with the 'respect' demanded by husbands and
accorded in return for his contribution to the household budget;
nevertheless, there are indications that changes in the definition of
the wife's role are taking place. Despite the fact that they continued
to 'respect' their husbands, the majority of women interviewed
nevertheless felt that they had the right to disagree with them,
rather than meekly follow their orders. Of course, if a husband is
reluctant to accept a renegotiation which would imply a relative
improvement in his wife's position within the family, he may
threaten to or actually withdraw his financial support and/or
threaten or commit physical violence on his wife. Both economic
and physical sanctions are mechanisms employed by husbands to
maintain 'an acceptable level of respect'.

What are the principal differences between the two sub-groups?
The women in the sub-group employing the housekeeping-
allowance system had sought wage-work in order to be able to buy
items which both they themselves and their husbands defined as
being beyond the minimal standard of consumption permitted by
the husband's wage. In addition, wage-work outside the home was
sought in order to establish a certain degree of autonomous income
generation, so as to avoid having to be always asking the husband
for money for each and every article the woman considered necessary
either for herself or the home. Finally, this type of work gave the

wife a degree of protection against loss of self-esteem and the feelings of humiliation associated with minimal social and economic power. Nevertheless, husbands do not readily permit their wives to take up outside wage-work; permission seemed to have been given in the majority of cases after a long process of persuasion, supported by promises on the part of the wife that her household obligations would not be neglected, that the children would not suffer and that the husband would continue to be treated in a respectful way. In this sense, industrial outworking, undertaken in the home itself, appears to threaten the position of the husband and the 'normal' completion of household tasks far *less* than women's wage-work in factories.

Nevertheless, wives who are wage-working for the reasons described above face a series of difficulties and obstacles in the process of redefining their relationships with their husbands. In the housekeeping-allowance model, the contribution of the husband is reserved for the basic and essential family expenditures, whilst the contribution of the wife is assumed to be for additional or extra items. The very nature of this form of money allocation contributes to the material and ideological reproduction of asymmetrical gender relations in the domestic sphere; the fundamental role of the husband as the economic provider remains untransformed and, indeed, may even be reinforced. Additionally, under such conditions, a wife would find it extremely difficult to justify, either in her own or her husband's eyes, economic or social behaviour which the husband considered to be 'disrespectful'. These women are still defined as 'maintained' and, as such, would normally avoid any outward show of new-found economic independence or increased purchasing power, for fear of this being interpreted as an attempt to humiliate their husbands and diminish his status both inside and outside the family. When the dominant conjugal ideology proved to be insufficient to control the behaviour of the wife, her 'good behaviour' could be assured by the use of the less subtle means already indicated, namely the withdrawal of his financial support to the family and/or the use of physical force against his wife. In all spheres, women's decision-making power remains at a minimum, as we saw for the group of women who contribute less than 40 per cent of the family's total expenditure under the common-fund model.

Even if the above analysis indicates that there are considerable limitations on the changes in conjugal relationships which are made possible by a woman gaining access to an independent income, the conclusion cannot be drawn that such changes that do occur are insignificant for the individuals concerned. Changes in the definition of roles of husband and wife and changes in expectations and levels of consciousness do not automatically give rise to a new style of family life and organization. It should be emphasized in particular, that capitalist/sexist society places at the disposal of the husband a series of resources which can be used to resist female incursions on his 'ancestral' and traditional rights: the husband's resources are economic, coercive and ideological, and include the manipulation of women's fears and of the insecurity women experience as a result of the acceptance and internalization of their own subordination. Women, of course, are capable of counter-attacking with the traditional weapons of the oppressed: the creation of guilt feelings on the part of the husband and the children through evidence of absolute devotion to the household and to the family, as well as the use of simulated sexual frigidity and acts of contempt and/or disregard for their husbands. Family interaction is normally characterized by latent tensions which can explode into violent arguments and/or physical fights. It should come as no surprise, therefore, that 60 per cent of the women interviewed considered their marriage to be a failure and that 50 per cent of the women would have separated from their husbands at some point during their marriage.

What, then, is the relationship between industrial outworking (and the corresponding independent and minimal income derived therefrom) and the overall picture of women's subordination outlined above? The analysis has indicated that access to an independent income (albeit small) to be used for the purchase of necessary family (rather than individual) items of consumption has, to some extent, enabled women to re-establish their own self-esteem and build for themselves a new and different image of their role in the working-class family. Both sub-groups of women gave similar answers to questions relating to the importance that they attached to wage-work in this respect. All were agreed that women's wages made a significant contribution to increasing the family's income and, particularly, to assuring women a minimal degree of control over their own lives. This degree of control and the creation of a source of self-esteem was achieved through struggle and was something to which women were committed. Ninety-five per cent of the women interviewed said that they would continue to work even if their husband were to increase the size of his contributions to the household budget. They answered in the affirmative because they had learnt through experience that the money provided by husbands is always subject to control, such that any increase in the husband's contribution would be accompanied by attempts to ensure an even greater control by the man over the economic and social spheres of family life.

Women's Industrial Outworking: Some Final Thoughts

One of the important conclusions to be drawn from the previous section is reflected in the fact that perhaps one of the most basic and positive results of women's incorporation into the labour market through industrial outworking was found in the sphere of self-esteem, i.e. an enhanced sense of well-being and usefulness on the part of the women interviewed, corresponding to a small amount of ground gained by those women in the administration of an improved household budget or in the more independent use of their own outside earnings. The study of different forms of household-income distribution clearly showed, in the case of those families operating with a common fund, that when the wife makes a significant and stable monetary contribution to the household budget, her access to an independent income facilitates the renegotiation of the terms of interaction within the family. Such a renegotiation may result in increased decision-making power for the woman in certain areas and her redefinition not only of her husband's rights but also of her own. When husbands relinquish their positions as exclusive economic providers to the family, combined with the generalized deterioration of conjugal relations which this often involves, the potential for such a renegotiation is increased.

In the case of those women who received some sort of housekeeping allowance, this form of household-income distribution tended to reinforce the pre-existing gender hierarchy with the result that the decision-making power of the wife remained extremely limited. Nevertheless, irrespective of the system of 'internal' income distribution used by the family, the small amount of earnings available to the working wife provided her with at least some minimal influence over the conjugal situation and tended to diminish the damage normally caused to her self-esteem by her overall economic dependence on her husband. In this sense, industrial outworking is better for working-class women than having no paid work at all, since the latter situation places women absolutely at the mercy of the unstable and often capricious monetary contribution of their

husbands, not to mention his verbal criticism and physical violence.
However, compared to the other 'external' forms of women's
proletarianization (e.g. in factories and workshops and even as rural
day-labourers) domestic assembly-work clearly has its limitations.

Despite the alienation involved in factory work, not only does the
female factory worker or day-labourer receive a minimum legal
package of benefits and a certain degree of trade-union protection,
but she is also drawn out of domestic 'seclusion', brought for the
first time into collective labour and encounters more propitious
conditions for the further development of class, trade-union and
gender consciousness, not to mention the basics of organization
experiences which are denied in their entirety to women in domestic
assembly-work.

Women's factory employment can have the impact within the
household sphere of challenging the most traditional definition of
the roles of mother and wife. The woman leaves the house and,
despite their mother's absence, the children do not immediately fall
ill; this thereby helps to break the taboo of 'outside' work and
through certain shifts in the organization of domestic life substitutes for the maternal role are created. The woman, despite her
double working day (which also exists in the case of industrial
outworking), nevertheless gains in consciousness as well as financially; her wages, however small, give her the possibility of a certain
degree of independence and putting an end to what may have been
an intolerable marital situation.

The implications of a woman's involvement in industrial wage
work are not, however, reproduced in the case of industrial
outworking. First of all, this is because of the minimal contradictions generated between the woman's roles as worker and mother.
Under these circumstances, the woman can continue defining
herself in the traditional manner with little likelihood of her
self-definition being challenged and without the seeds of doubt or
experimentation being sown. Thus, the woman remains at home,
dominated by the regular rhythm of domestic work and continually
worrying that her husband may object to her working at home for
wages. The woman works apparent miracles with her time and
energy, so that her husband is never in any doubt that the necessary
household chores are being satisfactorily performed. In fact, this is
one of the main reasons why married women with small children
prefer industrial outworking to other, better-paid 'outside' wage-
work. From this point of view, the women interviewed showed
considerable enthusiasm for industrial outworking (even if I had my

doubts!). Nevertheless, the low level of wages and the employment insecurity characterizing industrial outworking (with the exception of four of the fifteen garment outworkers interviewed) clearly helps to explain the limited change which has taken place in marital relations and gender roles.

In conclusion, given the conditions sketched in this chapter, if women in general are socialized or 'programmed' to accept both the image and the reality of gender dependency in the economic, emotional and sexual spheres, their integration into the labour market through their involvement in industrial outworking (based as it is on the continuation of that dependence) only provides her with the most minimal means of eroding that dependency, mainly in the form of enhanced self-esteem and confidence.

With regard to the future, and taking into account that recent reports have shown that in certain branches of industrial production, subcontracting and the use of industrial outworkers appears to be on the increase, the likelihood of an improvement in the pay and working conditions of industrial outworkers is probably rather remote. The reasons for this can be seen in the following example: Senora T of Colonia Moctezuma and four neighbours had a meeting in January 1982 with their local supplier in order to ask for an increase in the rate paid for their assembly of plastic products. As a result of their complaints, the intermediary subjected them to verbal abuse, refused to provide them with further work and brought down upon them the anger and scorn of other women in the same district who were also industrial outworkers for the same company and were supplied by the same intermediary. The reason for their anger was that the amount of work given to Colonia Moctezuma as a whole was reduced in order 'to issue a general warning against such protest and demands'. The 'beneficiaries' of this minor struggle were women from another district (Villa de Guadalupe) where the supplier's intermediary had increased the supply of materials and taken on new outworkers. Even if some type of trade-union organization were possible, which must be regarded at present as an Utopian hypothesis, it is relevant to ask whether these forms of quasi-proletarianization, in which there is virtually no possibility of wage rises and in which training is entirely neglected (except in the case of tailoring), should really be defended or would other avenues be more promising, involving different forms of mobilization of women, the formulation of different demands (in the health and educational sectors and in the sphere of community politics) and the training of women in other types of paid labour which transcend the limitations imposed by industrial outworking?

These conclusions based on the study of domestic and marital relations and of the experiences and perceptions of working women underline the importance of clearly linking our analysis of *class* relations with that of the relations of *gender* and *generational* subordination which characterize the domestic sphere in general and the work undertaken there in particular. It is only in this way, by uncovering the dialectical relationship between the sphere of labour and that of the household, that the likely consequences of urban 'informal-sector-based' employment-promotion policies (however well-intended) can be more clearly identified. Without such an analysis little if any attention will be given to the fact that such policies are likely to produce the absolute minimum of benefits for the women workers themselves who ostensibly constitute the 'target group' of these policies. There are other types of urban employment which do not depend for their 'success' on the reproduction of an ideology which assigns to women a gender identity which itself is based upon a subordinate definition of the woman as wife and mother. These alternative forms of employment could contribute in a much more effective manner, if not to the liberation of women, at least to the gaining of sufficient ground for that liberation struggle to be successfully fought in the future.

Notes

This chapter was presented at the World Congress of Sociology, Mexico City, 1982. It was translated by Chris Gerry.

1   Research was made possible by the support of the Ford Foundation, although the conclusions drawn and the opinions expressed in this chapter are not necessarily shared by that institution.

One-hundred-and-forty women industrial outworkers were interviewed, belonging to 137 families, thereby giving information on a total of 870 individuals. A questionnaire covering all 140 women was used to collect data on the size of family groups, labour relations, occupational background, unpaid domestic work and perceptions, norms and values relating to the woman's labour and domestic situation. A second questionnaire (usually accompanied by taped, open-ended interviews) was applied to a selection of 60 women (53 wives and 7 independent female heads-of-household) in order to collect information on domestic expenditure, resource flows within the household, survival mechanisms, decision-making power, marital relations, as well as perceptions of the woman's situation in general. In order to obtain the degree of detail characterizing this second survey, it was necessary to make several visits to the households in question, in order to establish a level of confidence and rapport commensurate with the often personal and delicate nature of the subject under study. The sociological and anthropological aspects of this research were directed by me and I also undertook the interviews in collaboration with R. Cohen and G. Gatica. Economic aspects of the study were the responsibility of Lourdes Beneria, who also interviewed the employers, managers, and workshop proprietors involved in the subcontracting and the industrial outworking which formed the study's focus.

2 Goodman and Redclift (1981) in an interesting study of the problems of social change in the agrarian sector, present and evaluate these two interpretations of articulation and the contributions of the corresponding authors. See chapter 2, *Theories of Capitalist Transition and Underdevelopment.*

3 See Philips and Taylor (1980) and Roldán (1982) for a further development of these ideas.

4 Philips and Taylor conclude by saying:

> Clearly at one level, the argument that the capital–labour relation is not a gender relation is correct; inasmuch as the capital–labour relation is a *value relation,* it is not a relation between people at all, but between abstract quantities of dead and living labour. The circuit of capital, as a value circuit, is not the story of real men and women entering into concrete social relations with one another, but an account – *abstracted from these relations* – of changing value forms . . . As a process which occurs in time, over time, a capitalist labour process is embedded in history, in inherited social relations. As a *concrete historical* process, the capitalist labour process must situate itself within existing patterns of social dominance and sub-ordination.

5 In Heyzer (1981) reference is made to a large number of studies which, together, demonstrate the fact that women's participation in the informal sector is extremely high. Moser and Young (1981: 60–1) add that this high level of female participation is at its highest in the lowest echelons of the sector, e.g. unpaid family labour in workshops and small enterprises, but is rarely seen in the form of independent female producers and entrepreneurs.

6 The definition of ascriptive gender relations is the one provided by Whitehead (1979: 11), in which, to describe the position occupied is to describe the gender. Normally and in general, such ascriptive gender relations relate to kinship relations (wife/husband, mother/

father, sister/brother, etc.). In other social relations, on the other hand, the gender aspect is not ascriptive, because gender is a characteristic which may or may not be present depending on the situation.

7   In particular, see Covarrubias and Muñoz (1978), de Riz (1975), Elú de Lenero (1975), Garcia et al. (1979, 1982), Jelin (1974), Recchini et al. (1976), and Rendón and Pedrero (1976), on various aspects of the relationship between family circumstances (marital status, number of children, class position of the head of household, parental relations, etc.) and women's insertion into the labour force.

8   This section is based on Beneria (1982), even though the conceptualization of industrial outworking as a form of quasi-proletarianization presented in this chapter is different.

9   In order to ensure that there was a connection between the woman's involvement in industrial outworking and the struggles undertaken by the family group, a series of detailed questions were addressed to the family members concerned. For detailed tabulations see Roldán (1982).

10 Information relating to the female heads-of-household in their struggles for social reproduction is not presented here but forms the basis for a separate article.

11 By working class, in a strict sense, we understand wage earners excluded from control over money capital, physical capital and labour power (i.e. those occupying working class positions within the social relations of production) but who are employed in private or State enterprises, engaged in the production of goods and services for the market (61 per cent of the sample). Members of the working class in a broad sense are: (1) wage earners who occupy working-class positions within political and ideological apparatuses, i.e. positions which are excluded from either the creation or execution of State policy and ideology (Wright 1978) (e.g. employees in the State administration, a clerk in the army, policemen, low-ranking soldiers, etc.); (2) some of these, it may be argued, occupy 'contradictory' locations within the political apparatuses and not a simple working-class position, but we do not have reliable information to make this assessment; and (3) those who provide personal service in exchange for money income (e.g. gardeners, chauffeurs in private residences etc.). These categories comprise ten per cent of the sample.

The petty bourgeoise is defined as having economic ownership and possession of the means of production, but no control over the labour power of others, since no labour power is employed. This term includes several types of self-employed in the manufacturing, service and commercial sectors, e.g. 'carpenter, garage-owner, ironmonger and one peasant. None of these heads-of-household employed unpaid family labour in their premises and for this reason no further qualifiications based on kin relations were made in the text.

12 The remaining heads are those involved in quasi-proletarianization processes (e.g. outworkers in the garment trade), pensioners and the temporarily unemployed.

13 Exceptions to this rule tend to be related to the internal composition of the groups and the socio-biological phase which they reached, but a detailed discussion is beyond the scope of this chapter.

14 The data upon which this section is based was derived from the 60 interviews undertaken with 53 wives and seven female heads-of-households, using the methodology of questionnaire, tape-recording of interviews, multiple visits and participant observation referred to in footnote 1. This chapter is confined to a discussion of the 53 cohabiting wives.

15 In *The Allocation of Money and the Structuring of Inequality in Marriage*, Pahl presents the conclusions of a large number of studies on this subject and makes the distinction between 'control' and 'budgeting'. This distinction has been used in the present chapter, though not in precisely the same way as she uses it. (Pahl 1982).

Part III

The Retreat of the State?

9

The Working Class and Small Enterprises in the UK Recession
Chris Gerry

Introduction

The gloomy predictions of those who see the current form of technological advance as the enemy of workers rather than their saviour may be only half right. Nevertheless, the future of many of the unemployed and those still to enter the labour market for the first time in the Western capitalist economies remains bleak indeed. Will they become permanent welfare recipients or will they be involved in some sort of rather marginal 'self-employment'?

If, in this context, the traditional forms of small enterprise are allowed or even encouraged to flourish, and 'new' forms emerge or are promoted, then wage-employment of some sort would tend to proliferate in the small-business sector rather than in the tradition-al, large-scale industrial enterprises. Were a more thriving small enterprise sector to be supplemented by an increase in 'new' forms of self- and collective-employment (e.g. co-operatives, community enterprises, etc.), a substantial quantitative and qualitative trans-formation of the sectoral distribution and importance of both self-employment and wage-employment could be foreseen. The sphere of 'self employment' (as conventionally understood[1]) has already become a significant arena of struggle between those who have been displaced from their traditional and relatively stable modes of income generation on the one hand and the State on the other.

The current world recession has seen a substantial acceleration in the internationalization of capital and the relocation of capitalist production, due to the fact that profitability has been severely squeezed. This process is part and parcel of the heightened competition made necessary by the continued search for profit under conditions of declining world demand (see Glyn & Harrison 1980: 5–33). In this context, new types of small enterprises have proliferated within 'national' economies at the same time as large national and transnational companies have initiated their own responses to the crisis. These responses have characteristically included the 'externalization' of a significant part of the labour and labour-associated costs previously borne by the company itself, either by making workers redundant (with or without the introduction of technological innovation) and/or by 'farming out' work previously undertaken within the large company to smaller pre-existing or specially created enterprises.

Additionally, other small enterprises (more commonly associated with what has been termed the 'black economy') have appeared, as redundant workers, unable to maintain subcontractual links with their former employers and unable to find alternative wage-employment, have established for themselves less 'formal' modes of income generation, not necessarily in conformity with current Health and Safety, registration, fiscal or other regulations and requirements imposed by the State.

Aside from these two types of small enterprises (former employees becoming dependent subcontractors, and black occupations which infringe Social Security, fiscal and other norms), another form of small enterprise has emerged or flourished as a result of the recent boom in microcomputers, biotechnology and the service activities associated with them.

There are also the already-established or newly initiated enterprises of a more 'traditional' character (in retail distribution, transport, construction, personal services, etc.) which have managed to survive the intensification of the competition associated with the deepening crisis.

It should be emphasized at the outset, however, that the preliminary classification sketched above ignores the very substantial 'rump' of small enterprises, spread across virtually all branches and sectors of manufacturing and services, who have continued to play a very significant role in the provision of commodities for the domestic market and for export. More importantly, these conventionally defined small enterprises continue to employ a very substantial proportion of wage- and salary-earners; estimates vary (according to the definitions and techniques used) from two-and-a-half to five million employees in the UK. These relatively small companies have also been seriously affected by the recession and have experienced bankruptcy, severe reductions in their labour forces, and may even have attempted some of the technological or other forms of restructuring more normally associated with large industrial concerns.

The comments which follow (and in particular those found in the third and fourth sections of this chapter) refer in particular to the types of newly emerging or reconstituted small enterprises (legitimate and black) mentioned above, rather than to the 'rump' of relatively classical, small-scale enterprises. Nevertheless, to the extent that policies favouring *or* discriminating against small enterprises (of whatever variety) will be forthcoming as part of State-promoted restructuring, some of the trends indicated below may well have significance for that 'rump' in the longer term. This emergence and/or reconstitution of particular types of small enterprises raises at least two important questions.

First, to the extent that the black economy constitutes (or will constitute) a significant component of the aggregate small-business sector (broadly defined in terms of both numbers active/employed and value added), the State will wish to ensure that any initial fiscal losses it may incur due to non-registration, fraud, etc., can be progressively reduced to manageable proportions. Paradoxically, this would probably mean that increased personnel would have to be deployed inside the Civil Service so as to improve the 'policing' of the 'new self-employed', at a time when public-sector employment in general is subject to substantial financial and manpower cuts.

Second, to the extent that small businesses, whether they are created on an inadvertent or a voluntary basis under conditions of economic recession, may increasingly adopt 'unconventional' organizational and institutional forms (e.g. autonomous producers, consumer and worker co-operatives), it will be in the State's interests to ensure that the institutional, legal and 'policing' provisions which govern the role, status and scope of such new forms, are constantly monitored, improved and updated in order to guarantee that those involved continue to respond to the State's fiscal, economic and ideological initiatives, in a direction consistent with the interests of the ruling class.

Gorz (1982) concludes that there will, indeed, be a struggle for the political 'space' which such new organizational forms will create. This chapter attempts, among other things, to argue that the struggle between these new (and not-so-new) forms and the State will also be over the distribution of the surplus produced by such enterprises. The struggle is not primarily over whether or not to promote smaller 'national' firms (and if so, to what extent); it is fundamentally concerned with providing the surest foundation for the renewed growth of capital, whatever form of restructuring this may require. A 'dependent renaissance' of the smaller-scale-enterprise sector is, under current conditions, absolutely vital to any strategy of rapidly accelerating accumulation. While the boom years of the late 1950s to late 1960s saw a trend towards a relative dissolution of the smaller enterprise in many sectors, the deepening crisis of the mid 1970s onwards have seen their flourishing in a number of quite different branches of economic activity, ranging from the 'high tech' micro-electronics sector to the 'alternative' (co-operative, individual/artisanal) organization found in some of the declining traditional branches.

It is therefore to be expected that this struggle for the largest share of the surplus generated by such new 'smaller' enterprises will take on different forms and will proceed differently and with varied tactics on both sides (i.e. State and small enterprises) according to the type of enterprise in question (i.e. legitimate/traditional, legitimate/technological, legitimate/'alternative', or black) and upon the specific economic and political circumstances of the moment. For example, while high-tech micro-enterprises linked to the consumer, intermediate goods or machinery/robotics markets will probably play a very important role in supporting (both with inputs and in terms of risks and costs) any industrial growth and restructuring in the UK, and therefore will need to be both controlled *and* encouraged, the encouragement offered to co-operatives, management-buy-out and other 'rescue operations' in the more traditional and declining sectors may be more apparent than real, more cosmetic (in terms of catering to regional, unemployed and other lobbies) than concrete. Thus the debate over the current status and future role of small enterprises is an important one, with considerable implications for both class analysis and politics.

The Historical Background to the Current Interest in Small Businesses

In the third quarter of the nineteenth century, Britain was at the height of its industrial and international trading power. From its own labour force had emerged the world's first working class and, at that time, a large minority (if not the majority) of that labour force remained 'self-employed', in the generally accepted sense of the word. Late Victorian social historians and commentators agreed that these apparently independent producers were nevertheless thoroughly exploited under capitalism without yet being fully subsumed under the increasingly dominant wage-labour relations of factory-based, capitalist commodity production.

When viewed from the 'inside', the typical small workshop of the period would seem to conform to our stereotyped image of craft or artisanal production – still relatively unmechanized, having a division of labour and a status-hierarchy which corresponds to differences in age and skill-level, and dominated by a pervasive and seemingly pre-capitalist set of relations of personal dependence and paternalism. Seen, however, from the 'outside', namely from the viewpoint of their commercial relations with other enterprises (suppliers and buyers) and with the final consumer, such small enterprises and their 'petty entrepreneurs' give the impression of being, more often than not, little more than satellites of the factory system of machinofacture and objective adjuncts to the industrial wage-labour force. However, despite the apparent convergence between the working conditions of those in 'traditional crafts' and trades and those labouring for wages in factories, a considerable gulf existed in ideological terms between the skilled workers in the two sectors on the one hand and between the small working proprietors and their factory-owning counterparts on the other hand.

In his classic work *The Condition of the Working Class in England* Engels suggests that the apprentices in nineteenth-century Birmingham's small workshops were:

> quite as badly off under the small employers as under the manufacturers, with the single difference that they, in turn, may become small employers, and so attain a certain independence – that is to say they are at best less directly exploited by the bourgeoisie than under the factory system. Thus these small employers are neither genuine proletarians, since they live in part upon the work of their apprentices, nor genuine bourgeois, since their principal means of support is their own work. This peculiar midway position (of such small employers) . . . is to blame for their having so rarely joined wholly and unreservedly in the . . . labour movement. (1969: 225–6)

Despite the fact that the activities of small enterprises were progressively integrated into the process of capital accumulation of the larger and more mechanized factories, and the last significant vestiges of generalized, *competitive* capitalism largely removed, small proprietors nevertheless remained ideologically much closer to the relatively newly-installed bourgeoisie than to the working class. Naturally, this commitment was neither unreserved nor without its contradictions, but it remained relatively strong as long as they were permitted to retain at least some of the formal and subjective trappings of independence, and as long as small enterprises were occasionally proffered certain material concessions. For Engels, the rapidly maturing capitalist mode of production was forced to wage war simultaneously on two fronts: first against the growing militancy of the working class and, second, against the potential competition of the 'puny, dwarfish and circumscribed capital' of the small, self-employed producers. Marx referred to the assets of these poor autonomous producers as 'the pygmy property of the many' (Marx 1976: 762).

Evidently, those owning and/or working in small enterprises in nineteenth-century Europe constituted a social layer no less subject to change, decomposition and reconstitution than any other section of society. This was true irrespective of the rhythm of capitalist boom and recession. Parallel to his more famous analysis of the differentiation of the Russian peasantry, Lenin (1972: 536) argued that a middle stratum of workshop proprietors, domestically based workers and similar producers was being continuously created, absorbed into the growing proletariat and again reconstituted on the margins of a developing capitalism. Thus the small proprietor and petty producer was equally susceptible to the possibility of being cast one day into the ranks of proletariat and the next day back into the satellite outposts of the factory system, or even into penury and vagabondage. Lenin concluded that 'the development of forms of industry, like that of social relations in general, cannot but proceed very gradually among a mass of interlocking, transitional forms and seeming reversions to the past.' Indeed, later observers concluded (on the basis of evidence from the period of the crisis and recession of the 1930s) that it was equally possible for wage-workers to be cast into the ranks of the 'pygmy proprietors' when capitalism was in crisis, as it was for the reverse process to take place in times of boom and capitalist expansion. The persistence of a significant 'autonomous' sphere of small-scale production and services (acting either as a refuge for workers displaced by the crisis and/or by new technology, or as a 'launching pad' for would-be entrepreneurs) and the continuous ebb and flow of workers in and out of the wage-labour force, to some extent explains the continuous influence of petit-bourgeois values and ideas on the labour movement in general and on ostensibly proletarian parties in particular.

But what of the petty entrepeneur, pygmy proprietor and micro-businessman in recent years? How well or ill have they fared in the post-World-War-Two, long boom and subsequent recession? What has been the relative weight of this sphere as either the launching pad or 'rubbish dump' for labour relatively surplus to capital's direct requirements? Why the current economic, political, ideological, fiscal and general academic interest in the small-enterprise sector? It seems unlikely that social analysts, politicians, journalists and political activists have all been affected with the same atavism and nostalgia for the 'good old days' of localized, atomistic competition (which, indeed, may never have existed). Does this current preoccupation imply that there is a generalized and recognizable attempt on the part of many different sections and strata of society to some extent to turn back the tide of alienating, exploitative and oppressive industrialism, be it monopoly capitalist, State capitalist or 'bureaucratic' in nature?

Clearly, elements of some of the above perspectives can be found in and behind recent public pronouncements on the small-enterprise sector. However, a large number of the books, articles, speeches and editorials on this theme can be interpreted in quite a different manner, i.e. as an offensive (of a relatively more ideological than material character) on the part of those sections of the ruling class whose interests and prospects have been most severely prejudiced by the current chronic recession. Nevertheless, the strategy is not purely ideological inasmuch as a part of its objectives must necessarily relate to a discriminatory bolstering of the economic prospects, not only of the UK's international interests but also those of certain existing and emergent fractions of non-internationalized capital which remain important to the political constituencies which have (or it is hoped will) supported the general interests of the ruling class.

If we are to understand the importance of the preoccupation with small businesses, co-operatives, self-help enterprises, etc., not to mention the black economy and the European informal sector, we should at least take account of the long historical pedigree attached to the theme.

As is the case with all such debates, the discussion of the role and significance of small-scale producers and 'micro-capitalists' has stressed and then de-emphasized various aspects of the overall problem in response to changes in the real world and our understanding of it. Early reflections on small-scale production (whether of urban craft-workers or rural small cultivators) often had their roots in some form of opposition to the detrimental social and distributional impact of either the development of agrarian capitalism and/or rapid capitalist industrialization. Though it was never a central theme in his major works, Marx nevertheless contributed significantly to the earlier stages of this debate (see e.g. the appendix to Marx [1976:1014–38] and the section in his *Grundrisse* [1972: 471–514]).

First published in 1899, Kropotkin's *Fields, Factories and Workshops Tomorrow* argued that the eventual industrialization of the entire globe was inevitable and that the most logical and desirable form for such a process to take would be that based upon a combination of small-scale agricultural and manufacturing units, geographically dispersed and predominantly oriented towards the satisfaction of relatively localized markets and 'popular' requirements. Such a qualitatively different form of industrialization was preferable, he suggested, to a continuation of the centralizing and wealth-concentrating tendencies of the capitalist industrialism upon which the exploitation and misery of the majority was based.

The Russian narodniks of the same era believed that national prosperity and its increasingly equitable distribution could be best assured in the long term on the basis of the village agricultural, handicrafts and political community (the *mir*), thereby allowing Russia somehow to bypass the worst effects of the alienation and exploitation of capitalist industrialization. Indeed, Lenin's *The Development of Capitalism in Russia* had the political objective of proving that such a project for 'bypassing' the worst effects of capitalism neglected the simple fact that the process of capitalist industrialization was much further advanced at that time than the narodniks believed.

In the 20 years following World War Two, the majority of Western Europe's colonies became independent, stimulating thereby a considerable interest in countries such as India and Nigeria in the means by which a more rapid and comprehensive industrialization process could be engendered. As an integral part of this preoccupation, the potential role of indigenous small enterprises in economic growth and social development received considerable attention, on the part of local planners, policy-makers, academic researchers and certain branches of the newly established international agencies. The aim of the analyses which followed was to estimate the contribution which might be made by the small-enterprise sector (in terms of output, investment and employment) to the difficult process of late industrialization.

To an even more limited extent (such was the influence of the pro-industrialization lobby both in the 'core' and the 'peripheral' economies), certain international bodies took up the 'cottage industry' theme, though without according it any really serious priority in the process of 'national economic development'. Such agencies focused upon the hypothesis that the ubiquitous handicrafts worker (and to a lesser degree, the peasant and petty trader) in underdeveloped countries might be mobilized in such a way as to at least mitigate the worst traumas of an underdevelopment which was assumed to be transitory, at least until such time as 'take off' was achieved.

Nevertheless, it rapidly became apparent that promotion of such cottage industries (while perhaps adding somewhat to the aggregate output generated within the national economy) by no means guaranteed that the benefits of such support would be necessarily enjoyed by those working in that sector. This was, after all, the era in which the poor were to be placated by the promise of benefits via the 'trickle-down effect', based upon a process of 'national economic growth' of a country whose role in the international division of labour was to remain substantially untransformed.

By the early 1970s, the small-enterprise sector in the ex-colonial economies suddenly became the focus of renewed attention. As part of its 'World Employment Programme', aimed at, among other things, the analysis of why capitalist industrialization had failed to provide sufficient 'modern-sector' employment in less-developed countries, the International Labour Office launched a series of studies of what it termed the 'urban informal sector' in Africa, Asia and Latin America: the term 'informal sector' had first been applied to the urban economy in such countries by Hart (1973) and was subsequently extended by the ILO and similar agencies to the rural areas of the Third World.

The conclusion drawn by many of these studies and the later policy experiments was that, with certain administrative and managerial reforms, accompanied by an injection of funds and technical know-how, the small enterprise sector could be transformed from a stagnant and 'involutive' complex of 'coping mechanisms' of the poor into an authentic engine of economic growth. Put another way, small-scale production could constitute, if properly stimulated, an additional source of economic surplus for less-developed economies, without prejudicing too much the (albeit minimal) emphasis being placed on income redistribution (see e.g. the ILO's 'Kenya Report' of 1972).

However, out of this same ILO programme (accompanied by a considerable number of independent research projects and their conclusions) there emerged a minority view concerning the current role and future potential of the small-enterprise sector.[2] The 'incapacity' of these micro-enterprises to 'contribute as fully as they might' to national economic growth (it was maintained) was more illusory than real. Were the relations existing between so-called informal sector activities on the one hand and the local and foreign capitalist and State enterprises normally identified with that process of national economic growth on the other hand to be rigorously analysed and fully taken into account, it would become clear that the major problem was not that the informal sector had limited capacity for generating value, but that insufficient of the growth generated within the sector was, in fact, retained by its 'members' in particular, or by the poor in general. At a less abstract level, this implied that the existing relations between small 'pre-capitalist' and larger (national and transnational) capitalist enterprises were themselves the major obstacles to any sustained economic growth with an explicit redistributional emphasis.

Policies which suggested that a few administrative reforms and a selective 'tinkering' with the status quo would unleash the pent-up productive energies and enterprise of small-scale producers were characterized by the 'alternative paradigm' as being either naive and short-sighted, or downright cynical in their objectives. Under capitalism, the promotion of such enterprises would have two asymmetrical but interconnected results: (1) for the minority of already relatively successful protocapitalists, there would be privileged and subsidized access to the few economic niches in which local capital could thrive; and (2) for the majority of petty producers, there would be a spurious form of promotion involving an eventual loss of all but formal autonomy in production, progressively substituting more direct capitalist exploitation for the 'transfer of value' which was already taking place in the sphere of circulation. In this latter case, while the 'pygmy property of the many' would retain a veneer of independence, the small workshop and its proprietor and workers would be transformed into 'disguised wage-workers' (Gerry 1980; Gerry & Birkbeck 1981), contributing more to the process of capital accumulation *outside* its own limited sphere of autonomy than to the much-vaunted 'internal' growth which was expected of the informal sector by the ILO.

These increasingly subordinated and proletarianized ex-petty producers would not even have the relatively limited benefits enjoyed by the small number of genuine wage-workers active in the modern-sector factories and offices (e.g. Health and Safety legislation, pension schemes, insurance, trade-union rights, etc.) Thus the continuation of apparently pre-capitalist production relations inside the workshop were not only compatible with but also 'functionally beneficial' to capital accumulation outside the small-enterprise sphere.

The integration of certain small enterprises into the process of capital accumulation (it was argued) would involve the provision of an additional 'subsidy' to capitalist production: certain labour and labour-associated costs could be 'externalized' through the widespread use of subcontracting and 'satellite' workshops (thereby reducing enterprise labour costs per unit of output), while the remaining informal sector enterprises would continue to produce a wide range of relatively cheap wage-goods for a significant section of the urban population (and, to a limited extent, for the peasantry), thereby (and in a more general and pervasive manner) holding down the costs of reproducing labour power. Thus the reformist and incrementalist approach to 'promoting' the informal sector seemed to further the interests of capitalist production and capital accumulation, at the quantitative and qualitative expense of the living and working conditions of those ostensibly 'targeted' for promotion.

At the same time, and to some extent as a 'spin-off' from the analysis of the development problems of Europe's former colonies, a number of writers in Europe and North America began to assess the contribution which the small-scale organization of production, consumption and community issues might make to stemming the floodtide of excessive centralization, bureaucratization and concentration of wealth and power in the 'core' capitalist economies. Two of the names most often associated with this 'left libertarian' critique of industrialism are Schumacher (1973) and Illich (1971, 1973, 1981).

However, for as long as the post-war, long boom continued, albeit at a diminishing pace, and government policy on energy, the environment and related issues appeared to be at least marginally responsive to popular pressure and public opinion, any head-on challenge to 'modern industrial civilization' was to be dismissed by the ruling orthodoxy as the irrational, pessimistic and Utopian ramblings of hippies, dissidents, neo-Luddites and armchair revolutionaries, all of whom were oblivious to the managerial problems of the 'real world'.

With the onset of the most severe period of capitalist crisis and recession since the 1930s, and the recognition that the slump was likely to be both protracted and profound, such ideas have gained considerable additional support and legitimacy. Economists began to speculate as to whether the small-scale sector of 'autonomous' producers in the 'core capitalist countries' expanded only in response to the exigencies of an economic recession (e.g. ex-clerks selling matches on street corners or the classical industrial reserve army) or whether it also expanded on the back of boom and expansion (e.g. de Oliveira 1984). The first conclusions drawn from these speculations were rather equivocal, and it soon became clear that both hypotheses were partially correct – at least at a superficial level of analysis (i.e. both boom and slump could provide stimuli to particular forms of small autonomous enterprises). Thereafter, the analysis continued at a more detailed level, posing questions relating to precisely which activities tended to flourish in recession and which benefited from economic boom.

Though the theme of rapid technological progress and its impact on 'the future of work' remained a constant feature of many analyses, the general focus shifted away from the largely sectoral issues of health, energy , arms expenditure, etc., to broader and more fundamental questions concerning the very organization of society and the orientation of the economy, i.e. the manner in which material life is and was to be produced and reproduced, as opposed to the incrementalist aim of reforming the distribution of income and wealth within the given system.

The Current Recession and the Role of Small Enterprises

In the run-up to the 1979 UK General Election, small businessmen and businesses became one of the more prominent topics of debate, discussion and party manifestos. All the major political parties vied with each other for the votes of both the 'traditional', small entrepreneur (shopkeepers, tradesmen, small specialist manufacturers, transport operators, builders, etc.) and the small but growing caucus of 'hi-tech', would-be entrepreneurs. *The Guardian* newspaper had already established its weekly Small Business Page with the appealing acorn logo (a reference to the adage that 'from acorns do great oaks grow') and, since then, many more of the 'quality newspapers' have followed suit. *The Financial Times,* for example, devotes its daily Management Page on one day each week to small-business advice, articles and problems.

As the recession intensified, the bourgeois press gave emphasis to articles and editorials dealing with 'the shape of post-industrial society' and 'life without work', as well as the new opportunities which were becoming available for the establishment of 'a firm of one's own' in the era of new technology. The press attributed great dynamism to what was, after all, a minute portion of the small-business community. As the apparent bottom of the recession was reached without any strong evidence of a future upturn manifesting itself, more references were made to the sponsored efforts and/or self-activity of those who had been made redundant (Local Enterprise Schemes, Business Start-up Programmes, etc.) as well as to those who had unsuccessfully attempted to enter the wage-labour market for the first time ('teenage' entrepreneurs, self-help alternatives to Youth Opportunity and Training Schemes). Conspicuous by its absence has been any sense of the *connections* between the 'new technology', the savage reduction in employment, the growth of legitimate small enterprises as well as that of the black economy, the proliferation of 'moonlighting' and 'hobbling' among the unemployed, the Conservative government's privatization strategy, the cuts in public expenditure and the restructuring of what was still euphemistically called 'British' capital within and outside UK national boundaries.

It would be naive and simplistic to suggest that all the major political parties (and the class fractions and/or combinations of capitals on whose behalf such political formations speak) had to a greater or lesser extent come to the same conclusion, namely that greater priority and support should be accorded those enterprises which not only offer the best opportunities for profit-making or foreign-exchange earning under the current conditions, but also to those which may be able to generate some degree of 'national' economic and employment growth, thereby mitigating some of the worst 'national' impact of the recession. Rather, the depth and character of the crisis has made it necessary for the ruling class to make provision for the burden of 'economic recovery' to be borne to an unprecedented extent, not merely by the working class (in the form of unemployment and reduced real incomes) but also different sections of that amorphous 'middle class', in the form of opportunities to establish or consolidate enterprises intimately connected with the hoped-for upturn in economic activity, opportunities which will almost certainly involve a substantial transfer of risks and costs from the largest national and multinational companies to the above-mentioned firms (see e.g. de Oliveira [1984] on Brazil). Regardless of the ideological 'trimmings', the objective is the same across the board, with differences of emphasis regarding the precise degree to which different classes and class-fractions will benefit from or bear the cost of the process of capitalist restructuring.

Nevertheless, were such a material impact to be effected, then some 'national' growth in output and employment might be forthcoming; were the effect of such a strategy to be predominantly ideological, it would at least provide a welcome boost to the morale of certain sections of the labour force and to certain types of existing and potential entrepreneurs. Such a hypothesis at least takes account (albeit implicitly) of the fact that, in the currently hostile and depressed international economic climate, it has so far been the larger enterprises with a capacity for the international mobilization and transfer of assets and resources which have set the tone for the overall process of restructuring and relocating production. Consequently, it is to be expected that such a process of restructuring (involving, for example, support for fractions of international capital whose presence in the UK is to be encouraged or consolidated via the provision of both cheapened labour power and a private support network of small enterprises able to service cheaply technologically advanced national, privatized branches of multinational or 'foreign', capitalist production) would be capable of creating new niches for small enterprises, just as many of the more traditional niches had been narrowed in previous periods of boom and capital concentration.

The response of transnational capitalist enterprises to the economic recession has been to pursue some or all of the following policies (with varying degrees of success):

1 the national rationalization and international relocation of production (Massey & Meegan 1982);
2 the restriction and/or shifting of major product lines;
3 the introduction of new technology (without or alongside productivity deals and job losses) facilitated by the downturn in labour militancy;
4 the conversion of substantial blocs of industrial capital into

finance capital (particularly during the period of internationally extremely high interest rates); and

5   the reappropriation of productive capacity which had previously been relinquished in favour of national capital in the now heavily indebted 'newly industrialized countries' (e.g. Mexico).

As part of its strategy to lift both national and internationalized branches of national economies out of their protracted recession, the ruling class will be required to make improvements to the levels of nationally generated and retained surplus. However, as suggested above, the effect should not be mistaken for the cause; such 'new national growth' as takes place will be the result and by-product of the overall strategy to bring large, internationalized capital out of its crisis. Modifications in the priority accorded relatively 'small', 'national' or even 'alternative' enterprises will constitute neither the dominant trend nor the principal objective of the strategy; nevertheless, the weight to be attached to 'national growth policies' will vary according to the degree of cohesion between small capitalists' economic activities and the vehicles they adopt for the furtherance of their political aims. Given the fragmented and heterogeneous nature of the economic branches in which small entrepreneurs are found, and their propensity to adopt equivocal and vacillating political positions across a broad spectrum of petit-bourgeois and bourgeois parties, such a cohesion is rather unlikely. The more nationally focused efforts mentioned above will tend to emphasize several quite distinct sectors of the 'national' economy for quite different reasons:

1   the sector of relatively 'backward' and weakened enterprises (both privately and 'publicly' owned) which is principally but not exclusively oriented towards the domestic market;

2   financial, advisory and technical service enterprises, principally but not exclusively oriented towards the demands of large trans-itional companies active in the country in question and/or oriented towards the export market (i.e. 'invisibles', techno-logical advice, and related services) (these enterprises may not be 'small' in terms of capital or labour employed); and

3   other components of the small-business sector believed to have the potential for rapidly generating a relatively high rate of accumulation and/or relatively substantial employment growth, regardless of their branch of production.

It may be in this (relatively medium-term) sense that governments have come to recognize that smaller capitalist enterprises have a positive role to play in the preservation of some sort of national accumulation process. After all, despite the fact that the nation state (whether developed capitalist, Third World or, to a lesser extent 'centrally planned') has become increasingly impotent relative to the progressively more internationalized world economic system, individual governments nevertheless are forced to respond both materially and ideologically to the political and social processes taking place within their own national boundaries. No national government, no matter how involved in or dependent upon the international economy the classes it represents may be, can afford to ignore completely the interests which are bound up in the national economy. It is precisely in this context − the contradiction between increasing involvement in the international economy and political dependence upon a nationally/territorially defined social and political structure − that the debate on small-scale enterprises has to be seen.

Since many of the surviving national branches of production in the UK, (including nationalized industries) have been disproportionately weakened by shrinking domestic and overseas demand for their products, heightened competition and, to some extent, by government policy itself, a higher profile given to the promotion of smaller enterprises, co-operatives, etc., is likely to further intensify competition in the home market among 'nationally oriented enterprises' themselves and between such enterprises and transnationals seeking to further penetrate that national market. This does not augur well for the type of results often naively predicted by those who foresee a new hey-day for the smaller enterprise and the boot-straps capitalist. Doubtless there will be redoubled demands for protectionist, domestic trade policies from some quarters, combined with appeals for more government help in penetrating overseas (and particularly Third World) markets: hence the recent appearance of policies in the UK and Western Europe which appear to be simultaneously 'open' for certain branches of production and 'protectionist' for others.

The Left's Response So Far: Goodbye to the Working Class?

What has been the response of socialists to the debate on 'the future of work' in general and the resurgence of a wide range of legitimate, alternative and black small-scale activities? Two recently published and crucial contributions to the debate are worthy of mention, not because they address themselves specifically to this question, but because they explicitly demand a fundamental rethink (in both theoretical and practical political terms) on the part of those socialists active in the labour movement and trade unions, Left political parties and the environmental, anti-nuclear and disarmament campaigns. The reassessment which Bahro (1982) and Gorz (1982) encourage focuses explicitly upon the capacity of the contemporary working class to act as the major agency of current political struggle, future social transformation and the eventual construction of a socialist society.

Gorz primarily offers a reappraisal of recent changes in the labour process under capitalism, and their impact upon the consciousness and combativity of the working class as conventionally defined. Bahro attempts to update orthodox socialist thinking in the light of what he terms the current pre-eminence of 'external contradictions' (by which he means those between the 'North' and 'South' and between the East and West) over the class contradictions which socialists have normally identified as being of central importance and concern. Bahro's 'external contradictions' threaten to destroy humanity irrespective of class divisions though nuclear holocaust, economic stagnation and de-development due to excessive arms expenditures and/or ecological deterioration.

In articles written at the end of 1982 for *'The Guardian,'*[3] Hobsbawm has echoed the controversy raised by Gorz and Bahro concerning the present and future role of the working class as an agency of social and political transformation, with particular reference to the British situation. In their separate ways, each of these authors poses crucial questions relating to some or all of the following issues: national economic decline, increasing unemployment in the advanced capitalist countries, the likely impact of the 'new' technology (microchips, 'robotics', etc.) on future patterns of employment, the current and much debated decline in the consciousness and militancy of the working class, the decline of the traditional 'labour' and left social democratic parties, and the corresponding rise of the 'new' parties of the recession.

Nevertheless, despite some or all of these issues being raised in an extremely thought-provoking manner, their interrelationships are not given much emphasis by Gorz, Bahro and Hobsbawm, nor have these authors suggested any concrete proposals and/or solutions, except for rather vague discussions of possible political realignments embracing traditional sections of the labour movement along with a myriad of other 'interest' groups. Thus, certain strategies are proposed but these are, in themselves, extremely problematical. The common thread of the three contributions is the thesis that the working class as such (i.e. as conventionally defined, in particular, by Marxists) has been, or is being superseded as the agency for any future socialist transformation of society.

For Gorz, this 'supersession' can be explained by the particular form, scale and pervasiveness of the contemporary capitalist labour process, which renders workers' traditional forms of struggle and organization (as well as their level of consciousness) inappropriate to the tasks of transforming society. For Bahro, the supersession of the working class as a revolutionary agency of change is explained in terms of the eclipsing of 'internal' (i.e class) contradictions by 'external' ones: namely between East and West over nuclear arms and between North and South over the global distribution of wealth which is produced and reproduced by the contemporary, capitalist, international division of labour. As a consequence, Bahro sees the struggle of mankind for survival itself as the pre-eminent concern, rather than any specific struggle of the working class for political and economic supremacy. The political implications of his thesis are that movements which are based narrowly upon the working class and (or?) its representatives are doomed to failure: broader movements based upon all those who feel threatened by nuclear attack and/or man-made ecological disasters, it is argued, are the only ones with any real hope of success.

For Hobsbawm, the decline in the political and revolutionary role likely to be played by the working class in the transformation of society has been the result of two interconnected factors: the substantial increases in its material standard of living during the post-World-War-Two long boom, and the qualitative impact on consciousness originating in the ostensible quantitative contraction of the class, as industrial employment has tended to give way (in the West) to a more pervasive white-collar, service-oriented type of employment.

A large number of criticisms can be levelled at this view of the 'shrinking working class', only a few of which can be dealt with here. Briefly, however, it should be stressed that:

1   So called 'national' working classes may be shrinking numerical-
    ly due to the currently high levels of unemployment, and the

impact (albeit slower than predicted) of new technology; but this ignores the fact that even during the current world crisis, the size of the 'world' working class, corresponding to the highly internationalized world economic system, is undoubtedly continuing to grow.

2   The pure numerical strength of the working class is a highly inaccurate measure of its political strength and level of consciousness; UK manufacturing employment now constitutes less than half of the total wage-labour force but, as long as one is operating outside the conceptual framework of bourgeois democracy (in which so-called political power is normatively correlated with numerical strength as expressed in voting patterns) it is entirely legitimate to cite such cases as the Russian Revolution, in which a working class both absolutely and relatively smaller than that currently found in the UK (approximately three million) was instrumental in the Bolshevik seizure of power. Thus the high (though relatively diminished) membership of the UK working class still constitutes a potential political force of considerable, indeed potentially determining, significance.

3   The assumption that white-collar or 'service-sector' workers are in some way *less* working class, or have fundamentally different or lower levels of political consciousness, cannot be made without reference to some empirical evidence; aside from the fact that a historically changing, rather than a static ahistorical social category is under scrutiny here, the most cursory glance at recent acts of industrial militancy in the white-collar and service sector is sufficient to invalidate this assumption.[4]

Clearly, an evaluation of the 'shrinking-working-class thesis' is absolutely central to the theme under discussion here: do we say 'farewell to the working class' as such and thereafter embark upon a search for some other donkey on which to pin the 'revolutionary' tail? Perhaps it would be more constructive to ask whether, both now and in the past, our confidence in being able to so correctly specify the location and boundaries of the working class has perhaps been misplaced?

The restoration of socialists' confidence in being able to identify, politically adapt to and – most important of all – influence the changing material and ideological contours of the working class, of course involves a move away from restrictively mechanical and dogmatic formulæ for 'class membership'; but it does not necessarily mean throwing the working-class baby out with the stagnant, analytical bathwater. We need to question just how sensitive to changes in capitalism itself have been our previous class analyses. Having made that reassessment, the historical trends in the boundaries of the working class *of* itself can be dialectically related to changes in the class *for* itself, i.e. its willingness and capacity to enter into struggle with the ruling class.

None of this added sensitivity to changing material and ideological circumstances needs prejudice the rigour which should characterize any analysis of political and socio-economic change. Gorz, Bahro and Hobsbawm appear to be saying that a new route to socialism is required, and that a prerequisite of this redirection is the discovery of a new 'vehicle'. Despite the 'new' route, vehicle and 'guides', the 'old' map (of class contours, boundaries and potentialities) continues to be used with (misplaced) confidence. If the working class is shrinking, are we then to talk with equal confidence (and not for the first time) of a 'new' capitalism? How easily this terminology elides with that of those who purvey the concept of the 'post'-industrial society. The crucial point is that Marxist analysis and the socialist transformation which it seeks to both inform and bring about, requires a continuous process of map-correction which results from concrete experience rather than from sterile theorizing.

Gorz, Barhro and Hobsbawm in their various ways challenge the relevance of the working class to contemporary political struggles and, in the final analysis, its role in the overthrow of capitalism and the construction of socialism. Yet there are only very vague and 'woolly' references to the likely identity and characteristics of those who would assume (or share) the burden of responsibility for this historical transformation. Gorz speaks continuously of 'the movement', Bahro of the Greens and even the 'Multicoloured', while Hobsbawm is content to refer to the 'broad unity' which will be required between all progressive groups (among which he includes the majority of reformists). At best, they suggest that the working class alone cannot fulfil the role of the revolutionary agency of social transformation. At worst, the working class disappears into the background of such a project and is supplanted by, rather than supplemented by, various other social groups (with allegedly 'cross-class' characteristics), such as the peace movement, environmentalists and, indeed, all those who adhere in principle to social democratic ideas. It is perhaps Gorz who comes closest to identifying those whom he believes will play the role of agents of 'revolutionary change' when he refers to a new 'non-class of non-proletarians', though further than this he appears unwilling to move.

Clearly, not all of those who have either been forced out of wage-employment or who have voluntarily switched from the positions classically occupied by workers in the capitalist labour process, have subsequently found it possible to transform themselves into small or medium-sized entrepreneurs in the private sector. It may have been the aspiration of some, but it turned out to be the reality for relatively few. School-leavers, for example, often found themselves working for small (and some not-so-small) capitalists, as a new type of contract labour inspired by the Youth Opportunities Scheme and its variants. Equally, not all of these badly affected by the recession have been wage employees: many small businesses (and a not inconsiderable number of major companies) have disappeared. The birth and death rates of small enterprises appear to have more or less matched one another in recent years, indicating a process of proliferation through high turnover rather than through numerical expansion of small businesses. Seen from a longer historical perspective, the number of 'small companies' (employing less than 100 workers) has declined from around 300,000 in the 1930s to around 70,000 in 1973.

Does this mean that ex-entrepreneurs have been proletarianized by the recession, or have they merely been made redundant? If they have moved into wage-employment, have they retained strong, ideological residues of their previous 'autonomous' status, despite the fact that they are now selling their labour power to capital? Does this also mean that many ex-employees, having been made redundant, have moved into the lowest echelons of self-employment, trading their previously proletarian status for a 'middle-class' one? The lack of information, analysis and, above all, clarity in many of the studies of small businesses makes the investigation of such questions extremely difficult — hence the crucial importance of analysing this sector, not merely as an academic exercise devoid of any 'real-world' objective, but more importantly as a means of exposing some of the very substantial holes in the thesis of the 'disappearing working class'.

Such an analysis of the small-business sector would help to clarify many of the processes and interconnections mentioned (but posed in fragmented form) by Gorz, Bahro and Hobsbawm. In this way, a more accurate assessment could be made of the strengths and weaknesses of the working class, the 'labour movement' and its representatives. Only after such an assessment will it be possible to make judgements concerning the ostensible decline of the working class and its politics. Perhaps the conclusion will be drawn that it is the politics of some of the self-styled spokespersons of that movement that has become marginal to the realities of the contemporary working class; it cannot have gone unnoticed that the title of Gorz's book *Farewell to the Working Class* is ambiguous, inasmuch as it can be interpreted either as an elegy to a spent political force or as a proclamation of a personal class trajectory.

In order, therefore, to assess the validity of the analyses presented by these three authors, and the implications of their proposals (whether theoretical or practical), it will be necessary to carefully examine those commentators who, like Hobsbawm, believe that workers today are politically unstable and volatile, despite the fact that those 'same' workers voted consistently for social democratic and workers' parties in the past. Were the same question to be posed in Gorz's terms, it would seek to identify of whom precisely the new 'non-class of non-proletarians' consists. Put in Bahro's terms, the socio-economic composition and political ideology/ideologies of the peace, anti-nuclear, environmental, ecology and devolution movements (in which he places so much faith as the means of averting barbarism) would need careful analysis before the working class could be so easily relegated or sidelined as an element of only secondary importance in the struggle to transform and transcend capitalist society.

A serious answer to this type of question would require that the above layers, strata and segments of contemporary society (heterogeneous as they undoubtedly are in class terms) be analysed 'in action' and 'in formation'. In other words, both these groups and the working class itself need to be 'assessed' in the very process of responding politically, organizationally and economically to the current crisis, taking both offensive and defensive initiatives in order to adapt to and challenge the conditions and processes which have been produced by the State's 'management' of the recession in favour of the restructuring (rather than the supersession) of capitalism.

One of the implications of seeing these various social layers 'in formation' or 'in motion' would be that an analysis would be required of the emergence and activities of what might be called the 'new parties of the recession', such as the Greens in West Germany and, in a very different way, the SDP in Britain. These new political groupings are themselves engaged in struggle: the policies which they currently espouse may have some impact in the near future, not only to the extent that some of these parties may be able to exert some influence on (or in) government, but also inasmuch as they hope, through such policy proposals and objectives, to draw voters and members away from the traditional bourgeois, petit-bourgeois and reformist 'labour' parties (and, incidentally, away from any revolutionary party explicitly espousing the overthrow of capitalism).

For Hobsbawm, for example, any rebuilding of confidence and combativity on the Left in the current circumstances would require a substantial redefinition of what constitutes 'the Left', enabling larger components of traditional and 'new' social democracy to be both ideologically and materially incorporated. Such a formula is currently rejected by Bahro, on the grounds that West German social democracy is already in terminal decline and has nevertheless maintained an overt hostility to Green theory, practice and policies.[5] For him, it is the extraparliamentary movements and the 'unorthodox' political parties which make up the potential political breeding ground of the Greens; incorporating these groups under the Green umbrella could allow considerable influence to be exerted by the Green Party inside the Bundestag, perhaps becoming an effective and autonomous opposition pressing for radical change. Only Gorz (1982: 116), however, emphasizes the fact that this will involve a struggle, though he fails to seriously raise the question of political power in his discussion:

> The State can only cease to be an apparatus of dominion over society and become an instrument enabling society to exercise power over itself with a view to its own restructuring, if society is already permeated by social struggles that open up areas of autonomy, keeping both the dominant class and the power of the State apparatus in check. The establishment of new types of social relations, new ways of producing, associating, working and consuming is the fundamental precondition of any political transformation. The dynamic of social struggles is the lever by which society can act upon itself and establish a new range of freedoms, a new state and a new system of law.

Yet Gorz remains vague about the form these 'new ways' of producing and organizing will take, how they will be created and co-ordinated, and by whom. Though he identifies political power (albeit implicitly) as the main objective of 'social struggles', he does not shed much light on the process by which this power will be either ceded (by the bourgeoisie) or seized (by his 'non-class of non-proletarians', one assumes). Gorz also remains equivocal concerning the way in which these initiatives will manage to keep State power in check, which is partly due to the fact that he underestimates the extent to which many of the 'alternatives', 'initiatives' and other options currently on offer have been formulated by institutions of the very State he seeks to capture, precisely in order to prevent the emergence of any real autonomy being expressed by the mass of the population.

The debate over the so-called 'disappearing working class' and its alleged supersession as an agency of social transformation has a serious deficiency – its lack of a rigorous and comprehensive analysis of the small-enterprise sphere, its forms of persistence/adaption and its scope for accumulation. In order to provide such an analysis in the terms outlined above, it is important that the small-business sector (and, though not identical, Gorz's own 'sphere of autonomy') be seen as a current and future battleground (in material and ideological terms) between classes. Such an approach would demand an examination of the strengths and weaknesses, strategy and tactics of groups which sought to carve out their own autonomy (whether in a 'new' form or an old one). *A more important focus of attention, however, should be the stratagems and weaponry deployed by the ruling class* to ensure that this sphere of autonomy neither suffocates for lack of accumulation opportunities (because this would place an insurmountable burden on larger capitalist enterprises to accumulate at rates which they are currently unable to attain and in markets which they cannot readily expand) nor develops a level of real (rather than merely formal) autonomy which might prejudice the benefits which the ruling class gains from its economic and juridicial relations with small units of production.

Recession, Restructuring and the Small-Enterprise Sector

If massive unemployment can be seen then as part of the same process of capitalist restructuring on a world scale of which recent technological initiatives also form an important part, then the depressing predictions concerning the future of the currently unemployed, those yet to attempt to find wage-employment and, indeed, those still with wage-work, should be viewed in a somewhat different light from the semi-obscurity which much of the recent literature has cast on this subject. The pessimists may not, in fact, be half right for at least two reasons. First, microchips and robots do not of themselves create unemployment, which is largely the result of a world economic crisis which has significantly sharpened the contradictions between potential productive capacity and basic human needs (such as available work and a reasonable income); ruling classes at national levels have set in motion their specific strategies for revivifying their own economies (and their international interests) in the hope that these unco-ordinated initiatives will somehow produce a global economic upturn. Second, the impact of new technology has been felt much more slowly than expected, in part due to the crisis-related limitations on new investment, but also due to resistance to its use on the part of both workers and management.

If small enterprises (as conventionally understood or Gorz's so-called new forms of organization) are permitted or even encouraged to flourish as part of the crisis strategy, then wage-employment of some sort may also grow in this sector, relative to its stagnation or decline in large-scale industry. This sphere of both 'new' self-employment and wage-work has already become a significant area of struggle between those displaced from their traditional and, in the past, relatively stable modes of income generation on the one hand and the State on the other. Rank Xerox, for example, announced plans in 1983 to make many of its middle managers partially autonomous, by helping them to set up consultancy firms which would provide services to companies (including Rank Xerox) outside of the two or three days for which the managers were to remain contractually tied to the company. Thus additional services (over and above the absolute minimum) are provided at individually competitive consultancy rates, without the 'inconvenience' of the social and other costs (e.g. perquisites) normally associated with management and other employment.

The 'sphere of autonomy' generated by capitalist crisis (to some extent State-managed as part of the capitalist restructuring which is vital to the system's recovery) will be extremely heterogeneous, especially in terms of the degree of 'autonomy' characterizing its constituent enterprises and activities. Small enterprises established by the former employees of major firms and continuing in the same sub-branch of activity may be 'fully autonomous' only on the surface. Their new-found freedom would amount to little more than being an extension of the factory for which they previously worked (though now bearing many more of the direct and indirect costs and risks) and, though formally self-employed, the majority of such small businessmen would be almost as integrated into their former company's activities as they were as salaried staff. However, they would now, in all likelihood, be employers themselves, and therefore able to pass on the cost burdens which they had recently begun to shoulder. Who, ultimately, would experience the lack of autonomy implicit in lower real wages, weakened or non-existent bargaining power and the ideological backward step of working under more 'personalized' relations of production, but the relative minority of redundant workers who are fortunate to find wage-work in this new and booming sector?

However, the news is not all bad for small businesses: recent government policy in the UK has quite clearly favoured a process of progressive internationalization of 'British' capital, which has involved not only the relocation of productive activities and investments abroad but also an internationalization through the conversion of industrial to finance capital; between 1979 and 1981, for example, UK holdings abroad rose from £8 billion to £28 billion, not least because of the relaxation of capital export restrictions. Nevertheless, the UK government has also found it necessary to simultaneously provide an employment-creation framework which allows enterprises of all sizes (including the smallest firms) to take advantage of cheap and relatively unskilled labour, through, for example, the Youth Opportunities Scheme and similar policies. In the same vein, a certain number of small enterprises have been able to avail themselves of Enterprise Zones established by investment-anxious and employment-hungry local and metropolitan councils.

Though it is still too early to estimate the real material impact of the recession and the plethora of make-work, reduce-the-unemployment-statistics, provide-cheap-labour and promote-new-business schemes (such as YOPs, Enterprise Zones, science parks and small business promotion) there is little doubt that, even were no real quantitative success to be achieved in the creation of a small-business sector able (if not always willing) to absorb many of the labour and labour-associated costs of the larger capitalist companies, it might nevertheless still have an appreciable ideological impact. Were such a strategy to be relatively successful in providing cost-reductions and cost-transfers, it would have simultaneously achieved two objectives. First, the strategy would have resuscitated and revitalized a number of mechanisms of exploitation (chain subcontracting, outworking, monopsonistic subcontracting between many micro-enterprises and one larger buyer of semi-finished goods, etc.) which previously were somewhat residual in the majority of branches of industry. Second, the strategy would have encouraged the emergence of a 'new' work ethic, namely that of self-employment (despite its often low degree of autonomy) as a form of income generation increasingly more typical than wage-employment.

Such a scenario has obvious dangers for large sections of the currently employed, the unemployed and those yet to try their 'luck' in the labour market; it also threatens those who have actively criticized and struggled against the policies and strategies which have accompanied the current economic recession. The danger here is that 'the Left' will be easily satisfied with a purely intellectual search for its 'lost' working class and will continue to search long after the changes implicit in the above tendencies have become concrete.

Those analysing the impact of the recession from a Left perspective should resist the temptation to say 'farewell to the working class' and should seriously reconsider their statements concerning the imminent disappearance of that class as an economic ⁄and political force with which to contend. They should perhaps consider the possibility that a phenomenon which has accompanied the current recession and high levels of unemployment is the emergence of a 'disguised proletariat', outside the major factories and offices, ignored by and ignoring the trade-union movement, whose objective conditions are highly similar to those we associate with classical capitalist exploitation, yet whose ideological position is increasingly individualist and petit-bourgeois, rather than collectivist and proletarian.

The analysis of this 'disguised proletariat' has its roots firmly in classical Marxist propositions concerning the industrial reserve army, rather than in the political alliances between bishops and bricklayers proposed by Left reformists and Eurocommunists. This same analysis has also been enriched by recent debates concerning classes in contemporary capitalist society (see e.g. Ohlin Wright 1976). From this perspective, it appears that, rather than confronting a working class whose physical presence and/or influence is shrinking to the point of disappearance, the working class is merely becoming 'less visible' to those whose reformism has been left standing by the speed and depth of the recent capitalist crisis and subsequent downturn in political militancy and struggle.

A large proportion of those in 'disguised wage-employment', working *with* but not (in any contractual or juridical sense) *for* capital, will appear to occupy the ground which is commonly (but incorrectly) identified with the legitimate small-enterprise sector and/or the less-legitimate so-called black economy. Here we come full circle – back to the need to analyse the current role, position and dynamic of the small-enterprise sector in the context of profound economic recession and capitalist restructuring, remembering that the focus of analysis will be units of production in which the relations between micro-entrepreneurs and their workers will be central, and in which the relations established between such enterprises and the *rest* of capitalist production and exchange will be vital to our understanding.

If the traditional parties and/or the 'new parties of the recession' are eager to capture these social layers as a political constituency, then the existing and up-and-coming generation of micro-entrepreneurs have to be offered at least some minimal material incentives within an acceptable, attractive and relevant ideological framework. This will be rather difficult to achieve in the current context of capitalist restructuring, but it is a nettle which must be grasped if the battle for the 'hearts and minds' of new micro-entrepreneurs *and* their workers is to be won by a political coalition different from that which today dominates the State, and offering a different social distribution of the new, higher level of accumulation.

Socialists must not only be aware of the likely implications of a ruling-class victory in this process of capitalist restructuring and the ideological inroads into the working class it implies; they must also be aware of the implications of a social democratic or 'alternative' victory and its limitations. By initiating the investigation of an important strand in the bourgeoisie's current strategy, we should hope for and work towards not merely new theoretical conclusions, but also a real political response to the threat. The quality and direction of such a political response will depend crucially on what sort of analytical approach is adopted, however. If political action is rooted in the notion of a 'disappearing working class', its parameters will be quite different from political action rooted in an approach which takes account of the shifts in workers' (and others') consciousness resulting from the recession and of the corresponding ruling-class strategy, but which does not accord *subjective* aspects of consciousness supremacy over the *objective* factors which condition that consciousness. In other words, we must understand the nature of the current crisis and recession, understand how the small-business sector fits into it (from the structural and the strategic viewpoints), and be aware of the dangers of confusing a concrete strategy for restructuring capitalism with some sort of renaissance of the small self-employed 'master' and the corresponding 'withering away' of the working class.

Notes

1 See in particular the essay by MacEwan Scott for an extensive analysis of the problems concerned with the analytical specification and empirical identification of this category.

2 For a detailed discussion of contending theoretical and policy-related views on the informal sector/petty commodity production in less-developed countries, see Moser (1978). For an extremely detailed analysis of the difficulties of operationalizing the concept of the informal sector, see Bremen (1976).

3 *The Guardian* 27 September 1982 (on the state of 'the Left' in Western Europe) and 20 December 1982 (on 'working-class nationalism'). *The Guardian* articles were shortened versions of Hobsbawm's contributions to *Marxism Today,* October 1982 and January 1983.

4 Examples of white-collar militancy in the era of the so-called 'decline of the working class' abound: in the late 1960s, following dockers' and dustmen's strike actions, there were the first teachers' strikes; in the early 1970s, civil servants and local government officers took industrial action; and a major civil servants' dispute took place in 1982.

5 However, with Willi Brandt's recent successes, culminating in an invitation from the co-ordinating committee of the German peace movement to speak at one of its Autumn 1983 major rallies, the SPD is clearly making strenuous efforts to win back the support it had previously lost (partly as a result of its attitude to disarmament) by capturing leadership positions in the German peace movement.

10

How Do Ways of Life Change?
Francis Godard

The Demise of Civil Society?

It is generally accepted that trends towards mass culture and the atomization and privatization of civil society constitute a major theme in the current evolution of ways of life. However, diagnoses are inconsistent and accounts differ according to the allegiance of the analyst: as representing the State and its institutions; business or management institutions; or the State, firms and other institutions collectively. Thus, we have on the one hand an account of the degeneration of civil society and on the other, the emergence of new types of sociability, or both.

Some authors identify a total rupture between civil society, the State and large-scale institutions of production and management. Thus, in Habermas' terms, we are witnessing a dislocation in the 'public sphere'. The totally atomized society they detect, dominated by a variety of State institutions, consequently gives rise to forms of regressive or crisis behaviour, the best illustration of which can be found in the 'social-narcissistic' trends of the 'cultural revolution' of the 1960s. The diminished investment in terms of paid work and related disaffection with trade-union structures that have been identified might be read as a sign of individualist passivity. Others, however see these phenomena as a sign of vitality. They invite us to witness the positive affirmation offered by various tactics of resistance beyond the confines of the discourse and strategy of political and trade-union apparatus. They urge us to decode the subterfuge of everyday practice and penetrate the network of counter-disciplinary tendencies in the face of omnipotent, large-scale organizations (for an excellent analysis of these points see Caroux 1982).

A more romantic reading suggests that the Achilles heel of the logic of domination lies in the multiplicity of subversive tactics employed by individuals. De Certeau for instance refers to the 'dispersed creativity' of 'unrecognized producers, poets in business' and describes 'the horizontal proliferation of micro-activities where the consumers' ways of doing things have their own subtle wit.' In examining the transient reality of everyday practices, de Certeau suggests that we are 'exploring the nocturnal side of societies'.

Elsewhere, research inspired by Illich sees alternative life-styles of a hedonistic, entrepreneurial or innovative kind as a rejection of mystifying political discourse and an attempt to regain possession of the individual's own life where that is possible, namely in the private sphere.[1]

The work of Rosanvallon represents a synthesis of these two perspectives and characterizes these phenomena in terms of their ambiguity, stating that they are 'a sign of reactionary retreat, an entropic way of life and at the same time a blueprint for new forms of social relationship marked by the search for greater social proximity and criticism of oppressive "collectivism"' (Rosanvallon 1981: 133). He stresses the capacity of civil society to withstand dislocation and argues that the development of new ways of life would involve further pressures upon the 'hidden shock-absorbers' provided by the various forms of secondary socialization, particularly the 'underground networks of familial solidarity'. He argues that to remedy the crisis of the welfare state 'there is no alternative but rapprochement with society itself. Intermediate social ties must multiply and individuals must be reincorporated into networks of direct solidarity in order to strengthen the social fabric' (Rosanvallon 1981: 133). Since, according to Rosanvallon, self-determining socialism is not on the agenda, the issue is one of defining the conditions for a post-social democratic compromise whose central object would be 'the forms of the political and the social'. This compromise, which should allow for the 'expression of negotiated alliances' is inseparable from 'the constitution of a genuinely democratic public sphere'. It should also provide increased opportunities for experimentation within civil society on the basis of reduced demand for State-provided collective services and a neutralization of political and trade-union conflicts which might be replaced by State–client compromises.

Rosanvallon defines the terms of the debate on the crisis and recomposition of civil society thus: neither economic liberalism nor self-determining socialism (an objective postponed for the longer term) but the creation of a new public sphere on the basis of a 'post-social democratic' compromise. Many social science studies seem more or less to accept these terms of debate. However, it is often difficult to disentangle prescription from description in analyses where the two are inextricably linked. The most prescriptive note is struck in the Californian perspective on the solution to the crisis. The Anglo-Saxon analysis of the informal economy is more descriptive, while the French tendency to romanticize everyday life leads to a certain æstheticism. The tenor is significant here because although, as I would claim, the common denominator of sociological analysis is the double postulate of fragmentation and the dissociation of the social from the State, polity and economy, the conclusion is sometimes that it is precisely this state of affairs which calls out for change, while other conclusions present dissociation as the very condition for a solution to the crisis.

My hypothesis is that an intellectual project is gradually taking shape which, from very different starting-points, involving a variety of themes and taking a number of paths, forms a distinctive method for approaching and solving the current crisis. I will now review a number of these analyses.

The Thesis of the 'Social' Worker

One text which is especially pertinent to the trends described above is the discussion on the relationship of the factory to civil society by Berra and Revelli (1980). In summary, the thesis developed by these authors centres on the 'crisis of the political centrality of the large factory *vis-à-vis* workers' behaviour' (p 112). The crisis in question is that of the Fordian model of society, in which the mass-worker was a hegemonic figure in the world of labour. This worker figure embodied the process through which the factory provided a sphere for socialization and the formation of workers' identity, and through which the rationality of the factory was imposed on the totality of individual behaviour. Thus a direct link existed between the sphere of production and the sphere of social reproduction.

Into this factory culture came a new 'territorial culture' which led to the substitution of the Fordian worker by the 'social' worker. A new generation of workers entered the factory with 'substantial trappings of behaviour structured *entirely* by the centrality of reproductive practices external to the productive universe of the factory' (p. 122). Hence, forms of resistance mature within the social instead of emanating from the collective worker. The factory ceases to be the carrier of any kind of hope; it confronts the worker as 'an alien power, a tear in the fabric of social relations and a break in the thread of subjectivity' (p. 154). The class is fragmented into a multitude of private individuals and its labour is shattered into 'myriad subterranean circuits'. The family again becomes a central place, 'a non-subject community . . . capable of determining and reproducing the emergent subjectivity of productive subjects' (p. 118).

One cannot of course deny the appearance of new practices in the world of the worker. The recourse to informal work, the increase in absenteeism, the rejection, especially among young people, of the old values linked with factory work are clear examples. Neither should one neglect the decomposition of the Fordian model (described by Aglietta): a combination of Taylorist processes, family norms (based on the monogamous family, stablized by consumption habits and structured by housing and car ownership) and a well-regulated game of wage negotiations. However, it is legitimate to ask whether the crisis does not also extend to the analysis itself. Does the problem encountered in analysing the emergence of new modes of existence according to genuine evidence of major shifts in social composition simply lead us to deduce that 'the social' (a new entity unaccompanied by any other kind of process) is falling apart? Was there ever a mythical epoch in which the 'worker figure' was reducible to nothing but the labour force (Pialoux 1981)? The analysis of transformations in class relations, kinship relations and the material conditions of existence has quite simply been left out, as though it was necessary to fragment the analysis after the manner of the politics of 'resistance', which are themselves totally fragmented. If we follow this path there is little prospect of illuminating the 'nocturnal side of societies'.

It is clearly fruitless to seek to advance alternatives to the thesis of the autonomy of civil society, the fragmentation of the processes of reproduction of the labour force,[2] or the idea that the attenuation of the productive system is tending to shape every aspect of social life. Similarly, it would be foolish to try and reduce the analysis of kinship relations to the inexorable mechanisms of the reproduction of the labour force, in order to show that factory discipline penetrates everyday life to the extent of defining the logic around which the entire system of family practices (the reproduction and mobilization of the producer of surplus value and his dependents [Pendaries 1980]) is articulated.

The old debate, expressed in these terms, is finished. This is not to say that the problems have been resolved, quite the opposite. Recent work by Combes (1981) shows clearly that criticism of the analysis which takes the reproduction of the labour force as its starting point has often been developed through the elaboration of a theoretical scheme which remains basically unchanged. It is claimed either: (1) that by refining the analysis of positions within the relations of production the homogeneity of the practices of production and reproduction are more clearly expressed; or (2) complex systems of mediation are introduced between a cause (location in the production process) and an effect (practices of reproduction); or (3) there is an attempt to show the various effects which consumption can have on production. Combes argues that analysis of the relationship between production and consumption or, at another level, between work and the family, when seen in terms of reciprocal relationships between autonomous spheres of activity, rests on a flawed conception of the problem. We need, therefore, to abandon this systemic paradigm of research into reciprocal interactions (others would say input and output) between family and occupational life, which uses an empiricist approach to investigate the family variables which intervene in occupational life and the occupational variables which intervene in family life. Other modes of analysis must be found. I would put forward two major priorities for theory.

First, we have to rethink the relationships between production and reproduction, without reducing production empirically to the factory sphere, as the locus of class relations and capital–labour relations in particular, or reproduction to the family sphere as the locus of kinship relations. One could advance other objects of research to 'show' how each type of social relationship is fashioned *from the inside* by the totality of other social relations, e.g. to show how kinship relations are completely interwoven with class relations, how class relations integrate sexual relations and how the shift in the relationship between sexes in society itself shapes the relationship between kin. The work of Combes and Haicault (1982) marks the significant theoretical advance in this sense. It lays particular stress on the fact that the family cannot be understood as the sole functional unit for the reproduction of the labour force subject to the 'needs' of production nor, it should be said, as the source of new-found conviviality, but rather as the stake in both sex and class relationships. The starting-point must be the totality of the processes by which human beings (and not just material products) are reproduced and that requires a revised theoretical definition of the totality of social relations through which this reproduction is organized.

One might then see that the modifications of relationships between the sexes within the family proceeds through the transformation of these relationships in society at large particularly through their relationship to work and paid labour (Bleitrach and Chenu 1982). One might also see that patriarchal authority relations cannot be modified within the kinship system without simultaneous change at the workplace and within the education system. Furthermore, one might see that changes in kinship relations, which are so fundamental to ways of life, are inextricably linked to change in the mode of reproduction of individuals and their dependents. Here I will take a very concrete example: the nature of personal projects and 'family strategies.' Overwhelmingly these are class struggles in miniature along individualist, everyman-for-himself lines. The aim may be promotion at any cost, status for oneself and one's dependents, or daily opposition to social subordination through all kinds of informal work. In a society which traps the vast majority of individuals and their dependents in a game of social life and death for the most mundane aspects of their daily existence, kinship ties will never be independent of the corporate strategies which families have to develop in their efforts to avoid failure or to achieve a measure of 'success'. The rejection which some young people are expressing may also be, in a confused way, a rejection of these skirmishings. When research is able to demonstrate all of this, and much work is already under way, it may be possible to encourage each and everyone, in their family or community, to work with greater enthusiasm towards the invention of new social relationships.

Second, on another level, I want to suggest that the stress on the emergence of the figure of the social worker runs the great risk of deflecting us away from an urgent task for current research, namely that of understanding the movements towards the recomposition of the world of labour and the internal diversification which they entail. There are two complementary lines of research which could be opened up.

The first would involve clarifying the whole range of possibilities which technological change entails, especially the introduction of automation. There is no reason to fatally accept the dualism in the world of work between highly qualified workers who are well integrated into the factory on the one hand and workers (especially female workers) with few qualifications who are condemned to an unstable existence on the other. Although analysis must seek to understand these tendencies, it equally has a duty to understand the opposite trend including, for example, strikes by unskilled workers or the demand for training and skills among young workers of both sexes. Ultimately, the thesis of the social worker seems to rest on the notion of inexorable de-skilling and thus on disinvestment in work by the great majority of workers.

In taking this approach, the proponents of this thesis only see what the thesis allows them to see: universal disaffection concerning work. The failure to notice those young people who are keen for occupational training and factory work is simply another form of blindness. In fact the two tendencies coexist in the current situation and, quite frequently, even within the same individuals. The essence of the problem is therefore to arrive at an understanding of the contradictory potentials which characterize this situation. This becomes impossible if one has already reached the conclusion that deskilling on a large scale is an irreversible process. In this case, all that is left is to prescribe research into new social relationships elsewhere and describe the emergence of new forms of resistance in civil society. This merely reinforces the idea of a battle lost on the field of the enterprise. I cannot stress this point too strongly: I do not pretend that the phenomena of disaffection with regard to work or struggles within the enterprise are imaginary, but that they are presented unidimensionally, as the consequence of a process (of massive deskilling) *already* achieved, rather than as one pole in a dialectic inherent in the open situation in which we *still* find ourselves.

The second line of research would involve analysing the emergence of new worker figures or the industrial labour force in general, on the basis of the actual constitution of the workers' world in different countries. One cannot talk of a crisis of working-class identity or its relationship to industrial work without understanding the heterogeneity of the workers' world in terms of these modes of constitution. Constant reference is made to the classic figure of the traditional worker (*ouvrier de métier*) and the associated working-class culture. Whilst there is some justification for this it would be wrong to overlook certain basic facts: in France, one-third of workers who were aged between 40 and 59 in 1977 came from rural backgrounds; only 50 per cent of skilled workers and 40 per cent of unskilled workers were sons of workers (as opposed to approximately

75 per cent and 74 per cent respectively in Great Britain) (Thelot 1982). This implies that we should treat the image of a traditional working-class milieu entirely focused on the factory with some caution. Similarly, with the most working class of all workers – the son of a worker – entering the factory at 14, in an industrial region, was there ever a time when his identity was completely merged with the factory? Rancière (1981) gives a useful reminder of the opposite view. He shows how working-class dreams, struggles and writing contain a vision of a world without workers' interests, an aspiration to live other than as a worker. This other tension between the claim to working-class identity and the refusal to reduce identity to this is deeply embedded in workers' consciousness. New forms are taking shape and it is these which we must seek to understand.

Warning: Neo-familism

The analysis of kinship relations and family practices is of crucial importance to the problem posed here for several reasons.

Firstly, this is the field of research which affirms the specificity of the 'private' sphere *par excellence*. This is based on the postulate that a field of specific interrelations defines and constitutes a distinct social space or on the thesis of the withdrawal of individuals into a place of refuge (the family) within a world in crisis. Second, (and here the sociological literature on the family is particularly abundant), a great many analyses based on hypotheses of the rejection of civil society or the retreat into the 'private sphere' fail to encompass the profound changes in kinship relations and family practices which are currently taking place. Finally, it is my view that the development of the research perspective which I propose (below) under the general heading of the dualism of the socialistic alternative (*l'alternative socialitaire*) is parallel to the emergence of a kind of sociological neo-familism. This neo-familism takes a variety of forms. Futurologists like Toffler,[3] for example, have given a lead as far as the evolution of wage-labour is concerned. They see the nuclear family (among the salariat as well as among manual workers and those in small private firms) as a new work collective, in terms of hypotheses about the evolution of the labour process linked with the development of informatics and the emergence of what he calls the 'electronic household'. Production in the 'third wave' does not require personnel to be concentrated at the place of work. With the proliferation of domestic computers, employees will no longer need to come together in large-scale units of production.

Similar technological opitimism is to be found in analyses like those of Pahl (1980) who suggests that we are moving towards increasing privatization of modes of consumption, especially as a result of technological innovations. These already make it possible for families to acquire machinery which functions in a non-collective mode and the trend is likely to continue. For me, and many others, technological optimism goes hand in hand with economic and political pessimism, to the extent that, having posited the insoluble crisis of the Welfare State, endemic upward pressure on the cost of public services (but private services too) and technocratic inflexibility in the organization of public services, the solution proposed is domestic responsibility for the large majority of socialized and collective services. There is a tendency, as in the case of Roustang (1982) to quote well-known sociological studies[4] which show that mutual aid within the family (especially the extended family) is preferred to 'external services' or reliance on collective services, in order to suggest a familistic solution to the crisis of the Welfare State. Within the same perspective, he takes up the theme of work-sharing and proposes, along with many other solutions like the reduction of working time, the development of part-time work. The argument is that this solution would reduce dependence on collective services and thus lead to a rediscovery of personal autonomy.[5]

It should be noted that these prescriptions and proposed solutions to the crisis in employment and welfare have a certain force because their appeal to reality is based on examples of individuals and families who are already choosing this kind of response. Although civil society is obviously ripe with such choices, however, they should not be allowed to obscure the equally significant alternatives which it also contains. Part of the problem is to show the contradictory dynamic at work. At another level, some Californian sociologists call for the construction of a 'new public sphere' which would begin with the reconstruction of the household unit.[6] Roustang shares this perspective to some extent when, having defined the isolation of the nuclear family cell, he proposes that it should be reinserted into a refurbished social fabric enriched by the life of the neighbourhood and the regeneration of multiple exchange of services within neighbourhoods.

Is it therefore appropriate to talk of neo-familism? The point here is certainly not to try and find a perfect classification for trends in research. In this case at least, as Friedmann and Ehrhart's lively critiques of theorists of the informal economy (designated Radical Romantics) have so clearly shown, there is no homogeneous research trend. Moreover, these authors base their criticisms on the fact that to postulate the appearance of new ways of life in terms of the development of domestic occupations is to postulate a process of privatization of social life when the problem is precisely to obtain the domestic group's return from its exile from civil society. My question, however, is do not both cases involve some sort of dissociation of the domestic group from the totality of social relations? First, we are given a description of autonomous families, then a prescription for additional links with the rest of the social body. To raise the problem of the organization of the domestic group as a micro-society without simultaneously posing the question of the nature of the social relationships which constitute it, is in effect to preclude any understanding of the relationships between this group and other groups, or between the mode of familial sociability and other, extra-familial modes of sociability except in the empiricist sense of a relationship between a family interior and a societal exterior. Apropos the domestic group, moreover, there is something of a paradox in assuming such an increase in autonomy when one of the salient features of the last 15 years has been the development of female employment and the continuation of female activity after the birth of children, when the pressure of the feminist movements is *beginning* to achieve for women a more substantial presence in public life and when the socialization of children is increasingly taking place outside the domestic group. At the very time when women and children, the two most captive members of the bourgeois family, are beginning to experience freedom from this captivity, there are those who persist in arguing for a process of autonomization. Just when women can *begin* to participate in social life in their own right, as individuals rather than by virtue of their role in a family (as mother, wife, daughter), why is it that *familial* participation in public life, or rather, participation according to membership of the family group, is being advocated?

Analytical neo-familism therefore reinforces ideological neo-familism. However, if neo-familism is to be found at this second level, it is certainly not in the sense of a classical and conservative familism which would preach a return to the old forms of the family. This yearning for the past no longer has intellectual credence and neo-familism would be the first to criticize the 'capitalist holy family' or to detail the new kinds of role-sharing between the sexes. Nevertheless, the domestic group remains the place of autonomy and individual liberty and, at the very least, it could become the basic cell of a future democracy. It seems, moreover, that interchangeability of roles between the sexes within the domestic group is already something of a reality and that, for some, it amounts to a declaration that definitive changes have occurred in family organization.

All this is affirmed without any further analysis of the social relationships which pertain among kin, or of the changes which have been affecting the domestic group for the last 20 years or so. When use is made of the findings of the more serious studies of the family (like those of Pitrou) it is selective. Therefore, in using the term neo-familism, we are describing both the empiricist tendency to consider the domestic group in itself as a field of autonomous interaction and the ideological tendency to make the family nucleus the focus of civil society's resistance to every kind of domination. In this respect, at least, the thesis of the autonomization of civil society is perfectly congruent with the 'post-social-democratic' approach of Rosanvallon.

Liberation Through Informal Work?

A similar inclination to argue for the autonomy of civil society is to be found among the theorists of dualism but in this case it is based on the opposition between paid labour and unpaid labour. A wide range of research perspectives and problems as well as hypotheses exist but the theoretical slant is the same.

Roustang (1982) shows how the economic advisers to the former government of Raymond Barre 'discovered the virtues of conviviality, the tertiary sector and system D' after having dropped the idea of liquidating non-competitive sectors in favour of leading sectors, designating as theorists of economic and social dualism. Sociological theories of dualism have developed in parallel with economic theories of dualism and this author is justifiably cautious about jointly designating as theorists of economic and social dualism those who subscribe to what I call a dualism of last resort and those who hold to what I describe as the dualism of the socialistic alternative.[7] The former propose to alleviate the crisis at the margins. In practice this means alleviation without any impact on the logic of organization or the valorization of 'competitive and high technology' economic sectors subject to international competition. They propose to lighten the burden on enterprises and in particular the burden associated with the various demands of labour which sometimes take the form of obligations to the State (public services). Finally, they call for self-sufficiency in civil society, hence dissociation. The latter affirm the need to separate the formal and informal sectors in order to preserve the informal and to provide new forms of autonomy and sociability.

The middle, post-social-democratic approach attempts to reconcile the two theories of dualism: one response to the crisis is to reduce the costs of reproduction of the labour force by every possible means. One way of doing this is to increase the self-production of services by households. If this can be done with pleasure and enjoyment, inventing more convivial social relations in the process, two birds are killed with one stone. If women can also be persuaded to work half-time, or share their work with other women, then that makes three. We can now appreciate what is at stake theoretically: the analysis of domestic labour and, beyond this, the analysis of the allocation of work between the formal and the informal sector.

An assertion which seems to attract unanimous support is that consumption (i.e. practices which arise from the sphere of consumption) is a form of production. This assertion is at the centre of the theoretical problems posed by the formal–informal dualism thesis. However, it conceals more than a few ambiguities. Let us consider the neo-classical economic approach to consumption in Becker's (1965) principal theories, including the refinements made by his followers. Here consumption is no longer simply considered as a combination of expenditure and saving but also as an activity or labour which depends on a range of technologies of consumption. As Cot (1982) has pointed out, the family is the privileged terrain of this new discourse. It is constituted juridically by contracts made in the marriage market and then becomes a small business which can be analysed in terms of a 'function of domestic production'.[8]

Although we cannot elaborate on the theme, it is worth remembering that the new micro-economic theories of the consumer, human capital and non-market social relations, far from being a special stage in the development of neo-classical economics, are central to the resurgence of economic liberalism and to the project of neo-liberal society. Confronted with the failure of the Keynesian remedies for the crisis, the crisis of the Welfare State, this approach advocates the disengagement of the State (from all except monetary policies), the restoration of mechanisms of market regulation *in combination with* the extension of theoretical models of economic analysis (following familiar formal categories of action) *to the totality of social behaviour.*[9] At the same time, the hypothesis of the existence of an equivalent market for all the goods and services produced within the family is advanced. The concrete subject is obscured by the economic subject which is itself confused with the capitalist. Civil society thus finds unity and homogeneity behind this figure (for further elaboration of these points see Andreff et al. 1982). All this is well illustrated in the study by Lemennicier and Levy-Garbova (1981) in their attempt to develop an 'autarchy-market' model of choice. The authors tell us that 'the existence of an equivalent market for goods and services produced under autarchy is a crucial hypothesis in the model. Without it, arbitration would not exist.' If this is accepted, then the formal model of rational behaviour can be applied: 'The choices concerning female activity are thus guided exclusively by the comparison of costs and relative efficiency of autarchy and the market considered as alternative ways of obtaining the products useful to the household' and the whole set of axioms for analysis of practices associated with it: maximization of utility and choice under conditional constraints, as in the new theory of the consumer, a considerable refinement of the analysis of constraints and rational choices.

Consumption is a kind of production: this is also affirmed in other quite different perspectives, including that of some theoretical feminists whose aim is to achieve recognition of the value of work performed by women within the household, and in theories of informal work which try to emphasize the central importance of domestic work in economic analysis (Lefaucheur & Barthes 1983) The logical consequence of such an approach is to propose the monetary evalution of the domestic work carried out in a country. This was done in France in 1981 by Fouquet and Chadeau. The method of calculation is not neutral because with different measurement techniques it is possible to obtain very different results. In particular, it is not indifferent from the point of view of the definition of the economic subject which it implies. Let us take two examples.

If domestic production is assessed according to the value of goods and services produced as the cost of acquiring them in the market, then one is assuming 'a complete commodification of domestic production' and treating the family as a small business. If one estimates the time spent in domestic work at the level of wages which the person (in this context, a woman at home) could expect to receive in the same time as an employee, then the economic subject is the productive subject. The difference is of more than marginal significance. Other authors have criticized an approach which reduces unpaid work to domestic work, showing how domestic work is itself inscribed in the totality of informal activities.[10]

There is much at stake behind these theoretical and technical debates, from the reduction (or increase) in the cost of reproduction of the labour force to the reduction of unemployment by a different allocation of labour. I wonder, however, if to leave it like this is not to accept a blinkered view of the problem of ways out of the crisis. At the most fundamental level I believe that to pose the problem in this way is restricted to the extent that it reduces individuals to their quality as labour or, more generally, to commodities.

Each individual is defined by a cost of reproduction and every practice can be reckoned in terms of a monetary equivalent. Consequently, the totality of individual activities can be broken down into a series of steps which allow for the calculation of costs and benefits. Conviviality is then *juxtaposed*. This is how theory comes to reflect capitalism's tendency to reduce social relations to their exchange value, in short to money. It is not a matter of pure mystification because the reduction of human activities to an abstract equivalent is inscribed in the logic of capitalism.

However, human activities are not reducible to this dimension alone. Certain authors, such as Mingione, Pahl and Kendé (1975, 1978) have emphasized this in refusing to regard all practices as economic practices *sensu stricto*. They propose to return to 'the fundamentals of economic activity' in distinguishing between domestic productive activities and unproductive domestic activities.[11] Boulding (1972), on the other hand, presents the transfer economy, with the family as its main agent, as the alternative to the exchange economy.[12] This leads me to several observations:

1 The distinctions employed by authors like Mingione, Kendé or Boulding appear to be indispensable. Those of Boulding are incorporated in a dualistic vision which distinguishes between the formal exchange economy and the informal economy of gift and transfer. However, it is apparently forgotten that even the *productive activities, exchange relations* or *market relationships* referred to can never be reduced to the abstraction of exchange value.
2 One cannot simply juxtapose spheres of practices and social relations by assigning activities of use and effect exclusively to the non-market sphere and the strict law of value and commodities to the sphere of market activities.
3 The various dimensions are involved in every practice and in

each sphere of activity. One cannot simply juxtapose the two or seek to change the one (the non-market sphere) without affecting the other.

4 Ultimately, to say that consumption is production or to differentiate market and non-market relationships or productive and unproductive activities amounts to complete abstraction unless, at the same time, one asks what is being produced and reproduced by these relationships and these activities.

In my view, the meaning of these domestic activities and social relationships only finds expression in terms of a specific form of reproduction which is not simply that of material goods but also that of human beings and actual, unique individuals within families. Furthermore, market relationships are realized through specific social relationships. In this connection it should be noted that the analyses mentioned above refer to a sort of pure economic space and never include in their analysis of domestic and informal practices the analysis of contradictory relationships of class, kinship and sex. In point of fact the problem is to be able to define the social relationships which are constitutive of family life 'as being both specific and "capitalist"' (Bourgeois et al. 1978). Beyond the various forms of exchange, reciprocity and transfer, it might then be possible to see forms of domination and of effective dependency.

Other lines of research are being pursued in France which could pave the way for alternative theories and indicate the potential for more profound changes in our societies. First, there are the studies previously mentioned which seek to analyse and define more clearly the social relationships linked to the reproduction of persons, and thereby aim to grasp the modalities of their transformation. Second, there are studies which deal with the reproduction of human beings and actual individuals in what is described in France as an anthroponomic perspective. This is a way of thinking about the processes of global development and the liberation of human beings which embraces all the dimensions of their existence from occupational qualifications to styles of loving, without attempting to circumscribe a priori the places where change might occur. Finally, there are studies which set out to understand the emergence over long periods of time of new historical forms of individuality and the matrices of practices which they support. The issue here is:

no longer monadic individuality, which was firmly established at the beginning of the last century (the form of individualistic individuality whose modes of reproduction are dominated by monetary exchange; nor the 'restricted' individuality of the pre-capitalist forms of society, a form of individuality defined entirely by a stable position in the line of descent and the local community); but a self-determining social individuality, whose actual representatives today are actors, spectators and intellectuals. (Casanova 1982)

When it Comes to New Ways of Life, Can We Afford to do Things by Halves?

Let us return to the post-social democratic thesis. I will rely mainly on Gorz's *Farewell to the Working Class* (1982) which, in my view, is one of the most illuminating sources on the current of thought we are dealing with here. The thesis consists of an ideologico-political perspective and a dualistic hypothesis. The *ideologico-political perspective* is the establishment of new types of social relationship and new ways of life including consumption and work. Here there is little cause for disagreement. However, these new social relationships are only to be established in civil society. There will be no attempt to break down, weaken or substantially alter the functioning of the State apparatuses. In the realm of material production and paid employment there will simply be an effort 'to work in the most dignified, the most efficient way possible and therefore with the minimum number of hours.'

Will self-determination mean nothing more than this? Must genuine freedom be sought elsewhere, especially outside paid employment? The hypothesis which follows from this is that it is possible to invent new social relationships in civil society outside market relationships without changing the apparatuses of the State and production and therefore the class relationships which they crystallize. However, *this is only possible if there are two distinct spheres,* according to the hypothesis of the dualistic organization of social space.

Gorz has chosen to call these the sphere of heteronomy and the sphere of autonomy.[13] The former defines activities which are owed to society, rewarded by a salary and require a minimum of personal investment: a kind of curse for the individual. The latter consists of activities which are ends in themselves, not bound by market relations: a kind of blessing. In the sense that heteronomy is indispensable for maintaining an efficient system of production planned in such a way as to satisfy 'primary' material needs it is a necessary evil. It is the sector of the large-scale enterprise and the 'inevitably depersonalizing division of labour', of narrow specialization accelerated by automation. The author appears to be convinced that there is no point in hoping to radically change relationships between people within the enterprise and no point in struggling against irreversible deskilling; we simply have to try and spend as little time as possible in this hell.

However, Gorz does not at any point slide into a form of communitarian anarchism. He denounces new-style traditional communities where love for the father or charismatic leader is transformed into the most tyrannical form of submission possible because they make the individual subject to complete approval by power and the law and deny him any sphere of freedom. He also denounces the risks of tribalism, the poverty of communitarian autarchy. Out of this comes the fundamental notion that a sphere of necessity which is objectified in universal social obligations is clearly taking shape. This leaves a better defined sphere of autonomous choice which is protected from the working of the rules in the heteronomous sphere.

According to Gorz, the advantage of this clear distinction is two-fold: on the one hand, the spirit of creativity acquired in the autonomous sphere would make individuals 'rebel against the hierarchical division of labour'. We must ask whether this has anything but romantic significance since it is apparently necessary to accept heteronomy as such, as a guarantee of maximum productivity? Why this option in particular? One could just as well say, following the theory of compensatory activities, that the possibility of creative self-expression in an autonomous sphere will counterbalance the accumulated frustrations of the heteronomous sphere and thus make them more supportable. On the other hand, the possibilities of discovery and new forms of communication in heteronomous labour would prevent 'community life from becoming impoverished through a sort of entropy'. However, can we conceive of activities conducted in terms of totally alienated social relationships as effectively enriching the activities of the autonomous sphere?

Let us consider the idea that in certain spheres of activity the individual possesses no control whatsoever over his existence, whilst in others he regains total possession. The tensions internal to each field of practices and the contradictory dynamic of the processes which work in one or the other direction are concealed. This is no less true of the factory than the family. Moreover, it involves closing one's eyes to, or at least averting them from, the fact that at each moment (or in each field of practices) actual individuals are the site of this contradictory dynamic between the processes of possession and dispossession of the control of their existence. Of course one cannot stop there. The processes which are constitutive of this contradiction have a different impact depending on the particular configuration of social relationships in which they occur, whether the factory or the family. Instead of making an a priori division of social space into spheres of autonomous and heteronomous practices would it not be possible to try and grasp the dialectic by which, on the one hand, individuals are mobilized[15] materially, financially, morally and effectively to organize their life and give it overall meaning and, on the other, are simultaneously mobilized by structural processes of vast scope which evolve over long periods and involve social groups on a very large scale?

This is precisely the orientation of an empirical research project into the life cycles of male and female workers in large-scale enterprises in the metallurgical industry in France, which I and others have initiated.[16] Our task is to find alternative methods and techniques of empirical analysis which neither lead to a romantic and metaphysical phenomenology which sees everyone as reinventing their life on a daily basis, nor to a despairing acceptance of the absolute subordination of everyday practices to the harsh exigencies of structural processes.

Prophetic discourses on the convulsions or the restiveness of civil society are no longer enough. We must not hesitate to go deeper into the analysis of social practices and ways of life, for the further one advances in this direction the greater one's awareness of the enormity of what is at stake for society.

By way of conclusion, I would say that I have had to use a broad brush to picture certain sociological issues. The problems call for nothing less than a clear understanding, not just of present society but of the civilization which is being given birth under our eyes, and the nature of the modalities which will lead us out of this current global crisis. The debate which began with questions about the meaning of the new practices appearing in European societies illustrates the way in which all theories prescribe as well as describe. It is in the very nature of modes of theorization in the social sciences. Descriptions which strive to be neutral, empiricist and guided by facts and yet ignore the potential changes which are written into the situations described, amount to prescriptions for the maintenance of the prevailing order.

What is at stake in the critical analysis which I have presented here is not just the fact that prescription – in this context, the autonomization of civil society and the creation of new social relations with it – is inscribed in the description of this civil society. It is not simply the fact that these prescriptions–descriptions obscure certain phenomena. It is the more fundamental fact that to describe the withdrawal of civil society into itself as a unilateral and non-contradictory phenomenon is to reduce a priori the range of potentialities inscribed within civil society.[17] Is this not to prescribe the hopelessness of significantly changing the logic (of functioning) of the large-scale apparatuses of production and control of the State machine? Can we change ways of life without also changing the ways of producing and governing?

Notes

This chapter was kindly translated by Howard Davis.

1 The journal *Autrement* specializes in 'miniature revolutions' and is the forum for current debate on these movements. For example: Les revolutions miniscules, *Revue Autrement* 29, Paris, Feb. 1981.

2 cf. Mingione on p. 19 of this volume.
  In this sense the cycle of reproduction of the labour force is already shattered: it no longer constitutes the link between the cycle of accumulation of capital, on the one hand, and the various subsistence economies and societies on the other. This is the starting point for the elaboration of our hypothesis that the increasing complexity and articulation of present-day societies gives rise to an important process of social fragmentation.

3 Toffler (1980:364) states:
  The rise of the prosumer, the spread of the electronic cottage, the invention of new organizational structures in business, the automation and de-massification of production, all point to the home's re-emergence as a central unit in the society of tomorrow – a unit with enhanced rather than diminished economic, medical, educational, and social functions.

4 In actual fact, those of Pitrou (1978).

5 Roustang (1982: 218) states:
  At present, there are scarcely any part-time posts except in unskilled work but does it necessarily follow that the development of part-time work would contribute to a decline in qualifications? Almost certainly not. It is likely that people

who have experienced greater autonomy in their lives will find
it hard to accept, even for a few hours per day, being subject to
poor working conditions or authoritarian work organization.

6 cf. Friedmann & Ehrhart (1982: 33–4):

But important as it is, the reconstruction of the household is
not the final objective. In order to produce its life, the
reconstructed household must enter into joint activities with
others, creating appropriate institutions of a political nature
that will ensure the accountability of both the state and the
economy to the people organized for a political life. And so the
reconstruction of the household cannot be confined to the
periphery of the capitalist system; it cannot take place in the
domain of civil society where the household's functions are
merely those of reproduction. An active role for the household
demands that return from our exile in civil society to the
center of the intersecting domains of public action.

7 It should be clear that I am referring here to the kind of dualism
which distinguishes between the formal sector (that of paid-
employment) and an informal sector (that of underground work),
with each individual of the household operating entirely within one
or the other sector, and not the kind of dualism which distinguishes
between social categories according to whether their main activity is
conducted within the primary or secondary sector, with reference to
the theory of labour-market segmentation.

8 Cot (1982: 140) states that 'Final satisfactions, made up of conviviality, goods and non-market services, sleep or procreation, result from
the 'productive consumption', of 'two factors of production', market
goods and non-market time . . .'

9 To quote a single example of this proposition, Lemennicier (1980)
writes: 'Let us follow Becker in assuming that a person marries if,
and only if, the share of goods consumed as a result of being married
exceeds that which would have been received in remaining single.'

10 Without question, the most thorough and, in this sense, most
pertinent attempt is that by Mingione (this volume) which extends
Pahl's work (this volume) in the direction of a more refined
conceptualization of activities in the informal sphere.

11 Kendé (1978: pp 206–25) puts forward a distinction between:

domestic productive activities (those which come strictly
within the sphere of economic analysis) and others. An activity
is considered to be productive when the person who performs
it (or who receives the benefit) could be replaced by any other
person and if that person can claim compensation when they
are not a member of the household under consideration. The

activity is 'unproductive' whenever this substitution cannot be made (e.g. study, games, exercise), or when the service emanates from a giving of the personality which makes no claim for reciprocation (maternal love).

12 The family is by far the most important agency in the gift economy. The gift economy is an economy of unilateral transfer. In an exchange I give you something and you give me something; in a transfer, I give you some sort of economic good and you give me nothing in the way of an economic good in return. Transfer is a growing and highly significant element in the economy. Without it society could not survive and children would all perish. (Boulding 1978:21–37)

If, in certain cases, exchange does take place, it is then a question of non-contractual exchange, which Boulding (1978:21–37) defines as reciprocity: 'One can define reciprocity simply as non-contractual exchange, mutual exchange of gifts or presents, or one-way transfer, A giving something to B without conditions and B giving something without conditions to A.'

13 The former assures the programmed and planned production of everything necessary to individual and social life, with the maximum efficiency and least expenditure of effort and resources. In the latter sphere, individuals autonomously produce non-necessary material and non-material goods and services, outside of the market, by themselves or in free association with others, and in conformity with their own desires, tastes or fantasies. (Gorz 1982:97)

14 Gorz states that the dissociation of spheres is necessary to preserve the autonomous sphere. Sceptics might be inclined to suggest that it is also essential for the preservation of the heteronomous sphere.

15 For a definition of this concept of mobilization see Godard and Cuturello 1980; Godard 1983.

16 *Transformations des Modes de Vie et Division du Travail: Analyse des Cycles de Vie des Familles dans le Monde Ouvrier.* This research is being carried out by D. Bertaux, P. Bouffartigue, D. Combes, F. Godard, M. Haicault, A. Jeantet, J.R. Pendaries, M. Pinçon, P. Rendu and H. Tiger. It is financed by the Ministry of Housing and the Urban Environment, and will be published (1984) as: *Comme on fait sa vie: familles ouvrières, histoires d'amjourd' hui.*

17 I continue to use the term for the sake of simplicity but, as I stated earlier, it is not one which I find particularly suitable in its current usage.

References

Abdullah T. & Zeidenstein S. (1981) *Village Women of Bangladesh: Prospects for Change*. Pergamon Press, Oxford.

Ahmed Z. (1980) The plight of rural women: alternatives for action. *International Labour Review*, July–August.

Allen S. (1981) Invisible threads. *IDS Bulletin*, vol. 12 (3). (41–7)

Allum P. (1973) Politics and Society in Post-war Naples. Cambridge University Press, Cambridge.

Alonso J. (ed.) (1980) *Lucha Urbana y Acumulación de Capital*. Casa Chata, Mexico.

Amsden A. (1980) *The Economics of Women and Work*. Penguin, Harmondsworth.

Andreff W., Cot A.L., Frydman R., Gillard L., Michon F., Tartarin M. (eds) (1982) *L'économie Fiction contre les Nouveaux Economistes*. François Maspéro, Paris.

Anthias F. (1980) Women and the reserve army of labour: a critique of Veronica Beechey. *Capital and Class* 10, 50–63.

Aranda J. & Arizpe L. (1981) The 'comparative advantages' of women's disadvantages: women workers in the strawberry export agribusiness in Mexico. *Signs* 7 (2), Winter, 453–73.

Arizpe L. (1982) Relay migration in the survival of the peasant household. In Safa H. (ed.) *Towards a Political Economy of Urbanization in Third world Countries*. Oxford University Press, Delhi.

Bagnasco A. (1977) *Le Tre Italie*. 11 Mulino, Bologna.

Bagnasco A. (1981a) Labour market, class structure and regional formations in Italy. *International Journal of Urban and Regional Research*, 5 (1), 40–4.

Bagnasco A. (1981b) La questione dell'economia informale. *Stato e Mercato*, 1 (1).

Bahro R. (1982) *Socialism and Survival: Articles, Essays and Talks, 1979–1982*. Herche Books, London.

Banaji J. (1977) Modes of production in a materialist conception of history. *Capital and Class*, 3.

Barrett M. & McIntosh M. (1980) The 'family wage': some problems for socialists and feminists. *Capital and Class,* 11, 51–72.

Basso P. (1981) *Disoccupati e Stato* Angeli, Milano.

Becker G. (1965) A theory of allocation of time. *Economic Journal,* 75 (September), 493–517.

Beechey V. (1977) Some notes on female wage labour in capitalist production. *Capital and Class* 3, 45–66.

Beechey V. (1978) Women and production: a critical analysis of some sociological theories of women's work. In Kuhn A. & Wolpe A.M. (eds) *Feminism and Materialism,* pp. 155–97 Routledge & Kegan Paul, London.

Beechey V. (1979) On patriarchy. *Feminist Review* 3, 66–82.

Beechey V. (1983) What's so special about women's employment? A review of some recent studies of women's paid work. *Feminist Review* 15, 23–45.

Bell D. (1973) *The Coming of Post-industrial Society.* Basic Books, New York.

Beneria L. (1979) Reproduction, production and the sexual division of labour. *Cambridge Journal of Economics,* 3, 203–25.

Beneria L. (1982), Industrial Home Work and Gender Relations. Unpublished final report.

Beneria L. & Sen G. (1981) Accumulation, reproduction and women's role in economic development. *Signs,* 7 (2), 279–98.

Benholdt-Thomsen V. (1981) Subsistence production and extended reproduction. In Young, K., Wolkowitz, C. and McCullagh, R. *Of Marriage and the Market.* C.S.E., London.

Bernstein H. (1979) African peasantries: a theoretical framework. *Journal of Peasant Studies* 6 (4), 421–43.

Berra M. & Revelli M. (1980) Absentéisme et conflictualité: l'usine reniée. Crise de la centralité de l'usine et nouveaux comportements ouvriers. In *Usines et Ouvriers,* Collection Luttes Sociales. François Maspero, Paris.

Bilac E. (1978) *Familias de Trabalhadores: Estrategias de Sobrevivencia.* Sao Paulo.

Blackaby F. (ed.) (1978) *De-industrialization.* Heinemann Educational Books, London.

Bleitrach D. & Chenu A. (1982) Y a-t-il une nouvelle personnalité féminine? *La Pensée,* 228, July–August, 44–57.

Blood R. Jr & Wolfe D. (1960) *Husbands and Wives.* Collier Macmillan, New York.

Bose A.N. (1974) *The Informal Sector in the Calcutta Metropolitan Economy.* World Employment Working Paper, ILO Geneva.

Boserup E. (1970) *Women's Role in Economic Development.* Allen & Unwin, London.

Bosquet M. (1980) Le chemin de la liberté. *Le Nouvel Observateur,* 812 (2 June), 40–1.

Boulding K.E. (1972) The household as Achilles' heel. *Journal of Consumer Affairs*, 2.

Boulding K.E. (1978) Réciprocité et échange: l'individu et la famille dans la société. In Michel A. (ed.) *Les Femmes dans la Société Marchande*. PUF, Paris.

Bourgeois F., Brener J., Chabaud D., Cot A., Fougeyrolles D., Haicault M. & Kartchevsky-Bulport A. (1978) Travail domestique et famille du capitalisme. *Critiques de l'Économie Politique*, 3, April–June, 3–23.

Bradby B. (1982) The remystification of value. *Capital and Class*, 17, Summer. 114–33.

Braverman H. (1974) *Labor and Monopoly Capital*. Monthly Review Press, New York.

Bremen J.A. (1976) A dualistic labour system? A critique of the informal sector concept. *Economic and Political Weekly*, 2, 48–50.

Britten N. & Heath A. (1982) *Women, Men and Families: Proposal for a New Social Class Classificaton*. Paper delivered to the British Sociological Association Conference, Manchester.

Britten N. & Heath A. (forthcoming) Women, Men and Social Class. Department of Social and Administrative Studies, Oxford.

Bromley R. (1978) The urban informal sector: why is it worth discussing? *World Development*, 6 (9/10), 1033–9.

Bromley R. & Gerry C. (eds) (1979) *Casual Work and Poverty in Third World Cities*. John Wiley & Sons, New York.

Bruegel I. (1979) Women as a reserve army of labour: a note on recent British experience. *Feminist Review*, 3, 12–23.

Bruno S. (1979) The industrial reserve army: segmentation and the Italian labour market. *Cambridge Journal of Economics*, 3, 131–51.

Brusco S., Capecchi V. et al. (1980) *Sindacato e Piccola Impresa in Italia*. De Donato, Bari.

Brusco S. & Sabel C. (1982) Artisan production and economic growth. In Wilkinson F. (ed.) *The Dynamics of Labor Market Segmentation*. Academic Press, London.

Buck N. (1981) *An Admiralty Dockyard in the Mid-Nineteenth Century: Aspects of the Social and Economic History of Sheerness*. Final report to the SSRC, Urban and Regional Studies Unit, University of Kent at Canterbury.

Burns S. (1975) *Home Inc. The Hidden Wealth and Power of the American Household*. Doubleday & Co., Garden City, New York.

Burns S. (1977) *The Household Economy*. Beacon Press, Boston.

Business Week (1978) The fast growth of the underground economy. 13 March, 73–7.

Business Week (1982) The underground economy's hidden force. 5 April, 64–70.

Bustamante J. (1979) Emigracion e inmovilidad. *Uno Mas Uno*, 14 May 1979.

Bustamante J. (1979) Estado legal de indefension. *Uno Mas Uno*, 26 June 1979.

Calza Bini P. (1977) *Economia Periferica e Classi Sociali*. Liguori, Naples.

Cardosa-Khoo J. & Khoo K.J. (1978) *Work and Consciousness: The Case of Electronics 'Runaways' in Malaysia*. Paper presented to the Conference on the Continuing Subordination of Women in the Development Process. IDS, University of Sussex, Brighton. (Forthcoming in Young K. (ed.) *Just One Big Happy Family.*)

Caroux J. (1982) Des nouveaux mouvements sociaux à la dérobade du social? *Cahiers Internationaux de Sociologie*, LXXII, 145–57.

Carrillo J.V. & Hernández A.H. (1981) *La Industria Maquiladora en México: Bibliografiá, Directorio e Investigaciones*. Monographs in US–Mexican Studies, University of California, San Diego.

Casanova A. (1982) Individualité, biographie, société. *La Pensée*, 228, July–August, 29–43.

Castells M. (1973) La urbanización dependiente en América Latina. In Castells M. (ed.) *Imperialismo y Urbanización en América Latina*. Gustavo Gilli, Barcelona.

Castells M. (1976) *La Cuestion Urbana*. Siglo XXI, Mexico City. (Revised edition.)

Castells M. (1981) *Capital Multinacional, Estados Nacionales, Comunidades Locales*. Siglo XXI, Mexico City.

CENSIS (1978) *Rapporto sul la Situazione Sociale del Paese*. Censis, Rome.

Centro de la vivienda y estudios urbanos (CENVI) (1981) *El trabajo no asalariado en la produccion y consumo del espacio urbano*. Mexico City: unpublished paper.

CENSIS ISFOL CNEL (1976) *L'occupazione Occulta*. Censis, Rome.

Cetro R. (1977) Lavoro a domicilio a Pomigliano d'Arco. *Inchiesta*, 33.

Chadeau A. & Fouquet A. (1981) Peut on mesurer le travail domestique? *Economie et Statistique*, September, 29–42.

Chen, M. Guznavi R., (1979) *Women in food-for-work: the Bangladesh experience*. World Food programme, Rome.

Chincilla N.S. (1977) Industrialisation, monopoly capitalism and women's work in Guatemala. In Wellesley Editorial Committee (eds) *Women and National Development: The Complexities of Change*. University of Chicago Press, Chicago.

Choain C. & Jacquemart J. (1982) Perception et répression du travail noir. In *Travail Noir, Productions Domestiques et Entr'aide*. Observation du Changement Social. Lille ATP du CNRS, Lille.

Cleaver H. (1983) Tesis sobre la teoría Marxista del valor de trabajo. *El Gallo Illustrado*, Sunday supplement, *El Día*, 10 April 1983, 7–14.

Collidà A. (1979) Città meridionale e sovraurbanizzazione. In Accornero A. & Andriani S. (eds) *Gli anni '70 nel Mezzogiorno*. De Donato, Bari.

Combes D. (1981) *Représentations des Rapports de Production et Approches des Modes de Vie*. Centre de Sociologie Urbaine, Paris. December.

Combes D. & Haicault M. (1982) *Production et Reproduction, Rapports Sociaux de Sexes et de Classes.* Paper delivered to the Tenth World Congress of Sociology, Mexico City.

Connolly P. (co-ordinator) (1977) *Investigación sobre Vivienda,* vol. 4, *El Capital en la Producción de Vivienda.* COPEVI, Mexico City.

Coordinadora Nacional del Movimento Urbano Popular (CONAMUP) Various documents 1980–83.

Comisión para la planeacion de las zonas marginadas (COPLAMAR) (1979) *Normas minimas de educacion y capacitacion.*

Cornuel D. (1980) Propositions pour une Theorie duale de l'Economie Informelle. Unpublished paper, University of Lille.

Cot A.L. (1982) Nouvelle économie, utopie et crise. In Andreff et al. (eds) *L'économie Fiction contre les nouveaux Economistes.* François Maspéro, Paris.

Covarrubias P. & Muñoz M. (1978) Algunos factores que inciden en la participación laboral de las mujeres de estratos bajos. In *Chile, Mujer y Sociedad.* UNICEF.

Coward R. (1983) *Patriarchal Precedents.* Routledge & Kegan Paul, London.

Daly A.A. (1904) *The History of the Isle of Sheppey.* Reprinted by Arthur S. Cassel, 1975.

de Barbieri M. (1978) Notas para el estudio de trabajo de las mujeres: el problema del trabajo doméstico. *Demografía y Economíca.*

de Certeau, M. (1980) *L'invention du quotidien,* tome 1, *Arts de faire.* Union Générale d'Edition, Paris.

Deere C.D. (1976) Rural women's subsistence production in the capitalist periphery. *Review of Radical Political Economics* **8** (1), 9–17.

Deere C.D. & de Janvry A. (1978) A Theoretical Framework for the Empirical Analysis of Peasants. Working Paper No. 60, Giannini Foundation, University of California, Berkeley.

Deere C.D. & Léon de Leal M. 1982. Peasant production, proletarianization and the sexual division of labour in the Andes. In Beneria (ed.) *Women and Development, the sexual division of labour in rural societies.* Praeger, New York.

de Grazia R. (1979) El trabajo clandestino: un problema de actualidad. *Revista Internacional de Trabajo,* **99**, 1649.

de Janvry A. (1975) The political economy of rural development in Latin America: an interpretation. *American Journal of Agricultural Economics,* **57** (3), August.

de Janvry A. & Garramon C. (1977) The dynamics of rural poverty in Latin America. *Journal of Peasant Studies,* **4** (3), 206–15.

de Leonardo M. & Guerra M. (1978) Mujer, familia y sociedad: viscitudes de la proletarización y politización femeninas. *Estrategia,* **20**, 78–88.

Delphy C. (1977) *The Main Enemy.* Women's Research and Resources Centre, London.

de Marco C. & Talamo M. (1976) *Lavoro Nero.* Mazzota, Milan.

de Oliveira F. (1984) A critique of dualist reason: the Brasilian economy after 1930, in Bromley R.J. (ed.) *Planning for Small Enterprises in Third World Cities*. Pergamon Press, Oxford.

de Riz L. (1975) El Problema de la Condición Femenina en América Latina: la Participación de la Mujer en los Mercados de Trabajo. El Caso de México. Unpublished paper, Mexico City.

Dixon R. (1978) *Rural Women at Work: Strategies for Development in South Asia*. John Hopkins University Press, Baltimore.

Edholm F., Harris O. & Young K. (1977) Conceptualising women. *Critique of Anthropology*, 3 (9/10), 101–30.

Edwards R.C. (1979) *Contested Terrain*. Basic Books, New York.

Edwards R., Gordon D. & Reich M. (eds) (1976) *Labor Market Segmentation*. Lexington Books, Massachusetts.

Edwards R., Gordon D. & Reich M. (1982) *Segmented Work, Divided Workers*. Cambridge University Press, Cambridge.

Elú de Lenero M. (ed.) (1975) *La Mujer en América Latina*. Sep/Setentas, Mexico.

Engels F. (1969) *The Condition of the Working Class in England*. Panther Paperback, London.

Esteva G. (1983a) Los tradifas o el fin de la marginación. *El Trimestre Económico*, 50 (2), April–June, 733–70.

Esteva G. (1983b) Leer políticamente el capital. *El Gallo Ilustrado*, Sunday Supplement, *El Día*, 10 April 1983, 3–6.

F.L.C. (Federation of Construction Workers) (ed.) (1982) *La Camorra e il Mercato Edilizio*. FLC, Naples.

Feige E.L. (1980) How big is the irregular economy? *Cudernos Económicos de Información Comercial Española*, 564–5, August–September 156–64. Spanish translation.

Feige E.L. (1981) A new perspective on macroeconomic phenomena: the theory and measurement of the unobserved sector. *Cuadernos Económicos de Información Comercial Española*, 16, 117–39. Spanish translation.

Ferguson A. & Folbre N. (1981) The unhappy marriage of patriarchy and capitalism. In Sargent L. (ed.) *Women and Revolution: The unhappy marriage of Marxism and feminism*, 313–38. Pluto Press, London.

Ferman L.A. & Berndt L. (1981) The irregular economy. In Henry S. (ed.) *Can I Have It in Cash?* Astragel Books, London.

Ferman L.A., Berndt L. & Selo E. (1978) Analysis of the Irregular Economy: Cash Flow in the Informal Sector. Unpublished report to the Bureau of Employment and Training, Michigan Department of Labor and Industrial Relations. The University of Michigan – Wayne State University, Ann Arbor, Michigan.

Ferman L.A. & Ferman P.R. (1973) The structural underpinnings of irregular economy. *Poverty and Human Resources Abstracts* 9 (March), 13–17.

Fernandez-Kelly M.P. (1978) Mexican Border Industrialisation, Female Labour Force Participation and Development. Unpublished.

Foudi R., Stankiewicz F. & Vaneecloo N. (1982) Chômeurs et économie informelle. In *Travail Noir, Productions Domestiques et Entr'aide*. Observation du Changement Social, Lille ATP du CNRS, Lille.

Fouquet A. & Chadeau A. (1981) *Le Travail Domestique*. Essai de quantification, archives et documents. INSEE, Paris.

Friedmann J. & Ehrhart S. (1982) *The Household Economy: Beyond Consumption and Reproduction*. Paper delivered to the Tenth World Congress of Sociology, Mexico City.

Fröbel F., Heinrichs J. & Kreye O. (1980) *The New International Division of Labour*. Cambridge University Press, Cambridge.

Galbraith J.K. (1974) *Economics and the public purpose*. Deutsch, London.

Galbraith J.K. (1982) *El Origen de la Pobreze de las Masas*. Diana, Mexico City.

Gallino L. (ed.) (1982) *Occupati e Bioccupati*. Il Mulino, Bologna.

Gappert G. & Rose H. (eds) (1975) *The Social Economy of Cities*. Sage Publishers, Beverley Hills and London.

Garcia B., Muñoz H. & de Oliveira O. (1979) Migración, familia y fuerza de trabajo en la Ciudad de México. *Cudernos del CES.*, **26**.

Garcia B., Munoz H. & de Oliveira O. (1982) *Hogares y Trabajadores en la Ciudad de México*. El Colegio de México/UNAM, Mexico City.

Garcia Ogalde J (1982) *Consulta popular sobre el capacitacion para el trabajo* Instituto de estudios economicos y sociales, Mexico.

Gardiner J. (1975) Women's domestic labour. *New Left Review* **89**.

Gerry C. (1974) *Petty Producers and the Urban Economy: A Case Study of Dakar*. World Employment Working Paper, ILO, Geneva.

Gerry C. (1979) Small scale manufacturing and repairs in Dakar: a survey of market relations within the urban economy. In Bromley R. & Gerry C. (eds) *Casual work and Poverty in Third World Cities*. John Wiley & Sons, Chichester.

Gerry C. (1980) Petite production marchande ou salariat déguisé? Quelques réflexions. *Revue Tiers Monde*, 21 (82), April–June.

Gerry C. & Birkbeck C. (1981) The petty commodity producer in Third World cities: petit bourgeois or 'disguised proletarian'? In Bechhofer F. & Elliott B. (eds) *The Petite Bourgeoisie: Comparative Studies of the Uneasy Stratum*. Macmillan, London.

Gershuny J.I. (1977) Post-industrial Society: The Myth of the Service Sector. *Futures,* April, 103–14.

Gershuny J.I. (1978) *After Industrial Society: the Emerging Self-service Economy*. Macmillan, London.

Gershuny J.I. (1979) The informal economy: its role in industrial society. *Futures,* 11(1) February, 3–15.

Gershuny J.I. (1983) *Social Innovation and the Division of Labour*. Oxford University Press, Oxford.

Gershuny J.I. & Miles I.D. (1983) *The New Service Economy*. Frances Pinter, London.

Gershuny J.I. & Pahl R.E. (1979) Work outside employment: some preliminary speculations. *New Universities Quarterly,* 34 (Winter), 120–35.

Gershuny J.I. & Pahl R.E. (1981) Work outside employment. In Henry S. (ed.) *Can I Have It in Cash?* Astragel Books, London.

Gershuny J.I. & Thomas G.S. (1984) *Changing Times: Activity Patterns in the UK, 1937–1975.* Oxford University Press, Oxford.

Giddens A. (1981) *A Contemporary Critique of Historical Materialism, vol. 1, Power, Property and the State.* Macmillan, London.

Gimenez M. (1982) The oppression of women: a structuralist Marxist view. In Rossi I. (ed.) *Structural Sociology.* Columbia University Press, New York.

Gimenez M. (1977) Population and capitalism *Latin America Perspectives* iv, 4.

Ginatempo N. & Fera G. (1982) *Autocostruzione Marginalità o Proposta.* Casa del Libro, Reggio Calabria.

Glyn A. & Harrison J. (1980) *The British Economic Disaster.* Pluto, London.

Godard, F. (1983) *Sur le concept de mobilisation.* GERM-CERCOM, Marseille-Nice.

Godard F. & Cuturello P. (1980) *Familles Mobilisées.* Collection Texte Intégral, Plan Construction, Paris.

Goddard V. (1981) The leather trade in the Bassi of Naples. *IDS Bulletin,* 12 (3).

Goodman D. & Redclift M.R. (1981) *From Peasant to Proletarian: Capitalist Development and Agrarian Transitions.* Basil Blackwell, Oxford.

Gorz A. (1982) *Farewell to the Working Class: An Essay in Post-industrial Socialism.* Pluto, London.

Graziani A. (1978) The mezzogiorno in the Italian economy. *Cambridge Journal of Economics,* 2, 355–72.

Greenfield H.I. (1966) *Manpower and the Growth of Producer Services.* Columbia University Press, New York.

Gutmann P. (1977) The subterranean economy. *Financial Analysts Journal,* November/December, 26, 27 and 34.

Gutmann P. (1978a) Are the unemployed, unemployed. *Financial Analysts Journal,* September/October, 26–9.

Gutmann P. (1978b) Professor Gutmann replies. *Financial Analysts' Journal,* November/December, 67–9.

Gutmann P. (1979a) The subterranean economy. *Taxing and Spending,* April, 4–8.

Gutmann P. (1979b) Statistical illusions, mistaken policies. *Challenge,* November/December, 14–17.

Gutmann P. (1980) Latest notes from the subterranean economy. *Business and Society Review,* Summer, 25–30.

György A. (1975) Multinational corporations world wide sourcing. In Radice H. (ed.) *International Firms, Modern Imperialism.* Penguin Books, Middlesex.

Hanger J. & Moris J. (1973) Women and the household economy. In Chambers R. & Moris J. (eds) *Mwea: an Irrigated Rice Settlement in Kenya.* Weltforum Verlag, Munich.

Hardy D. & Ward C. (forthcoming) *Arcadia for All* (provisional title).

Harloe M. & Paris C. (1982) *The Decollectivisation of Consumption, Housing and Local Government Finance in Britain, 1979–1982.* Paper delivered to the Tenth World Congress of Sociology, Mexico City.

Harris O. (1981) Households as natural units. In Young K., Walkowitz C. & McCullagh R. (eds) *Of Marriage and the Market: Women's Subordination in International Perspective.* CSE Books, London.

Harris O. & Young K. (1981) Engendered structures: some problems in the analysis of reproduction. In Kahn, J.S. & Llobera J. (eds) *The Anthropology of Pre-capitalist Societies.* Macmillan, London.

Harrison J. (1973) The political economy of housework. *Bulletin of the Conference of Socialist Economists.*

Hart K. (1973) Informal income opportunities and urban employment in Ghana. *Journal of Modern African Studies,* 11, 61–89.

Hawrylyshyn O. (1976) The value of household services: a survey of empirical estimates. *The Review of Income and Wealth* 2 (June), 101–31.

Hawrylyshyn O. & Adler H.J. (1978) Estimates of the value of household work, Canada 1961 and 1971. *The Review of Income and Wealth,* 4 (December), 333–55.

Heinze R. & Olk T. (1982) Development of the informal economy. *Futures,* June. 189–204.

Henry S. (ed.) (1981) *Can I Have It in Cash?* Astragel Books, London.

Heyzer N. (1981) Towards a framework of analysis: Women and the informal sector. *IDS Bulletin,* 12 (3), 3–7.

Himmelweit S. & Mohun S. (1977) Domestic labour and capital. *Cambridge Journal of Economics,* 1. 15–31.

Hobsbawm E. (1982) The State of the Left in Western Europe. *Marxism Today,* October. 8–15.

Hobsbawm E. (1983) Working Class Nationalism. *Marxism Today,* January. 13–19.

Hugon P. (1980) Le secteur 'non-structure' ou 'informel' des économies des pay du Tiers Monde. *Revue Tiers Monde,* April–June, 3–9.

Humphries J. (1977) The working class family, women's liberation and class struggle: the case of nineteenth century British history. *Review of Radical Political Economics* 9 (3) (Autumn), 25–41.

Humphries J. (1977) Class struggle and the persistence of the working-class family. *Cambridge Journal of Economics,* 1, 241–58.

Ifeka-Moller C. (1975) Female militancy and colonial revolt: the womens war of 1929, Eastern Nigeria. In S. Ardener (ed.) *Perceiving women* 127–57. J.M. Dent, London.

Illich I. (1971) *Deschooling Society,* Penguin, Harmondsworth.

Illich I. (1973) *Tools for Conviviality.* Fontana, London.

Illich I. (1981) *Shadow Work.* Marion Boyars, London.

Ingrosso M. (1979) *Produzione Sociale e Lavoro Domestico.* Angeli, Milan.

INSEE (1978) *Données Sociales.* INSEE, Paris.

Institute of Sociology, University of Turin (1977) *Politica del Lavoro e Seconda Professione.* Bookstore, Turin.

Institute of Sociology, University of Turin (1980) *Laurare due volte, Study and Research,* Bookstore, Turin.

International Labour Office (1972) *Employment, Incomes and Inequality: A Strategy for Increasing Productive Employment in Kenya.* ILO, Geneva.

International Labour Office (1980) *Women in Rural Development: Critical Issues.* ILO, Geneva.

IRES-CGIL-DAEST (1981) *L'evoluzione delle Strutture Economiche della Campania.* CGIL-Campania, Naples.

Jallade J.P. (ed.) (1981) *Employment and Unemployment in Europe.* Trentham Books, Staffordshire.

Jelin E. (1974) La Bahiana en la fuerza de trabajo: actividad doméstica, producción simple y trabajo asalariado en Salvador, Brasil. *Demografía y Economia,* 7 (3).

Jenkins C. & Sherman B. (1979) *The Collapse of Work.* Barrie and Rockliff, London.

Karlechevsky-Bulport A. (1978) Travail domestique et famille du capitalisme. *Critiques de l'Economie Politique,* 3 (April–June), 3–23.

Kendé P. (1975) Vers une évaluation de la consommation réelle des ménages. *Revue Consommation,* 2.

Kendé P. (1978) Les biens et les services autoproduits dans la consommation de ménages français. In Michel A. (ed.) *Les Femmes dans la Société Marchande.* PUF, Paris.

King K. (1974) Kenya's informal machine makers: a study of small scale industry in Kenya's emerging artisan society. *World Development,* 2.

Komarovsky M. (1967) *Blue Collar Marriage.* New York.

Kowarick L. (1977) *Capitalismo e Marginalidade na America Latina.* Paz e Terra, Brazil.

Kropotkin P. (1974) *Fields, Factories and Workshops Tomorrow.* Ward C. (ed.), George Allen & Unwin, London.

Kumar K. (1978) *Prophecy and Progress.* Allen Lane and Penguin Books, London and Harmondsworth.

Lafuente Félez A. (1980) Una medición de la economía oculta en España. *Boletín de Estudios Económicos de Deusto,* 3, December.

Lay C. (1982) *Napoli: Il Terremoto Quotidiano.* (Preface by Pugliese E.) Loffredo, Naples.

Leacock E. (1981) History, development and the division of labour by sex: implications for organization. *Signs,* 7 (2), Winter. 474–491.

Le Bars J.J., Camus G., Gosset A. & Nottola Y. (1980) *Essai d'Analyse des Causes Socio-économiques du Développement du Travail au Noir dans les*

348   *References*

Travaux du Bâtiment. SEDES-CORDES, Paris.

Le Brun O. & Gerry C. (1975) Petty producers and capitalism. *Review of Africal Political Economy*, 3.

Lefaucheur N. & Barthes A. (1983) Modes de vie, pratiques familales et consommation: travail et familles. In *Recherches et Familles* Colloque National, Ministère de la Recherche et de l'Industrie. Secrétariat d'Etat chargé de la Famille auprès du Ministère des Affaires Sociales et de la Solidarité Nationale.

Lehman D. (1980) Proletarización campesina: de la teorias de ayer a las prácticas de mānana. *Nueva Antropologie*, 4 (13–14), May, 65–86.

Lemennicier B. (1980) La spécialisation des rôles conjugaux. Les gains du mariage et la perspective du divorce. *Consommation, Revue de Socio-Economie*, 1 (January–March), 27–72.

Lemennicier B. & Levy-Garboua L. (1981) L'arbitrage autarcie-marché: une explication du travail féminin. *Consommation, Revue de Socio-Economie*, 2.

Lenin V.I. (1972) *The Development of Capitalism in Russia.* Collected Works, Vol. 3. Lawrence & Wishart, London.

Leon P. (1980) *Economia Sommersa . . . Modelli di Sviluppo e Qualità della Vita: l'Approccio degli Studiosi Italiani.* Paper presented to the Seminar of the Consiglio Italiano per le Scienze Sociali (CISS) on Economia Sommersa, Nascosta, Sotteranea, Invisible, Informale: Molte Realtà o una Sola?, Rome.

Lessa C. (1970) Marginalidad y proceso de maiginalización. *Cuadernos de la Sociead Venezolana de Planifación*, 82–83.

Liguori M. & Veneziano S. (1982) *Disoccupati a Napoli.* ESI, Rome.

Lim L. (1978) *Women Workers and Multi-national Companies in Developing Countries: The Case of the Electronics Industry in Malaysia and Singapore.* Occasional Paper No. 9, University of Michigan.

Lipton M. (1980) *Family, Fungibility and Formality.* Paper delivered to Workshop on Women, the Working Poor and the Informal Sector, Institute of Development Studies, University of Sussex, April.

Litwak E. (1980) Occupational mobility and extended family cohesion. *American Sociological Review*, 25 (1).

Lomnitz L. (1975) *Como Sobreviven los Marginados.* Siglo XXI, Mexico City. (English translation: *Networks and marginality: life in a Mexican shantytown.* Academic Press, New York 1977.)

Long N. & Richardson P. (1978) Informal sector petty commodity production, and the social relations of small scale enterprise. In Clammer J. (ed.) *The New Economic Anthropology.* St. Martin's Press, New York.

Loutfi M. (1980) *Rural Women: Unequal Partners in Development.* International Labour Office, Geneva.

Lowenthal M.D. (1975) The social economy in urban working class communites. In Gappert G. & Rose H. (eds) *The Social Economy of Cities.* Sage Publishers, Beverley Hills and London.

Lowenthal M.D. (1981) Non-market transactions in an urban community. In Henry, S. (ed.) *Can I have it in Cash?* Astragel Books, London.

Lustig N. (1981) *Distribución del Ingreso y Crecimiento en México: un Análysis de la Ideas Estructuralistas.* El Colegio de México, Mexico City.

MacEwan Scott A. (1979) Who are the self-employed? In Bromley R. & Gerry C. (eds) *Casual Work and Poverty in Third World Cities.* John Wiley & Sons, Chichester 105–29.

Manpower Services Commission (1983) *Labour Market Quarterly Report.* February.

Margulis M. (1980) Reproducción social de la vida y reprodución de capital. *Nueva Antropología,* 4 (13–14), May.

Margulis M. (1982) Reproducción de la Unidad Doméstica, Fuerza de Trabajo y Relaciones de Producción. Unpublished.

Margulis M. et al. (1981) Fuerza de Trabajo y Estrategias de Supervivencia en una Población de Origen Migratorio. Unpublished.

Martínez Vazquez J. (1981) El negocio de los topos. *Actualidad Económica,* 1206, 7–13 May.

Marx K. (1972) *Grundrisse.* Penguin/New Left Books, Harmondsworth and London.

Marx K. (1976) *Capital,* vols 1 and 2. Penguin/New Left Books, Harmondsworth and London.

Massey D. & Meegan R. (1982) *The Anatomy of Job Loss: The How, Why and Where of Employment Decline.* Methuen University Paperbacks, London.

McGee T. (1979) The poverty syndrome: making out in the Southeast Asian City. In Bromley R. & Gerry C. (eds) *Casual Work and Poverty in Third World Cities.* John Wiley & Sons, Chichester.

Meillasoux C. (1980) Economías del autoconsumo. *Nueva Antropología* 4 (13–14), May, 9–46.

Meillasoux C. (1981) *Maiders, Meal and Money.* Cambridge University Press, Cambridge.

Mendras H. (1980) Economie et Sociabilité. *CNRS. Archives de l'ATP* Observation du Changement Social, 3, 121–36.

Michalet C-A. (1976) *Le Capitalisme Mondiale.* Edition Presses Universitaires de France.

Mies M. (1980) Capitalist development and subsistence reproduction: rural women in India. *Bulletin of Concerned Asian Scholars,* 12 (2), 3–14.

Mies M. (1981) Lace, Class and Capital Accumulation. Unpublished paper, Institute of Social Studies, The Hague.

Mingione E. (ed.) (1977) *Ricerca Sociologica sui Poli di Sviluppo Industriale nel Meridione,* 6 vols. Duplicated FORMEZ, Rome.

Mingione E. (1981) *Mercato del lavoro e occupazzione in Italia dal 1945 ad oggi.* CELUC, Milan.

Mingione E. (1982) *Informalization and Restructuring: the Problem of Social Reproduction of the Labor Force.* Paper delivered to the Tenth World Congress of Sociology, Mexico City.

Mingione E. (1983) Informalization, restructuring and the survival strategies of the working class. *International Journal of Urban and Regional Research,* 7 (3).

Minian I. (1981) *Progreso Técnico e Internacionalización del Proceso Productivo: El Caso de la Industria Maquiladora de Tipo Electrónico.* Centro de Investigaciones y Docencia Económica, Mexico City.

Mitra A. (1977) The status of women, *Frontiers,* 18 June.

Moctezuma P. (1981) Las luchas urbano-populares en la coyuntura actual. *Teoría y Política* (5), July–September, 101–24.

Moltocalvo M.A. (1980) La economía irregular: una primera aproximación al caso español. *Revista Española de Economía,* July–September.

Molyneux M. (1979) Beyond the domestic labour debate. *New Left Review,* 116 (3–27).

Morris L. (1983) *Renegotiation of the Domestic Division of Labour in the Context of Male Redundancy.* Paper presented to the Annual Conference of British Sociological Association, Cardiff.

Moser C. (1978) Informal sector or petty commodity production? Dualism or dependence in urban development? *World Development,* 6 (9/10). 1041–64.

Moser C. (1980) Women's work in a peripheral economy: the case of poor urban women in Guayaquil, Ecuador. Paper presented to Institute of Development Studies Workshop on *Women, the Working Poor and the Informal Sector.* Brighton, Sussex.

Moser C. (1981) Surviving in the suburbs. In *Women and the Informal Sector. Institute of Development Studies Bulletin,* 12 (3), July.

Moser C. & Young K. (1981) Women of the working poor. In *Women and the Informal Sector. Institute of Development Studies Bulletin.* 12 (3), July. 54–62.

Muñoz H. & de Oliveira O. (1979) Algunas controversias sobre la fuerza de trabajo en América Latina. In M.T. Katzman & J.L. Reyna (eds) *Fuerza de Trabajo y Movimientos Laborales en América Latina.* El Colegio de México, Mexico City.

Muñoz H., de Oliveira O. & Stern C. (1977) Migración y marginalidad occupacional. In Muñoz H. Oliviera O & Stern C et al. *Migración y Desigualdad Social en la Ciudad de México.* El Colegio de México/ UNAM, Mexico City.

Myrdal G. (1957) *Economic Theory and Underdeveloped Regions.* Harper & Row, Torchbook Editions, New York.

Myrdal G. (1975) *La Pobreza de las Naciones.* Siglo XXI, Mexico City.

Navarro B. & Moctezuma P. (1980a) Accumulación de Capital y Utilización de 'Espacio urbano' para la Reproducción de la Fuerza de Trabajo. Tesis de licenciatura, Economics Faculty, UNAM,, Mexico.

Navarro B. & Moctezuma P. (1980b) Clase obrera ejercito industrial de reserva y movimientos sociales urbanos de las clases dominadas. *Teoria y Politica* 2.

Negrete M.E., Partida V. & Puente S. (1982) *Estructura Económica y*

Problación Economicamente Activa en la Ciudad de México. Colegio de México, Mexico City.

Nelson N. (1980) *Why Has Development Neglected Urban Women?* Pergamon Press, Oxford.

Nun J. (1969) Sobrepoblación relativa, ejército industrial de reserva y masa marginal. *Revista Lationamericana de Sociología,* 5 (2), 178–236.

O'Connor J. (1973) *The Fiscal Crisis of the State.* St. Martin's, New York.

O'Connor J. (1974) *The Corporations and the State.* Harper, New York.

O'Higgins M. (1980) *Measuring the Hidden Economy: A Review of Evidence and Methodologies.* Outer Circle Policy Unit.

O'Laughlin B. (1974) Mediation of contradiction: why Mbum women don't eat chicken. In Rosaldo M & Lamphere L (eds) *Women, Culture & Society* 301–18. Stanford University Press, Stanford.

Paci M. (1973) *Mercato del Lavoro e Classi Sociali in Italia.* Il Mulino, Bologna.

Paci M. (ed.) (1980) *Famiglia e Mercato del Lavoro in una Economia Periferica.* Angeli, Milan.

Paci M. (1982) *La Struttura Sociale Italiana.* Il Mulino, Bologna.

Pahl J. (1982) *The Allocation of Money and the Structuring of Inequality within Marriage.* Health Services Research Unit, University of Kent, Canterbury.

Pahl R.E. (1980) Employment, work and the domestic division of labour. *International Journal of Urban and Regional Research,* 4 (1), March, 1–20.

Pahl R.E. (1984a) *Divisions of Labour.* Basil Blackwell, Oxford.

Pahl R.E. (1984b) The restructuring of capital, the local political economy and household work strategies; All forms of work in context. In Gregory D. & Urry J. (eds) *Social Relations and Spatial Structures.* Macmillan, London.

Pahl R.E. & Dennett J.H. (1981) *Industry and Employment on the Isle of Sheppey.* HWS Working Paper, Work Strategies Unit, Beverley Farm, University of Kent at Canterbury.

Pahl R.E. & Missiakoulis S. (1984) *On the Measurement of the Domestic Division of Labour.* (forthcoming).

Pahl R.E. & Wallace C. (1982) The restructuring of capital, the local political economy and household work strategies: all forms of work in context. Paper presented to the Tenth World Congress in Sociology, Mexico City.

Pala A.O. (1977) Definitions of women and development: an African perspective. *Signs,* 3 (1), Autumn. 9–13.

Palmer I. (1977) Rural women and the basic needs approach to development. *International Labour Review,* 115 (1), 97–107.

Palmer I. (1979) New official ideas on women and development. *Institute of Development Studies Bulletin,* 10 (3).

Papanek H. (1977) Development planning for women. *Signs* 3 (1), 14–21.

Pearson R. & Elson D. (1981) Nimble fingers make cheap workers: an analysis of women's employment in Third World export manufacturing. *Feminist Review*, 7, 87–107.

Pedrero M. & Rendón T. (1982) El trabajo de la mujer en México en los sesentas. In *Estudios Sobre la Mujer*. SPP, Mexico City.

Pendaries J.R. (1980) *De l'Indéductibilité de Pratiques Sociales.* Notes pour un débat autour de 'Familles Mobilisées'. Collection Texte Intégral. Plan Construction, Nice.

Perlman J. (1976) *The Myth of Marginality.* University of California Press, Berkeley and Los Angeles.

Philips A., Taylor B. (1980) Sex and skill: notes towards a feminist economics. *Feminist Review* 6.

Phizaclea A. (1981) Migrant women and wage labour: the case of West Indian women in Britain. In West J. (ed.) *Work, Women and the Labour Market*. Routledge & Kegan Paul, London.

Pialoux M. (1981) Force de travail et structure de classe: à propos de 'usines et ouvriers-figures du nouvel ordre productif'. *Critiques de l'Economie Politique*, 15–16, April–June, 162–87.

Pitrou A. (1978) *Vivre sans Famille? Les Solidarités Familiales dans le Monde d'Aujourd'hui*. Privat, Toulouse.

Portes A. (1978) The informal sector and the world economy: notes on the structure of subsidised labour. *Institute of Development Studies Bulletin*, 9 (4), June, 35–40.

Portes A. & Walton J. (1981) *Labor, Class and the International System*. Academic Press, New York.

Programa Regional del Empleo para América Latina y el Caribe (1981) *Sector Informal: Funcionamiento y Políticas*. PREALC, Santiago, Chile.

Pugliese E. et al. (1976) La struttura del settore calzaturiero a Napoli. *Inchiesta*, 22.

Quijano A. (1971) Polo marginal y mano de obra marginalista. CEPAL, Santiago.

Ramondino F. (1978) *Napoli, i Disoccupati Organizzati Raccontano*. Feltrinelli, Milan.

Ranciére J. (1981) *La Nuit des Prolétaires*. Fayard, Paris.

Recchini Z. Santu R. & Wainermann C. (1976) Participación de las Hogeres en la Actividad Económica en Argentina. CENEP, Buenos Aires.

Remy D. (1975) Underdevelopment and the experience of women. In Reiter R. (ed.) *Towards an Anthropology of Women*. Monthly Review Press, New York.

Rendón T. & Pedrero M. (1976) Alternativas para la Mujer en el Mercado de Trabajo de México. INET, Mexico City.

Roberts P. (1979) The integration of women into the development process: some conceptual problems. *Institute of Development Studies Bulletin*, 10 (3).

Robinson J. (1964) *Economic Philosophy*. Penguin Books, Middlesex.

Robinson J. & Converse P.E. (1972) Social change reflected in the use of time. In Campbell A. & Converse P.E. (eds) *The Human Meaning of Social Change.* Sage, New York.

Robinson J., Converse P.E. & Szalai A. (1972) Everyday life in twelve countries. In Szalai A. (ed.) *The Use of Time.* Mouton, The Hague.

Rodman H. (1967) Marital power in France, Greece, Yugoslavia and the United States: a cross-national discussion. *Journal of Marriage and the Family,* 29 (2) 320–36.

Rogers B. (1980) *The Domestication of Women: Discrimination in Developing Societies.* Tavistock, London.

Roldán M. (1981) Trabajo asalariado y condición de la mujer rural en un cultivo de exportación.World Employment Programme Working Paper, Geneva.

Roldán M. (1982) Subordinación genérica y proletarización rural: un estudio de caso en el noroeste mexicano en las trabajadoras del agro. In de Leon M. (ed.) *Debate Sobre le Mujer en America Latina y el Caribe,* vol. 2. Colombia.

Roldán M. (forthcoming) Domestic outwork, patterns of money allocation and womens consciousness a case study of domestic outworkers in Mexico City, in K. Young & C. Moser (eds) *Women; Work and Consciousness.*

Rosanvallon P. (1980) Le développement de l'économie souterraine et l'avenir des sociétés industrielles. *Le Débat,* 2 (June), 15–27.

Rosanvallon P. (1981) *La Crise de l'Etat-providence.* Le Seuil, Paris.

Roustang G. (1982) *Le Travail Autrement, Travail et Mode de Vie.* (Preface by Rosanvallon P.) Dunod, Paris.

Rowntree M. and Rowntree J. (1970) More on the political economy of women's liberation. *Monthly Review* 21 (8), 26–32.

Saba A. (1980) *L'industria Sommersa.* Marsilio, Padua.

Sachs J. (1980) *Les Temps Espace du Développement.* Paper delivered to CISS seminar, Rome.

Safa H. (1981) Runaway shops and female employment: the search for cheap labour. *Signs,* 7 (2), Winter.

Safa H. (1982) (ed.) *Towards a Political Economy of Urbanisation in Third World Countries.* Oxford University Press, Delhi.

Safilios-Rothschild C.A. (1967) A comparison of power structure and marital satisfaction in urban Greek and French families. *Journal of Marriage and the Family* 29 (2), 345–52.

Sahlins M. (1972) *Stone Age Economics.* Aldine, Chicago.

Santos M. (1975) *L'espace Partagé.* Ed. M. Th. Génin, Paris.

Saunders P. (1983) *Beyond Housing Classes: the Sociological Significance of Private Property Rights in Means of Consumption.* Working Paper No. 33, Urban and Regional Studies, University of Sussex.

Sauvy A. (1980) Les comptes souterrains (Eurépargne). *Problèmes Economiques,* 1702.

Seccombe W. (1974) The housewife and her labour under capitalism. *New Left Review,* 83.

Secretaria de Programacion y Presupuesto (S.P.P.) (1982) *Estudios sobre la mujer.* Mexico City.

Secretaria de Trabajo y Prevision Social and PNUD/OIT (1977) *Algunas interpretaciones sobre el sector marginal o informal urbano.* Mexico City.

Segalen M. (1980a) Faire construire. Résistance et contre-pouvoirs familiaux en Bretagne. *Economie et Humanisme,* **251** (January–February), 40–9.

Segalen M. (1980b) Maisons et Jardins: Sociabilité et Economie Informelle à Saint-Jean Trolimon. Unpublished.

Sen A. (1981) *Poverty and Famine.* Oxford University Press, Oxford.

Sen G. (1980) The sexual division of labour and the working class family: towards a conceptual synthesis of class relations and the subordination of women. *Review of Radical Political Economies,* **12** (2), 76–86.

Singer P. (1979) Desarrollo y empleo en el pensamiento latinoamericano. In M.T. Katzman & J.L. Reyna (eds) *Fuerza de Trabajo y Movimientos Laborales en América Latina.* El Colegio de México, Mexico City.

Singer P. (1980) *Economía Política del Trabajo.* Siglio XXI, Mexico City.

Skolka J. (1976) Long-term effects of unbalanced labour productivity growth. In Solari L. & du Pasquier J.-N. (eds), *Private and Enlarged Consumption.* North Holland, Amsterdam.

Sría de Programacion y Presupuesto (1982) *Estudios Sobre la Mujer.* SPP, Mexico City.

Stack C. (1974) Sex roles and survival strategies in an urban black community. In Rosaldo M. & Lamphere L. (eds) *Women, Culture and Society.* Stanford University Press, Stanford, California.

Stolcke V. (1981) *The Unholy Family: Labour Systems and Family Structure – The Case of Sao Paulo Coffee Plantations.* Paper presented to La Conferencia sobre Aspectos Teóricos del Parentesco en A. Latina, Ixtapan de la Sal, Mexico, 1981.

Stoler A. (1977) Class structure and female autonomy in rural Java. In The Wellesley Editorial Committee *Women and National Development,* University of Chicago Press, Chicago and London.

Szelenyi I. (1981) Structural changes and alternatives to capitalist development in the contemporary urban and regional system. *International Journal of Urban and Regional Research,* **5** (1), 1–14.

Thelot C. (1982) *Tel Père, tel Fils? Position Sociale et Origine Familiale.* Dunod, Paris.

Thrift N.J. (1983) On the determination of social action in space and time. *Society and Space,* **1** (1), 23–57.

Tievant S. (1982) Vivre autrement: échanges et sociabilitié en ville nouvelle. In *Cahiers de l'Observation du Changement Social,* vol. 6. Editions de CNRS, Paris.

Tinker I. (1976) The adverse impact of development on women. In Tinker I. & Bramsen M.B. (eds) *Women and World Development.* Praeger, New York.

Toffler A. (1980) *The Third Wave.* Collins/Pan Books, London.

Tokman V.E. (1979) Dinámica de mercade de trabajo urbano: el sector informal urbano en América Latina. In M.T. Katzman & J.L. Reyna (eds) *Fuerza de Trabajo y Movimientos Laborales en América Latina*. El Colegio de México, Mexico City.

Topalov C. (1979) *La Urbanización Capitalista*. Edition Edicol, Mexico City.

Touraine A. (1977) La marginalidad urbana. *Revista Mexicana de Sociología*, **39** (4), 1105–42.

Vanek J. (1974) Time spent in housework. *Scientific American*, **231**, 116–20.

Vázquez Arango C. (no date) *El Crecimiento de la Economía Oculta*. Unpublished paper, Madrid.

Vergopoulos K. (1978) Capitalism and peasant productivity. *Journal of Peasant Studies*, **5** (4), 446–65.

Wallace C., Pahl R.E. & Dennett J.H. (1981) *Housing and Residential Areas on the Isle of Sheppey*. HWS Working Paper, Work Strategies Unit, Beverley Farm, University of Kent at Canterbury.

Weiner A. (1979) Trobriand kinship from another view: the reproductive power of women and men. *Man*, **14** (NS), 328–48.

West J. (1982) *Work, Women and the Labour Market*. Routledge & Kegan Paul, London.

Whitehead A. (1979) Some preliminary notes on the subordination of women. *IDS Bulletin*, **10** (3).

Whitehead A. (1981) I'm hungry mum: the politics of domestic budgeting. In Young et al. (eds) *Of marriage and the market*, CSE Books, London.

Wright O.E. (1976) Class boundaries in advanced capitalist societies. *New Left Review*, **98** July–August.

Wright O.E. (1978) *Class, crisis and the state*, New Left Books, London.

Wrigley E.A. (1967) A simple model of London's importance in changing English society and economy, 1650–1750. *Past and Present*, **37**.

Yanagisako S. (1979) Family and household: the analysis of domestic groups. *Annual Review of Anthropology*, **8**, 101–205.

Young K. (1978) Modes of appropriation and the sexual division of labour: a case study from Oaxaca, Mexico. In Kuhn A. & Wolpe A.M. (eds) *Feminism and Materialism*, 124–54. Routledge & Kegan Paul, London.

Youssef N. (1974) *Women and Work in Developing Societies*. Population Monograph Series, University of California, Berkeley.

Index